Confidential
Confidential

THE INSIDE STORY OF HOLLYWOOD'S
NOTORIOUS SCANDAL MAGAZINE

SAMANTHA
BARBAS

CHICAGO
REVIEW
PRESS

Published by Chicago Review Press Incorporated
814 North Franklin Street
Chicago, Illinois 60610
ISBN 978-0-912777-54-2

Library of Congress Cataloging-in-Publication Data

Names: Barbas, Samantha author
Title: Confidential Confidential : the inside story of Hollywood's notorious
    scandal magazine / Samantha Barbas.
Description: Chicago : Chicago Review Press, 2018. | Includes bibliographical
    references and index.
Identifiers: LCCN 2017061185 (print) | LCCN 2018003706 (ebook) | ISBN
    9780912777559 (adobe pdf) | ISBN 9780912777566 (kindle) | ISBN
    9780912777573 (epub) | ISBN 9780912777542 (cloth)
Subjects: LCSH: Confidential (New York, N.Y.) | Tabloid newspapers—United
    States—History—20th century. | Sensationalism in journalism—United
    States—History—20th century.
Classification: LCC PN4900.C65 (ebook) | LCC PN4900.C65 B37 2018 (print) |
    DDC 051—dc23
LC record available at https://lccn.loc.gov/2017061185

Typesetting: Nord Compo

Printed in the United States of America
5 4 3 2 1

CONTENTS

Introduction v

Part I

1 The Education of a Publisher 3

2 The Age.. 17

3 *Confidential*.. 21

4 Winchell and Rushmore................................. 35

5 Asbestos... 46

Part II

6 The Dream Factory...................................... 57

7 Hot Hollywood Stories.................................. 67

8 Hollywood Research Incorporated....................... 81

9 Gossip 96

10 The Legal Department 101

11 1955 109

12 Hollywood... 125

13 The Curious Craze................................... 143

14 Public Service....................................... 155

Part III

15 Libel 163

16 Freedom of the Press 176

17 The Post Office.. 184

18 The Peak 195

19 The Decline... 204

20 Slander.. 215

Part IV

21 The Kraft Committee 223

22 Criminal Libel....................................... 233

23 The Trial 251

24 The End and the Aftermath 273

25 Conclusion 281

Notes 295

Selected Bibliography 343

Index 353

INTRODUCTION

IN 1955 *I LOVE Lucy* was one of America's most popular TV shows. Its comic depictions of the trials and tribulations of married life enchanted millions of viewers each week. The program was based on the actual marriage of fiery redheaded comedienne Lucille Ball and her husband, Cuban-born bandleader Desi Arnaz. Fan magazines and Hollywood gossip columns mirrored their off-screen and on-screen personas. To fans, Lucy and Desi were just as devoted to each other in real life as they were on television.

The sleazy gossip magazine *Confidential* shattered the illusion. Its January 1955 cover story, "Does Desi Really Love Lucy?" revealed Desi's flings with prostitutes. "Desi is most certainly a duck-out daddy," wrote *Confidential*. He "sprinkled his affections all over Hollywood for a number of years. And quite a bit of it has been bestowed on vice dollies who were paid handsomely for loving Desi briefly, but presumably as effectively as Lucy."[1]

Confidential's next issue featured a sensational story about a torrid interracial liaison between Sammy Davis Jr. and Ava Gardner, who was then married to Frank Sinatra. "Some girls go for gold, but it's bronze that 'sends' sultry Ava Gardner," *Confidential* reported.[2] Later that year, *Confidential* revealed how Joe DiMaggio and Frank Sinatra broke into an apartment where they thought Marilyn Monroe, DiMaggio's ex-wife, was having an affair. The infamous event would go down in Hollywood history as the "Wrong Door Raid."

At a time when homosexuality was one of society's greatest stigmas, *Confidential* made waves by outing celebrities. *Confidential* revealed heartthrob actors Van Johnson and Tab Hunter as gay. Actress Lizabeth Scott was spotted among "Hollywood's weird society of baritone babes." Liberace was outed in "Why Liberace's Theme Song Should Be 'Mad About the Boy.'"[3]

Bob Hope slept with a floozy, according to *Confidential*. Errol Flynn installed a two-way mirror in his mansion that he used to spy on visitors having sex in the guest bedroom. Ava Gardner and Lana Turner took part in a rollicking threesome with a Palm Springs bartender. Eddie Fisher entertained "three chippies" in a hotel room. Kim Novak slept her way to stardom. Mike Todd cheated on his wife, Elizabeth Taylor, with a stripper; Liz cheated on Mike with actor Victor Mature. Frank Sinatra was the "Tarzan of the Boudoir" because of the bowls of Wheaties he ate between rounds of lovemaking.

In the 1950s, *Confidential* magazine, America's first celebrity scandal magazine, revealed stars' misdeeds and transgressions in gritty, unvarnished detail. Deploying a vast Los Angeles–based network of informants and tipsters, publisher Robert Harrison destroyed Hollywood's carefully constructed image and created a massive media empire. *Confidential* became the bestselling magazine on American newsstands, surpassing *Time*, *Life*, and the *Saturday Evening Post*.[4] "Everybody reads it, but they say the cook brought it into the house," Humphrey Bogart famously quipped.[5] By 1955, when *Confidential* published the "Wrong Door Raid" story, the magazine had nearly sixteen million readers.[6]

Confidential's spectacular rise was followed by an equally spectacular fall. Stars filed multimillion-dollar libel suits against *Confidential*, and California prosecuted the magazine for obscenity and "criminal libel," publishing false statements with an "intent to harm." The charges culminated in a star-studded 1957 trial, later described as the O. J. Simpson trial of its time. The state forced *Confidential* to tone down its gossip; shortly after, Harrison sold the magazine, and *Confidential*'s career was over. But its legacy lives on in our obsession with gossip and celebrity scandal.

Confidential was the founder of sleazy celebrity gossip journalism in America. This book tells its story and reveals how the magazine revolutionized celebrity culture and American society in the 1950s and beyond. *Confidential* was the forerunner of *People*, the *National Enquirer*, and TMZ.com, and it was raunchier and more outrageous than all of them. With its wild red-yellow-and-blue covers, screaming headlines, and tawdry stories, *Confidential* exploded the pristine, candy-coated image of movie stars that Hollywood and the press had sold to the public. It transformed America from a nation of innocents to a more sophisticated, worldly people, wise to the phony and constructed nature of celebrity. It shifted reporting on celebrities from an enterprise of concealment and make-believe to one that was more frank, bawdy, and *true*.

The 1950s were an age of conformity and conservatism—the era of Mickey Mouse and *Leave It to Beaver*, of suburbia, anticommunism, and "family values"—

and *Confidential* tore through all of that like a wrecking ball. *Confidential* blew the top off America's prim, upright self-image, and it ushered in the skepticism and cynicism toward authorities, images, and ideals that would come to define American life in the 1960s and after. *Confidential* redrew the boundaries between private and public life and the limits of public expression. It marked the end of an era of *hush-hush*—of secrets, closets, and sexual taboos—and the beginning of our age of tell-all exposure. *Confidential* shattered America's complacency and exploded its innocence. In doing that, it lay the foundations of our own more jaded, weary times.

Confidential magazine was the brainchild of Robert Harrison, one of the unsung media pioneers of the twentieth century. The son of Russian Jewish immigrants, a ladies' man, and a slick nightclub playboy, Harrison started his career in the 1940s when he published the first pinup magazines in the country. By the end of the decade, Harrison, renowned as the "cheesecake king," was publishing six different girlie magazines.

In the early 1950s, Harrison decided to expand his empire with an "exposé" magazine revealing sensational stories about crime, sin, and urban vice. Promising to go "behind the scenes" and reveal facts that were *stunning, hideous, naughty, taboo, torrid, daring, shocking, sinful,* and "100% true!," *Confidential* debuted in 1952. The racist, homophobic, right-wing publication became famous for exposing communists and for outing homosexuals in politics and high society. Playing to the public's worst fears and taboos, *Confidential* hit a nerve. But it wasn't until *Confidential* started reporting on movie stars that it became a true sensation.

Before *Confidential*, Hollywood was literally a dream factory. As depicted in fan magazines and the mainstream press, movie stars were icons of perfection, wholesomeness, and Americana. Though they might have lived more glamorously than Main Street, at heart they were "just folks"—they paid off their mortgages, doted on their children, and never cheated on their spouses. The powerful film studios, deploying an army of press agents and "fixers," concealed messier, dirtier truths. Los Angeles cops and judges were paid to ignore stars' domestic violence, partying, and drug abuse. The studios sent pregnant, unmarried actresses off to have secret abortions. Hollywood spared no expense to conceal homosexuality, considered the most scandalous transgression of all. Dependent on the studios for advertising and access to stars, the press colluded in the cover-up, even though most journalists knew the real story.

When *Confidential* arrived on the scene, this system of spin and deception was starting to crumble. A 1948 Supreme Court decision forced the studios to sell off their profitable theater chains, and competition from television led to plummeting film attendance. Studios had fewer resources to invest in publicity, and they began to release actors from their long-term contracts. Many stars were losing the protection for their images that the studios had once provided. The Hollywood publicity machine was breaking down, and Harrison brilliantly exploited it.

Confidential Confidential tells the story of Robert Harrison's little magazine that could, how it rose from a seedy fly-by-night pulp magazine to become one of the bestselling publications in the country and a major phenomenon of the 1950s. It describes the scoops, scandals, sins, and wreckage—of stars' marriages, careers, and egos—and the legal war that led to the magazine's inglorious takedown. It explains how *Confidential* transformed America's relationship to celebrity, privacy, the media, and sexuality; how it reshaped journalism and popular culture; and made us who we are today.

It's not an easy story to write. History's record keepers have not been good to *Confidential*. Archivists didn't have the foresight to save copies of the magazine; only one library in America has a complete run.[7] Harrison left behind no personal papers, and *Confidential* preserved no records. The court documents have been put away in the storage vaults of Southern California courtrooms, untouched for decades. This account draws on never-before-published court records, FBI files, archival papers, and thousands of newspaper and magazine articles.[8]

Weaving together cultural history, journalism history, film history, and legal history, *Confidential Confidential* is the authoritative history of *Confidential* magazine, famously described by journalist Tom Wolfe as "the most scandalous scandal magazine in the history of the world."[9] It is about a simpler, more innocent time, and how *Confidential* upended it, undermining Americans' ideals and dreams, dethroning their idols and contradicting the things they thought were true. It is an important story, and a juicy story. And now it can be told.

PART I

1 | THE EDUCATION OF A PUBLISHER

ROBERT MAX HARRISON, THE future publisher of *Confidential,* was born on April 14, 1904, in Manhattan. His parents, Benjamin and Pauline, had migrated from Latvia fourteen years earlier. Benjamin was born in 1867; Pauline Isralowitz was born in 1871. The name "Harrison"—after President Benjamin Harrison—was bestowed on them by an Ellis Island immigration official. A tinsmith by training, Benjamin took up work at the Duparquet, Huot & Moneuse Co., a well-known maker of heavy-duty kitchen equipment for hotels and restaurants. It was steady, well-paying work, and he held the position until he retired.[1]

In 1894 the couple had their first child, Helen. Gertrude was born in 1897. In 1899 the couple had their third daughter, Ida Ettie, who went by Edith. When Bob was born, the family lived in a tiny tenement apartment at 112 East 98th Street in a working-class neighborhood populated by German, Italian, Irish, and Jewish immigrants. A few years later the family moved to Hewitt Place in the Bronx, another poor immigrant area. By 1920 the family had relocated again, this time to a section of West 108th Street in Manhattan filled with high-density tenement buildings.[2]

Little is known about Harrison's childhood; he said almost nothing about it. He did have an eager and early interest in girls. Harrison doted on neighborhood sweethearts and was an ardent fan of the pretty chorines and Ziegfeld girls who were pop culture icons in that era. Although Harrison was bar mitzvahed and raised in a religious family, he didn't practice as an adult, and Judaism played little part in his life.[3]

3

Like most children of recent immigrants in New York at that time, Harrison spent hours on the street. The street was his playground and classroom; there he learned how to think on his feet, to fight, and to sell. Most poor immigrant kids worked odd jobs on the street—singing for pennies, running errands, peddling fruit, shining shoes. They grew up listening to the cries of street vendors and pushcart peddlers, learning that, in the words of historian David Nasaw, it was "the salesman's job to pitch and the customer's to resist."[4]

Harrison was a born hustler—a "kid who always saw a commercial angle," as he put it. At the age of ten, he watched subway riders exiting a station in a rainstorm. He set up an umbrella rental stand. It was his first business venture.[5]

When Harrison was fifteen he came up with a "magazine"—*Harrison's Week End Guide*, a pamphlet listing hotels and other lodging for people taking road trips in New York and New Jersey. Automobiles were still a novelty back then; roads were just being developed, and most people weren't familiar with hotels. He drew up the pamphlet and took it to a printer, who signed a publishing contract. It wasn't long before he realized he'd been ripped off. The printer ran it off and "that was the last I ever saw of it," he recalled. "That S.O.B. stole it from me. And I thought I was gonna make a lot of money on it."[6]

Harrison went to public grammar school, then to Stuyvesant High School, just emerging as one of the city's leading public high schools. He excelled at English but flunked math. High school education wasn't required, and after two years Harrison dropped out to work as an office boy in an ad agency. His father opposed it. Religious and steeped in old-world values, Benjamin believed that a man should have a useful trade, like welding or carpentry. Advertising and publishing were just "air businesses," he snickered. Harrison felt guilty about disappointing his father, and it pushed him to succeed in his publishing career. When he achieved fame with his magazines, he'd tell friends, "My father wouldn't believe I'd ever be this important."[7]

Sometime in his teens, Harrison discovered he had a passion and "flair" for writing. That interest took him to Columbia University, where he studied English and literature in the evening division. In 1921 he took his first job in publishing, as an office boy at Joseph Pulitzer's *New York World*. Three years later Harrison went to work on a scandalous new tabloid called the *New York Evening Graphic*.[8]

The 1920s was the great age of the tabloid in America. By the end of the decade, several cities had tabloid newspapers, with the most prominent and influential published in New York. Presented as cheap amusement for working-class audiences, tabloids offered readers a potent daily dose of crimes, mysteries, murder trials, and scandals announced with garish photos and ninety-six-point headlines. In an era of flappers, jazz, cars, and speakeasies—of urbanization, sexual liberation, and cultural upheaval—tabloids embodied the whirlwind mood of the times and the hard rhythm of the cities where they took root and flourished. Tabloids were the "journalistic mirror" of their time, wrote one critic. They were as "expressive of modern America as World Series baseball, skyscrapers, radio, . . . taxicabs, and beauty contests." With gusto and abandon, they defied the norms and practices of conventional journalism, with its staid tone and dry, straightforward factual reporting. Unlike traditional newspapers, focused on politics, business, and world affairs, tabloids dealt in matters of the heart and everyday life, the "things that people talk about on the streets and in their homes." Their animating principle was that "no matter what his background and education, a man is governed by his emotions."[9]

The 1920s wasn't the first time sensationalistic journalism had attracted an audience. The pre–Civil War era had the penny press, cheap newspapers offering fantastic tales of murders, seductions, and other urban mayhem. The 1890s saw "yellow journalism," perfected by the Hearst press, with enormous scare headlines, lavish pictures, and blatant fictions offered as news. The *National Police Gazette*, a little pink paper described as the "greatest journal of sport, sensation, the stage, and romance," was the forerunner of the 1920s tabloids. The *Gazette*, which crested between 1880 and 1910, was the first publication to feature divorce stories and to embellish newsprint with woodcut illustrations of such titillating subjects as bare-knuckled pugilists, showgirls, and gun battles.[10]

The *New York Daily News*, the nation's first tabloid, debuted in 1919. In 1924 William Randolph Hearst launched a rival, the *Daily Mirror*, promising "90 percent entertainment, and 10 percent information." Later that year Bernarr Macfadden introduced the *New York Evening Graphic*. Diminutive and muscle-bound, "a crazy Irishman with a mane of long hair," a food-faddist and exercise junkie so obsessed with health that he was nicknamed Body Love, since the late 1800s Macfadden had published a string of magazines devoted to fitness, nudity, and sex, including *True Story*, the nation's first "true confession" magazine. The *Graphic* burst on the scene with all the sweaty, hurling bravado of its founder. "We intend to interest you mightily," announced its opening editorial. The paper would "flash . . . like a new comet" across the publishing landscape.[11]

Like the *Daily News* and the *Mirror*, the *Graphic* reveled in stories about deviance, torture, violence, and crime. But its sex was seamier, its scandal more scandalous, its crime more gruesome, and its claims more bogus than its tabloid rivals:

GIRLS NEED SEX LIFE FOR BEAUTY

WEED PARTIES IN SOLDIERS' LOVE NEST

KIDNAPPED SCHOOLGIRL, 12, FEARED SLAIN BY FIEND

MY FRIENDS DRAGGED ME INTO THE GUTTER

> Sunk into the depths of loneliness, Ann Luther, motion picture actress, is today in hiding in Hollywood. Since she lost her $1,000,000 suit against Jack White, wealthy motion picture producer, she has been, she says, "sick at heart." Once trustful of her fellow beings . . . she has turned against the world in bitterness. Yet, in her breast burns the desire to have the truth set right before the world, and it is her story of tragedy and battle that she reveals today for the first time to GRAPHIC readers.[12]

Drawn in by the lurid headlines, readers stayed on for the *Graphic*'s regular features—its confessional fiction, prize contests, sports news, comic strips, and illustrations of women in various states of ecstasy and undress. Everything was written in Jazz Age slang: women were "shebas," "red hot mammas," or "broken butterflies." When death or misery stalked a family, *Graphic* reporters and "picture hounds" were set on the trail. Parents were shown drooped over the limp body of a dead child; bandage-swathed victims were depicted scattered in the streets, writhing in pain. The *Graphic*'s front page was usually straddled by a bathing beauty whose "heaviest piece of raiment is the caption," one critic quipped. Macfadden told his editors he wanted sex in each issue—"big gobs of it."[13]

NOTHING BUT THE TRUTH, the *Graphic*'s motto, was often incanted but rarely followed. The *Graphic* did do some investigative journalism from time to time; a famous exposé of fraud in the Miss America Pageant led to the contest's temporary closure in 1925. But a good deal of the *Graphic* was faked. When editors didn't have a story, they made one up. If they didn't have a photo to go with a story, they made that up, too. Photographs were cut apart and put back together; heads and bodies were superimposed and faces retouched. Perhaps the most infamous "composograph" came out of the 1925 trial of socialite Kip Rhinelander, seeking an annulment of his marriage on the ground that his wife hadn't told him she was black. The wife was ordered to take off her clothes in court to show the color of her skin. A chorus girl posed in a reenactment of the scene, and the photo was retouched to look as if it had been taken on the spot. *Editor and Publisher* declared it the "most shocking news-picture ever produced by New York journalism."[14]

The *Graphic* indeed "flashed like a comet." It rose brilliantly, reaching a circulation of over two hundred thousand in 1926, but it flamed out after only eight years. Old-guard moralists saw the *Graphic*'s run-riot worldview as an assault on truth, privacy, and traditional values—"certain . . . to disrupt the home, ruin the morals of youth and precipitate a devastating wave of crime and perversion"—and the law came crashing down. New York authorities went after Macfadden for publishing a "lewd" newspaper, in violation of the state penal code. Over $12 million in libel suits were filed against the *Graphic*, making it the most sued publication in history to that time. Department store advertisers, the backbone of the New York dailies, had no interest in the "Porno-*Graphic*," and Macfadden struggled to find advertising. While the *Daily News* and the *Mirror* continued to publish into the 1930s, the *Graphic* shut its doors in 1932 at a loss of $8 million.[15]

By that time, Harrison was long gone. He stayed at the *Graphic* for only eight months. What he did at the paper and why he left is shrouded in mystery. It was rumored that he left under less than honorable circumstances: according to *Esquire*, he was discharged "because he happened to introduce his immediate superior to a girl who gave him not only love but also the disease which is thought by some to be no worse than a bad cold." It was "one of the few instances in . . . history . . . in which an employee was fired primarily because of the carelessness of the employer."[16]

––––––––––

Harrison's time at the *Graphic* left an impression on him. The paper's outrageous ballyhoo spoke to him—it had a swagger and ballsy style that Harrison the street kid could relate to. The *Graphic* was Harrison's journalism school, and it taught him the basics of publishing: how to paste up pages, edit copy, and write headlines. It also gave him his lifelong business philosophy: sex sells. From that point on, the idea of becoming a publisher fixed brightly in his mind. Harrison fantasized about running his own newspaper or magazine, but the path there wasn't entirely clear.[17]

For the next decade and a half, Harrison bounced unhappily around a series of dead-end sales and advertising jobs. The 1930 census listed him as a twenty-six-year-old dress salesman, living with his parents. After that he worked in an ad agency, writing copy for banks. He wrote brochures for Cook's Tours and tried selling song lyrics. He eked out a living, but he was restless and bored. "When I tried to sell dresses or went into other businesses, to me it was a job I had to get to at 9 o'clock, and at 5 o'clock I couldn't get out fast enough," he recalled. He longingly perused *Variety* and its column Literati, on magazines, writers, and the publishing industry. "I was trying to find myself. I was always hoping to go into business for myself. I felt there was no future in working for anybody else."[18]

In 1935 Harrison began his journey back to publishing when he took a job as an ad salesman at the Quigley magazines. Martin Quigley Jr. was publisher of *Motion Picture Herald* and *Motion Picture Daily*, trade publications for the movie industry. Second only to *Variety* in their circulation and influence, Quigley's magazines reported on box office returns, legal and production issues, government relations, censorship, and other matters of interest to the film industry. Quigley, a devout Catholic, had been one of the authors of the Motion Picture Production Code, a code of self-regulation for the film industry that was based on Catholic principles and adopted in 1930. A response to threats of film censorship, the code forbade the glorification of crime in films and the depiction of such taboos as drug use, miscegenation, and homosexuality.[19]

Harrison worked hard for Quigley. In addition to selling advertising space, he helped Quigley start a short-lived magazine called *Teatro El Dia*, a trade publication for the Latin American film industry. As a promotion, Quigley transferred Harrison to his Hollywood office. He hated it. Compared to New York, Hollywood was a "dull town," in Harrison's opinion. "The tempo wasn't like New York." "There was no night life and I like night life." Disgusted, he returned to New York in one week.[20]

When he got back he called up Eddie Jaffe, a well-known press agent, and asked him for cheesecake photos of stage actresses he represented. Harrison collected them, and before long he came up with the idea of starting a girlie magazine. In the evenings when he finished his work for Quigley, he stayed in the office and used the typewriter to write up his material. In late 1940 he was ready to launch the magazine. Harrison asked Jaffe to keep quiet, to protect his job with Quigley. But Jaffe sent a news release to *Variety*, and on Christmas Eve Quigley fired Harrison. With a $500 loan from his sister Helen, a secretary, Harrison started his own publishing company in the two-bedroom apartment he shared with Helen.[21]

––––––––––

It didn't take much to start a girlie magazine in those days. All you needed was a little for pulp paper and some black-and-white printing. There was no need to pay reporters, and cheesecake photos, circulating widely in an underground market, could be had for nearly nothing. In the 1920s and '30s, publishers in ramshackle offices on the edges of the publishing industry had filled newsstands with magazines with titles like *La Vie Parisienne*, *Artists and Models*, *Hot Dog*, *Hi-Jinks*, *Snappy Stories*, *Cupid's Capers*, *Wild Cherries*, *Capt. Billy's Whiz Bang*, *Gay French Stories*, and *Paris Nights*. A modernized version of the *Police Gazette* offered racy pictures of showgirls along with true-crime fiction and sporting news.[22]

There were always opportunities in the field because publications were constantly going out of business. Publishing obscene and "indecent" material was a crime. Throughout the country, municipal authorities canceled the licenses of newsdealers who sold cheesecake magazines. In the 1930s Mayor Fiorello LaGuardia ordered New York garbagemen to pick girlie magazines off newsstands and trash them.[23]

In 1941, five months before America's entrance into the World War II, Harrison's *Beauty Parade* hit newsstands. Although pinup pictures had appeared in calendars and in centerfolds in pulp magazines, *Beauty Parade* was the first American publication devoted exclusively to pinups. Harrison hired top pinup artists Earl Moran, Billy DeVorss, and Peter Driben to paint portraits of beautiful, long-legged girls for his covers. For publicity, he sponsored a tour of each month's cover girl to army camps and enlisted burlesque stars Sally Rand and Gypsy Rose Lee as publicity "ambassadors." As a stunt, they put silk stockings between the pages of every fifth copy of the first issue. It was a smash; the first issue sold out in just two hours.[24]

Curvy, good-looking showgirls and actresses modeled for Harrison. Freelance photographers took pictures of them stripped to their bras and panties. The women posed for little, sometimes for nothing but the exposure. Harrison's models were busty—especially so, since he taped their breasts together. Harrison was a "nut about . . . cleavage," recalled pinup icon Bettie Page, who worked for Harrison during her early career. He would make her hold her breasts together and "they would put 2-inch-wide tape all across. I hated that, and so did the other girls who posed for him."[25]

Girlie magazines boomed during the war, when pinup girls became icons and symbols of the home front. The government sent out millions of pinup pictures to GIs as morale builders, reminders of what they were fighting for. *Beauty Parade* spawned a host of cheap imitators with titles like *Grin*, *Gags*, *Hit*, *Halt!*, *Army & Navy Fun Parade*, *Laff*, *Hello Buddies*, *Showgirls*, and *Glamorous Models*. Between 1943 and 1946 Harrison launched four more magazines featuring "naked women and jokes, on a 60-40 ratio," as one columnist quipped. The year 1942 saw *Eyeful*, a magazine of "Girls, Gags, and Giggles." "We were going to call it 'An Eyefull and an Earfull,'" Harrison said. "But we changed it to Eyefull."[26]

In 1943 Harrison started *Titter*, "America's Merriest Magazine," featuring "Gals and Gags, Bevies of Beauties, Barrels of Fun." The title came from "a very famous cartoon," Harrison said. "It's this woman with the big bust walking down the theatre aisle, and the caption read: 'And a big titter went through the audience.'" In 1944 Harrison launched *Wink*, featuring "Girls, Gags, and Gayety." After the war Harrison introduced *Flirt*. When his magazines took off, he moved his office from his apartment to a small space behind a freight elevator in a building at 201 West 52nd Street. The walls were adorned with girlie photos and the garish covers of *Wink*, *Flirt*, *Eyeful*, and *Beauty Parade*.[27]

In the summer of 1945, Harrison met Edythe Farrell, editor of the *Police Gazette*. The first woman editor of the *Gazette*, Farrell was a minor celebrity in the publishing world. Under her editorship, the *Gazette*'s circulation skyrocketed from 38,000 to 250,000. A fiery woman who worked like a whirlwind, Farrell introduced Harrison to sadomasochism and fetishism by giving him a copy of Richard von Krafft-Ebing's bondage treatise *Psychopathia Sexualis*. Harrison told her he didn't "dig that kind of stuff" but admitted it could appeal to readers.[28]

Harrison hired Farrell from the *Gazette*, and his magazines transformed. Models donned corsets, long-haired wigs, and six-inch heels with ankle straps. Pictures showed men whipping women, women hitting women with milk bottles and bowling pins, women being spanked, and women in chains. A typical photo spread, "Links of Love," depicted a half-dressed woman in manacles: "Nora Brendt . . . dramatically depicts this slave study of a pathetic pretty who little realizes that the links which bind her are wrought of pure love, since she is the captive of a Sultan who has admired her fervently from afar."[29]

Commercial artists would be "quietly working away on some layout when a door would open and in would tramp some margarine-faced babe in a brassiere, panties, and spike heels, with a six-foot length of chain over her shoulder, dragging it over the floor," one of Harrison's editors recalled. "You'd be trying to write a caption and you'd look up and this gal would be walking through pulling 20 yards of chain, and Bob would come out in his bathrobe . . . yelling 'Let's do a fanetta (posterior) shot' or 'Let's do a buzzoom (bosom) shot,' and the photographer would be crawling up a ladder to shoot down the girl's cleavage." In the midst of it all were Harrison's sisters Helen and Edith, who worked as his secretaries. They treated him like a little boy, following him around the office, listening to his complaints, and reminding him to eat his dinner. One of Harrison's employees wrote a play based on an average day in the office but gave up trying to produce it when he realized he could never convince anyone that a place like that really existed.[30]

In the tradition of the *Evening Graphic*, a good deal of Harrison's material was faked. A photo spread in *Titter* titled "Model Records Daring Death Leap" depicted a woman "falling" from a seven-hundred-foot Chicago skyscraper, her skirts flying. The photo was of course staged, shot in Harrison's office. To save money, Harrison often modeled for his magazines. In the June 1949 issue of *Beauty Parade* he was depicted as a "leering wolf" in a two-page photo spread. In a feature called "Babes in Bras" he appeared in a work jacket toiling over a drawing board, as "Jules Latour, the famed bra designer at work." In other spreads he was shown as a "guitar-strumming troubadour," an inmate of a mental hospital, a man spanking a woman, a man being spanked by a woman, and a "male model illustrating the proper art of how to kiss a woman."[31]

In June 1946, Harrison launched *Whisper*, a cross between a detective, scandal, and pinup magazine. It was the most unique and adventurous of Harrison's publications, and it presaged *Confidential*. Its subtitle was *Knows All; Shows All, the Inside Story, True Facts Revealed!* In addition to pinups, *Whisper* featured exposé and "true confession" stories about sex, drugs, and vice, such as "A Decade of Hollywood Sin," "Rejuvenation Through Male Hormones," "Fate of Faithless Wives," "Your Impotence May Be Mental," "How Reefer Parties Breed Vice," "Marriages Without Men," and "Abortion Doctors Exposed." Like all Harrison's magazines, its advertisements—for sex manuals, weight loss programs, baldness remedies, and girlie photos ("real photographs of smart pretty girls in snappy poses!")—targeted the magazine's audience of white, working-class, middle-aged men with vivid imaginations and a hunger for love.[32]

Some of *Whisper*'s stories were true, but most were "make-believe stories . . . of mental adventure," Harrison admitted. *Whisper* once ran a story about "White Indians" in the Rockies. There was no such thing as "White Indians," but it was a "cute idea that if you got into the Rockies somewhere there would be beautiful white girls who were White Indians." The story was illustrated with photographs. "We got some girls and dressed them in Indian costumes. Shot the pix ourselves. Six months later we were still getting calls. 'Hey,' the guy would say. 'Hey, I'm on my vacation in Wyoming. I seen one of them White Indians you wrote about.'" The whole thing, Harrison confessed, was "a nice fraud."[33]

As a publisher Harrison was shrewd, meticulous, and demanding. He saw his magazines as an expression of himself, and they reflected his fetishes, quirks, and unusual tastes. Harrison was obsessed with bad puns, which he saw as sophisticated. If he were about to run a picture of a bikini-clad girl holding a knife, he'd come up with a caption like "Knife Work If You Can Get It." For a shot of a girl swathed in bandages, he'd write, "My Mummy Done Told Me." Nervous and neurotic, Harrison chain-smoked, paced, and gnawed constantly on bits of food. A perfectionist and workaholic, he worked sixteen hours a day, every day, hovering over his photographers and retouchers. Office conditions were hectic, and there was constant turnover on the staff.[34]

Harrison still talked like the streets, in a Broadway promoter's accent. He was "rude, crude, and unlettered," one of his editors remarked. His language was "studded with profanity and language one finds chalked on the walls in cheap washrooms." With him things were "damn right" or "hell no." People were "geniuses" or "clinkers." He told dirty jokes in a coarse, scratchy voice. When you talked to him, you "did not get a warm and fuzzy feeling," recalled the son of one of his editors. Harrison wasn't stupid, but he was desperately naïve about current events. Once asked his opinion on politics, he said, "I like Ike and everybody else. All that stuff is as foreign to me as Europe is." Harrison was "incapable of any abstract reasoning or evaluation," a friend observed. His greatest strength was his salesmanship—he had an "infallible instinct for stuff that would sell."[35]

By 1947 "Broadway Bob" was earning $100,000 a year, a fortune at the time. Pundits predicted a decline in pinups after the war, but business was thriving, Harrison told the press: "You can now buy semi-clad girls on wallpaper, on playing cards, liquor glasses, ties, or towels." Harrison spent lavishly on fine suits and shirts from the luxury tailor Sulka. With his sister Helen and her new husband, Dan, he took up residence in a nine-room apartment in Manhattan's elegant Parc Vendome. He mounted an oil painting of a nude man and woman, the original painting for one of his magazines, over his bed and built a miniature nightclub in his living room, featuring tables with checkered tablecloths, a long bar, and zebra stripes, in the image of the nightclub the El Morocco.[36]

Harrison lived for nightlife—he was a "major playboy," recalled his friend and lawyer, Al DeStefano. Accepted into New York's "Café Society," he became a regular at elite hot spots like the Stork Club, the Colony, and his favorite, El Morocco, where he hobnobbed with high society and Broadway stars amid fake palm trees, zebra-patterned upholstery, and bare-shouldered girls stepping the latest rhumba. He usually came in with one of his models on his arm; "it made him feel like the Duke of Broadway," said a friend. Society columns portrayed him as an aggressive playboy, and he regarded the publicity with "childlike delight." In 1951 Harrison took Bettie Page to the Beaux Arts Ball at the Waldorf Astoria hotel. On Harrison's suggestion, she wore a pair of black fishnet stockings, panties, high heels, and twin telephone dials over her breasts.[37]

Harrison dated his models, sometimes a few at a time, showering them with gifts and vacations. But his career was his only true love, and he had no interest in marriage and a family. Girlfriends were appalled by his self-focus. "If you didn't talk about magazines you had to talk about him," said burlesque star Sherry Britton, who dated Harrison briefly. "Conversation with Bob concerns Bob and his dream fulfillments. If he makes a hundred thousand a year he's thinking in terms of a million next year." June Shirley Frew, a five-foot-eight blonde model from Canada, was Harrison's steadiest partner. Harrison met her in 1946, when she was twenty-four and modeled for his magazines. In 1947 Broadway columnist Earl Wilson described Frew as a "Montreal socialite." She posed for *Whisper*, she said, "because I wanted to shock my very staid Canadian family." Frew returned to Canada in 1948, then came back to the United States later that year, describing herself to immigration officials as Harrison's "fiancée." Although the press referred to her as "Mrs. Harrison," the two never married. Frew stayed with Harrison through the *Confidential* years.[38]

By the age of forty-five, Harrison was a well-groomed fast-talker full of confidence and salesmanship. Five-foot-eight, clean-shaven, with a deep sunlamp suntan, Harrison had a beak nose and narrow eyes, bright white capped teeth, slicked-back hair, and a modestly receding hairline. He was a "muscular, handsome, slender man . . . faultlessly attired in well-tailored clothes . . . barbered and manicured to a high polish." "Heavy hoods of skin hang down over the corners of his eyes . . . his voice is low and underscored by ill-concealed snorts and hacks. His clothes are those of an immensely prosperous manufacturer of nail enamel, wrought of expensive fabrics, and a trifle sharp," reported *Esquire*. The nation's premiere publisher of girlie magazines, Harrison was renowned as America's "cheesecake king."[39]

By 1950 Harrison's career was surging beyond his wildest dreams. Giddy with success, he plotted more stunts, more fame, more profits, and even more outrageous publications. But his cheesecake glory came to a sudden halt when his accountant told him his magazines were broke. "We had six magazines . . . [and when they] start losing money for a few months, you can lose hundreds of thousands of dollars and not even know what happened," Harrison recalled.[40]

One reason was competition. The end of wartime paper rationing and a prosperous postwar economy led to an increase in magazine publishing. In 1949 the number of girlie magazines was at a record high. Harrison's rivals were not only cheesecake magazines, but also new general interest men's magazines like *Modern Man*, a forerunner of *Playboy*, which featured fiction, humor, and photos of well-known actresses and models without the smutty jokes and bad puns in Harrison's magazines.[41]

Legal problems also cut into Harrison's profits. Presaging his later experience with *Confidential*, Harrison had several run-ins with the law. In 1949 Cleveland banned all six of Harrison's publications for violating an ordinance against obscenity. The New York Society for the Suppression of Vice took Harrison to court several times, and for a while Mayor LaGuardia ordered Harrison's magazines off New York newsstands.[42]

In 1949 North Adams, Massachusetts, forced news dealers to stop selling Harrison's magazines. In Bloomington, Indiana, officials pressured newsstands to remove them. In 1952 a judge held a Coney Island newsdealer criminally liable for selling Harrison's publications, which he deemed "lewd, indecent, and obscene." Parents in Newark witnessed their kids poring over *Wink*, *Titter*, and *Beauty Parade*, and they complained to authorities. Harrison went to a PTA meeting to appease them. He told them: "we weren't interested in having children get their hands on our magazines. And . . . if they did, there was no harm. I could see where a child of 10 could imitate a stabbing, but what could he imitate in a girlie picture?" They quickly dropped their complaint.[43]

Postal inspectors threatened to revoke Harrison's mailing privileges on grounds of obscenity. Harrison retained noted civil liberties attorney Morris Ernst to represent him. Ernst went to Washington and talked with Roy Frank, the Post Office's head lawyer. Frank demanded they remove the "spicy" ads and said that "61 pages of solid girlie stuff was too much." Harrison and Frank came to an agreement. Harrison put more clothes on his models, and the lustier ads were pulled.[44]

Harrison was also sued for libel. A *Whisper* article from 1950 portrayed "gangs, prostitution, and thrill-seeking whites" in Harlem. "Right next to ritzy Park Avenue are streets more dangerous for a white man to walk through after dark than the wildest bushland in Africa," it said. "A tremendous number of crimes are committed by the kid gangs of Harlem . . . deadly wars are constantly being fought between rival hoodlums in dark streets and side alleys."[45]

Harlem leaders brought suit, branding the article "lurid and sordid trash," and "vicious, slanderous, and defamatory." "What excuse do the editors of *Whisper* offer for having printed this scandalous material?" asked the editors of a prominent African American newspaper. "What does the magazine intend to do about counteracting the effects of this scandalous piece, which if given any consideration could easily set race relations back at least 50 years?"[46] Faced with these threats to his girlie empire, Harrison began thinking up a new magazine.

2 | THE AGE

CONFIDENTIAL MAGAZINE GREW, like a weed, out of the dark and paranoid soul of the early 1950s.

It was an unsettled, turbulent time. America had been transformed by the war, and was grappling to make sense of the changes it wrought. After the war, communists advanced in Europe and Asia, and in 1949 the Soviet Union exploded an atomic bomb. President Truman initiated loyalty investigations of federal employees, and the nation descended into a Red Scare. In 1947 the House Un-American Activities Committee began investigating alleged communist activity in Hollywood. Right-wing politicians warned of a communist "fifth column," and the Justice Department issued a list of communist-affiliated organizations, a virtual blacklist used to deny employment. By 1949 the Red hysteria was so intense that a majority of Americans believed that the government should take all steps to rid the nation of communists, "even if innocent people should be hurt." Over half the population agreed that "all known communists should be jailed."[1]

In 1950 the United States entered the war in Korea, a proxy war with the Soviets. The following year Senator Joseph McCarthy proclaimed the existence of Soviet agents in the State Department and launched a virulent witch hunt of communists in government. McCarthy gained an enormous following, and his tactic of "Red-baiting"—falsely accusing his opponents of communism—came to define the era's politics. State and local governments urged citizens to "name names" and rat out each other as "subversives." Corporations, schools, and labor unions set up their own "loyalty checks" to ferret out not only communists but anyone seen as left of center: New Dealers, labor leaders, civil rights activists, pacifists, atheists. Communists lurked everywhere, the public was told, disguised as ordinary citizens, "in factories, offices, butcher shops, on street corners, in private business," said Truman's attorney general J. Howard McGrath. The Republican Party, out of power since the 1930s, regained Congress and the presidency by preaching anticommunism, "traditional values," and the American way of life.[2]

The mood of the times was deeply conservative—patriotic, righteous, and buttoned-down. Americans' confidence and stability had been shaken by the war, and their goals and dreams reflected their weariness: owning one's home, entering the middle class, and enjoying cars, televisions, and other fruits of the postwar economy. For the first time, white-collar jobs outnumbered blue-collar jobs. The number of families moving into the middle class increased by over a million a year. There was an exodus from cities as new homes with picket fences and two-car garages popped up like dandelions across the suburban landscape. In 1953 *Fortune* magazine hailed an "economy of abundance" never before seen in history.[3]

Church attendance reached record highs, Bible sales skyrocketed, and "In God We Trust" became the nation's official motto. Nearly three quarters of Americans were members of a church or religious group. The family was celebrated as the bedrock of society, a safe haven in a threatening and unstable world. The male ideal was the breadwinner—staunch, emotionless, and dominating—while women were to be glamorous housewives who kept their homes spotless, doted on their children, and remained youthful and optimistic. Under the ideal of the "feminine mystique," women were to find fulfillment not in education or paid employment, but in their own "femininity"—"sexual passivity, male domination, and nurturing maternal love."[4]

Marriage rates rose, and almost half of brides were teenagers. The birth rate peaked—the "baby boom." Sexual norms, on their face, were old-fashioned and repressive. There was a preoccupation with premarital chastity that reached a near frenzy, and a moral panic around all forms of so-called deviant sex, from extramarital sex to homosexuality. Conservative groups launched "purity" movements to cleanse all traces of sex from popular culture.[5]

It was a time of complacency, simplicity, and conformity. In many parts of the country, people knew their neighbors and left doors unlocked. An idealistic public put its faith in God, home, family, and nation. It was an age of big dreams, big hopes, and big heroes: baseball players, presidents, pop singers, and especially movie stars, the most beloved celebrities of all. Male icons were tough and manly—John Wayne, Joe DiMaggio, Ernest Hemingway—while female role models were demure, submissive, and perky, like the fictional housewife June Cleaver of the sitcom *Leave It to Beaver*. Mass media reinforced America's feelings of optimism and superiority with bright images of prosperity and contentment: happy housewives, harmonious families, gleaming consumer products, and big cars roaring down newly built highways, virtual symbols of the nation.

At the same time, there was a deep current of anxiety and restlessness that even TV couldn't shake. By 1950 the bomb, and fear of the bomb, were an integral part of American life. Terrified families built fallout shelters in their backyards, and children were taught to "duck and cover." The usually optimistic Reverend Norman Vincent Peale spoke of an "epidemic of fear and worry" in the United States. "Our nation," warned a civil defense pamphlet, is in a "grim struggle for national survival and the preservation of freedom in the world."[6]

There was also the domestic fallout from the war to deal with. Over six million women had entered the workforce during the war. Though most returned home at war's end, for many women paid employment stoked yearnings for independence and dissatisfaction with the housewife role. Many African Americans enjoyed greater job opportunities and prosperity during the war, leading to political activism, postwar racial tension, and calls for civil rights. Wartime disrupted families and marriages, creating space for nonmarital sex, including gay and lesbian relationships. Cities burgeoned during the war, and with them came delinquency and crime. In the 1950s, "containment" became the metaphor of the day—containing the spread of communism through aggressive foreign policy, and containing the social upheaval unleashed by the war.[7]

However naïve and idealistic Americans might have been, at the same time they were losing their innocence. Made increasingly world-wise from their war experiences and new Cold War realities, the public was growing up. Americans were realizing that appearances weren't all that they seemed; beneath pleasing, placid images lay more complex and disturbing truths. Wartime had led to more fluid social identities—women working in factories like men, minorities making inroads into white society, many people recognizing themselves, for the first time, as not exclusively heterosexual. "Passing" became a motif in popular culture—blacks disguising themselves as white, Jews passing as gentiles, gays passing as straight, communists masquerading as loyal citizens.[8] Facades of sexual propriety often concealed less-than-respectable behavior, the public was learning; the truth about sex would begin to seep out through rock and roll music and racy paperback novels, Alfred Kinsey's sexuality studies, and new men's magazines like *Playboy*. The wool was being pulled off eyes as crime, sex, and vice became more visible in an increasingly global, urban, complicated world.

Postwar America was a mass mediated society, saturated by radio, television, movies, and print media. Never before had mass communications exerted such influence over the nation's preferences, habits, and ideals. Television was introduced to most homes in the early 1950s and it became the most popular form of entertainment. At a time when Americans had more leisure and disposable income than ever, the circulation of print publications reached record highs. Celebrity dominated American culture, and actors, politicians, and other public figures were relying on publicists to promote attractive personas. A growing, sophisticated advertising industry spent $9 billion annually to churn out persuasive images of products and people.[9] Wearied by wartime propaganda, and savvy to the workings of publicists, marketers, and admen, Americans were becoming conscious—and distrustful—of "spin." At the same time they enjoyed their bubble of innocence, the public was fascinated with going "behind the scenes"—with exposing, informing, shattering facades, tearing down fronts, and seeing the "real truth" behind illusions. This is where *Confidential* came in.

3 | *CONFIDENTIAL*

IN THE STORY HARRISON told the press, *Confidential* was inspired by the Senate hearings on organized crime, the famous "Kefauver committee hearings" of 1951 that made the Mafia a household name in America. Like much of what Harrison said about himself and *Confidential*, this story isn't completely true.

The years after the war witnessed a major boom in organized crime. Just as legitimate business flourished in prosperity, so did the mob. By the early 1950s, the Mafia had infiltrated virtually every big city, practically untouched by federal authority. Prosecution had been left to local law enforcement, and it varied wildly from place to place.[1]

Alarmed by reports of brutal mob killings and a virtual Mafia "supergovernment" controlling hundreds of communities, Democratic Senator Estes Kefauver of Tennessee launched a committee to investigate labor racketeering in interstate commerce. Meeting in fourteen cities in 1951 and interviewing more than eight hundred witnesses, the committee made startling discoveries. Americans of all races, religions, and ethnicities, including seemingly respectable businessmen and politicians, were enmeshed in organized crime. Local Democratic administrations were tied up with the mob, and in some cities it was impossible to tell where official authority ended and the mob began.[2]

In Miami, the Kefauver committee found gambling everywhere, from restaurants to cigar stands. In Kansas City, it confronted, in Kefauver's words, "a place that was struggling out from under the rule of law of the jungle." In Chicago it heard stories about bribing and illegal gambling among the city's police force. The hearings were made even more spectacular by

21

their broadcast on the new medium of television. Local stations interrupted programming to cover two days of hearings featuring "hoodlums of every description . . . [and] the records of their dealings with murderers, dope peddlers, [and] gamblers."[3]

In New York, Mafia kingpin Frank Costello testified before the committee. His lawyers objected to filming his face; cameramen instead zeroed in on his hands. On live television, Americans watched Costello fidgeting and nervously tapping his fingers while he dodged the committee's questions. Virginia Hill, a former moll to the late mobster Bugsy Siegel, was the star of the "Kefauver show." Clad in suede gloves and a mink stole, she recounted "fellas" who showered her with money and racetrack tips. Unruly and defensive, she screamed at photographers as she left the courtroom, "I hope the fucking atom bomb falls on every one of you!"[4]

There had never been anything like it. Never before had the public witnessed crime and vice so nakedly exposed. Nearly thirty million viewed the gossipy tittle-tattle, larger than the audience for the World Series that year. People deserted department stores and movie theaters during "Kefauver hours." Schools dismissed students to watch the hearings, and housewives turned bridge sessions into "Kefauver parties." "The week of March 12, 1951, will occupy a special place in history," *Life* wrote. People had "suddenly gone indoors . . . into living rooms, taverns, and club rooms, auditoriums, and back offices . . . there, in eerie half-light, looking at millions of small frosty screens, people sat as if charmed."[5]

"When the Kefauver Committee was conducting its TV hearings, I saw people were nuts about it," Harrison recalled. "I mean everybody: office workers, housewives, average people [got] wrapped up in watching characters they'd read about—thieves, prostitutes, racketeers—get up on the stand and be questioned." It was then, he said, that he realized Americans were fascinated with crimes and their backstories—with sex and sin "behind the scenes." There was "excitement and interest in the lives of people in the headlines and getting behind the story."[6]

In the wake of the hearings, Harrison said, he came up with the idea for an "exposé magazine"—a muckraking magazine "that told the stories that the newspapers did not tell, or other magazines did not tell." It would reveal "inside, gossipy stuff"—"injustices in government, corruption in government, products that defrauded the public, [and] the antics of well-known people . . . any and all subjects of interest to the public that their family newspaper did not give them." Five or ten years earlier there might not have been an audience for it, but in 1951, he believed, America was "ready for it."[7]

While the Kefauver hearings might have alerted Harrison to a ready market for scandal and gossip, there was another origin to *Confidential*, one that Harrison never revealed. Harrison stole the idea from a series of wildly popular, nasty exposé books, the *Confidential* series, that was topping bestseller lists in the early 1950s.

Between 1948 and 1952, four books with *Confidential* in their titles made headlines: *New York Confidential* (1948), *Chicago Confidential* (1950), *Washington Confidential* (1951), and *U.S.A. Confidential* (1952). Now largely forgotten, they were a sensation in their time. Written in a crude, muckraking style, they offered an alleged "behind the scenes" exposé of deviance, crime, and corruption in American cities. Lascivious, right-wing, racist, sexist, homophobic, and largely false, they depicted America as weak and diseased, infected by communism, crime, and liberal thinking. In their pages, communists, spies, criminals, gays, intellectuals, New Dealers, African Americans, and women joined together in a sinister conspiracy to subvert the nation. The books sold more than seven million copies and introduced a new nastiness, viciousness, and sexual smearing into politics and popular culture.[8]

Authors Jack Lait and Lee Mortimer were no strangers to sleazy journalism. Both worked for the right-wing, sensationalistic Hearst press and were part of a network of government officials and conservative journalists who stoked the Red Scare. Lait, editor of the Hearst tabloid the *New York Mirror*, started his career reporting on Chicago's underworld in the 1920s and was considered one of the leading newspapermen of his generation. Mortimer, twenty years Lait's junior, was his colleague on the *Mirror*, where he wrote a column called New York Confidential. A small man "known for his feuds and night club fisticuffs," Mortimer was a friend of Harrison's and an early editor of *Beauty Parade*. He gained national fame in 1947 as the journalist Frank Sinatra punched outside a plush Hollywood nightclub for calling him a communist and a "dago."[9]

The *Confidential* books were written as "travel guides," not for the actual traveler but the armchair traveler—the conservative reader of middle America ready to be shocked by sin and vice in the nation's big cities. In breathless prose, they described "reefer parties," prostitution houses, gambling dens, and gay "dives" that flourished by night but that weren't visible to the casual observer. Their existence was nothing new, Lait and Mortimer wrote, but the mainstream press was too timid to report it.

For the most part, they were right. Most magazines and newspapers of that time *were* restrained, held back by their conservative business backers and the norms of polite society. "All the news that's fit to print" was by today's standards very little. Afraid of offending the sensibilities of the average reader and the advertisers who courted those readers, news media exercised vigorous self-censorship. Gritty details about rapes, suicides, prostitution, and murders were excluded. If sex crimes were reported, they were described only in euphemistic, watered-down terms. "Taboo" subjects, of which there were many, were treated delicately or avoided altogether: interracial relationships, drug use, "deviant" sex.

There was also a big cover-up around public figures. In the large, mainstream papers of the day, the unseemly activities of public officials were almost always suppressed. There was a gentleman's agreement between the press and the powers that be that scandalous material, especially involving sexual transgressions, would never make it to print. The extramarital affairs of Presidents Warren Harding and Franklin Roosevelt were famously concealed by the press corps. Fear of reprisals and liability for libel, journalistic ethics (such as the American Society of Newspaper Editors' professional code stating that newspapers should not invade privacy solely for "public curiosity"), and the desire to not upset the relatively naïve ordinary reader meant that newspapers rarely revealed indiscretions, even though reporters knew all about them.

Venturing into taboo topics, prying into privacy, with their "eye at every keyhole from the Bowery to Park Avenue," Lait and Mortimer claimed to tell "the truth about the mobsters and molls, B-girls, strippers, clippers and gyppers, cops and robbers, politicians, bums and slums, dope and delinquency." They purportedly trolled slums and back alleys for information, and got their tips from cabbies and bellboys. The news was so hot it had to be whispered. The books were infamous for their intimate, *hush-hush* tone, *confidentially* and *on the QT.*[10]

In *Washington Confidential*, the smears went political. Lait and Mortimer accused the Roosevelt and Truman administration of turning the nation's capital into a hotbed of communism, drunkenness, whoring, and corruption. In wild, interracial, homosexual orgies, liberals and communists—"fairies and Fair Dealers"—seduced "initiates" to their faith. An entire chapter denounced the civil service as "infected" by homosexuals. *Washington Confidential* was so controversial that the federal civil service launched a publicity campaign to defuse it.[11]

U.S.A. Confidential, a bestseller, attacked the entire country. "Greedy groups and misguided ninnies are turning [America] into a nightmare," Lait and Mortimer alleged. "Conditions of . . . crime, graft, and organized racketeering have spread over virtually the entire nation. . . . Differing only with climate, population, and other local and regional circumstances, we found prostitution, perversion, and protected political extortion in hamlets, counties, and states as rotten as in the big cities. . . . The country is in the grip of the Mafia, tighter than ever . . . politics on all levels everywhere we found crooked, raw, and shameless. . . . Our youth is unbridled, hopped up, sex-crazy, and perverted."[12]

Thick with misogyny, the *Confidential* books complained that women everywhere—"in farm houses, factories, furnished rooms, and in furs"—were "promiscuous and predatory." "Negroes," who purportedly committed about half of the nation's crimes, were knee-deep in corruption and leftist politics.[13] Lait and Mortimer reserved their greatest animus for gays and lesbians. Homophobia leered from almost every page of the *Confidential* books.

Long regarded as too sinful to be discussed, homosexuality was just beginning to appear in the press and public discourse. There was enormous naïveté surrounding sexual orientation. Most Americans of the time hadn't heard of homosexuality and didn't understand it even when it was explained to them. Homosexuality emerged as a topic of interest with the greater visibility of gays and lesbians during the war. The military had offered an opportunity for many Americans to explore their sexuality, and the rise of cities in wartime fostered large urban gay communities. Same-sex attraction was put on the nation's front pages in 1948 by Dr. Alfred Kinsey, whose report on Americans' sexual practices announced that more than a third of men had engaged in homosexual activity. Psychiatry, gaining in prestige and authority, rushed forth with new explanations for same-sex attraction. Once considered a moral issue, homosexuality was being described as a "neurosis" that could be cured with psychotherapy, electroshock treatment, and massive injections of hormones. "No one is born sexually deviated," *Time* magazine explained in 1950. "Sexually aberrated individuals can be treated [by] psychoanalytic psychotherapy."[14]

Not only an individual problem, homosexuality was cast as a social menace linked to other ills caused by war and its aftermath, including the breakdown of communities, rising crime, and the weakening of the family. "Behind a wall erected by apathy, ignorance, and a reluctance to face facts, a sinister threat to American youth is fast developing," *Coronet* magazine announced in 1950. "Unlike disease and crime, this threat, until very recently, was seldom discussed in public; its existence was acknowledged only in whispers—and in sordid police and prison records." More than eight million Americans were said to be actual or potential homosexuals, and the number was allegedly on the rise. The main "reasons" for same-sex attraction, according to experts, were "glandular disbalance," "parental cultivation of infantilism in adolescents," "complicated economic conditions," and the "distortion of values produced by high-tension city life."[15]

In 1949 the State Department had dismissed ninety-one employees for "moral turpitude," the vast majority for homosexuality. The Senate subsequently authorized a formal inquiry into "moral perverts" in government. The Senate's report linked homosexuality to communism, alleging that gays would be security risks because they would be easy targets for blackmail; they would readily divulge secrets to spies rather than risk exposure of their sexual identity. Like communists, homosexuals purportedly feigned normality to fit into society. Both worked insidiously to corrupt the young, and their infection was contagious. "You can't hardly separate homosexuals from subversives," said Senator Kenneth Wherry of Nebraska. "Mind you, I don't say every homosexual is a subversive, and I don't say every subversive is a homosexual. But a man of low morality is a menace in the government, whatever he is, and they are all tied up together. . . . There should be no people of that type working in any position in the government."[16]

Drawing on the Kinsey report and the Senate hearings, Lait and Mortimer described homosexuality as a hidden, flourishing "epidemic" spread by communists and other "subversives." "Confidentially, many men aren't men," they announced. "The entire nation is going queer!"

> The unsophisticates who think of queers as prancing nances with rouged lips and bleached hair will not believe us. . . . Any cop will tell you that among the fairies he arrests are tough young kids, college football players, truck-drivers, and weather-bitten servicemen. An admiral tried to rape a young soldier on the street in Honolulu. Many queers are married, fathers of families. . . . A particularly sanctimonious U.S. Senator from an Eastern state is known to follow youths as young as his grandchildren into rest rooms.[17]

More than six thousand homosexuals were on the government payroll, they claimed. Though they didn't name names, Lait and Mortimer exposed high-ranking officials as "deviates." "A man of almost Cabinet rank in the Defense Department is . . . a pervert with bivalent tendencies, a two-way performer," they alleged. One of the most "startling surprises" of their investigations, they said, was that more women were "sexual deviates" than men: "Sapphism has gone underground into the ranks of secretaries, file clerks, telephone gals, the five-and-dimes, and the female armed service. . . . Lesbians in heat are more combative than the ordinary garden variety male. Uncooperative girls are often raped."[18]

The *Confidential* books would be hard to take seriously if it weren't for their enormous readership. Lait and Mortimer spoke powerfully to frightened and confused Americans, the same audiences whose fear and bewilderment drew them to the hatemongering of McCarthy and his ilk. Lait and Mortimer weren't petty, small-time zealots mouthing off to small-town audiences. Their filth was "boosted by every drugstore and bookstore, and peddled by Hearst," warned John Mallan in the *New Republic*. They were in the big business of hate, backed by big money, with full-page advertisements in the *New York Times*.[19]

As *U.S.A. Confidential* shot up bestseller lists, Harrison had his inspiration. "*Confidential!*' he shouted one day in the office. "I've got it! *Confidential!* It can't miss!"[20]

———

Exposed: LOVE IN THE U.N.!

Confidential

UNCENSORED AND OFF THE RECORD Dec. 25¢

O'DWYER: SAINT OR SINNER?

SHOWGIRL SELLS SHARES IN SELF

ATHLETES ARE LOUSY LOVERS!

HOODLUMS' PARADISE

When it debuted in late 1952, *Confidential* was one of the most frank and edgy exposé magazines to ever appear on newsstands. *Wikimedia Commons*

In the first half of 1952, Harrison and Al Govoni, Harrison's chief editor, mocked up Harrison's new magazine. Govoni, a former reporter for the *Police Gazette*, had been with Harrison Publications since 1949.[21] Harrison and Govoni worked diligently, trying out new ideas and scrapping them over and over again. The first issue of *Confidential*, subtitled *Uncensored and Off the Record*, hit newsstands in September.

Printed on cheap pulp paper in a garish blue, red, and yellow color scheme, *Confidential* was striking. Its headlines, in a square and rugged font, were bold and stark, often ending with exclamation points in pairs or tripled. Big black-and-white photos ran with almost every article, punctured by screaming yellow arrows targeting the site of a crime or a "love nest." Blurry, grainy, close-up photos showed their subjects in an unflattering, even gruesome, light. *Confidential* wasn't the first publication to use this style. The *Police Gazette* and *Click* magazine, which had its life in the 1930s and '40s (with headlines like "Marijuana: A Roadside Weed Now a National Menace," and "How Deaf Mutes Make Love"), had a nearly identical look.

Nor was *Confidential* the first exposé publication. Early twentieth-century muckrakers had published exposés of government and business corruption in magazines such as *McClure's* and the *American Magazine*. Less respectable pulps such as the *Police Gazette*, *Friday* ("the weekly magazine that dares to tell the truth!"), *Sensation* ("stories no other magazine dares to print"), *Inside Stuff*, and Harrison's own *Whisper* wrote about salacious subjects in a breathless "tell-all" style. (At the time *Confidential* debuted, the *Police Gazette* had just launched a multipart series, "Hitler Is Alive!") There were also picture-heavy tabloids like the *New York Daily News* and the *New York Daily Mirror*, the *Evening Graphic*'s former competitors. In many cities, highly partisan, short-lived "scandal sheets" did sensational reporting on crime, vice, and corruption.

But with its wild, outrageous, vicious claims, *Confidential* would outdo them all. Taking on forbidden topics—especially taboo sex—in a lurid and randy style, *Confidential* was one of the most frank and edgy exposé publications to ever hit newsstands, and it would be the first to go mainstream.

Openly defiant of polite society and untethered to big business interests—Harrison relied on the same seedy advertisers for correspondence courses, sex manuals, and weight loss products showcased in his girlie magazines—*Confidential* would go where mainstream journalists retreated, revealing a world that was *stunning, hideous, sensational, naughty, exclusive, taboo, torrid, daring, intimate, shocking, sinful, sordid,* and *horrifying*:

> The bunk is going to be debunked! In this, its first issue, *Confidential* will open your eyes and make them pop. It pulls the curtain aside and takes you behind the scenes, giving facts, naming names, and revealing what the front pages often try to conceal!
>
> Here you will read about the famous who are infamous; about the glamorous who are de-glamorized; about the mugs and the mobs; about high society and low society. Yes, you may be shocked, but at least you'll get the truth without any trimmings. You'll get plain talk without double talk. You'll get what you've always wanted to get—the real stories behind the headlines—uncensored and off the record! . . .
>
> We hope you'll like *Confidential* and tell your friends. If you don't like it, tell us. We love truth—which is why *Confidential* contains no fiction. It's all fact![22]

The first issue of *Confidential* was ripped straight from the Kefauver hearings and the Lait and Mortimer books. An entire section of Issue Number One offered an "Underworld Expose." The article "Hoodlums' Paradise" presented a "frank, uncensored report" of the mob-owned town of Hot Springs, Arkansas, "a devil's brew of notorious mobsters, gamblers, strip-teasers, and dirty peep shows!" "What Virginia Hill Didn't Tell Kefauver" promised "the real lowdown on plenty of the things the Cinderella Girl of the underworld didn't talk about." "Monte Carlo of the Air" by "Carlton Mitchell"—most *Confidential* articles ran under pseudonyms—reported that a gambling ring had invested $3 million to run casinos in airplanes, "9,000 feet in the sky." Harrison claimed, outrageously, that the article "drove that operation out of New York. I covered that one myself and took pictures in the airplane with a concealed camera."[23]

"Rackets," another section, exposed swindles and hoaxes in everyday life. "Highway Larceny" described a "flim-flam by dishonest gas station attendants who swindle motorists out of $300,000,000 a year. . . . One of their favorites is the oil-can flim-flam. Attendants always want to check your oil when you drive into a station for gas." So-called "public service" stories exposed corruption and social injustices. "I Was Tortured on a Chain Gang!" described conditions in a Georgia prison camp. The article was purportedly written by "George Drexel," wanted by the state for escaping a chain gang. It featured a gruesome photo of Drexel, his back whipped and lacerated. "Devil's Island for Boys" reported on an Arizona prison where young inmates were forced to walk barefoot through the scorching desert, their heads shaved. "Some people will say it can't happen here . . . But it does! For the sake of the youth of America, read this shocking report," the story urged.[24]

Like Lait and Mortimer's books, *Confidential* seethed with racism and misogyny. An article titled "They Pass for White!" described blacks "passing" as Caucasian as the "biggest, most fantastic, and most pathetic trick ever played on the white race. For more than 20 years, some five million negroes have been living a big white lie. They've turned their backs on their own race and crossed over the line to the world of the whites—and very few of the so-called Superior Race ever realizes it," the article reported breathlessly. "Let's Abolish Common Law Marriage" warned the magazine's mostly male readership about "the most dangerous booby trap ever set for bachelors—common law marriage," "an incredible situation wherein money-hungry females can persuade courts to declare them common law wives, often on the very thinnest of evidence. . . . If YOU are a bachelor, WATCH YOUR STEP!"[25]

From the start, *Confidential* was preoccupied with homosexuality, which remained its signature issue and enduring theme. This, in its own right, made it a landmark; no publication of the time wrote about it so unrelentingly, crudely, and obsessively. A photo essay in the first issue, "The World's Queerest Wedding," described as a "*Confidential* exclusive," displayed pictures from an alleged "wedding" of two male homosexuals in Paris. "The blushing bride wore silk and lace—and also happened to be a man!" read the subtitle. The couple was shown cutting a wedding cake and throwing a bouquet ("floral decorations included pansies"). A "waltz between bride and groom signal[ed] [the] start of festivities which went on for hours. . . . Everyone was very gay."[26]

Confidential's second issue featured its very first article outing a star as homosexual, "Is It True What They Say About Johnnie Ray?" Ray, an up-and-coming pop star, a crooning, crying songster who made teens swoon, was a closeted homosexual who had been arrested in 1951 in Detroit for accosting and soliciting an undercover vice squad officer in the restroom of a burlesque house. The press paid little attention to the arrest, since Ray was an obscure performer at the time. It wasn't until his hit record *Cry* appeared later that year that Ray became a star, and rumors swirled around his sexuality.

Confidential alluded to the arrest and reported on Ray's alleged appearances in women's clothing:

> There were scores of persons in Detroit who could swear they had seen this youngster cavorting on the stage of a nightclub made up and outfitted down to the last scarlet fingernail in a girl's attire. A suave, sophisticated audience in New York's internationally known Copacabana Club had also seen him "in drag," a cynical Broadway term for a man who dresses as a woman. . . .
>
> There can be no doubt that, like millions of other men in this nation, Ray finds his quotient of "maleness" a serious challenge at times. . . . Could a skilled psychiatrist revamp his personality to eliminate these outbursts of femininity?[27]

Confidential, noted the fledgling gay magazine *One*, "says nothing directly in affirmation of whether Johnnie is or isn't [gay], but readers see a host of strange rumors, suggestions, hints, and quotations of 'certain well-known people' all of which sum up to one answer."[28]

Harrison brought most of his girlie magazine staff with him over to *Confidential*. His sister Edith Tobias was his secretary and editorial assistant, his sister Helen Studin was office manager, and her husband, Dan, was circulation manager. The name "E. Studin" was listed on the masthead as a "researcher." Dark, mustachioed thirty-eight-year-old Al Govoni, the son of Italian immigrants from Lowell, Massachusetts, was *Confidential*'s managing editor for most of its run. Jay Breen, a genial, husky reporter for United Press Syndicate, wrote freelance for *Confidential* until he went to work for Harrison full time in 1954. Breen, who would later go on to become associate editor, was *Confidential*'s most prolific and important writer. By 1955 he wrote more than half its stories. Breen had both a way with words and a serious alcohol problem. His drunken binges often forced delays in the magazine's production schedule.[29]

Confidential magazine, Harrison boasted, was cutting-edge investigative journalism put together by "newspapermen and writers with a ... consuming passion for facts." In reality, most of what appeared in *Confidential* was stolen or faked. Harrison's writers freely ripped off other people's books and articles. A freelancer hired to report on the Mafia, a subject she knew nothing about, did her research by calling someone who had written a book on the Mafia and asking him if she could crib it. Some articles were completely false. At weekly staff conferences, editors and writers would discuss "Harrison dream-stories." "We would kick around an idea for a phony story," recalled one editor. "Something that couldn't very well be disproved."[30]

A photo spread showed a bikini-clad woman poised to assault a photographer at a Hollywood nightclub. The picture showed a "Swedish starlet, being groomed for the big time by a major film company, who took a bit too much booze ... and romped outside the Mocambo in her scanties. Her name is Tia Carlson of Stockholm. Rather than offend a big movie advertiser, this news was killed!" In reality, the girl was a model, and the man was a *Confidential* writer. The article "Gangster Ghouls" revealed how the mob was making grave-robbing into an industry. A caption read: "Former ... hoods Vito Ligi, left, and Joe Carr play coy after their arrest." The man posing as Ligi was a *Confidential* editor. Harrison was "Joe Carr."[31]

Even though *Confidential* claimed to be "100% true," Harrison issued scores of retractions. "The Mob Moves in on Show Business," in the second issue, offered an exposé of mob tie-ups in the music, jukebox, and nightclub industries. Singer Tony Bennett's manager was "a character called Ray Muscarella," a talent handler who worked in the trucking business on the side. Muscarella used his mob connections to get Bennett's record into eighteen thousand jukeboxes simultaneously, according to *Confidential*. "The juke boxes involved, for the most part, are owned and/or operated by the mob."[32]

Muscarella wasn't pleased, to put it mildly, and after the article came out he and an associate went to Harrison's office. Harrison turned white when he saw them; it's rumored they hung him out the window by his heels. Harrison threw up his hands and admitted he made a mistake. "From now on, I'm gonna read every article we publish," he said. The following issue ran a retraction with the headline, "When we make a mistake, it's a beaut."[33]

The mistakes and faking got so bad that the staffers rebelled. They asked to have their names taken out of the magazine. The correct names were listed on the first issue, but after that pseudonyms appeared for many of its editors. They were ashamed of having their names in *Confidential*.[34]

4 | WINCHELL AND RUSHMORE

CONFIDENTIAL WAS A FLOP. Its first print run was only 150,000 copies. In 1952 forty-seven magazines had circulations of more than one million. *Confidential*'s closest rival, the *Police Gazette*, circulated more than 300,000. In their heyday, Harrison's girlie magazines sold over 250,000 copies per issue.[1]

Harrison was frankly ashamed by the first issue of *Confidential*. He knew he needed to tone down the faking and hokum; he needed better writing and better publicity. For the latter, he went to Walter Winchell. Egotistical and career-obsessed, gossip columnist Winchell would promote anyone who flattered him. And a Winchell plug, Harrison knew, was "money in the bank."[2]

Since the 1920s, Walter Winchell had been America's best-known gossip columnist and foremost news personality. Millions read his syndicated column, listened to his radio show, and watched him on television. Winchell had actually started his career on the *Evening Graphic* in the 1920s, though Harrison never met him at the time. At the *Graphic*, Winchell penned one of the first celebrity gossip columns in the country, titled Your Broadway and Mine. Written in an abrupt, fast-paced patter, filled with his trademark "Winchellisms"—"welded" and "middle aisled" meant married, "Reno-vated" was divorced —the column described the private lives of stage and screen stars, socialites, and other public figures. Quipped *The Outlook* magazine in 1929, Winchell commented on "which couple is about to agree to a separation, what distinguished member of Broadway society is Reno-bound . . . in quest of a divorce, which homes are anticipating blessed events . . . and other odds and ends of private gossip such as respectable newspapers do not print."[3]

Though small-town gossip columns had long reported on the comings and goings of society figures, Winchell was the first to apply those techniques to Broadway and Hollywood, fast becoming focal points of the public's curiosity and interest. Winchell's column was very much like an old-fashioned society column, except that the figures he wrote about came from America's new "society"—models, showgirls, mobsters, singers, dancers, and movie stars who socialized in fashionable nightclubs, mugged for the camera, and modeled modern values of conspicuous consumption and sex appeal. Winchell created a pantheon of idols, lifestyle icons for the nation to emulate and discuss. He was the pioneer of the celebrity gossip column and one of the architects of American celebrity culture.

When Winchell moved to the Hearst-owned *Daily Mirror* in 1929, he skyrocketed to fame. As part of the Hearst syndicate, Winchell's column appeared in more than two thousand papers, with a daily circulation of nearly nine million. His Sunday night radio broadcasts—with his greeting, "Good evening Mr. and Mrs. America, from border to border and coast to coast and all the ships at sea," issued in a brisk staccato reached over fifty million listeners. Winchell "knew more about celebrities in every stratum and more things about them than any other living man in this country," according to *Time*. He was a household name and a "national institution." Winchell became a celebrity in his own right, even playing himself in a 1937 movie, *Wake Up and Live.*[4]

"If a thing is true, or even half true," Winchell often said, it was material for his column, "no matter how private or personal it may be." He ran news about the troubles of couples that hadn't yet filed for divorce and reported suicides that wouldn't have made the papers. But Winchell didn't print all that he knew. Winchell famously suppressed the sexual infidelities of New York mayor Jimmy Walker. He often held back material he thought would be destructive to families and relationships, saying he never printed anything that might wreck a happy marriage. If Winchell saw a married man or woman dallying with a romantic interest in a nightclub, he'd conceal it unless he had reason to believe that the marriage was already on the rocks.[5]

Winchell was one of the most gargantuan personalities in New York journalism, a world where big egos were as common as split infinitives. Though physically diminutive—lean, with beady eyes and a narrow, foxlike face—his arrogance, drive, and compulsion could fill up a room. Volatile, compulsive, and restless, Winchell had hard blue eyes, a nasal voice, and enormous energy, which he channeled into chain-smoking, tapping his feet, and pacing. Each night he would scour the city looking for news, then come back to his apartment and sleep fitfully for as long as his nerves would allow. Winchell's brash and hard-driving manner endeared him to his millions of fans, but colleagues found him cold, fickle, and narcissistic. He talked endlessly about himself, ruminating over his insomnia, eating habits, and likes and hates, accompanying his monologues with facial expressions, gesturing hands, and darting fingers. He believed that everyone read his column and was aghast when he found out they didn't. Career was for Winchell, as it was for Harrison, a "driving demoniac obsession."[6]

In the late 1930s, Winchell began devoting less space in his column to celebrities and more to politics. He became an opinionated pundit, offering aggressive and pointed commentary on world affairs. Winchell had been a staunch supporter of FDR and the New Deal, and supported intervention in the war in Europe. Winchell was also an advocate of civil rights and attacked the Klan and other racist groups. But after the war, Winchell's politics shifted. After Roosevelt's death, Winchell no longer had contacts in the White House. He turned on President Truman and accused the administration of being infiltrated by communists. Anticommunism became his cause célèbre. Winchell was an outspoken supporter of Joseph McCarthy and FBI head J. Edgar Hoover, who often leaked information to Winchell. Winchell used his column to launch unfounded allegations of communist activity against countless groups and individuals. When he found a target, he honed in on it viciously, smearing his opponent in column after column.[7]

Winchell's red-baiting cost him popularity, and by the early 1950s his career was on the decline. Always combative and controversial, his hard-right stance brought him even more feuds and enemies. Sensing his career was in a tailspin, he became insecure and depressed. Winchell sought to feed his ego like a starving man. He nonetheless continued to wield enormous influence. In the fall of 1952 he began broadcasting his Sunday night radio show on television, expanding his reach and power.[8]

For the first issue of *Confidential*, Harrison ordered his staff to court Winchell, to "butter the old boy up." A writer did a short piece praising Winchell, but Harrison threw it out because he thought it was too obvious.[9]

Harrison then came up with the idea of covering the "Josephine Baker affair." At the time, Winchell was in a feud with Baker, the African American dancer and actress who had risen to fame in Paris in the 1920s by entertaining while clad only in a girdle of bananas. Baker remained in Europe during the 1930s and '40s and became internationally renowned for her erotic dancing. She returned to the United States in 1951, where she was slated to perform in nightclubs and in New York's Strand Theatre.

The "Baker affair" had taken place in October 1951, when Baker and a group of white friends entered the Stork Club, the most famous and elite of the café society nightclubs and Winchell's virtual office. Sherman Billingsley, the club's owner, was racist and arrogant. Baker was seated but wasn't served, and she left in a fury. She publicized the insult the next day, intending it to be a pioneering civil rights case. Baker's press agent claimed that Winchell, who was in the club at the time, hadn't supported her and was complicit in the affront. Winchell was outraged at having been brought into the conflict and by the implication that he was indifferent to civil rights. NAACP head Walter White wanted Winchell to attack Billingsley, but he refused. Instead Winchell went after Baker, accusing her—with no basis—of being pro-fascist, a troublemaker, and a communist.[10]

Winchell's connection to the incident and his digs on Baker gave his many enemies an excuse to go after him. The journalist, publicist, and publishing world gadfly Lyle Stuart had recently started a tabloid called *Expose*, described in FBI files as a "rag sheet" that was "anti-Catholic, anti-Jewish, anti-religion, and antieverything." Stuart took the opportunity to settle an old grudge against Winchell, publishing a story, "The Truth About Walter Winchell," that described him as vain, egocentric, psychopathic, and "one of the greatest hoaxes ever put over on newspaper readers." The leading liberal paper in New York, the *Post*, another Winchell enemy, ran a series titled "Inside Winchell," commissioned by editor James Wechsler. The series debuted with a front page article depicting Winchell as "one of the loneliest men in the world." He was a sad character who "assumes that he knows everybody and everybody knows him." "He made the gossip column a respectable newspaper feature . . . but he spends much of his time justifying the existence of gossip columns and trying to prove he is a heavier thinker than Walter Lippmann," the article alleged. Winchell lashed back with an attack on Wechsler and the *Post*, which he denounced as the "Poo," the "Compost," and the "Postinko."[11]

"Winchell was Right About Josephine Baker!" *Confidential* announced. "Walter Winchell was virtually the only newspaperman in America who had the guts to stick his chin out and tell the world what a phony Josephine Baker was when she provoked the now-famous 'Stork Club Incident' last winter. For his pains, Winchell became an international target for charges of discrimination." *Confidential* alleged that Baker stirred up the Stork Club incident for publicity; she was a spotlight hunter, disappointed at not being flattered in the United States as she had been in France, and used the "honest fight against discrimination" to promote her career. According to the article, Baker was lucky to have been let in the Stork Club because Billingsley reserved it for "important people," and "anyone who didn't drop to their knees for her, personally, was lashed and vilified as being obviously biased against the color of her skin."[12]

Harrison marched the story over to Winchell's publicist Ed Weiner, who gave it to Winchell. Winchell was flattered, and he plugged *Confidential*. "Don't miss the next *Confidential* mag (about la Baker) due Feb 4," he wrote in his column in late January 1953. When the story came out, Winchell pumped *Confidential* on his TV show, holding up a copy of the magazine before six million viewers. The issue flew off newsstands. *Variety* reported that it sold out in sixteen to twenty cities, in some within forty-eight hours. "*Confidential* mag sold out the first 2 days following a Sunday-night teevy-radio plug for its expose of Josephooy Baker," Winchell announced. From then on, Harrison ran a Winchell article every issue. "We'd try to figure out who Winchell didn't like and run a piece about them," one *Confidential* writer recalled. "We had one in every issue. And [Winchell] kept on plugging *Confidential*. It got to the point where some days we would sit down and rack our brains trying to think of somebody else Winchell didn't like. We were running out of people, for Christ's sake!"[13]

There were rumors in publishing circles that Winchell was part of *Confidential*. That wasn't true, and Winchell was staunchly opposed to anyone thinking he had a hand in *Confidential*. Harrison recalled that one time he had advance notice that Winchell was going to plug an issue on his TV show, and he told his news distributor about it. The distributor sent a notice to news dealers to stock up on the issue because Winchell would be promoting it. Winchell was outraged because it made it look like *Confidential* had a deal with him.[14]

Despite Winchell's praise for *Confidential*, deep down he knew it was trash. Winchell got hundreds of letters from readers complaining about his connection to *Confidential*. He once dined with a group of *Time* editors who were enraged by his support of *Confidential* and asked him why he allowed himself to be identified with it. "They were in my corner when I needed friends," he said. Even Winchell recognized he'd been "driven to extremes" in getting involved with *Confidential*, wrote biographer Neal Gabler. When Winchell and Harrison met at Lindy's restaurant, he asked Harrison, "How the hell did I ever get involved with *Confidential*, I can't figure it out." He did it out of desperation: he was consumed by "anger and vengeance" and needed every means to carry it out.[15]

Walter Winchell made *Confidential*. *Confidential*'s circulation shot up more than five times in five months, going from 150,000 in December 1952 to 800,000 by the end of 1953. Winchell continued to champion *Confidential* that summer and fall, and he tracked and trumpeted the magazine's success. "A Broadway at 50th newsstand has 300 requests already for *Confidential* mag due the 17th," Winchell wrote in June 1953. "*Confidential* mag is getting richer. One Philly newsstand ordered 13,000 copies," he noted in September. *Confidential* was the "fastest selling Two-Biterature in town."[16]

Harrison's efforts to court Winchell took him to Howard Rushmore, Winchell's friend and a prominent writer for Hearst's *New York Journal-American*. Six foot four, gangly, and homely with sharp, angular features, Rushmore was a former communist turned zealous anticommunist, a wife-beater, a liar, and a vicious, unstable man. Rushmore would go on to become one of the driving forces behind *Confidential*.

Howard Rushmore was a troubled soul whose misery and self-loathing started young. Born on July 2, 1912, Rushmore grew up in poverty in Sheridan, Wyoming, where his parents were homesteaders. When he was fourteen, the family moved to Missouri. His father took a job at a brick plant, and Rushmore worked there in the evenings. During the early years of the Great Depression, he took to the rails as a hobo. "We rode in boxcars reeking of manure, in coal cars with black dust biting into our skin," he recalled. "We ate together in 'jungles,' huddling for protection against the cold. We drank dirty stew, and the hope went out of us."[17]

As a cub reporter on a local paper in Missouri, Rushmore wrote a moving story about an accident at the brick plant. A worker had been "ground to bits" under the revolving wheel. Later Rushmore covered the brutal lynching of a young black man in Kansas City and got to know communists who protested the lynching. He became interested in their work, and in 1935 Rushmore joined the Young Communist League. He went on to become state organizer of the Young Communist League in the Dakotas, then a writer on the *Daily Worker*, the Communist Party's major newspaper. By 1939 Rushmore was the *Daily Worker*'s official film critic, a high position within the communist hierarchy. He began dating Ruth Garvin, who wrote the women's column for the *Sunday Worker Progressive Weekly*. They married in 1936. Rushmore beat her, and they split up after he threatened her life at a party.[18]

Obstreperous and opinionated, Rushmore battled with the *Daily Worker*'s editors over news policy. The tension reached a head when Rushmore wrote an ambivalent review of *Gone with the Wind*. Remembering tales he had heard from his maternal grandfather, who'd been in the Confederate Army, Rushmore admired the movie. The communists didn't. "Any picture that supports the South can't be truthful," they said. They accused him of having "careeristic, mercenary, and antiworking class tendencies" as well as "anti-Negro sentiments" and anti-Semitic views. Rushmore was told to rewrite the review. Instead, he broke with the party. "I put the review in my pocket, wrote a short note of resignation and left the *Daily Worker* and the communist party forever," he wrote. His departure made the front page of the *New York Times*.[19]

The *Daily Worker* printed an attack on Rushmore. Not averse to turning a capitalist dollar, Rushmore marched over to Hearst's right-wing newspaper the *Journal-American* and told editors how he'd become disenchanted with communism. The *Journal-American* hired Rushmore, and he became Hearst's leading red-hunter, specializing in attacks on his former comrades. In the 1930s Rushmore was the first journalist to make a full-time job reporting on the communist movement. Rushmore "established means to watch party activities

almost like a police force," wrote Hearst columnist George Sokolsky. He allegedly knew more about what was going on inside the movement than every government agency except the FBI. In 1945 Rushmore married a beautiful blonde
former model, Marjorie Frances McCoy, a widow with two young daughters
who was working as a columnist at the *Journal-American*. His first wife tried
to have him arrested for bigamy, claiming she and Rushmore never divorced.[20]

In the 1940s Rushmore became a professional stool pigeon, traveling
around the country and appearing as a witness before official bodies investigating communism. In 1947 he became a key witness in HUAC's investigations
of the film industry. The following year Rushmore went before the Washington
State Committee on Un-American Activities, where he alleged that 150 government employees were operating a Soviet spy ring. He displayed a typewritten
document that he claimed was an FBI report. FBI agents asked him to produce
it. He showed them a letter that he himself had written.[21]

In the early 1950s Rushmore became one of the key forces behind Senator
Joe McCarthy's rise to power. The official liaison between the Hearst organization and McCarthy, Rushmore built up McCarthy in Hearst's papers and was a
major source of his information on alleged communists. When McCarthy took
the position of chairman of the Senate's Permanent Subcommittee on Investigations (PSI) in 1953, he hired Rushmore as his research director. McCarthy
asked the FBI to do a background check on Rushmore. It advised him that
Rushmore was an unreliable reporter, a "so-called specialist on Communist matters" who had a habit of embellishing rumors and drawing "heavily on his own
past experiences and imagination." "Rushmore's writings on communist matters have proved unreliable due to his tendency to sensationalize and blow up
fragments of information," read the report. It was the opinion of the New York
FBI office that "everything written by Rushmore on communist matters should
be heavily discounted as to veracity." McCarthy hired him nonetheless. The
Journal-American gave Rushmore a leave of absence to work for McCarthy.[22]

In the spring of 1953 Harrison called Rushmore at McCarthy's office in Washington. "Hello," he said over the phone. "This is Harrison. Publisher of *Confidential*."
"I've never heard of you," Rushmore snapped.[23]

Undaunted, Harrison told Rushmore he was renowned as an expert on anticommunism and wanted him to work on a story. Harrison was hoping to do a piece on *New York Post* editor James Wechsler, once a member of the Young Communist League and one of Winchell's enemies. Wechsler had allegedly recanted and professed to be an anticommunist. Winchell attacked Wechsler in his column, calling him a left-winger, communist sympathizer, and "fellow traveler."[24]

Rushmore told Harrison he was busy with McCarthy's committee and couldn't help him. Harrison pleaded with Rushmore, telling him he'd pay for him to come to New York and meet him. Rushmore flew there that night and took a taxi to Harrison's apartment. A small, sharply dressed man with slicked-back hair and a gleaming white smile opened the door. Over dinner, Rushmore told Harrison that he had been a card-carrying communist but reformed and was now an anticommunist. "Anyone who works for Joe McCarthy is good enough for me," Harrison grinned.[25]

Harrison convinced Rushmore to do the story. "The fact that James . . . Wechsler, the one-time member of the Young Communist League's national executive committee, is still editor of a daily newspaper which claims to be anticommunist can be regarded as a phenomenon in the annals of American journalism," Rushmore wrote. Wechsler claimed that he had severed all connections with communists, but the "ex-pink but can't prove it." "At this writing, 16 years after Wechsler says he threw over communism and became its enemy, he has yet to appear as a government witness in a public hearing and name a single individual he knew while a leader of the red conspiracy. Dozens of real ex-communists have done just that and have sent many spies and traitors on their way to the electric chair or to long jail terms," Rushmore taunted. Winchell announced gleefully in his column, "*Confidential* mag's next steamroller will flatten the N.Y. Compost editor James Wechsler." He began calling *Confidential* his "pet mag."[26]

In July 1953, Rushmore left McCarthy's committee. McCarthy found out Rushmore was using pre-hearing testimony for his articles in the *Journal-American*. Rushmore arranged with McCarthy's staff to channel information to him that would appear in the *Journal-American* several days before scheduled hearings. Outraged, McCarthy's chief counsel, Roy Cohn, ordered his staff not to release information to Rushmore unless it was cleared with him first. Insulted, Rushmore quit the committee.[27]

Rushmore continued to work for the *Journal-American* and used the paper to stage attacks on Cohn. He also worked part time for *Confidential*. Rushmore promoted *Confidential* on radio and TV and became the magazine's resident red-hunter. His articles praised Winchell and played to Winchell's causes, including tirelessly attacking Winchell's enemies and exposing purported communist "subversion."[28]

In "They Exposed the Cancer Chiselers," Rushmore celebrated Winchell's work for the Damon Runyon Cancer Society, a charity Winchell founded in 1946. Harrison obligingly became a contributor to the fund. That issue also featured an article on another Winchell foe, tabloid publisher Lyle Stuart. "You've never heard of him and his smear-sheet, but *Confidential* is alerting you to be on guard in case Lyle Stuart attempts to peddle *Expose* in your community," Rushmore wrote, alleging that psychiatrists deemed Stuart "egocentric," "narcissistic," and a threat to others.[29]

Rushmore's specialty remained "outing" communists in high places. "The Strange Death of J. Robert Oppenheimer's RED Sweetheart" tainted atom bomb developer Oppenheimer with the red brush, rehashing a decade-old scandal involving the suicide of his former lover, a medical student with communist ties. "There's Plenty of RED in the Harvard Crimson!" accused more than sixty Harvard professors—by name—of involvement with the Communist Party. "Times have changed in Cambridge," wrote Rushmore, "and the worried looks on the faces of old alumni who proudly send Sonny Boy off to *alma mater* is all too apparent. What's bothering the erstwhile proud parents isn't Junior's grades as much as it is the type of Marx made by his professors." "H. Rushmore's thesis on the Harvard Reds (in Confidential mag) sold out fast in Boston," Winchell wrote in his column.[30] In a nod to the magazine's new right-wing, McCarthyite focus, Harrison changed the magazine's subtitle to *Tells the Facts and Names the Names*.

By 1954 Rushmore's career at the *Journal-American* was deteriorating. He was fighting with management over his salary, as well as his ongoing attacks on Roy Cohn in his column and the big tabs he'd been running up at expensive nightclubs like the Stork Club. The paper also didn't like that he was writing for *Confidential*. Rushmore, chronically anxious, suffered from terrible ulcers. At one point he had an ulcer attack in a subway station and was forced to recuperate in Saint Clare's Hospital.[31]

In September, the *Journal-American* fired Rushmore, and he came to *Confidential* full time. The paper said it was for "economy" reasons. Rushmore told the press that the firing was due "to my criticism of Roy Cohn, plus my persistent exposures of the crackpots calling themselves McCarthyites." *Time* reported that Rushmore had become associate editor of a "Manhattan . . . magazine which thrives on sin, sex, and plugs from Hearst columnist Walter Winchell."[32] Harrison, always slightly embarrassed by his cheesecake reputation, was pleased with the intellect he believed Rushmore was bringing to *Confidential*, and he paid Rushmore more than he'd ever earned in his life.

Rushmore was grateful to Harrison and saw the position as a way to advance his anticommunist agenda. But he had reservations about Harrison and *Confidential* from the start. In many ways Harrison and Rushmore were similar—both were shrewd, flamboyant, and wildly opportunistic. Yet they were also opposites. Both men were liars, and they fibbed when it suited them, but for Harrison the lies were big and Barnumesque—he didn't believe them and didn't expect others to, either. Rushmore's lies were insidious, told with deadly seriousness, meant to humiliate and destroy. While Harrison was gregarious and social, Rushmore was a dour and moody loner. Though he seemed outwardly mild-mannered, with a slow and homespun speaking style, Rushmore had a violent temper and attacked others on the slightest provocation. Harrison reveled in his playboy reputation, while Rushmore saw himself as moral and upright.

Harrison was a simple man. He wanted one thing: to be a rich and powerful magazine mogul, and he pursued it with enormous drive and diligence. Rushmore was also career-driven, but his hunger for fame and influence was always mixed up with ideology. He'd adopt causes zealously, then abandon them when he felt he'd been slighted or insulted. He had a haughty, high opinion of himself. Rushmore was uncomfortable with *Confidential*'s tawdry sensationalism. "The publication left me unimpressed," Rushmore recalled after he left *Confidential* in 1955. "It was printed on cheap paper, [and] had a lot of garish photographs and articles with sensational titles." He also disliked Harrison's reputation as a publisher of "girlie books."[33] It wasn't long after Rushmore started *Confidential* that he was already looking for a way out.

5 | ASBESTOS

BY THE END OF its first year there was a noticeable change in *Confidential*. Harrison had dialed back some of the more obvious faking. Though the magazine was still screaming and spectacular, the "Harrison dream stories" had disappeared. *Confidential* continued to recycle other people's material, but there were also more earnest attempts at independent reporting. Harrison's staff dug up sources like birth certificates, arrest records, and court records, which became the basis of several *Confidential* exposés. Harrison also developed a network of professional journalists in New York, including Lee Mortimer, who fed him story leads and tips.[1]

At the same time *Confidential* was becoming more "journalistic," it was also becoming more sleazy, vicious, and crude. The magazine was a kaleidoscope of sin and sensation, offering lurid stories on urban vice, taboo sex, and muckraking "public service" articles exposing "rackets," corruption, and fraud. *Confidential* became a vehicle for character assassination, smearing politicians, actors, and socialites with scandalous revelations about their private lives, especially their sex lives. Harrison promoted the magazine as "hot," sending reviewers a pair of white canvas gloves stamped "asbestos" with each issue.[2]

Illicit sex remained *Confidential*'s foremost obsession. At a time when America's leaders panicked about promiscuity and "deviant" sex, *Confidential* presented readers a lurid vision of a nation running amok in sexual chaos. An article

46

titled "Scandal at the Waldorf" described a secret, "clever . . . call girl operation" run by stenographers at the Waldorf Astoria hotel. "For a pay-off, public
stenos will do more than type. And they know what to do for tired business
men who end a letter with a *proposition*, instead of a preposition!" "Tip Off on
Hat Check Girls" revealed the purported likelihood of hat check girls becoming
call girls—it was five times greater than girls who danced on a chorus line,
and thirty-one times more likely than a "run-of-the-mill girl," according to
Confidential's dubious statistics. In *Confidential*'s paranoid world, scheming,
conniving women looked for every opportunity to defraud gullible, love-struck
men. "Operation Diaper: Call 'Em Daddy" described the "latest gimmick" of
"Broadway beauties": how "modern Jills are giving guys the chills by ending
their romances in the maternity ward, then hauling the dads into court for
payoffs lasting 18 years!"[3]

Interracial romance became a regular topic in *Confidential*. It was one of
the most controversial subjects of the time, combining two explosive issues, race
and sex. In the wake of the war and Nazi atrocities, and the desegregation of
the army after the war, many Northern whites had become sympathetic to the
cause of racial equality. The public was fascinated with cross-racial romance;
films like *Pinky* (1949) and the Broadway play *South Pacific* offered liberal,
enlightened portrayals of it. Yet Americans remained as intolerant of interracial marriage as they had been a hundred years earlier. According to polls,
only 1 percent of southern whites and 5 percent of whites outside the South
approved of marriage between blacks and whites.[4]

Confidential titillated readers with tawdry accounts of interracial sex
in entertainment and high society. Articles reinforced noxious stereotypes
about African Americans' alleged hypersexuality and the idea of innate hos-
tility between the races. Interracial relationships never involved real love, said
Confidential—only vengeance, deviance, or lust. A July 1953 article claimed
to offer "the first completely true," "shocking" story about "why the colored
blues singer" Pearl Bailey married Louie Bellson, a white musician nearly half
her age. It was to "get even with the white race."[5]

Jazz singer Billy Daniels, renowned for his recording of "That Old Black
Magic," had married socialite Martha Braun Daniels in 1950. Their stormy
union received a good deal of attention, especially in the African American
press, and by 1953 publications like *Jet* and the *Chicago Defender* were reporting

its breakdown. The couple divorced in February 1954. Martha sold her story to *Confidential*, which ran a first-person account, "White Women Broke Up My Marriage to Billy Daniels."

"Nymphomaniac" white women seduced her husband, according to Martha. "Individually and in squads . . . dozens of them, blondes, brunettes, and redheads, chorus cuties and society belles . . . married and single, beautiful, homely, and in-between. *And all of them white.*" White women trailed him outside his dressing room, and even approached him on their honeymoon. Billy reveled in their attention, taking them on two or three at a time. "I yawned at Dr. Kinsey's report on females. You can say my married life with Bill was mainly a brutal lesson in how lustful women can be and how vain the object of their sex-crammed hunger can get."[6]

Martha regretted giving *Confidential* the story and tried to buy it back. Billy claimed the article was a reason for cutting off alimony, since the divorce settlement stipulated she reveal nothing about their marriage. Harrison agreed to quash it, but the piece was more than halfway through its print run and couldn't be retracted. The article reached a far greater audience than *Confidential*'s eight hundred thousand readers. African American newspapers—the first media in the country to report on *Confidential*—announced the story with bold headlines: "Martha Braun Daniels' piece in the May issue of *Confidential* magazine almost scorches the paper it is printed on. It is really hot stuff!"[7]

In 1953 *Confidential* began a section called The Lowdown on High Society! The romances, divorces, and affairs of the ultra-rich had long been chronicled in society columns, but *Confidential* revealed their sex lives with disturbing frankness. FDR's son Elliot Roosevelt was a "problem child" mixed up with "blondes, brunettes, and bankruptcies." John Jacob "Jakey" Astor VI—"Fatso," to *Confidential* readers—was a filthy tightwad so cheap he wouldn't pay fifty dollars for a female escort. In 1953 the magazine featured a series on the marital troubles and custody battles of Bobo Rockefeller, heir to the Standard Oil millions, who won an astounding $5.5 million in a divorce settlement. According to Winchell, *Confidential* broke news of the Rockefeller divorce before newspapers did.[8]

The flamboyant, gay debauch Jimmy Donahue, heir to the Woolworth fortune, became one of *Confidential*'s favorite subjects. His wild sexual exploits provided endless fodder for the magazine. "Jimmy Donahue's Hush-Hush

Secret" told of a wild night on the town ten years earlier that resulted in a man's brutal assault. *Confidential* reported that in 1944 police found a serviceman named Williams sprawled face down and unconscious in a gutter, his hair crudely shorn. A district attorney's investigation revealed that Williams had been in a gay bar the night before and had met a foursome led by Donahue. After taking him back to Donahue's apartment and picking up a couple of men, "rough trade," the gang of four, in a "sadistic orgy," beat Williams up, cut off his hair, and dumped him near the Fifty-Ninth Street Bridge. The scandal "would have made national headlines, if it had not involved an heir to a $150,000,000 fortune. Just as money talks, it also can silence," *Confidential* wrote.[9]

In its "public service" stories, *Confidential* championed itself as the defender of the common man against frauds and "rackets." *Confidential* revealed alleged corruption at the Radio City Music Hall, the "Nation's Biggest Sweatshop," where unions were quashed and dancers earned only thirty-five dollars a week. According to *Confidential*, the Red Cross came back to communities it had bailed out and asked for its money back. Alcoholics Anonymous was a "fairy tale," more effective as a pickup joint than a cure—a "faster spot for a pick-up than the best saloon in town!" *Confidential* claimed to deplore criminals and swindlers, yet described their tactics in lurid detail. One article reported on a scheme to bilk the government out of tax dollars using a fake name and fictitious employer. "How They Tap Your Phone" explained how to tap phones and the equipment needed, including "a length of wire with clips on the ends" and "a .01 microfarad condenser."[10]

Harrison began running so-called health exposes in every issue. The synthetic hormone diethylstilbestrol, used in chickens, could make a "virile man effeminate," *Confidential* reported. "Informed authorities are wondering just how many of the 4,380 homosexuals separated from the armed services in less than three years got that way from eating this insidious drug that robs males of their manhood." *Confidential* joined the public debate over smoking, a response to new evidence linking it to cancer. The dangers of cigarettes had long been a pet cause of Winchell, who publicized the link between smoking and cancer and denounced the tobacco industry for suppressing the findings. "Pills That Kill the Smoking Habit" revealed Big Tobacco's efforts to quash news of a recently invented antismoking pill called Flavettes: "The odds are that up until now you haven't heard of these pills. The reason is that the millions of dollars spent annually in cigarette advertising have been an effective block to public knowledge of the anti-tobacco discoveries. Running ads for such pills is, in the eyes of the nation's big magazines, tantamount to killing the goose that lays the golden eggs."[11] On the smoking issue, *Confidential* was years ahead of its time.

———————

Confidential continued to profit from the homosexual panic, fueled by the government's persecution of gays and lesbians. In 1953 President Eisenhower issued an executive order barring gay men and lesbians from federal jobs, and the Justice Department developed a plan to weed out homosexuals, alcoholics, and other "subversives." The FBI established connections with local police departments to bar homosexuals from government employment and coordinated with local vice squads in entrapment raids and arrests. Employers dismissed workers suspected of homosexual tendencies, and police surveillance teams arrested scores of men and women under the guise of laws against vagrancy, lewdness, and disorderly conduct. Official action gave the green light to vigilante groups, and acts of hatred and violence were reported throughout the country.[12]

There was perhaps no greater stigma. Gays and lesbians defied the exaggerated gender ideals of the 1950s, with virile, dominating men and submissive, ultrafeminine women. They pointed up the fragility of marriage and the nuclear family, the purported foundations of American society. Homosexuals became scapegoats for a host of social anxieties, and the panic damaged not only those who lost their jobs, lost face, were jailed, or committed suicide, but millions of Americans, gay or not, whose families and friendships were ruined by allegations of homosexuality or fears of being accused.

Brazenly, *Confidential* claimed that gay men had "infiltrated" important industries and institutions. "The Lavender Skeletons in TV's Closet," from July 1953, described the purported "invasion" of the TV industry by gay men. "The way they have jam-packed television confirms a prediction by the eminent Dr. Kinsey that homosexuality is increasingly vastly." "As of this writing, the lavender and lace-shirt situation has frantic executives of the big networks desperately hunting for a solution and a way to keep the truth out of camera range," *Confidential* wrote.[13]

In "Hollywood, Where Men Are Men—and Women Too!" "Juan Morales" (Howard Rushmore) alleged that "things have gotten so out of hand in this new Sodom-on-Sunset Boulevard that you can't tell the he-men from the she-men without a scorecard."

> No one knows, for sure, how many fairies there are in Hollywood. The town is loaded in high places with people who have bivalent tenden-cies . . . and while it poses a problem for the police and psychiatrists, it's a helluva lot tougher on the women. They never know, when they go out with a man, whether they're dating a Jack or a Jill. Personally, we liked the good old days in Hollywood when Fanny was a name and pansy was a flower![14]

By the end of 1953, *Confidential* had outed four prominent public figures as gay, and there were more to come. Some of the disclosures were already public, either through rumor or from being part of an arrest record. Some of the allegations were true; many were debatable. In every case they were scandalous—any accusation of homosexuality was.

In July 1953, *Confidential* recounted the criminal record of "Big Bill" Til-den, one of the greatest tennis players of his generation. In 1946 Tilden had been caught soliciting a fourteen-year-old boy. In 1949 he was arrested for picking up a sixteen-year-old hitchhiker.

> Nobody would dare question the greatness of Big Bill, the last to retire from the Golden Age of Sport . . . but there was an abnormal contributory factor to Tilden's amazing longevity in competition, 35 years of championship or near-championship form. . . . Tilden's dissipation was always with juveniles who had to go to school the next day and consequently had to be in bed early. This practice earned Tilden two jail sentences, one of three months duration, one for a year.[15]

"How That Stevenson Rumor Started," written by Rushmore under the pseudonym "Joseph M. Porter," rehashed a rumor that Democratic presidential candidate Adlai Stevenson was gay. The allegations had been widely circulated the summer before the 1952 election. *Confidential* claimed to reveal the "scandalous source" of the rumor. According to *Confidential*, Stevenson's vindictive former wife, Ellen, had planted it. "*Confidential* now puts on record that *Ellen's rumor was a dastardly and deliberate lie.*"[16]

Rushmore's political loyalties wouldn't have permitted him to reveal the real source: J. Edgar Hoover. The Stevenson smear actually originated in Washington, where Hoover wanted to ensure Eisenhower and Nixon's election. On the day of Stevenson's nomination, FBI officials produced an extensive report of his alleged homosexuality. It claimed Stevenson had been arrested in Illinois and New York for sex crimes, that he went by the name "Adelaide" in gay bars in Chicago, and that Hoover put Stevenson on the "sex deviate" list he kept in his office.[17]

Though *Confidential* claimed outrage and deemed the rumor false, the story put the accusations in print and kept them in the public eye. *Confidential* said it ran the story as a "public service." "*Confidential* takes no political sides, but because the maligned candidate has been accepted by the country, even in defeat, as a statesman of the highest order, and may very likely run for office again, it presents as a public service, for the first time in print anywhere, the full, true, and exclusive story of that rumor and its origin."[18]

By the end of 1953 *Confidential* was flying off newsstands. Harrison got thousands of admiring letters, and fans were giving newsdealers orders to reserve copies of the next issue. Playing to the public's worst fears and taboos, *Confidential* had hit a nerve. "It's only a baby, five issues old, but *Confidential* is flexing its muscles these days like the brute in its ad who used to be a 97-pound weakling," observed the *New York Post*. "It is taking on some of the biggest and wealthiest personalities in the public eye."[19]

One testament to *Confidential*'s success was the criticism it was starting to generate. A few newspaper columnists were complaining vocally about its lewdness and crudeness. In September, the *New York Post* did a six-part series on *Confidential* commissioned by editor James Wechsler, payback for *Confidential*'s attack on him. The *Post* exposed Harrison's "girlie book" background and *Confidential*'s hoaxes and fakes, its "tendency to toy with the facts." A few disgruntled *Confidential* ex-employees had talked to the *Post*.

"Winchell's current passion in the magazine field, *Confidential*, is not yet a year old but already has a pretty good collection of skeletons rattling in its editorial closet," wrote the *Post*. "By skeletons we mean Wrongos, to borrow a word patented by [Walter] . . . and by Wrongos we mean not only 'exclusive inside stories' that fall somewhat short of the truth, but also stories that are neither 'exclusive' nor 'inside' nor new." "The business of telling a sex story without being pinned down to names, places, or dates was a tried technique employed by the same publisher on other magazines for 12 years. The production of *Confidential* for the mass market merely called for a conversion job on the assembly line. Blood and lust, in general, became blood and lust, in particular. With names, places, and dates."[20]

Winchell defended *Confidential* against the *Post*. "One of the gazettes in town complained that *Confidential* mag is too naughty," he wrote. "This convulses some of us who recall when the same indignant editor told *Time* mag that he planned to get circulation via the sin-and-sensations gimmick. The reporter doing the current series practically made a career out of interviewing prostitutes."

"Journalistically speaking, one of the biggest laughs lately is the *Post*'s all-out attack on *Confidential* magazine," opined a columnist for the *Brooklyn Daily Eagle*. "*Confidential* is a sort of poor man's peep show. But I seem to recall there was a period when the Jimmie Wechsler *Post* wallowed in sensual appeal. It reminded me of the palmy days of Macfadden's *The Graphic* when Bernarr would peddle anything if he thought he could corral some more circulation. People who attack sin need to sweat out a period of self-examination before they launch their rockets."[21]

Perhaps nothing revealed *Confidential*'s success more than the rise of imitators, including *Rave*, *Suppressed*, *Top Secret*, and *Behind the Scene*. By 1955 there were more than a dozen *Confidential* knockoffs.

All the copycats mimicked *Confidential*'s look, with bright covers, bold fonts, garish close-ups, oversized exclamation points, and titillating teasers. The stories were similar, covering topics that already appeared in *Confidential*. Like *Confidential*, the competitors were obsessed with sex, exaggeration, and innuendo. Some made their headlines sound lewd by using words that seemed perverted to the careless reader: "Judy Garland—Is She a Secret Hedonist? Is Ava Gardner an Unnatural Narcissist?"[22]

Rave, published by former literary agent Victor Huntington Howland, appeared right after *Confidential*, in April 1953. For years, it would remain *Confidential*'s closest competitor in sensationalism, notoriety, and circulation. The first issue featured articles on "How to Marry $100,000,000," "The Most Hated Man in Hollywood," "The Man Who Invented Big Bosoms," and "Saturday Night with Clark Gable." In August 1953, Harrison's former editor Edythe Farrell started her own *Confidential* knockoff, *Suppressed*.[23]

Top Secret magazine—"Hollywood, Broadway, TV, Café Society, International"—debuted in October 1953, put out by freelance writer Eugene Tillinger. *Top Secret* featured stories such as "The Intimate Life of Texas Millionaires," "What Life Did Not Print About Audrey Hepburn," "Gangsters in Exile," and "Sex Scandals Rock Communist World." It copied *Confidential* down to the Winchell plug. "America's best-kept secret of the past fifty years was shattered in one fell swoop with a historic broadcast over 500 TV and radio stations on November 13, 1953, when Walter Winchell lifted the veil that has long obscured possibly harmful effects of cigarette smoking. This was a great public service," it reported in "Ciggies—More 'Guilty' than You Think." Winchell promoted *Top Secret* in his column.[24]

Some of the *Confidential* imitators did well, but none of them could beat Harrison. He was always one step ahead; his material was more creative, titillating, and sensational. And that was never more true than when he decided to expose Hollywood.

PART II

6 | THE DREAM FACTORY

HARRISON NEVER INTENDED *CONFIDENTIAL* to be a celebrity gossip sheet. When he started the magazine, star exposés were far from his mind. But it wasn't long into *Confidential*'s career that he realized red-baiting articles and warmed-over stories about mobsters and socialites would get him only so far in the mass market. In the spring of 1953, Harrison began turning his attention to Hollywood.

That year fifty million Americans went to the movies each week. The celebrity news and gossip industry was thriving. More news came out of the film colony than any other American city except the nation's capital. More than four hundred men and women, working for the trade press, wire services, newspapers, magazines, and fan magazines, were accredited as Hollywood reporters.[1]

Most of the news they put out was distorted, if not totally false. Film studios pressured journalists to keep stars' transgressions out of the press—their infidelities, out-of-wedlock pregnancies, drug addictions, and homosexual relationships. The public consumed puffery, as fictional as movies themselves. *Confidential* was about to change that.

By the time *Confidential* arrived on the scene, movies were America's most beloved and influential form of entertainment. For more than fifty years, Hollywood and its stars had shaped Americans' habits, values, and ideals. Initially marketed as cheap entertainment for working-class audiences, in the early twentieth century films had been shown in five-cent "nickelodeons" to viewers entranced by the sheer novelty of moving images on the screen. By 1910 films became longer, more sophisticated, and narrative, and they began to feature actors. When actors developed fans, film studios got an idea. Although good publicity and good films sold tickets, the studios realized nothing drew audiences like stars. By 1915 the movie industry operated on a "star system," selling films by selling actors. Audiences would line up in droves to see a star, not the film; the film was the excuse to showcase the star. It worked—by the 1920s the film industry was a billion-dollar business, the fifth-largest industry in the country, and ninety-five million Americans went to the movies each week.[2]

Exuding "personality" and sex appeal, immersed in romance and conspicuous consumption, movie stars became heroes and role models, and an entire culture built up around them. Gossip columns, fan magazines, and newspaper reports tracked stars' activities, and they were worshiped by legions of fans. By 1920 reports of Hollywood marriages and divorces rated front-page headlines. Stars' glamorous activities offered an imaginative outlet for Americans seeking escape from their ordinary, humdrum lives. Film celebrities endorsed products, modeled lifestyles, and wielded enormous influence over the public's values, fashions, and buying habits. By 1930 more than 65 percent of Americans went to movies regularly. When Clark Gable took off his shirt in the 1934 film *It Happened One Night*, revealing that he wore no undershirt, the men's underwear industry went into decline. The movies, reported a 1935 study, were "not only the most universal form of recreation" for the public, but a "major source of ideas about life and the world in general."[3]

Like films, movie stars were industrial products put out by a massive factory system, a "studio system." By the late 1920s, five vertically integrated companies—Metro-Goldwyn-Mayer, Warner Bros., 20th Century Fox, Paramount, and RKO—dominated film production, distribution, and exhibition. The studios' financial headquarters were in New York, but their filmmaking activities took place in Hollywood. Vastly wealthy and enormously powerful, their expansive lots functioned like small nations. The extensive roster of studio personnel included not only actors, directors, writers, and film crews, but also lawyers, doctors, dentists, chiropractors, policemen, druggists, schoolteachers, and priests. Living like pashas in baronial castles and running their lots in near-Babylonian style, studio heads treated their actors like indentured servants.

Studios secured the services of top stars through seven-year contracts, which gave them the right to control virtually every aspect of their lives. We made you, the studio bosses would tell stars, therefore we own you.

Studio publicists manipulated stars' personas with surgical precision. When an actor was hired by a studio, the studio publicity department "typed" him—as a romantic hero, cowboy, rebel, or gangster, for example—and a "screen image" was created. The actor's name was changed. Stylists designed a new wardrobe and dyed his hair. Press releases were issued. One of the publicity department's most important jobs was making sure an actor's offscreen persona matched his on-screen image, which fans demanded. If an actor was tough and rugged in films, press releases described him as a hunter and fisherman in real life. "Studio biographies" offered phony accounts of actors' home lives—how they ate, dressed, and spent their weekends. Press agents planted the material in fan magazines, newspaper columns, and other media outlets.[4]

The images of stars' romantic lives were meticulously managed. Publicists screened actors' phone calls, arranged dates, and set up relationships. Outrageous stunts were concocted and performed. In the 1930s the 20th Century Fox studio engaged eight of its top stars, four men and four women, in a "libidinal round robin" in which they were paired off successively with one another. This was done solely for publicity. Studios fed news of the "couples'" unions and breakups to gossip columnists and fan magazines. The MGM publicity department operated like General Motors, actor Ricardo Montalbán quipped, "It was run with such efficiency that it was a marvel. It was done by teamwork; they could project the product, and the product was not any individual movie, it was the actor. They created a persona that they thought the public would like; they tailor-made the publicity to create a persona throughout the world."[5]

Fans wanted stars to be both extraordinary and ordinary, superheroes and "just folks." The studios delivered, presenting stars as sophisticated and glamorous yet also clean, honest, and upstanding. According to the studios, stars never used drugs, drank too much, or were adulterous. They were sober, hardworking, and faithful. In reality, there was a freewheeling attitude toward sex and drugs in Hollywood that industry leaders spared no effort to conceal.

In the early 1920s, a trio of Hollywood scandals rocked the world: actor Fatty Arbuckle allegedly raped and killed a movie starlet at a wild party, director William Desmond Taylor was mysteriously murdered, and heartthrob actor Wallace Reid died in a drug sanatorium. These incidents led to a nationwide outcry over "Hollywood morals" and the passage of film censorship laws. In several states, films couldn't be shown unless they were prescreened by a government board and granted a seal of approval.[6]

In 1922 the studios backed the creation of an industry-wide trade organization, the Motion Picture Producers and Distributors of America (the MPPDA, renamed the MPAA in 1945), charged with doing an internal "housecleaning" and promoting a clean-cut image of Hollywood. Under the leadership of Will Hays, former postmaster general, in 1930 the MPPDA began administering the Motion Picture Production Code, a code of self-censorship that prohibited depictions of rape, seduction, murder, homosexuality, and other themes that would likely offend film audiences. Studios implemented a strict "morality clause" in actors' contracts that read, "The artist agrees to conduct himself with due regard to public convention and morals, and agrees that he will not do or commit any act that will degrade him in society, or bring him into public hatred, contempt, scorn, or ridicule." A violation was grounds for dismissal, and stars' paychecks could be docked if they didn't live up to their image.[7]

With the MPPDA's help, the studios employed in-house "fixers" and made generous "contributions" to police and city officials to keep stars from being arrested or jailed. Whenever a star got into trouble, studio representatives sped to the scene before cops arrived. Every Monday, publicists defused rumors of domestic violence and cleared up drunk driving arrests that piled up over the weekend. The studios regularly arranged for unmarried actresses to have abortions. Hospitalizations for abortions were described to the press as "appendectomies," and stints in rehab as respites for "exhaustion." In 1935, when Loretta Young was impregnated by Clark Gable, her costar on the set of *Call of the Wild*, the MGM studio sent her to Europe to conceal her pregnancy. A Catholic, Young refused to have an abortion. She returned to America before the baby was born and gave birth in a secluded Hollywood bungalow staffed by MGM personnel. The baby was turned over to an orphanage. When the girl was nineteen months old, publicity head Howard Strickling arranged for Young to adopt her.[8]

When producer Anderson Lawler offered an undercover cop cocaine, thinking he was a male prostitute, 20th Century Fox studio head Darryl Zanuck stepped in and the charges were dropped. To cover up for Spencer Tracy, a violent alcoholic with a hair-trigger temper, MGM kept an ambulance on call at the studio. Bar owners and hotel managers were told to call Strickling if Tracy showed up drunk and rowdy. When the call came, the ambulance would leave with studio employees dressed as paramedics. They'd put Tracy on a stretcher and rush him away before anyone recognized him. When Clark Gable, drunk, crashed his car in Brentwood, hitting a pedestrian and killing her, Gable was shuttled away to a private hospital. It never made it onto the police blotter, and the dead woman's family was paid off. The power of the studios was enormous, "and it wasn't only the power to make movies or to anoint someone or make a movie star," recalled screenwriter Budd Schulberg. "They could cover up a murder. You could literally have someone killed, and it wouldn't be in the papers."[9]

Studios spared no expense to conceal stars' homosexuality from the public. Gay actors were forced to go out with female stars, and often to marry them. Studios orchestrated dozens of so-called lavender marriages. Hush money was paid to keep lovers quiet. Louis B. Mayer was infamous for his hatred of homosexuals, going as far as to launch a publicity campaign in 1933 to prove that at MGM "men were men." All single men were required to date starlets and be photographed looking brawny and tough. To suppress rumors that Robert Taylor was gay, Howard Strickling linked Taylor to actresses and planted stories about his affection for firearms and hunting. MGM linked Ramón Novarro to supposed sweethearts back home in Mexico. Stars who defied the studios suffered. When Novarro rejected Mayer's demand that he marry, his career plummeted. William Haines's refusal to marry and "play the game" led Mayer to cancel his contract.[10]

———————————

Print media—newspapers and magazines, gossip columns, and fan magazines—were key to the star illusion. Without them, stars wouldn't exist. And without stars, who brought them readers and advertising dollars, the media's own fortunes would tumble. It was a mutually beneficial relationship of spin, concealment, and deception.

By the late 1940s more than twenty fan magazines were sold on newsstands, including *Photoplay, Movie Mirror, Screen Book, Motion Picture Herald, Hollywood, Silver Screen, Screenland, Modern Screen, Picture Play*, and *Modern Movies*. Their total circulation was more than seven million, and the top magazines—*Photoplay* and *Modern Screen*—had more than a million each. Fan magazines were regarded by the film industry as one of the most important publicity outlets and the greatest "star builders." Their theme was family and romance, and the typical reader was a young, unmarried woman. Guided by the studios, they claimed to tell readers what stars were "really like"—how they spent their spare time, how they stayed good-looking, where they went on vacation, what they liked in a mate. Articles were corny, mawkish and sappy: "How I Feel About Love," by Shirley Temple; "No Sad Songs for Ronnie," about Ronald Reagan's storybook life; "Marriage Is Such Fun," about Veronica Lake and her husband. The fan mags were often described as "pablum"; reading a fan magazine, one writer famously quipped, was like "eating a banana underwater." Everything in the fan magazines was basically a rewritten press release. Studio publicity departments would call fan magazine writers periodically to "discuss ideas." This consisted of the publicists presenting a list of story suggestions, which the writers would hand over to editors.[11]

The enormously influential columnist Louella Parsons, a fat, hard-bitten, shrewish old biddy in her seventies, was queen of Hollywood celebrity reporting, with forty million readers in the early 1950s. Parsons had been the pre-eminent peddler of Hollywood news since the 1920s, when she signed on as a columnist with the Hearst news syndicate. Her rival Hedda Hopper—famous for her outlandish headgear and strident right-wing stance—appeared in seventy newspapers and had thirty-two million readers. Though Hedda and Louella described themselves as "gossip" writers, both women were effectively part of the film industry. With their daily squibs about actors' careers, vacations, families, dates, and marriages, they promoted stars like the fan magazines did, sugar-coating stories and gushing over storybook lives.[12]

Hopper and Parsons kept networks of insiders—nurses, ushers, Western Union clerks—and sometimes broke stories on stars' marriages and divorces, reporting them before the studios released their announcements. But they colluded with the studios in keeping wraps on seamier activities. Hopper and Parsons would "trade" a taboo piece of information, like an abortion, for a sensational but printable news item, like an impending divorce. Like most reporters, Louella and Hedda knew about virtually all of the skeletons in the closet and could have rocked the world if they revealed them. But they didn't want to or need to. They achieved massive readership by revealing tidbits of truths and half-truths while concealing 99 percent of the iceberg.

A handful of lesser columnists wrote on Hollywood for film industry trade journals, news syndicates, and newspapers. Sheilah Graham had a column, Sheilah Graham's Personal Report on the Stars, in the North American Newspaper Alliance and in *Screenland* magazine. Mike Connolly was a gossip columnist for the trade journal *The Hollywood Reporter*, and Army Archerd wrote for *Variety*. Jimmie Fidler's column, Jimmie Fidler in Hollywood, ran in the McNaught Syndicate, as did Leonard Lyons's Hollywood and Broadway column The Lyons Den. Dorothy Kilgallen's influential Voice of Broadway column, which also covered Hollywood stars, was syndicated by King Features. Hy Gardner wrote a column for the *New York Herald Tribune*, and Erskine Johnson's Hollywood Notes was syndicated by the Newspaper Enterprise Association. The trade paper columnists were somewhat more frank in their reporting, but they too colluded in the cover-up. If they wrote anything titillating about a star, it usually came in the form of a "blind item," alluding to salacious facts without revealing the names of participants. They knew better than to spill the beans. No one had an interest in incurring the wrath of the studios, their lifeblood and livelihood.

At the height of the studio system in the 1930s and '40s, there was a gentleman's agreement between the studios and the press that genuinely compromising information would never make it to print. The press rarely, if ever, printed scandal for fear of losing access to stars and studio advertising. When incriminating details did appear—like Robert Mitchum's 1948 arrest for marijuana possession—the studios swooped in to nip potential train wrecks in the bud, issuing strategic press releases and planting favorable accounts with Hedda, Louella, fan magazines, and newspapers. Press agents became "suppress agents."

The studios went as far as to set up a "credentialing system"—all journalists writing about Hollywood had to be approved by the MPPDA. Only journalists "noted for their honest and clean writing" would be on the "whitelist" of writers allowed access to studios and stars. If a writer "behaved," he was given a "Hays card." If he tried to publish anything unfavorable to the studios, his card was withdrawn. Star interviews had to be conducted with a studio representative present, and writers were forced to submit stories to studios for prepublication approval. There were strict taboos on writing about smoking, drinking, pregnancy, and sex. MGM deleted a passage from a story that said actress Virginia Bruce enjoyed dancing until the wee hours of the morning. Penciled in was the correction, "Virginia likes to get all her dancing over with by twelve o-clock." Writers who didn't adhere to the studios' "journalism rules" were banished from studio lots. "Reporters are in good standing on some of the lots only when they act as unpaid press agents for the studios," wrote the *New York Times'* Douglas Churchill, banned from the studios for his frank reporting. There was not a reporter in Hollywood, he said, who couldn't shake the country "by sitting down at his typewriter and recording merely a portion of the things he knows."[13]

Through the end of World War II, Hollywood was a celebrity factory, producing images of glamour and perfection for a credulous, starstruck public. But after the war, the star machine was beginning to break down. Between 1945 and the early '50s, the film industry suffered a series of setbacks that would lead, within a decade, to the demise of the studio system and its powerful image-making apparatus.

The advent of television devastated film attendance. In 1949 around 940,000 TV sets were in use; by 1950, there were four million. Spurred by technological developments, the strong postwar economy, a soaring birth rate, and the rise of the suburbs, after the war NBC, CBS, and ABC introduced regular prime-time television programming. In the postwar suburban boom, most new homes were built away from downtown centers and first-run movie theaters. Film-going was no longer a nightly or weekly ritual, but rather a special occasion. Film attendance fell from a record high of ninety million a week after the war to around forty-six million in 1950, and it continued to decline during the decade. From 1946, when entertainment-starved Americans paid $1.7 billion to watch movies, theater receipts scaled off year after year. By 1953 they were down to $1 billion, a 40 percent drop.[14]

Hollywood was tarnished by the congressional investigations into communism in the film industry, which started in 1947 and continued through the 1950s. Even though less than 1 percent of film personnel had any kind of communist affiliation, the accusations tainted the entire industry and tore the movie colony apart. Dependent on the financial support of conservative banking and industrial interests, as well as favorable press and public approval, MPAA head Eric Johnston succumbed to the pressure, creating a blacklist of alleged communist writers, actors, and other personnel who were banned from employment in Hollywood.[15]

There were also big-time moral scandals after the war. The nation was rocked by rumors of widespread drug use in Hollywood, news of Rita Hayworth's premature baby in 1949—the birth took place only seven months after her marriage to Prince Aly Khan—and in 1950, Ingrid Bergman's affair with director Roberto Rossellini while both were married, resulting in an out-of-wedlock child. The Bergman incident was particularly devastating, since she had a pure, upright image, having played nuns and saints in films. Bergman was publicly excoriated, even denounced on the floor of the US Senate as "an instrument of evil." In the conservative moral climate of the early 1950s, religious and civic groups such as the Catholic Legion of Decency revived their attacks on "Hollywood morals," and there were campaigns for film censorship that continued throughout the decade.[16]

To deal with the fallout, film industry leaders started a trade organization called the Motion Picture Industry Council (MPIC) under the leadership of MGM production head Dore Schary. In 1948 the MPIC embarked on an aggressive public relations campaign to counteract unflattering publicity. Whenever anything negative was printed about stars, the MPIC would rush out press releases championing the good work being done by the movie industry, such as contributing to worthwhile charities. The MPIC also started a program to "protect aspiring movie hopefuls" from "errors in personal and professional conduct." It would give "youthful newcomers to the movies" training on how to avoid scandal—"solid instruction in matters like personal deportment and public relations."[17]

The biggest jolt to Hollywood came from the US Supreme Court. In 1948, in *United States* v. *Paramount Pictures, Inc.*, the court declared that the studios held a monopoly over film production, distribution, and exhibition, and forced them to sell off their theater chains. This spelled financial disaster for the studios, since movie exhibition had been their main source of profit. Without guaranteed theaters to show films, the studios began to cut back on production and lay off personnel. Forced to cut costs, big studios let go of dozens of producers, directors, and writers. The contract system that had salaried producers, directors, actors, writers, and film crews broke down, and job security vanished.[18]

Between 1950 and 1953 more than three thousand movie theaters closed, and the number of studio workers declined by 15 percent. Warner Brothers eliminated half of its publicity department. In 1940 Hollywood produced more than 450 major films; by 1955 the number was down to 314. In 1945, 790 actors and actresses had been under contract to the major studios, but by 1954 there were only around 200.[19]

To the public, Hollywood still seemed a land of fantasy and glamour, and fans lavished admiration and affection on beloved celebrities—established stars like John Wayne, Gary Cooper, Jimmy Stewart, Spencer Tracy, Humphrey Bogart, Judy Garland, Katharine Hepburn, Jane Russell, Jane Wyman, and Elizabeth Taylor, along with newcomers Marlon Brando, Grace Kelly, Rock Hudson, Audrey Hepburn, Tony Curtis, and Marilyn Monroe. Under the slogan "movies are better than ever," the studios released a vast and impressive array of films, from dramas to westerns to comedies to musicals. Popular star "types" of the '50s included the handsome, charming leading man, epitomized by Gregory Peck, Tony Curtis, Ray Milland, and Spencer Tracy; tough guys like Burt Lancaster, Robert Mitchum, and Kirk Douglas; and "pretty boys" like Tab Hunter, Guy Madison, and Troy Donahue. Among the most beloved female stars were "bombshells" including Jayne Mansfield, Jane Russell, and Marilyn Monroe. Stars still seemed larger than life to their fans, but within Hollywood things were more restrained and sober. Moderation was replacing extravagance. There were fewer wild parties and people living beyond their means. Barbecues were replacing gold-plate dinners. "In the restaurants and the homes of the movie people, the talk about what's going on is confused," observed critic Bosley Crowther in the *New York Times*.[20]

Unprepared for the sudden change in status, many actors turned toward Broadway, formed their own production companies, or signed on for independent film ventures. Some did television appearances, which were plentiful but poorly paid. Stars who were released from the studios commissioned independent press agents to keep their names in the papers. The studio publicity departments were still powerful—in 1954 there were 215 studio publicists, and the industry spent $12 million a year on publicity—but they no longer wielded the muscle they once did.[21] The gossip floodgates were about to open.

7 | HOT HOLLYWOOD STORIES

IN APRIL 1953 *CONFIDENTIAL* ran its first major article on a film personality—Howard Hughes, the eccentric aviation mogul, film producer, and owner of the RKO studio.

The article "Howard Hughes—Public Wolf #1" described "the World's Richest Bachelor" as an "unkempt, shy, and sick-looking man," so awkward that "he hires 'yes-men' to find 'yes-girls' for clandestine romance." "The girl won't have to worry about saying 'Yes' or 'No' to this famous gentleman for he has already dispatched a henchman to make sure her answer is 'Yes,'" *Confidential* wrote. Hughes allegedly had 164 girlfriends stashed in a "hidden harem" in Hollywood and was "bust-happy." He demanded that his women be bosomy young brunettes; "any girl with a bust of less than 36 inches" he considered flat-chested.[1]

Confidential was spot on. Hughes did commission scores of women in Hollywood for sexual favors, most of them under contract to RKO. Just like he collected airplanes, Hughes obsessively collected women, stashing them in the more than one hundred apartments, hotel rooms, and houses he owned around Hollywood.

Confidential's story on Hughes was titillating, but it wasn't a blockbuster— Hughes was well known for his bizarre and reclusive tendencies. In 1947 he had spent over four months alone, naked and unbathed, in a darkened studio screening room, continuously watching movies. Hughes' passion for the female bosom was no secret. Hughes had directed the 1943 film *The Outlaw*, censored because of revealing shots of Jane Russell's enormous breasts. Hughes was outraged nonetheless. The day the magazine came out, Hughes's staffers were ordered to comb newsstands and buy up every copy they could find. *Variety* reported that no copies of *Confidential* were available on Southern California newsstands because Hughes had bought all of them.[2]

A few months later, Harrison began pursuing Hollywood gossip with more gusto when he started a section called Hollywood Lowdown. Its first story debunked a rumor that circulated in newspapers several months earlier involving Frank Sinatra, Ava Gardner, and Lana Turner. All were among the nation's top stars, the favorite subjects of gossip columns. Sinatra, one of the most popular singers in the country in the 1940s, was about to appear in the film *From Here to Eternity*, which would relaunch his flagging career. Sinatra and Gardner, sultry star of high-profile films like *Show Boat* and *The Snows of Kilimanjaro*, had married in 1951, and their relationship was turbulent, to put it mildly, with ongoing, well-publicized spats. Sinatra had dated Turner before he married Gardner.

Back in October 1952, according to the press, Sinatra returned to his home in Palm Springs after a singing engagement in New York, sneaked into his house, and found Gardner and Turner together. He kicked them out of the house in a rage that was so noisy and violent that neighbors called the police. Newspapers reported the incident—SINATRA-AVA BOUDOIR ROW STORY BUZZES wrote the *Los Angeles Times*—but the details remained a mystery. Neither Gardner, nor Turner, nor Sinatra talked to the press about it after Louella Parsons reported in a headline that "Frank Sinatra and Ava Gardner separate after he finds her with Lana Turner," implying he'd discovered them in bed together. The rumor that Sinatra caught the women in a lesbian act was repeated with graphic details until it became practically an accepted fact in Hollywood.[3]

"Frankie Handed Hollywood One of Its Biggest Mysteries When He Booted His Wife and His Ex-Girlfriend out of the House. We Got to the Bottom of It!" reported *Confidential*. "Time, plus . . . some pretty involved sleuthing has cleared away the fog of Frankie's folly and now it can be told."

Confidential alleged that Sinatra didn't sneak into the house as reported, but rather walked in the front door, found the women sitting around in the living room drinking and making jokes about Sinatra, and "flipped his wig," since he didn't like the thought of them palling around. "Frankie didn't sneak in. There is nothing in Sinatra's career to suggest that he wouldn't make le entrance grande at any time. Most of the 'inside stories' when scrutinized carefully proved as thin as the hairs on Frankie's now not-so-celebrated cranium. The truth of the matter is that, being a very sensitive fellow he didn't like the idea of Ava and Lana getting together." Gardner and Sinatra were on good terms, *Confidential* reported, and Sinatra was visiting her in Africa as she shot *Mogambo* with Clark Gable.[4] *Confidential*'s article was amusing, but it was hardly a scoop.

But the next issue of *Confidential* did feature a truly scandalous story—"Why Joe DiMaggio Is Striking Out with Marilyn Monroe!" Appearing in August 1953, it was the most sensational piece in *Confidential* to date, and it doubled the magazine's circulation, bringing it to eight hundred thousand.

Marilyn Monroe—a bosomy cotton-candy blonde, kittenish and voluptuous—was one of the hottest stars in Hollywood and the most highly publicized actress of the year. To that time she had appeared in minor roles in a smattering of films like *The Asphalt Jungle* and *All About Eve*, none of them especially notable. But in 1953 she emerged on the scene with a series of films cementing her image as a sex symbol, including *Gentlemen Prefer Blondes*. Hedda Hopper called her the "cheesecake queen turned box office smash" and *Life* featured her on its cover. A series of wild publicity stunts enhanced her sexy reputation, including reporting to columnist Earl Wilson that she went around without underwear.[5]

Monroe and DiMaggio met on a blind date in early 1952 and began seeing each other seriously in March. He had just ended his career as a legendary New York Yankee; she was twenty-five and he was thirty-seven. Their relationship was enormously thrilling to the public; the couple became "the whole country's pets," constantly photographed and written about. By the end of the year, columnists were sure marriage was on the horizon. In early 1953, though, there were signs the romance might be cooling. Louella Parsons reported on February 12 that "as of this writing, Marilyn and Joe have iced—for good." It was rumored that Monroe's studio, 20th Century Fox, was trying to kill the relationship. Dorothy Kilgallen noted on February 20 that "Marilyn Monroe's friends feel her studio has won the battle to keep her from marrying Joe DiMaggio."[6]

According to *Confidential*, the reason DiMaggio "was fanning out like a bush leaguer with Marilyn" was Joe Schenck, the troll-like, seventy-six-year-old cofounder of 20th Century Fox and one of Hollywood's richest and most powerful men. Schenck opposed a Monroe-DiMaggio marriage, said *Confidential*. Schenck was Monroe's "Daddy." He "guides the luscious blonde's career, inspires her ambitions, lauds her triumphs, and lulls her fears." He was always there with a "paternal hug or a strong shoulder to cry on." "To others, Joe Schenck might be a bald-headed old man. To Marilyn he was, and is, the kind of guy every little girl wants—the man who snaps his fingers and gets results," *Confidential* explained.[7]

This wasn't the first time Schenck had played Papa to an attractive starlet, according to *Confidential*. The "stubby Galahad ha[d] been a knight in a cream-colored convertible for years from gals from six to 36." Schenck was once Daddy to Shirley Temple. Temple wanted a pony, and he had an English army major bring one from the Shetland Islands aboard the *Queen Mary*. Schenk threw lavish parties for many beautiful "fatherless females." *Confidential* revealed that the IRS once went after Schenck for his "fatherly interest in a shapely dancer" he met in Miami. He set the woman up as a secretary in Los Angeles, gave her a new car, and spent $8,000 furnishing a new apartment for her. He tried to take the expenditures out of his income tax.[8]

Confidential never mentioned sex, but the implications were obvious. Whether Monroe actually slept with Schenck is disputed, but there is no question that the two had a relationship that was at least partly sexual. Back in 1947, when her contract with 20th Century Fox expired, Monroe, then an unknown actress, resorted to the Hollywood party circuit. Monroe encountered Schenck personally during one of the infamous gin rummy games he hosted in his mansion, attended by top Hollywood executives. Schenck kept a bevy of young women at the mansion to entertain himself and his guests; Monroe became one of them. Large and bald, with a bulbous nose and deeply lined face, "a weathered bear of a man, aging but active, a bon viveur," Schenck gathered beautiful women around him "the way certain men prize fine stallions," in the words of Monroe biographer Anthony Summers. After a while, Monroe became Schenck's favorite girl, and she began seeing him outside of the parties. At one point she moved into his guesthouse. Schenck repaid her by winning her a six-month contract with Columbia Pictures. "Uncle Joe" remained a daddy figure to Marilyn, taking her under his wing and advising her on her career and romances, at one point even offering to marry her.[9]

The article was a bombshell. The damage was less to Monroe than to Schenck and the film industry. It was a shot across the bow, a message to Hollywood that Harrison wasn't going to play their game. Right after the article came out, syndicated columnist Jimmie Fidler warned the film industry about a new scandal sheet "certain to do . . . harm to the motion picture industry." Fidler cited the "disgusting" article, "Why Joe DiMaggio Is Striking Out With Marilyn Monroe," "so packed with rotten innuendoes that the stomachs of most people would be soured by reading it. . . . The writer of this story, not finding Marilyn Monroe sensational enough . . . rings in movie executive Joseph Schenk's life story . . . and spreads suggestive filth across most of the two full pages."[10]

"The movie moguls had better do something about mending the ways of its famous employees," Fidler warned. "Else I predict that . . . the nation's parents, already fed up with the immoralities of show business . . . will boycott movie theaters so thoroughly that they will never be able to open their doors again."[11]

———————

Emboldened by his success with the Monroe article, Harrison ran a string of Holly-wood articles in late 1953 and early 1954. Some were silly and harmless, like "The Sleeping Habits of the Stars," on what actresses wore to bed, from silk nightgowns to pajamas. "They Started in Their Birthday Suits" publicized well-known stories about Marilyn Monroe, Joan Crawford, Yvonne DeCarlo, and Sheree North having posed nude early in their careers—*sans* photographs, of course. One article described the latest Hollywood fad of breast implants. "What nature's forgotten is no longer fixed with cotton. Now Hollywood surgeons are fixing 'flats' and boosting more than morale!" reported "Custom Tailored Bosoms." According to *Confidential*, Tallulah Bankhead, Gloria Swanson, and Marlene Dietrich had gone to a secret hospital in Glendale where they received an "astonishing" new opera-tion involving "inserting a plastic material underneath the skin of the breast."[12]

At the same time, Harrison was making deeper forays into sin and scandal. A series of articles revealed titillating facts about stars that never made the press.

Confidential exposed Orson Welles, actor, director, and "boy genius" of *Citizen Kane* fame. Back in 1950, Welles had "discovered" the gorgeous young African American actress Eartha Kitt and cast her in his stage production of *Faust* in Paris. On opening night, he kissed her so hard onstage that her face and lips were swollen for days. The kiss was reported widely; Kitt told the story to *Look* magazine. But she didn't report what *Confidential* did—that the kiss was a form of punishment. *Confidential* reported—correctly—that Welles and Kitt had been lovers. Welles wanted to get back at Kitt for "catting around" with "passionate millionaires who flung diamonds, minks, and fancy cars at her tan tootsies." The Kitt incident became the entree to an all-out attack on Welles, described as lustful, fat, and filthy, with "an aversion to soap and water and an affinity for dirty fingernails." Welles had an insatiable sexual appetite, a lust for girls of "all sizes, shapes, and colors," including "femmes of ebony hue." He "may be built like a brewery truck horse, but he's caught up with an awful lot of fleet-footed fillies," *Confidential* reported, describing his "torrid" relationship with Italian actress Lea Padovani while he was married to Rita Hayworth.[13]

"Lana Turner: Why They Love Her and Leave Her" recounted Turner's tumultuous relationships with Bob Topping, Lex Barker, Greg Bautzer, Artie Shaw, Turhan Bey, Stephen Crane, Tyrone Power, and Fernando Lamas. Both on and off screen, Turner was a seductress, noted for her sensual figure, platinum blonde hair, *femme fatale* demeanor, and tendency for serial relationships. Fans knew about the men *Confidential* wrote about; Turner had been married to four of them. But *Confidential* revealed bitter fights and how some of the relationships were abusive—Turner suffered gashes, broken bones, and black eyes. Turner brought it on herself, said *Confidential*. She was "Filmdom's No. 1 party girl," with an insatiable desire for "kicks," an "uncontrolled urge for high living, liquor, love and late hours. . . . She was uninhibited in her choice of playmates" and attended many parties where the "guests were of mixed color."[14]

In early 1954, *Confidential* was one of the first media outlets to reveal the failing marriage of Roberto Rossellini and Ingrid Bergman. Their relationship had been in the news since 1950, when Bergman, then married, had an affair with Rossellini, her director on the film *Stromboli*, that resulted in an out-of-wedlock child. She divorced her doctor husband to marry Rossellini. In 1953 columnists and fan magazines were hinting that the marriage was on the rocks. "You've heard the rumors—now read the facts . . . behind the impending crack-up of the most notorious love affair of the century!" *Confidential* announced. The magazine divulged unsettling details behind the impending break-up: Rossellini brutally abused Bergman, including hitting her in public and insulting her to the point of tears. At night their neighbors heard smashing plates and shouting voices that lasted till dawn.[15]

Mario Lanza, star of *The Great Caruso* (1951) and widely regarded as the greatest operatic tenor of his time, was depressed, alcoholic, reclusive, wildly temperamental, and a binge eater. The public got some inkling of this when the press reported vaguely on a series of "explosive incidents" in 1953, including Lanza's refusal to show up on the set of *The Student Prince*, which led MGM to fire him. *Confidential* reported that Lanza was indeed a mental case—a confirmed "looney," a repulsive drunk "with a roving eye and often uncontrollable emotions." One minute he flew into rages, and the next he was "laughing uproariously at some joke and patting a chorus girl's posterior." *Confidential* described how Lanza once consumed twenty-eight box lunches on an MGM movie set in Santa Monica, then leaped into the ocean and almost drowned. "Mario Lanza is such an emotional problem child that many of his friends have expressed the belief a psychiatrist should slow him down," *Confidential* opined. "His ego is astounding."[16]

Red Skelton, famed for his brilliant slapstick, was one of the most popular TV comics. In 1953 reports of his personal struggles and marital problems began to surface in the press. In June *Screenland* reported that Skelton was in bitter spats with his wife, allegedly the result of hard work and long hours. In early 1954 Skelton made national news when columnists reported that he "accidentally" shoved his right arm through a glass shower door. *Confidential* revealed one source of Skelton's woes: he was a hard-core, two-fisted alcoholic. "When Skelton goes off on a bat, because he is anxious about his TV show or a movie, he gets rambunctious," *Confidential* reported. "He has violent arguments with his wife while consuming scotch in the morning instead of coffee." At times he got wild and whipped out a pistol. "Several times in the past year, Skelton has galloped through the house, waving the gun and staggering." *Confidential* also blew the lid off something Skelton's publicists had worked hard to keep out of the press: his penchant for dirty movies. A notorious prankster, Skelton projected porn films onto the blank wall of the garage next door to his house; nude, gyrating images could be seen by anyone driving down Sunset Boulevard.[17]

In March 1954 *Confidential* ran its very first story that claimed to out a movie star as gay. It was a milestone not only in the magazine's history but also in all of Hollywood history.

The target was Dan Dailey, an accomplished dancer and Broadway veteran who started his career at MGM back in the early 1940s. After serving in the war, Dailey moved to 20th Century Fox, where he starred in musicals such as *Mother Wore Tights*, *When My Baby Smiles at Me*, and *Give My Regards to Broadway*. Acclaimed for his song-and-dance talents, Dailey nonetheless remained a second-tier player, never achieving the status of his more prominent costars Gene Kelly, Donald O'Connor, and Betty Grable. Nor was he a heartthrob. In 1953 *Modern Screen* answered a letter from a fan asking, "Do the girls in Hollywood consider Dan Dailey a great catch?" The answer was a definite no.[18]

Tall and lanky with a boyish grin and tousled blond hair, Dailey first appeared in Hollywood gossip in 1949, after the failure of his second marriage. In "Why Dan Dailey's Marriage Failed," in *Modern Screen*, Hedda Hopper portrayed Dailey as a sympathetic character who had lost his marriage to the demands of a movie career. His 1951 admission to the Menninger Clinic for psychiatric problems garnered a good deal of attention. But Dailey's frank admissions to reporters about his mental health crisis neutralized the rumor mill in subsequent years. Dailey's film career marched on steadily, with starring roles in *What Price Glory* (1952), *The Pride of St. Louis* (1952), and *Meet Me at the Fair* (1953). In 1953 fan magazines were still running articles on his psychiatric breakdown and journey to recovery. *Modern Screen* described Dailey as a devout Christian and "man of faith," his mental illness healed by religion.[19]

In November 1953 Dorothy Kilgallen, writing for *Screenland*, also reported this small item:

> Dan Dailey went to a house party in San Fernando Valley attired in women's clothing which he had borrowed from the 20th Century Fox wardrobe department as a gag. He was picked up by the Encino police department and had to talk his way out of an overnight stay in the local jug.[20]

"What are the troubles of the fun-loving, gay Dan Dailey? What was he doing in that car that sparked the tongue-wagging in movietown?" asked *Confidential*. "*Confidential* can reveal the true tale."

The article described Dailey's marital troubles and how he began to hit the bottle when his wife left him. At the Menninger Clinic, psychologists discovered the root of his problem: he was incapable of having a "lasting, successful relationship with a woman." After his discharge from the clinic, Dailey had an affair with actor Keenan Wynn's wife Beetsie, and they agreed to get married. Beetsie got a fast divorce and waived alimony rights. Dailey then announced that he couldn't marry her. "You see, he was 80 percent willing to be with women. But that other 20 percent—well he just liked to pal around with the guys," *Confidential* reported.

> While Beetsie wept and Wynn stormed, Dailey was back having a ball. And he was becoming more uninhibited, more daring. Often he went to stag parties. One night, for the hell of it, he decided to go to a stag costume party in a dress. This was dandy—except that after the party, Dailey, with too many drinks under his girdle, still wore the dress, high heels, and wig.
>
> . . . There's a law, you know, against men wearing women's clothes in public. They call it 'in drag.' . . .
>
> Dailey has since become more surly and antagonistic. He makes no secret of being a Hollywood heel. His friends hope that soon he will decide to go into psychoanalysis to solve his problem permanently. Thousands do every year—men and women who, because of early childhood maladjustments, have anxieties, perversions, and fears. Sometimes they aren't sure whether they're adults or children, men or women. . . . Hollywood hopes Dailey will seek psychiatric help soon. Until then, he's Hollywood's problem child—who may wind up in the headlines.[21]

Confidential was right that Dailey was a cross-dresser. According to film historian William Mann, Dailey's habit of wearing women's clothes—whether for gags or otherwise—was legend in Hollywood. The composer André Previn recalled in his biography how Dailey turned up drunk and in female clothing for the press screening of *It's Always Fair Weather* in 1954. According to Previn, when Dailey drank too much, "he was given to putting on smart little frocks. It was a sort of hobby, like stamp collecting."[22] *Confidential* would run a story on another Dailey cross-dressing incident in 1957, "The Night When Dan Dailey Was Dolly Dawn."

It's unclear whether Dailey was actually bisexual or gay. He was a private person and left few clues about his personal life. *Confidential* didn't say outright that Dailey was gay, but it implied as much. Most Americans at that time weren't savvy enough to distinguish between cross-dressing and homosexuality; to them, Dailey was "queer," and that was enough to taint him. On March 5, 1954, columnist Erskine Johnson noted that 20th Century Fox lawyers were contemplating legal action over "an eye-popping article about Dan Dailey in a sensational magazine."[23]

By the summer of 1954 the film industry was beginning to realize the magnitude of the threat it faced with *Confidential*. The magazine's September issue, appearing on newsstands in July 1954, released two "Confidential Exclusives." The first was an outing story, "The Untold Story of Van Johnson," by Howard Rushmore. The second offered shocking allegations about the private life of Rita Hayworth.

Six foot two, blond and boyish, Van Johnson was not America's image of a homosexual. A bobby sox heartthrob back in the 1940s, *Photoplay* had named him the magazine's beefcake pinup of 1945, and Gallup polls reported him the fastest-rising male star in the country. He played the "red-haired, freckle-faced soldier, sailor, or bomber pilot who used to live down the street" in films like *A Guy Named Joe*, and a string of films with musical comedy star June Allyson and actress-swimmer Esther Williams. After the war Johnson's career continued steadily. Between 1950 and 1954 he made fourteen films for MGM, earning close to $500,000 a year. Tired of being assigned to juvenile roles even though he was thirty-six years old, Johnson decided in 1954 not to renew his MGM contract and instead went freelance, working the Las Vegas nightclub circuit to earn money on the side.[24]

When Johnson was hired by MGM in 1942, Louis B. Mayer realized he had a "problem" on his hands. Johnson, who had started his acting career on the stage, had been notorious on Broadway for his homosexual affairs. According to screenwriter Arthur Laurents, Johnson had also been caught "performing in public urinals" in Hollywood. Mayer knew it wouldn't be long before the studio had to pay someone to keep quiet about Johnson's sexuality. Believing that Johnson could be "cured" by a good-looking woman, he threw attractive starlets at him, to no avail.[25]

In 1943 Johnson was badly hurt in an auto accident. He spent a month recuperating at the home of his best friend, Keenan Wynn. While recuperating, he became friends with Wynn's first wife, Evie. Mayer heard about it and sent for Evie. Johnson "will only marry you," Mayer told her. "I'm here to see if we can't work something out." Mayer told Evie that if she divorced Wynn and married Johnson, the studio would help Wynn, who was on the verge of being laid off from the studio. Evie divorced Wynn and married Johnson.[26]

"Now—for the first time—the Hush Hush story of Van Johnson can be told," wrote *Confidential*. "The idol of the nation's gals of all ages during World War II was an admitted homosexual."

According to *Confidential*, Johnson disclosed his sexual orientation when he was called before the draft board. What he told his draft board is unknown, but a few days later, the Selective Service called the FBI to investigate whether Johnson was lying about his homosexuality to evade the draft.

"Van told the FBI he didn't want to be a homosexual. And he added that he was making a desperate effort to return to normal living," *Confidential* wrote. "In one of the most unusual 'kiss and tell' stories in the history of the FBI, Van gave a full account of his relations with women . . . including a well-known musical comedy star."

Johnson went back to Hollywood, and the FBI continued their investigation. Johnson later reported to the Los Angeles FBI field office "that he was continuing his desperate effort to rid himself of his abnormality." "But it took another tragedy in Van Johnson's life before he succeeded," wrote *Confidential*. That was the automobile accident, in which Johnson fractured his skull. Amazingly, he survived.

Johnson went back to the draft board to be reclassified on grounds of physical disability. The FBI didn't intervene because the question of whether he was gay was no longer important to his draft status. "The simple classification of 4-F puts a finis to the story of a man's fight against himself," according to *Confidential*. The magazine implied that Johnson had since "recovered" from his homosexuality. Since the war, he'd "made many movies and to the few who know his triumph over tragedy, he seems almost a new man, filled with a vibrant confidence."[27]

"How Rita Hayworth's Children Were Neglected," a signed story by Jay Breen, dropped a bombshell on the bombshell's public image.

Voluptuous, red-headed Hayworth, nicknamed "the love goddess," had been the nation's most glamorous screen idol during the early 1940s and the most popular pinup girl for GIs during the war. With films like *Cover Girl* (1944) and *Gilda* (1946), she became the Columbia studio's top star and one of the biggest box-office attractions in the world. But in the late 1940s Hayworth's popularity went into decline as her off-screen struggles eclipsed her career. After divorcing Orson Welles in 1947, with whom she had one daughter, Rebecca, she fell in love with Prince Aly Khan, leader of the Ismaili Muslim sect, and traveled around Europe with him. Moralists criticized her for cavorting around with a married man, and worried about her fitness as a mother. In 1949 Hayworth married Khan and they had a daughter, Yasmin. Tired of his chronic infidelity, Hayworth filed for divorce, which was granted in January 1953, and she was awarded full custody of Yasmin.

Hayworth then took up with the Argentinean-born Dick Haymes, a one-time crooner and minor screen star who had blown all his money, and was an alcoholic, deeply in debt, and nicknamed "Mr. Evil" in Hollywood. When Hayworth married Haymes in September 1953, he was being pursued for non-payment of child support, and the government was threatening to deport him. After the wedding, Hayworth and Haymes lived in a rented home in Greenwich, Connecticut. When they decided to move to the Plaza Hotel in New York, a deputy sheriff held most of their personal belongings, claiming that they owed back rent and had inflicted thousands of dollars of damage to the house. Once in New York, the couple was exhausted and decided they needed a vacation. Hayworth sent the children to stay with Dorothy Chambers, an acquaintance of Haymes who had been a babysitter for the girls. Hayworth and Haymes sped off to Florida.

Chambers ran an antique business in White Plains, New York, in a seedy neighborhood of motels and rooming houses. Her home was dilapidated, filthy, and completely unguarded. A neighbor reported the children's whereabouts to the Westchester County Society for the Prevention of Cruelty to Children, and after two intense days of scrutiny, the society's child protection director filed a formal neglect petition.[28]

In April 1954, Hayworth appeared before a New York judge to answer allegations that she had neglected Rebecca and Yasmin. The judge concluded that although Hayworth hadn't been directly guilty, the children had suffered neglect and that the child protection society's complaint was "fully justified." He ordered Hayworth's daughters to remain in his court's jurisdiction until she could eliminate their disgraceful living conditions.[29]

Hayworth's fans turned out to support her en masse, blaming the charges on "busybodies." For a while, the neglect charges actually boosted Hayworth's popularity. Noted one columnist, "Whoever touched off the neglected children charge against Rita Hayworth gave her a headache but did her an unexpected favor. Millions of citizens who were bored with Rita's past boners suddenly switched to her side—refusing to swallow the allegation that she was an unloving mother—and became her staunch defenders in the battle for public sentiment." Fan magazines described Hayworth as the victim of a vicious plot and Chambers as a "wonderful woman."[30]

"It was a shocked and disbelieving nation that picked up its newspapers late this spring to read the incredible story of Rita Hayworth's children," announced *Confidential*. She "cried 'foul,' and set off a nationwide debate as to whether she was being persecuted or whether the little girls had, in fact, been neglected. . . . Spread before you on these pages are authentic pictures which settle that argument for all time. . . . These are pictures a whole world who discussed the case never got to see and this is a report never before put in print."

One of the neighbors who called the child protection society had also called *Confidential*. On March 18 Jay Breen, tipped off by the neighbor, had gone to the house disguised as a potential renter. Wearing a soiled robe, Chambers answered the door, invited him into the kitchen, and offered him a jigger of Scotch out of a grimy bottle. The kitchen table was crowded with boxes of food and greasy dishes. Even though she'd never seen him before, she pointed out the window to show him Hayworth's daughters.

The next day Breen returned with a *Confidential* photographer who took pictures showing Yasmin playing in a sink filled with dirty dishes and sitting on a dingy porch digging in a basket of garbage. She slept in a room so littered with boxes of clothing that she had to climb over them to reach her bed. Across the street from the house was a marshy dump, heaped with huge boulders and surrounded with seven-foot-high weeds.

While the two girls were living in sordid conditions, *Confidential* reported, Haymes and Hayworth were spending their money lavishly—dining at El Morocco, and at Maud "Chez Elle," one of Manhattan's most expensive restaurants. Haymes tipped a restaurant doorman five dollars to watch his dog. "Were Rita Hayworth's children neglected? You've seen the pictures, you've read the facts. Now, you be the judge!" *Confidential* advised.[31]

The article was truly damning. Fans now confronted undeniable proof that Hayworth had in fact neglected her children. "Pages 41, 42, and 43 of the September *Confidential* . . . will shock those of Rita Hayworth's defenders who believed that whatever mistakes she made, she would never be a neglectful mother," Dorothy Kilgallen noted on July 8, 1954. "And the accompanying text makes it clear that the White Plains neighbors who brought the plight of Yasmin and her half-sister Rebecca to the attention of the Westchester County Society for the Prevention of Cruelty to Children were not mere busybodies."[32]

When the issue sold out, Harrison announced a new policy for *Confidential*. "We've got to have more Hollywood stories," he told his staff. "The hotter the better. . . . We need hot, inside stories from Hollywood that make our readers whistle when they read them and say 'we never knew that before.'" Harrison told his staff to spend more money getting inside stories on "Hollywood personalities and on homosexuals." He announced *Confidential*'s new criteria for running a story: "Is the star's name big enough and well-known enough to sell the magazine?"[33]

8 | HOLLYWOOD RESEARCH INCORPORATED

"HOT HOLLYWOOD STORIES" WAS now the name of the game at *Confidential*. Their pursuit led Harrison to create an extraordinary news network—a gossip network—unprecedented in journalism and the history of Hollywood.

Harrison assembled an army of informants in Los Angeles—private detectives, prostitutes, valets, maids, bartenders, waiters, hairdressers, unemployed extras, and screenwriters. His niece Marjorie Meade and her husband, Fred, were installed in Hollywood to head *Confidential*'s gossip-collection operations, called "Hollywood Research Incorporated." HRI paid informants handsomely for tips, and the juicier the better. Harrison capitalized on the decline of the studios and their once-airtight publicity system. Everywhere his informants went, they found people willing to tell the truth about stars, and the studio guard dogs weren't always there to protect them.

Hollywood became a "beehive of private eyes, tapped telephones and recording machines."[1] There were detective agencies throughout the city doing business for *Confidential*. Maids employed in celebrity households went to work with secret recorders. Chauffeurs, doctors, and hairdressers were spying on their movie star clients and sending tips to HRI. Gossip had always circulated in Hollywood, but it was now being collected and channeled to HRI for publication in *Confidential*.

At the beginning of *Confidential*'s Hollywood coverage, Harrison had relied mostly on professional journalists for gossip. Most *Confidential* informants had been reporters for Los Angeles newspapers or Hollywood correspondents for news syndicates, privy to secrets they were forbidden to print.

Florabel Muir was one early contributor to *Confidential*. A tough-talking, hard-boiled "newspaper dame"—described by a colleague as "red haired and horse faced"—Muir covered the film industry for the *New York Daily News*. Ezra Goodman, who wrote on Hollywood for *Time* magazine, also gave tips to *Confidential*, as did Goodman's longtime mistress, Aline Mosby, the Hollywood correspondent for the United Press International news service. Between 1952 and 1954, Mosby pseudonymously wrote twenty-four stories for *Confidential*.[2]

Leo Guild, who wrote the television column in the trade paper *The Hollywood Reporter*, contributed to *Confidential*, as did Mike Connolly, a shy, soft-spoken, forty-year-old former reporter who wrote the *Reporter*'s Rambling Reporter column. *Newsweek* described Connolly as the most influential columnist within the film industry, "Hollywood's unofficial arbiter, prosecutor, talent scout, trend spotter, and social registrar" who got "the pick of the trade items, the industry rumors, [and] the policy and casting switches." His was the best-read gossip column in Hollywood; "no respectable Hollywood breakfast table would be without it." Connolly regularly fed Harrison gossip because he was gay and closeted, and afraid of being outed by *Confidential*. The tradeoff was an open secret in Hollywood.[3]

Harrison was constantly trying to enlist top-flight journalists, both as tipsters and as writers. These efforts almost always failed. Most reputable journalists didn't want to get involved with *Confidential*, even under pseudonyms. Harrison tried unsuccessfully to hire Kendis Rochlen, who wrote a column called Candid Kendis in the *Los Angeles Mirror*. He considered her "very brilliant and witty." Harrison was also impressed by Jimmy Cannon, sports writer for the *New York Post*, and Murray Kempton, who wrote on labor and social issues for the *New York Post*. He put out feelers ("I thought he might want to earn a little something on the side"), but Kempton never responded. Agnes Underwood, city editor of the *Los Angeles Herald-Express*, also declined to write for *Confidential*.[4]

Maurice Zolotow, a former reporter for *Billboard*, was renowned as one of the best writers on the entertainment industry. Harrison told Rushmore that he wanted to "get him." Rushmore doubted Zolotow would actually work for *Confidential*, but arranged a dinner for the three of them at the Colony restaurant.

"After a good deal of reconnoitering, Mr. Harrison finally came to the point," Zolotow recalled. "'In doing your research, you must run into a lot of stuff you can't use in your books and articles.'" Harrison's eyes gleamed: "'I mean like the kind of stuff I can use . . . you know, about homosexuality and like that.'"

"My main impression of that dinner," Zolotow said later, is that "Harrison seemed queer for queers. He kept asking me, 'Who's homosexual? Who's perverted?'"

"Look, you don't have to do the work," Harrison said. "You don't write the story. You just type the idea on a piece of paper. We got men in the office that will write it up. Or you can telephone it in if you got an idea for a story. Nobody will know you gave us the idea. We could pay you in cash so no checks will be traced back to you. Don't worry about nothing. . . . You hear a good rumor, you phone it in to me personally and you got yourself five hundred dollars."

Zolotow said he couldn't work for *Confidential*; he wouldn't feel good about it. "You're making a mistake," Harrison replied. "You're a fat-headed chump." Harrison was irritated, resenting that he paid for a Colony dinner and got nothing out of it. He grumbled about it the next day. A week later Harrison called Zolotow. "Are you ready to go to work for us?" he asked. Zolotow was astonished.[5]

Shortly after the *Los Angeles Daily News* closed its doors in 1954, one of its staffers was in the California State unemployment office arranging to draw insurance checks while he looked for other work. He explained his plight to a female interviewer, who told him there was a reporting job available. "The editors of the magazine *Confidential*," she said, "are looking for a West Coast man, and I'm sure that you would be acceptable." Said the journalist, "Madam, if you will apply for a job in a brothel, I'll apply for the job with *Confidential*."[6]

In 1954 Harrison began planting the seeds of his "gossip network" when he sent Rushmore to Los Angeles to track down informants for *Confidential*. Rushmore made four trips, two that year and two in 1955. During the visits

Rushmore also attended Walter Winchell's TV broadcasts. Harrison wanted Rushmore to bring Winchell the latest issue of *Confidential* and ask if he could promote it on the show.[7]

Rushmore spent most of his trip getting in touch with reporters. A few agreed to submit ideas and stories on a freelance basis. Rushmore hired Florabel Muir and her husband, Denis Morrison, who wrote for the *Saturday Evening Post*. The Muirs eventually quit *Confidential*, claiming to be disgusted with it. Rushmore also went to the movie studios in search of gossip and contacts. To his surprise, the Universal-International studio wined and dined him and put a limousine and driver at his disposal. The result of the studio's benevolence was a series of exposés on it, including a blockbuster story on actor Rory Calhoun's criminal record.[8]

Shortly after Rushmore returned to New York, Harrison made a trip to Hollywood in August 1954. He was unhappy with Rushmore's journalist contacts, he said; their stuff was too "tame." Most of their tips came from the public record and could be used in the *New York Daily News* and the *New York Times*. They weren't "hot and . . . won't sell my magazines," he complained. The reporters "can't get the kind of material we want, they can't get the hot inside stuff or they won't get it. . . . That's what sells the book. That's what we have to have."[9]

Harrison set up shop at the posh Beverly Hills Hotel and focused on finding prostitutes and private detectives to work as informants. One important contact he made was Ronnie Quillan, a thirty-eight-year-old prostitute and madam who ran a well-known, high-priced call girl service. Quillan had bright red hair that was three feet long, plucked eyebrows, a perpetually drugged look, and was reported to work from a gold-trimmed address book containing more than a hundred names.[10]

Quillan, whose birth name is unknown (she adopted the stage name "Veronica Ainsley"), came to Hollywood in the 1930s as a bit actress and dancer. In 1939 she married screenwriter Joseph Quillan but divorced him in 1943, charging that he beat her. In 1944 she moved to Beverly Hills, where she began to work as a prostitute but tried to pass herself off as a "socialite." That year newspapers reported that "socialite Miss Ronny Quillan of Beverly Hills" had reported the theft of "$10,000 worth of furs, perfumes, and five dozen pairs of nylon hose" from her apartment. It would become one of her favorite publicity stunts—reporting to the police that tens of thousands of dollars of jewelry, furs, and cash had been stolen from her, only to later be mysteriously recovered.[11]

Quillan made national publicity in 1949 when newspapers reported that her ear almost was severed in a razor fight with French singer Roland Gerbeau. In December 1950, she was arrested for slashing singer Billy Daniels with a butcher knife. Daniels tried to rape her, Quillan told police. She later retracted the claim when medical examiners found there was no trace of rape. Quillan had been trying to shake down Daniels, with whom she'd been involved, for $5,000. On the night of the incident, Daniels went to Quillan's apartment at three in the morning, after he finished playing at the Mocambo nightclub. When he said he was leaving the apartment, she slashed him, then picked up a table lamp and threw it at him. According to Daniels, she'd been taking sleeping pills all night.[12]

Quillan met with Harrison four times in August 1954. Harrison called on her in her apartment in Hollywood; she also met him at the Beverly Hills Hotel. Quillan had been corresponding with Harrison since March that year, when she wrote to him about a *Confidential* story on Billy Daniels in which she'd been mentioned, calling it "completely false." Quillan asked Harrison to retract it, telling him she'd give him the true facts. Harrison told her he wasn't interested. When Quillan met Harrison in Hollywood, she told him she wanted *Confidential* to run her life story. Harrison declined, saying he wanted "juicy facts" about celebrities.[13]

Harrison convinced Quillan to feed him information from her network of "girls." According to Quillan, Harrison "wanted stories primarily dealing with the sexual activities of celebrities in the movie colony, [and] the more lewd and lascivious the story, the more colorful for the magazine." Between 1954 and 1957 Quillan contributed material for thirty *Confidential* stories.[14]

———————

Francesca De Scaffa, a dark, gorgeous twenty-four-year-old bit actress, became another key *Confidential* informant. De Scaffa, like Quillan, was a con artist and liar and may have been a prostitute. De Scaffa claimed to be a "Countess" of French and Chilean descent, born in Venezuela and educated in Paris. She boasted that she had met Mahatma Gandhi, who predicted she would have a brilliant film career, and had been engaged to a French prince and an Italian count. After the breakup of her marriage to actor Bruce Cabot in 1950, De Scaffa had affairs with Dominican playboy Porfirio Rubirosa, the Shah of Iran, Clark Gable, and Orson Welles, among others. She tried to launch a film career and appeared in minor roles in *On the Riviera* (1951) and *Captain John Smith and Pocahontas* (1953).[15]

De Scaffa told Harrison that she had access to every home in Hollywood and that she could get any story he wanted, even if she had to sleep with someone for it. Between 1954 and 1955, De Scaffa provided tips for several *Confidential* articles. Harrison paid De Scaffa more than $30,000. She later threatened to sue Rushmore and Harrison for libel when they brought up her name as a *Confidential* informant.[16]

Harrison also contacted several private detectives, including sixty-two-year-old H. L. von Wittenberg, who ran his own service, the Hollywood Detective Agency. Von Wittenberg did business mostly for divorce clients and was an old hand at wiretapping. Harrison asked von Wittenberg if he could do investigative work for *Confidential*. This would involve, in some cases, "bugging a place," and using hidden cameras—"magnetic eyes," Harrison told him. Harrison hired von Wittenberg for fifty dollars a day plus expenses. Von Wittenberg did one assignment for Harrison then quit, telling Harrison he thought the work "stank."[17]

During this period, Harrison made a few attempts at real investigative reporting. According to *Esquire*, Harrison approached a young woman reporter in New York and made her a "startling proposal." The woman had done a number of short pieces for *Confidential* under the name "J. Shirley Frew," which Harrison had bestowed on her. ("J. Shirley Frew" was the name of Harrison's girlfriend, June Frew.) Harrison was so impressed with her stories that he called her to his office and told her he had a big job for her. Actors Franchot Tone and Melvyn Douglas were then appearing in Broadway plays. He said he thought they were both notorious "wolves." He proposed to clad the woman in a fancy dress, mink coat, and costly jewelry, and then, with a detective present, send her to the actors' dressing rooms, where she would try to get each man to make advances on her. If she succeeded, she would get to keep the coat. This offer was made with Rushmore, Govoni, and a lawyer and secretary present.[18]

But by the end of 1954 Harrison had little need for undercover journalism; the gossip just flowed in. In addition to news from his growing network of tipsters in Hollywood, Harrison was receiving hundreds of random, unsolicited tips. Prostitutes, maids, neighbors, hairdressers, press agents, and former lovers with potentially incriminating information sent letters and made calls to the *Confidential* office. But Harrison still wasn't satisfied, he told Rushmore. He needed "hotter" information, and also a way to streamline, classify, and verify facts. He needed a separate "gossip agency," he said, a permanent "listening post" in Hollywood. He set out to create one.

In January 1955 Harrison asked Rushmore if he wanted to go to Hollywood and be in charge of the "listening post," the "Hollywood operation for *Confidential*." Rushmore declined; he couldn't do it because of his wife and kids, he said. But he agreed to take another trip to California to see if he could set up the bureau. During the trip Rushmore contacted more journalists and tracked down story leads.[19]

That visit contributed to Rushmore's disillusionment with *Confidential*. Harrison wanted to do a story on Joan Crawford, since he'd heard rumors that she abused her adopted son and daughter. "Our information is that she's mean to the kids," Harrison said. "Dig up everything." Harrison contacted Los Angeles reporter Jerry McCarthy to check out the Crawford story; McCarthy couldn't confirm it. The *Hollywood Reporter*'s Mike Connolly knew about the impending article and set up a meeting between Crawford and Rushmore to give Crawford a chance to refute it. Rushmore met Crawford in her dressing room at the Universal-International studio.[20]

"Sitting there in [Crawford's] cottage . . . I suddenly felt a surging wave of contempt for myself," Rushmore recalled. Rushmore told Crawford that *Confidential* wanted the story because it was "of public interest." Crawford was a celebrity, and the public had a right to know if she was abusing her children. But at the end of the two-hour conversation, Rushmore was convinced that Crawford was a "wonderful," "generous" foster parent. Rushmore persuaded Harrison to drop the story.[21] Rushmore never took any steps toward establishing the Hollywood "listening post." Fortuitously, around this time

Harrison's twenty-six-year-old niece, Marjorie, and her husband, Fred, were having financial trouble.

———————

Marjorie Tobias Meade was the daughter of Harrison's sister Edith and her husband Charles Tobias, an auctioneer. Born in 1927, Marjorie attended public grammar schools in New York City and dreamed of becoming an actress as a child. For two years she studied journalism at Pennsylvania State College, where she met Fred Meade, who'd just returned from flying with the Air Corps in Europe. Marjorie and Fred married in 1943 and settled in New York. Fred worked for his father's chinaware company while Marjorie raised their two children.[22] Marjorie was exotic and gorgeous in a movie star way, with narrow, elongated, blue-green eyes, smooth skin, and high cheekbones. Always flawlessly dressed, she had short, wavy dyed-red hair, thin, arched eyebrows, and a catlike grin. Fred, stocky and medium height, had wavy light brown hair, receding at the temples, that he greased back with pomade. He looked much younger than Marjorie, although he was three years her senior.

In New York, Marjorie was marginally involved with *Confidential*. She read gossip columns every day, and if she saw something Uncle Bob could use she went up to the *Confidential* office to give it to him. She also went to the office one or two days a week to see her mother and have lunch. Everyone at *Confidential* ate lunch in the office because they were too busy to go out.[23]

In 1954 Fred decided to go into the fiberglass building panel business, and he started his own company, National Fiberglass Products. As he discovered when he tried to sell fiberglass during a blizzard that winter, weather conditions in New York weren't good for fiberglass. He came up with the idea of operating his business out of California, and he told Harrison about it. Enthusiastic, Harrison said he would be happy to pay the cost of a two-way exploratory trip to Los Angeles if Fred and Marjorie could "take care of a few things" while they were there. Harrison told them that "he had some people [there], writers and one thing or another, that he had been in contact with previously." He wanted Marjorie to call them, extend his wishes, and ask them to send him stories they'd been working on. Marjorie was "to hustle them along, to see what the stage of their work was."[24]

The Meades made their first trip to Hollywood in January 1955. Harrison put them up at the Beverly Hills Hotel. During the ten days they were there, the Meades looked around for a distributorship for Fred's fiberglass panels. Meanwhile, Marjorie contacted Aline Mosby, Leo Guild, Mike Connolly, Columbia studio head Harry Cohn, Agnes Underwood, and H. L. von Wittenberg regarding *Confidential* stories. Connolly took them out to the Mocambo and offered them a tip.[25]

When people found out Marjorie was Harrison's niece, she was besieged with gossip. At a press party at the Beverly Hills Hotel, someone came up to her and said, "I've got a great story for your uncle, do you want to take it down?" They told him they had no way to take down information. The tipster told them to get a tape recorder, which they rented from von Wittenberg. She came up to their room and recorded the story.[26]

The Meades returned to New York, and Harrison asked them how things went. Fred told him the prospects for selling fiberglass were great and that he wanted to live in Los Angeles. Harrison replied that in addition to selling fiberglass he should try and cultivate material for *Confidential*. "Maybe you can accomplish two things at once," he said. The couple went back to Hollywood on another *Confidential*-sponsored trip in March 1955. On this second trip they made more contacts for Harrison. At parties and at the Beverly Hills Hotel, the Meades were again inundated with tips. Marjorie also did research for Harrison; she went down to newspaper morgues and checked legal records related to *Confidential* stories.

When the Meades got back to New York and looked more deeply into the fiberglass situation, they found it wasn't as good as they thought. There were several companies in Los Angeles manufacturing fiberglass cheaply, and freight rates from New York made it impossible to compete. Fred abandoned the idea of bringing fiberglass to California. When they told Harrison the business wasn't going to work, he said, "don't worry. I'm not going to leave you stranded. . . . I want to help you in any way I can."[27]

That summer, "Uncle Bob" paid for Fred and Marjorie to move to Los Angeles to work full time for *Confidential*. He rented them a luxurious eight-room

Spanish-style house on North Palm Drive in Beverly Hills, which would also serve as their office. Marjorie was given $5,000 to start up *Confidential*'s "gossip headquarters." A separate corporation was set up, both for tax purposes and to insulate *Confidential* from any liability the Meades might incur.[28] Harrison's New York attorneys sent the Meades to the Los Angeles attorney Birger Tinglof, and "Hollywood Research Incorporated" was formed. All of the stock was issued to Marjorie.

A "front" was set up for HRI. *Confidential*'s art department drew up a brochure saying that Hollywood Research Incorporated was a "news gathering organization in Hollywood supplying information to magazines." Harrison showed the brochure to Rushmore, who told him he didn't think anyone would be fooled by it. "Well, the attorneys feel that it will," Harrison said. The Meades sent out a form letter to every major magazine in the country, offering their services for research work.[29]

The purpose of HRI was both to collect tips and to check facts. The Meades were to pay informants for gossip, anywhere from a few hundred to a few thousand dollars, depending on how sensational it was. They paid by check or in cash, if the informant wanted to protect their identity. The Meades also worked on more than seven hundred "verification" assignments for Harrison. They searched material in the public record—land titles, birth and death records, criminal records—to confirm *Confidential* articles. They also coordinated fact-checking by Quillan, De Scaffa, von Wittenberg, and other informants, paying them generously for their work. Harrison spent between $1,000 and $5,000 to research and fact-check most stories. When it came to proving homosexuality, Harrison would spend thousands to check facts and line up witnesses. Informants were outfitted with state-of-the-art surveillance equipment—hidden cameras and miniature tape recorders that could be concealed in wristwatches or jacket lapels. "We have the exact time, exact date, the bungalow number, everything documented, just in case," Harrison boasted.[30]

On the advice of his lawyers, Harrison demanded that all informants sign notarized affidavits. The affidavits read, "I swear that all the events described in the above story are true and that I was a participant in these events." Fred Meade became a notary public. The affidavits—sometimes so scandalous that Harrison referred to them as "dynamite"—were kept in a locked file cabinet in the *Confidential* office. Harrison always tried to get multiple witnesses to corroborate scandalous facts. "Remember that a witness can be bought off,"

Harrison said. "If we do a story about X, and [if] it's a very serious accusation, the person we did the story about might remember who that witness was and have him or her go to Europe and then sue. . . . So to offset that we have several investigators work and have several witnesses."[31]

Even though they'd be pilloried for their work for *Confidential*, the Meades' research for Harrison was thorough and systematic. One example can be seen in their research on a story on Mae West's alleged relationship with her former chauffeur Chalky Wright. In 1955 the Meades had gotten a package from Harrison containing a letter and a newspaper clipping. Harrison had taken the clipping and Scotch-taped it to a piece of paper. He circled a sentence with a green crayon—"Mae West's Newest Beau Is Bound to Cause a Bit of Talk." Harrison sent it along with a letter from "Dale Wright," dated November 11, 1954, and addressed "Dear Bob."

> Dear Bob: Here's a story that might fit your format. Some few years ago—perhaps 15—Mae West had a Negro chauffeur . . . named Jones. The driver-employer relationship soon developed into something a little more intimate, however, and rumor had it that Jones became her lover. One night at a party Jones demanded that Mae leave. She declined, after having a good bit to drink, and Jones knocked her down—and out—tossed her into the big limousine he drove for her and hauled her home. There were many such rumors at the time, most of them originating on the West Coast. I know some people who know about these incidents and they can be tied into a story on Mae West's Backstreet Love Life or some other such title. Whattya think?
>
> Incidentally, this chauffeur was a former prize fighter, which reminds me further that she was also linked romantically with Chalky Wright, another prize fighter, who is still active as a trainer in Los Angeles and perhaps can be persuaded to talk, for I'm sure he knows the whole story.[32]

Fred Meade tracked down Wright, interviewed him, and got a signed statement detailing the year and a half he spent living with West while working as her bodyguard and driver. West had been a boxing fan since the 1930s and helped support Wright's career; Wright went to work for West when his career ended. A private investigator accompanied Fred when he took the statement from Wright. Meade went to Bakersfield to talk with West's former road manager, and the investigator took him to prize fights and introduced him to boxers he knew.[33]

The article, "Mae West's Open-Door Policy," ran in the November 1955 issue. Illustrated with a large picture of Wright superimposed over a picture of West with outstretched arms, the article chortled that West's "favorite color combination" was black and white, and claimed that during the year Wright worked for West she showered him with elaborate gifts, purchased a house for his mother, and financed his divorce. *Confidential* didn't come out and state but implied a sexual relationship between West and Wright, as well as "a succession of feather, middle, and light-heavyweight fighters." The piece was deeply upsetting to West, who tried to distance her off-screen persona from her screen image.[34]

HRI's gossip came from Hollywood news correspondents, stars, directors, producers, cameramen, former studio publicists, photographers, fan magazine writers, room clerks, bellboys, waiters, cigarette girls, nurses, and secretaries. It came from friends of celebrities, enemies of celebrities, private detectives, policemen, and disgruntled maids and butlers. It came from hairdressers, decorators, valets, store clerks, chauffeurs, bartenders, and ushers. It came from wives and husbands, ex-wives and ex-husbands, prostitutes, paramours, and even brothers, sisters, sons, daughters, and parents.

Servants, the Meades found, were excellent tipsters. *Confidential* paid maids and butlers to bring recording devices with them to work. Stars were warned to check references carefully when hiring governesses. "During the past year several . . . have had painful experiences with a woman who takes a job for a few weeks or months, spies on the family's private life, and reports her findings to the scandal magazines . . . to make money on the side," reported one columnist. A governess at the home of Dean Martin's ex-wife gave a tip to *Confidential*. An interior decorator for a top celebrity was also source of tips. A Palm Springs bartender who sold stories about Joan Crawford, Lana Turner, and Ava Gardner made enough to open a small restaurant. Robert Tuton, a Hollywood maître d', gave the Meades information on his affair with Joan Crawford and was paid $750.[35]

Film extras, screenwriters, and bit actors became important sources for *Confidential*. Frank Goldberg, an unemployed Hollywood writer, sold the magazine information about actor Sonny Tufts. Actress Vera Francis sold facts about Edward G. Robinson. Allan Nixon, former husband of comedienne Marie Wilson, gave tips on several stars, and Fred Meade loaned him money. William Chaney, a film extra, confirmed stories about Mickey Rooney and Donald O'Connor. Prostitutes and "party girls" were prolific sources. Fred Meade actually flew to Dallas to pick up a tip from a prostitute who was living there.[36]

As Harrison's operations became more complex, he relied increasingly on private detectives. In the summer of 1954, Harrison hired Barney Ruditsky to give him tips on his clients. A frequent figure in the press, Ruditsky started his career in the 1920s as a New York City police detective on its "gangster-industrial squad." After retiring from the NYPD he moved to L.A., where he opened a small liquor store as well as a nightclub, Sherry's Restaurant on Sunset Boulevard, and his own private detective firm that became Hollywood's go-to. These ventures brought him into contact with the entertainment world and also the mob. In 1949 Mickey Cohen, a regular at Sherry's, was shot outside the restaurant in an assassination attempt. Ruditsky's agency collected on bad debts owed casinos, including Bugsy Siegel's Flamingo Hotel and Casino in Las Vegas. Ruditsky, called to testify at the Kefauver hearings, denied having ties to the underworld.[37]

In the summer of 1955, Harrison enlisted the services of Fred Otash, who became a key player in *Confidential*. Otash was the quintessential hard-boiled, ultra-macho postwar Los Angeles private detective, memorialized by 1950s novelist Mickey Spillane and, later, crime fiction writers like James Ellroy, author of the 1990 novel *L.A. Confidential*. Otash went around Hollywood in a chauffeured Cadillac full of women he called "little sweeties." He also drank a quart of Scotch and smoked four packs of cigarettes a day. He was a thug and a roughneck, a notorious playboy, and a virulent racist and homophobe whose speech was filled with profanities and epithets. A big, good-looking, thickly built man, six foot one and 220 pounds, Otash had wavy black hair, heavy eyebrows, cherub cheeks, and a perpetual smirk.[38]

Born in 1922, the sixth child of an impoverished Lebanese couple living in Massachusetts, Otash had been in the Marines during the war and was an expert in hand-to-hand combat. Caught behind enemy lines, he once fought his way back using his bare hands to kill a Japanese soldier. Upon discharge in 1945, he applied to the Los Angeles Police Department and became its "leg breaker." When William Worton took over the LAPD in 1949, he formed a "goon squad of ex-Marines to take care of organized crime figures"—to "take 'em off the bus, airplane, train, beat the shit out of 'em, and put 'em back on," in Ellroy's words. Otash was one of them. The chiefs gave him other "hairy" assignments—picking locks, climbing telephone poles, break-ins. He earned the title "Gestapo Otash" for harassing protesters and street speakers. "I used to give those commies a bad time when I walked the beat," he recalled. "We have certain laws that are in the book about speech-making . . . and I took advantage of those sections . . . and broke up . . . various conferences." In 1946 newspapers reported that Otash fired on a homeless man in Pershing Square after asking him about his draft classification, winging him in the arm and bringing him down on the sidewalk. Otash eventually became the LAPD's top "undercover man," making news by going out in drag one night in an effort to catch rapist Caryl Chessman, infiltrating a stolen car ring, and busting gangsters including Bugsy Siegel and Mickey Cohen.[39]

When he arrived at the department, Otash was immediately labeled a nonconformist, stubborn, and a "bullheaded sonofabitch." The chiefs—the "old guard," thick in corruption—cracked down on the "Young Turks," giving them nothing but bad news, Otash wrote in his autobiography. "I came into the department with a bunch of young guys who'd just fought a war and were in no mood for any bullshit from a bunch of armchair police generals." He outraged the top brass by being chauffeured to work in a limo owned by a girlfriend. William Parker, who took over as chief in 1950, despised him. "Parker was the kind of chief who'd order men out on an assignment with specific instructions that were a violation of his own 'by the book' procedures. Later he'd deny the orders had been his," Otash wrote. "The guy could have made three-star general in the Prussian army. All spit, polish, and brass." Parker put him on what the men called the "Merry Go Round," transferring him every thirty days from one precinct to the next.[40]

In 1948 Otash got in trouble for watching some "very big businessmen" play dice. He was in uniform, and the game got raided by the vice squad. The police trial board said he should have put the men in jail. Otash was found guilty of neglect of duty and suspended for sixty days without pay. He was warned to avoid associating with gangsters and prostitutes. "I'm a vice cop," he fumed. "Where am I supposed to get my information, from priests and rabbis?"

The following year, Otash got an off-duty permit to work as a store detective at the Hollywood Ranch Market on Vine Street. There he found actors like James Dean ripping off caviar and other expensive grocery items. The job was lucrative, and before long Otash was "driving a new Caddy . . . owned 25 or 30 tailor made suits, and . . . making it with some of the best looking broads in town." Parker revoked the permit, and Otash sued him. In 1954 Hollywood lawyer Arthur Crowley prepared a test case to challenge Parker's authority to control off-duty employment. But before the decision came down, Otash left the force.[41]

At some point in the early 1950s, Otash started doing favors for people in Hollywood. "You needed to get your girlfriend an abortion? Freddie's the guy. You needed to get a drunk-and-disorderly charge dropped? Freddie's the guy. You needed to break up a squeeze on a gay actor? Freddie's the guy," as Ellroy put it. Otash set up shop as a private investigator in 1954, opening the Fred Otash Detective Bureau at 1234 North Laurel Canyon. By 1955 Otash was earning about $100,000 a year working on divorce cases for socialites and movie stars, and doing investigations for well-known lawyers like Melvin Belli and Jerry Giesler. From the time Harrison hired Otash in 1955 to the time of the *Confidential* trial in 1957, Otash received more than $35,000 from Harrison, paid through the Meades' account.[42]

Otash trailed celebrities, photographed them with zoom lenses, and installed hidden cameras and recorders in their homes. "Sometimes we used helicopters," Otash recalled. "If something had to be done, I would get a master key made that would fit the trunk of a car. And I'd get someone very small—I'd use midgets sometimes—and I'd put them in the trunk of a car." He even put a midget on the floor of a back seat. For a story on Gary Cooper's alleged affair with Grace Kelly, Otash trailed the actor for two or three weeks. If a car was parked in a driveway and Otash couldn't get close enough to the house to find out when the car left, he'd put a Mickey Mouse watch under the back wheel. When the car pulled out, it would crush the watch, recording the time.[43]

Most accounts describe Otash as utterly sleazy, maybe even more sleazy than Harrison and Rushmore, but there were times when Harrison, Rushmore, and Otash agreed to withhold stories that wouldn't "be in good taste." Recalled Otash: "We had a beautiful love story about Kathy Hepburn and Spencer Tracy which was never used because we agreed that this was such a clean pure love affair that it would be best if we just kept it out of *Confidential*."[44]

9 | GOSSIP

CONFIDENTIAL WASN'T THE FIRST time vicious celebrity gossip had appeared in print. Scandalous news about entertainment stars—describing their sexual affairs, addictions, abortions, and other indiscretions—had long been in circulation. But it was limited, for the most part, to the underground press. Salacious tabloids and scandal sheets were stocked beneath grimy newsstand counters and sold to nervous-looking customers in brown paper wrappers. Considered vulgar, outrageous, and even legally obscene, they were quashed by authorities, sometimes within months. The gutter press teemed with smutty publications with lives as long as moths. What made *Confidential* different was that it took celebrity sleaze to the national stage. With shrewd lawyers, an "army" of informants, and a knack for gauging the tenor of the times, Harrison found a way to make nasty gossip mainstream.

———————

In 1916 a shady conman, drug addict, and lowlife named Stephen G. Clow became one of the first successful celebrity gossip peddlers in America when he started an influential, short-lived New York scandal sheet called *Broadway Brevities and Society Gossip*. Devoted to gossip of "stage, screen, and society," it was launched with the "aim of outshining anything in sensational journalism." Described as "an unequaled mirror of Broadway's restless life in all its shifting lights and shadows," its articles were devoted to the "detailed destruction of reputations." The amorous escapades of prominent actresses, producers, and playwrights, such as Florenz Ziegfeld, David Belasco, and Ethel Barrymore, were ruthlessly exposed. *Brevities* reported on the extramarital dalliances of prominent married men and women and revealed that actors had sexually transmitted diseases. Its specialty was descriptions of homosexuality in the entertainment world. In January 1924, it ran a thirteen-part series, "A Night in Fairyland," which exposed gay and lesbian nightlife in Manhattan. Clow obtained his material through spies and tipsters, "an amazing pirate's crew of men and women . . . from café hangers-on . . . to gilt-edged kingpins," one newspaper reported. "Broadway is honeycombed with swarms of spies who will sell information to anyone who will pay the price." The publication, sold at newsstands, was primarily for Broadway insiders, though it occasionally fell into the hands of ordinary readers. Noted one commentator, "many casual readers bought the magazine and read—with amusement, greedy interest, disgust, or frank incredulity . . .—items about this celebrity and that."[1]

Broadway Brevities was a shameless extortion racket. Clow approached prominent individuals and told them he had gossip he'd publish unless they bought advertising. If they did, they'd get a favorable write-up. A former Ziegfeld showgirl paid $150 to suppress a scandal. Film director D. W. Griffith's advertising manager bought $600 worth of advertising to prevent the tabloid from stirring up a controversy over the death of an actor in one of Griffith's films. Clow collected large sums from Paul Bonwit of Bonwit Teller department store fame, Percival Hill, president of the American Tobacco Company, banker W. Averell Harriman, and film producer Jesse L. Lasky. When his potential victims seemed unfazed by his threats, he'd tell them, "My runners get the dope on everybody."[2]

In April 1924 a federal grand jury indicted Clow on charges of misuse of the mails and conspiracy to use the mails to defraud. An all-star cast of witnesses appeared before the grand jury, including matinee idol Lowell Sherman, screen star Texas Guinan, musical star Elsie Janis, producer Lee Shubert, socialite Peggy Hopkins Joyce, and fight promoter Tex Rickard. Clow was found guilty and sentenced to six years in federal prison in Atlanta, where he spent two years. "Few things are meaner than to threaten publicly to blast the lives of private individuals by publishing their social or moral errors," the judge declared.[3]

Undaunted, after his prison stint Clow reemerged with an even seedier publication: *The New Broadway Brevities*, later renamed *Brevities: America's First National Tabloid Weekly*. This version of *Brevities* was a large, garish tabloid with lewd illustrations and blaring headlines. *Brevities* exposed vice, sexual habits, prostitution, corruption, and gay and lesbian life. Its covers and front pages, writes one magazine historian, promised "sweeping coverage of every form of depravity." Titles were crude, often written around double entendres: "Fair Gals Grab Stiffs! Chicago Gals Perform in Weird Exhibition Rites"; "Sissies Permeate Sublime Social Strata as Film Stars and Broadwayites Go Gay." A column titled Hollywood Lowdown appeared in a few issues. In 1932 the Licensing Commissioner for the City of New York, declaring the publication obscene, forced newsstands to stop selling *Brevities*, and it shut down shortly after.[4]

In Hollywood a small, sleazy underground press used similar shakedown tactics. In the early 1930s a writer-conman named Frederic Girnau printed outrageous lies about actress Clara Bow in his self-proclaimed "political weekly" the *Coast Reporter*. The *Reporter* denounced Bow as the mistress of several actors, including Rex Bell, a "cowboy lothario" she liked because he was "ambidextrous in the saddle." Girnau alleged that Bow had spent a night in a Tijuana brothel, where she initiated sex acts with two prostitutes. When there was no man around, she resorted to her woman servant. When there was no woman around, she turned to her dog. The articles about Bow ran in four issues of the gossip rag and were preceded by a purported affidavit bearing the signature of Daisy DeVoe, Bow's secretary, saying she had agreed to give Girnau a "true and honest story." Copies of *The Coast Reporter* were issued free to newsboys, and the paper was sold outside the Paramount studio's main gate.[5]

Girnau promised Bow that if she bought the paper for $25,000 he would stop publishing stories about her. Foolishly, he mailed copies to film industry leader Will Hays, several judges, and local PTA officials and was arrested by federal agents for obscenity and misuse of the mails. He served eight years in federal prison. According to Louella Parsons, these extortion schemes ran rampant in Hollywood. In 1931 a young male star paid $20,000 to keep a lurid story out of print. A leading producer at a large studio paid $1,700 to protect the good name of his stars.[6]

Perhaps the most notorious Hollywood scandal sheet before *Confidential* was *Hollywood Nite Life*, which had a brief, sordid life in the late 1940s and early '50s. The weekly tabloid, promising the "real truth, behind the news," described as a "nightclub gossip weekly," was funded by gangster Mickey Cohen with an initial $15,000 investment by Frank Sinatra. *Hollywood Nite Life* was run by Jimmy Tarantino, a former stringer for the boxing trade paper *The Knockout* and a member of "the Varsity," Frank Sinatra's original posse of hangers-on. According to Sinatra's FBI file, ex-welterweight Barney Ross, Sinatra manager Hank Sanicola, and Tarantino operated the magazine for six months until Tarantino acquired it. The tabloid—a strange combination of promotional puffs, Winchell-type gossip, and the occasional editorial blast on a disfavored star or director—circulated only in the show business community, "sort of a slimy version of *Variety*."[7]

A sleazy character who wore snappy suits and talked fast, Tarantino ran a tiny three-room office on Sunset Boulevard "filled with silent characters who stare out the window, puff cigarettes, and have whispered consultations with the editor," Aline Mosby wrote in 1948. His self-appointed crusade was to rid Hollywood of addicts. "Lately he's been smearing his front page with dope stories that would blister the print right off the blaringest tabloids," Mosby reported. In boldface capital letters read accusations like, "Not since the days of Fatty Arbuckle has Hollywood been faced with so dirty a mess. Sparks are growing into big, ugly, consuming flames. Miss G. and Mr. F. are only two of the many victims of dope addiction . . . also Mr. M." Tarantino referred to celebrities only by initials. He was especially vigilant about exposing Judy Garland's drug addiction. In the summer of 1948, he ran three front-page articles about "Miss G.," describing her as a "pill-head." The magazine was planted on the desks of studio chiefs and top producers. "*Hollywood Nite Life* has been tearing into everybody, and Jimmy mutters about movie stars' lawyers paying him visits. . . . He could also paper his office wall with threatening telegrams," wrote Mosby.[8]

Tarantino met his demise when, like Clow and Girnau, he got involved in extortion. "Salesmen" for *Hollywood Nite Life* began confronting celebrities, giving them the option of advertising or becoming the subject of an exposé. Among those approached were Johnnie Ray and Murray Chotiner, campaign manager for vice presidential candidate Richard Nixon, as well as newsstand owners and restaurant owners who would be "blasted" unless they bought advertising. Tarantino was indicted on extortion charges in January 1953, found guilty, and sentenced to San Quentin for fifteen years. *Hollywood Nite Life* was auctioned off later that year for a grand total of one dollar.[9]

10 | THE LEGAL DEPARTMENT

SINCE HIS "GIRLIE BOOK" empire, Harrison was no stranger to the legal risks of pulp publishing. His cheesecake publications were driven off newsstands for violating obscenity laws, and the US Postal Service rejected their mailing privileges for lewdness and indecency. The bans and lost mailing privileges were troublesome, but they weren't fatal to Harrison's operations. Harrison could just edit the text and put more clothes on his models to make the magazines acceptable to authorities.

But *Confidential*'s legal dilemmas were different. With its scandalous attacks on stars, it invited lawsuits for libel. A few big libel judgments, or even one, could potentially bankrupt the magazine. Even if plaintiffs didn't succeed, the cost of defending the magazine could be devastating. The fear of libel lawsuits led Harrison to take up an intense system of legal prescreening orchestrated by high-priced lawyers. Though the magazine was accused of lying, and sometimes did make up facts, it was one of the more carefully vetted publications on American newsstands.

Since the 1940s, Harrison had employed the New York law firm of Becker, Ross & Stone. After his skirmish with the postmaster general, Harrison always checked with his attorneys before printing anything racy. "It had to be acceptable to the Post Office," Harrison recalled. "If [the editor] said, 'Let's do a picture of a woman holding a whip,' I called my lawyer right away and said 'Is this legitimate? If he said it was legitimate it was fine with me."[1]

The firm worked with Harrison on *Confidential*. At *Confidential*'s height in the mid-1950s, Harrison paid Becker, Ross & Stone $100,000 a year. It was a small firm, with only twenty-five or thirty employees—fifteen lawyers and five law clerks. It had 250 clients, most of them nonpublishing companies.[2]

Albert DeStefano was Harrison's main lawyer. A 1938 graduate of the City College of New York, chubby, good-natured, gregarious DeStefano attended Fordham University School of Law and graduated *cum laude* in 1947. After law school, DeStefano got a master's degree in tax law from New York University, then became an associate, and in 1953 a partner in the Becker, Ross & Stone firm. Colleagues described him as a "scrappy, smart lawyer" who was "ethical and engaged" and "rather nebbish." He would go on to achieve a distinguished career as a corporate lawyer, specializing in mergers and acquisitions. DeStefano was not only Harrison's lawyer, but also a close friend. Harrison held many of his business conferences at El Morocco, the Stork Club, and the Harwyn Club. DeStefano accompanied him there, sometimes well into the night. They drank, people-watched, and talked about how to avoid lawsuits.[3]

Confidential's other lawyer was Daniel G. Ross, a graduate of Yale and Columbia Law School. A founder of the Becker, Ross & Stone firm, he specialized in corporate law. Ross, who wore finely tailored suits and horn-rimmed glasses, was dapper, cool, and sophisticated. He claimed that he never made a mistake in counseling Harrison on *Confidential*.[4]

Ross and DeStefano were involved with all aspects of *Confidential*, from giving financial and tax advice to overseeing the editorial process.[5] The lawyers sat in on editorial conferences, consulted with staff writers, and aside from Harrison, had the final say on what ran in *Confidential*. They also gave advice to Harrison about *Whisper* ("The Stories Behind the Headlines"), which Harrison continued to publish. By 1955 Harrison had converted *Whisper* from a pinup magazine into a tawdrier version of *Confidential*, a dumping ground for stories that weren't good enough for *Confidential*, or for warmed-over, rehashed *Confidential* articles. *Whisper* was housed in the *Confidential* office but had its own separate editorial staff.

Libel was Harrison's biggest legal concern, and it hung ominously over the magazine from the start. Harrison tacked up a little note behind his desk saying, "Watch for Libel." He carried $60,000 of libel insurance with European insurance companies, and kept a substantial reserve in the event of a libel judgment.[6]

For material to be libelous, it has to be both false and defamatory. To be defamatory, a statement has to be not just insulting to a person, but absolutely destructive to his reputation—it has to cause one's peers to "avoid, scorn, or shun" them. Certain kinds of material were considered so damaging to a person's reputation that they were libelous per se. Statements accusing someone of professional incompetence, being unchaste, committing a crime, or having a "loathsome disease" (a venereal disease) were libelous per se. Accusations of homosexuality were also libelous per se.[7]

Since there weren't yet First Amendment protections in libel law, as there would be after the 1960s, libel was a genuine threat to publishers. If a plaintiff brought a libel suit, the statement in question was presumed to be false; the burden was on the defendant to prove the truth, which was usually an expensive and difficult task. Publishers went out of business from large libel judgments. Editors and publishers described the "nightmare" of libel litigation. Journalism textbooks urged reporters to "lean over backwards" to avoid writing anything that "might possibly be construed as libelous," and to avoid "any words to which offense might be taken."[8]

By the time he started doing his Hollywood exposés, Harrison already faced libel suits and threats of suit. In 1953 the actor Paul Valentine told newspapers he planned to sue Harrison for an article titled "They Pay to Wear the Pants," about actresses who supported their husbands. The article alleged that "Lili St. Cyr, the stripper, is another beauty of show business who invariably falls for a non-working Romeo." Valentine, who was married to St. Cyr, claimed he had been under contract to the RKO studio at $500 a week. Publisher Lyle Stuart sued *Confidential* for $250,000 over the article by Howard Rushmore calling him an "admitted extortioner, a hate peddler, and a coddler of communists."[9]

When *Confidential* started its "hot Hollywood" stories, the lawyers began "libel checks," reading each issue closely and considering whether every sentence, article, and photograph could be libelous. Libel checks were de rigueur among major publishers. The *Saturday Review of Literature* noted in 1950 that the careful, pocketbook-conscious publisher "usually has every manuscript read by a libel expert before it is passed for manufacture." An error or lapse in this process could lead to an angry letter demanding satisfaction by the injured person, or by his lawyer, "who is either pressingly indignant or just pressing."[10]

Confidential's libel checks were thorough and meticulous. Ross and DeStefano often demanded that writers rewrite certain phrases; sometimes entire stories would be eliminated if they were too controversial. They also asked Harrison for proof of every statement. "I got lawyers that go over every word in my magazine and they make sure it's 100 percent libel proof," Harrison boasted. "There is not one word that goes into this book that is not thoroughly authenticated and documented."[11]

Every Confidential article originated in a "story conference." Confidential's stories typically began when a tip or affidavit came in to the New York office from an informant or from HRI. The lawyers and Confidential's staff met to discuss the information, and the editors would come up with a story idea. Sometimes a writer would come to Harrison with a pitch for a story, but that usually happened with the "public service" stories. With gossip stories we "work the other way round," Harrison explained. "We do the research on it, we get the facts, we get it backed up. Then we call a writer and we say: 'Here. These are the facts . . . take these facts and weave them into a nice fast moving story.' We call it a toboggan ride; we want someone to get interested right away and not to get off that toboggan until they are through."[12]

The writer assigned to work on the story attended the conference. The story line was usually decided on by Harrison, with contributions from other staff. The lawyers would weigh in on what should be taken out and what should be left in. The writer would then take the affidavit or a copy of the unsigned affidavit and write the first draft of the article.

Ross and DeStefano consulted with writers on language and phrasing. One strategy to avoid libel, they advised, was to qualify every statement. Articles were peppered with words like "maybe," "assuming," "probably," "reportedly," "perhaps," and "generally." Another strategy was to imply scandalous facts. In most stories, illicit sex was suggested but never directly stated. Confidential "says nothing with finality," observed Confidential imitator Top Secret magazine. "It doesn't come right out and claim. . . . Everything is left neatly up in the air, letting the heavy steel wrecking ball swing freely." As long as the core facts of a story were true, the lawyers told Harrison, writers could embellish them as much as they wanted. Harrison described it this way: "Once we establish the star in the hay and that's documented, we can say anything we want and I think we make the [stories] a hell of a lot more interesting than they really are. What's a guy gonna do, sue us and admit he was in the hay with the dame, but claim he didn't do all the other things we dress the story with?"[13]

The lawyers advised Harrison to always print less than he knew. If *Confidential* published a story accusing someone of having sex with a woman who wasn't his wife, it should withhold further details—that the lover was underage, for example. The threat that the whole story would come out in court was enough to deter most libel suits. According to Otash, what *Confidential* published was "thin stuff" compared to what the tipsters actually uncovered.[14]

Pictures also required care. *Confidential* didn't employ its own photographers or paparazzi; it bought photos from freelance photographers working for major newspapers or magazines, and occasionally from private eyes like Otash. Pictures weren't *Confidential*'s strong suit; rarely did photos add much to a story. Many images in the magazine weren't of stars, but of places—bungalows, apartments, and nightclubs where scandalous events allegedly took place. In the interest of avoiding liability, *Confidential* eschewed steamy and salacious photos. When it did run photos of stars, they were usually unflattering, showing them in unappealing poses—with their mouths agog, looking angry, disheveled, or drunk. Pictures could be just as libelous as words if they conveyed a false and defamatory meaning—as when unrelated images were juxtaposed to create scandalous implications, like the photo of Mae West superimposed against a picture of her black chauffeur Chalky Wright. Captions could be dangerous too. Harrison loved snarky, innuendo-laden captions; they could make up for a bland photo. For its expose of Desi Arnaz sleeping with prostitutes, *Confidential* used a picture of Arnaz and Lucille Ball cutting a cake at their tenth wedding anniversary. The caption noted Desi's skill with other kinds of "cheesecake."[15]

When the first draft of an article was completed, the writer, editors, and lawyers would convene. Govoni, dubbed "The Reader," would read the story out loud. Govoni had a deep, resonant voice, with perfect diction and timing. Harrison believed that if you read a story out loud, every weakness in it would stand out.[16]

After the first reading, there would be suggestions. The lawyers would examine the story in light of the affidavits and other documentation to see whether the writer had gone beyond the facts. The lawyers sometimes asked for additional affidavits, especially if any came from untrustworthy witnesses. Harrison spent most of *Confidential's* budget on lawyers, researchers, tipsters, and fact-checkers. Harrison would pay as much as $4,500 for an article, with $1,000 going to the tipster, $500 to the writer, $500 for pictures, and $2,500 for lawyers to nail down important facts.[17]

In addition to checking for libel, Ross and DeStefano read stories with an eye to obscenity. Publishing obscene material was a crime in almost every state, punishable by fines and jail time. Sending obscene material through the mails was a federal crime. Although some states were liberalizing the definition of obscenity, in most the legal standard for obscenity was strict—obscene material was whatever judges or police considered "lewd," "immoral," or "salacious." *Confidential's* lawyers cautioned the writers to be exceedingly cautious about violating obscenity laws and to avoid explicitly writing about sex.[18]

Ross and DeStefano constantly held back Harrison and the writers. Often they rejected stories if they thought they were based on hearsay. Some stories would be killed right off the bat if the lawyers thought they were too controversial. Harrison planned to do an article on Florabel Muir after he read an item in her column in the *New York Daily News* attacking *Confidential*. He wanted to expose her and her husband as former *Confidential* informants, printing canceled checks HRI had sent her. Rushmore, DeStefano, and Govoni persuaded Harrison that she was likely to retaliate and that it would be too risky to run the story.[19]

The writers put up the most resistance. When the lawyers told them an article needed a rewrite, they'd flip. "Why delete this? What's wrong with it?" they'd ask. In cases where the lawyers said a story might be obscene, the writers would point out passages in bestsellers that were just as risqué. "Now how can you restrict us . . . when this stuff is sold in public libraries, sold all over the country and is accepted?" they'd ask. One time after the lawyers recommended deleting entire paragraphs in an author's story, he gave them a disclaimer he wanted to put in with the article saying he relinquished all responsibility for it because it was the attorneys' work, not his own.[20]

Rushmore also battled with the lawyers. Rushmore complained that Ross and DeStefano refused to accept his word as proof of a story's authenticity.

In 1955 Harrison and Rushmore got into a bitter fight about an article on Eleanor Roosevelt. It was a vicious story that went back several years, alleging a relationship between Roosevelt and a black chauffeur, and there was no proof other than that Rushmore said it was true. Rushmore demanded that Harrison print the story, even though there was no documentation. When Harrison and the lawyers refused, he accused them of not running it because they were pro-Roosevelt. Rushmore also wanted to do a story on Marilyn Monroe sleeping with a photographer who was an alleged communist, which the lawyers turned down because there was no corroboration. Rushmore complained to a columnist for the *Detroit Free Press*: "The magazine uses a whole covey of legal eagles to steer away from libel suits. . . . Those lawyers have torpedoed . . . good stories."[21]

When Harrison and the lawyers agreed on the final text of an issue, it was sent to typographers who made up galley proofs. The proofs were set up on "boards," which were mounted along the wall in the editorial department, where the lawyers inspected them before they went out to the printer. There were about sixteen boards containing the entire issue.[22]

Everyone met one last time before the magazine went to press. Charlie, the elevator man in the building—a husky guy with a blond crew cut, *Confidential*'s "man in the street" critic—was invited to the conference, where Govoni read all the stories in a "voice like the narrator on *The March of Time*." Even at this stage there might be changes to the text. Harrison usually agreed to having the proofs changed at the last minute, which often resulted in the magazine being late. If the lawyers found something bad in the galleys, they would have to send them back to the typographers, which took twenty-four hours, and they would have to get an extension from the printer. De Stefano recalled that the lawyers were "much abused for causing [issues] to be late." The boards were sometimes air expressed to the printer in Chicago; if they were running late, one of Harrison's staff would personally carry the boards on a plane to Chicago.[23]

Confidential's lawyers also advised Harrison on the setup of the company. Though based in New York, *Confidential* had no connection to its printer, wholesaler, distributor, and sellers. The magazine was printed in Illinois by an independent publisher called the Kable Printing Company, and its entire press run was purchased by a wholesale distributor, the Publishers Distributing

Corporation, which sold the magazine to distributors in other states. This meant that *Confidential* couldn't be sued for libel in any state other than New York. Most of the magazine's copies were sold at newsstands, rather than by subscription; newsstand copies were distributed by truck, rather than mail, to head off potential problems with the Post Office.[24]

Harrison's lawyers became even more dear to him in 1955, when *Confidential* went after bigger stars, making even bigger, bolder, and more serious claims.

11 | 1955

THE YEAR 1955 WAS one of turbulence and innocence. The civil rights movement was galvanized by the brutal lynching of a fourteen-year-old African American boy named Emmett Till, sparking protest across the South. The Cold War heated up with the signing of the Warsaw Pact, a collective defense treaty between the Soviets and their Eastern European allies. The United States began bolstering anticommunist forces in Vietnam, the first nuclear-powered submarine cast off, and a series of fourteen nuclear test explosions, Operation Teapot, took place at a Nevada test site.

The Mickey Mouse Club debuted on ABC, and Disneyland opened in Anaheim, California. Ray Kroc opened his first McDonald's, and Coke appeared for the first time in cans. A Gallup poll declared 1955 the year of Mambo Mania—Americans were crazy for dancing the mambo.

In Hollywood, musicals, comedies, and war films reigned: *Oklahoma!, Guys and Dolls, The Seven Year Itch, Battle Cry.* As film attendance continued to decline—figures had dropped by 50 percent since 1946—studios developed new gimmicks like 3-D movies and widescreen film to lure audiences back to the big screen. Top stars included Grace Kelly, June Allyson, John Wayne, William Holden, Gary Cooper, Marilyn Monroe, Rock Hudson, Marlon Brando, and Clark Gable—all victims of *Confidential.*

Confidential went through that year like a wrecking ball, smashing idols, tearing down reputations, and devastating egos with articles revealing the misdeeds of the most beloved stars. By the end of the year, *Confidential* was selling more copies at newsstands than any other magazine in American history.

In 1955, *I Love Lucy* was one of the most popular TV shows in the country, and a beloved national icon. The program debuted in 1951, and in 1954, forty-five million Americans were tuning in to it each week. Lucille Ball and Desi Arnaz were the most widely viewed comedians in the history of show business.[1]

"The Arnazes live quietly in their home in Chatsworth in the San Fernando Valley, 20 miles from Hollywood, preferring sleep to nightclubs," wrote *Coronet* magazine in 1953. "Energetic Desi spends nearly every weekend fishing on his 34-foot launch, named, like everything they own, 'Desilu.'" Gushed a fan magazine, "To Lucille Ball, her children, her career, her money, her fame, are all important to her, but first and foremost in her book of values comes the success of her marriage to Desi."[2]

In reality, their marriage was volatile and tumultuous. It had been that way from the start. Ball and Arnaz, who were married in 1940, almost divorced in 1944 but reconciled before the decree became final. They continued to fight, and Arnaz had several affairs. Fan magazines insisted that the conflict was a thing of the past. "When Lucille and Desi Arnaz were first married there were many stormy scenes," *Screenland* reported in 1954. "And yet, even a roving husband can sometimes be made to stop roving if his wife is a smart little doll like Lucille Ball.... After almost every argument Desi would pack his clothes and move into a hotel room. Now he doesn't do that. What happened was that Lucille was able to convert him from a bachelor husband with too many privileges into a more domesticated animal." In February 1955, a ghostwritten, syndicated news article, "Lucille Ball Finds Grace Key to Lasting Marriage," claimed she'd turned her marriage around through her Christian faith. "I realized this was a three-way deal. Desi and I with God, and through God. Without Him, we were nothing."[3]

Confidential shattered the image. Its cover story, "Does Desi Really Love Lucy?" by "Brad Shortell"—Howard Rushmore—revealed Desi's flings with prostitutes. *Confidential* informant Ronnie Quillan, the Hollywood madam, baited Arnaz with some of her "girls" to bring up to date a story she sold *Confidential* about a night she spent with Arnaz back in 1944.

"Desi is most certainly a duck-out daddy," *Confidential* wrote. He had "sprinkled his affections all over Hollywood for a number of years. And quite a bit of it has been bestowed on vice dollies who were paid handsomely for loving Desi briefly, but, presumably, as effectively as Lucy."

Confidential described his encounter the previous August with a call girl in the Beverly Hills Hotel. "She was given about 30 seconds to admire the mirrored living room and its twin couches when Desi took her off to inspect another room." That incident was no isolated case. Another "pay-for-play-squab" had slept with him in 1951.

The heart of the article was an incident that happened more than ten years earlier, in October 1944. Ball had just filed for divorce. It never took effect because it was granted in California, where the couple had to live apart for a year before the divorce became valid. According to *Confidential,* they "slightly missed this cooling-off period by getting together the very first night after her decree."

During the year when the divorce could have become final, Arnaz slept with a prostitute, *Confidential* reported. At the time, he was an army sergeant stationed at Birmingham General Hospital in Van Nuys. In the cocktail lounge of the Ambassador Hotel in Palm Springs, he met a "dark-eyed temptress," and they spent the next five hours "smooching and drinking." The article claimed that Ball knew about the affairs but loved him anyway. "And Desi most certainly loves Lucy. It's just that, like a lot of other husbands, he's got a little extra—to go around."[4] *Confidential* hit newsstands at the same time as the December 1954 issue of *Look,* which featured a cover story, "Lucy and Desi, TV's Favorite Family."[5]

Ball was curious about the *Confidential* story and asked one of her staff to bring her a copy, explaining "Christ, I can't go out and buy it myself." She read it and was horrified. Arnaz burst onto the *I Love Lucy* set with a copy. "Look what those SOBs are saying about me now," he said. Later, with a friend, Ball broke down in tears.[6]

"Lucy was just distraught," her friend recalled. "She had her pride, and it was hard because she was just mad for Desi." In public, she remained silent. She, Arnaz, and another couple were at an industry dinner with Danny Kaye, singer Lily Pons, and conductor Andre Kostelanetz when Kaye said, "You made *Confidential!*" Pons didn't know what *Confidential* was, so Kaye told her, "It's a magazine about fucking." Ball was so upset that she was silent the rest of the evening.[7]

"I LOVE LUCY"

Does Desi Really

Television's best-known hubby is like a lot of other married men. He loves his wife, but "Oh, those other kids!" Here's an inside report on Desi's back-street babes that will have Lucy tearing her hair... or his!

"Desi most certainly loves Lucy. It's just that, like a lot of other husbands, he's got a little extra—to go around." *Author's collection*

By BRAD SHORTELL

EXACTLY WHAT MAKES a husband leave home is something that has been baffling wives since Adam and Eve. For an outstanding example, let's take one of the nation's most famous pops, Desi Arnaz, co-star of television's top show, "I Love Lucy" and legal partner of luscious Lucille Ball.

The jackpot question is: With a curvy, red-haired tid-bit like Lucy waiting for him at home, would Desi be foolish enough to prowl Hollywood like a bachelor wolf and, if so, why?

Just Wait Till Lucy Finds Out

Part of the answer is going to jolt the 45,000,000 fans of the show right out of their TV hammocks. For Desi is most certainly a duck-out daddy.

Why he does it is something you'd have to ask Arnaz. Close friends of his have been holding their breaths for years in fear that his scarlet-tressed wife may bring the discussion up any moment, possibly with a flat-iron in her hand. Lucy, they point out, is a lass with a temper to match her flaming hair and not one to shrug off a misbehaving Mister.

Desi has, in fact, proved himself an artist at philandering as well as acting, because Lucille is a clock-watching mama, the kind that checks her hubby's collar for lipstick when he comes home. And the couple have such a back-breaking work schedule to produce their weekly TV drama that Desi's had to sandwich in his sin.

Under the circumstances, he's done pretty well. Because behind the scenes, Arnaz is a Latin Lothario who loves Lucy *most* of the time but by no means *all* the time. He has, in fact, sprinkled his affections all over Los Angeles for a number of years. And quite a bit of it has been bestowed on vice dollies who were paid handsomely for loving Desi briefly but, presumably, as effectively as Lucy.

TURN THE PAGE →

Love Lucy?

The night Lucy won two prizes in the 1952 Television Academy Awards, her hubby came along, too, with a roving eye for any "prizes" he might find.

"Whatever joy remained in their marriage effectively ended" with the story in *Confidential*, wrote her biographer Kathleen Brady. "Lucy continued to hope that their lives would work out together and even prayed for it . . . but she no longer believed that staying with Desi was worth the sacrifice of herself. With the *Confidential* article, she felt she stood shamed before 'the public'. . . . She was forced to confront the details of his escapades . . . whether the facts of the piece were exactly as reported or not, Lucy knew the gist of it was true and she knew everyone else did as well." Arnaz denied the allegations. They divorced in 1960.[8]

One of *Confidential*'s favorite themes was interracial sex in Hollywood, and one of its most infamous stories in that vein was "What Makes Ava Run for Sammy Davis Jr.?," in March 1955. "Some girls go for gold, but it's bronze that 'sends' sultry Ava Gardner," *Confidential* reported.

Davis, a young, talented, flamboyant African American singer-dancer, was beginning his career on the nightclub circuit. Gardner's husband, Frank Sinatra, was his mentor. According to *Confidential*, Gardner and Davis were in the midst of a torrid sexual relationship. "Sexy, sultry Gardner topped herself last month when she popped up on the cover of a national Negro magazine with an article, under her personal byline, titled 'Sammy Sends Me,'" wrote *Confidential*. The article featured photos of Gardner and Davis together in a hotel lobby, including a picture of the two holding drinks and laughing. One picture showed Gardner with her foot up on the armrest of a chair Davis was sitting in; another showed him leaning over her in her chair.[9]

Confidential described an appearance at the Apollo Theater the previous fall, when Gardner appeared in a tribute to Davis. Hand in hand with Davis on the Apollo stage, she joked around for a few minutes, then "the pair pranced off into the wings, and after a couple of curtain calls, strolled out of the place on a date more sensational than anything advertised on the theater's marquee. . . . It was the first time Gardner had met Sammy on his home grounds but far from their first game. It would seem Sammy had begun 'sending' as far back as early 1952, when he played a series of Hollywood nightclub engagements." *Confidential* wrote that Davis was just one of many "dark-skinned gents" that "have been proving their powerful fascination for Ava for years," including Dizzy Gillespie and actor Herb Jeffries.[10]

Though most of *Confidential*'s articles had some basis in truth, this one seems to have been an outright lie. In the fall of 1954 Gardner had gotten a call from Davis. He was going to be named an honorary mayor of Harlem and wanted to have some celebrity friends at the Apollo Theater for the celebration. With several black entertainers and civic leaders, Gardner appeared on the stage, where she praised Davis.[11]

Davis called her shortly afterward and told her that a black magazine, *One World*, wanted to put him on its cover posed as Santa if he could get a star to be in the picture with him, which would be taken at a Christmas party at the Drake Hotel. Gardner agreed. After the pictures were taken, Davis and Gardner sat around having cocktails. The photographer caught a few pictures, which were published in *One World* with an article under Gardner's byline, "Sammy Sends Me as a Performer." *Confidential* drew on the provocative title but left out "as a performer."[12]

The article provoked a strong reaction, especially in the South. There were boycotts of Gardner's films, and the photos were even used as campaign material by Southern bigots against integrationist candidates. The *Confidential* story transformed Davis's image, marking the moment he became controversial. Before *Confidential*, the media depicted him as a "modest, clean-cut sweet young man," according to biographer Gary Fishgall. *Confidential* portrayed him as someone to watch carefully: "a cocky, swinging, fun-loving Negro who would stop at nothing to get what he wanted, even when his goal was a glamorous white movie star who had been married to his idol and friend." The *Confidential* article "went to the heart of mainstream America's greatest fears about black men."[13]

In May 1955 *Confidential* ran "The Secret's Out About Burt Lancaster," revealing the muscular heartthrob as a repulsive, violent lecher. Lancaster had played a tough army sergeant in the 1953 Academy Award–winning film *From Here to Eternity*. "It's estimated that no less than 8,000,000 American women went to see burly Burt Lancaster in his role of the tough top-kick in *From Here to Eternity*," *Confidential* wrote. "It's hard to say how many went home, sneered at their husbands, and retired to dreamland—to picture themselves wrapped in Burt's biceps. But the number must be considerable, judging by the thousands of letters he gets weekly from both married and single femmes. . . . Most of them just never knew how lucky they've been to miss a personal introduction to their hero."

Francesca De Scaffa was the source of the story. *Confidential* alleged that Lancaster attacked De Scaffa when she went with him to his dressing room to practice lines for a movie audition. He told her to take off her clothes. When she refused, he grabbed her by the shoulder, ripping the sleeve and shoulder of her dress. "Burt used to be a circus strong man and acrobat, so the climax was inevitable," *Confidential* wrote. "Francesca parted company from the sleeve and shoulder of her dress midst horrified squeals and muscular grunts. What followed was a scramble that could replace wrestling on TV overnight."

Confidential cited a childhood laced with violence and a similar account from actress Zina Rachevsky. Lancaster invited Rachevsky to his bungalow and tore off her clothes. She fought back, biting him so badly that he had to go to the hospital. "Burt's tendency towards clobbering cuties is rapidly becoming no secret at all among dames in the know in Hollywood. Some gasp with surprise upon meeting his wife and the mother of his five children. They fully expect to see Mrs. Lancaster wearing at least a pair of shiners, whereas she always shows up unbruised and seemingly quite happy. How she does it is one of movieland's favorite mysteries."[14]

Confidential was right. Lancaster drank heavily and was brutal to women. At a party in the early 1950s at the Columbia studios, an acquaintance remembered, Lancaster got drunk, lifted a woman high up above his head, then flung her to the ground. "It was terrible. Publicity people hushed it up. We got her into the hospital and the insurance covered it. It was pretty vicious," he recalled. Lancaster was on a trip to San Francisco with his young sons when he saw the copy of *Confidential* on newsstands. He told his wife that he "had to sue" but his lawyers convinced him that a lawsuit would just give the story more publicity.[15]

Even though he'd been on the screen for more than twenty years, Clark Gable remained one of Hollywood's top box office draws. When *Confidential* did its exposé of him in the summer of 1955, he was starring in two 20th Century Fox films (*The Tall Men* and *Soldier of Fortune*) and one from MGM (*Betrayed*). A womanizer and heavy drinker, Gable had fathered illegitimate children and had several run-ins with the law. But studio publicists convincingly portrayed him as gentlemanly and heroic.

In "The Wife Clark Gable Forgot," *Confidential* revealed Gable's brutal neglect of his first wife, Josephine Dillon, his former acting teacher. Gable married Dillon before he was a star, back in the 1920s. While Gable rose to stardom, Dillon continued teaching, and she fell into penury. She was seventy-one when the *Confidential* article came out. According to *Confidential*, Dillon was living in a dilapidated barn in North Hollywood. *Confidential* found her on a tip from De Scaffa, who was Gable's jilted lover. The story was De Scaffa's revenge on Gable.

Confidential described how Gable ignored Dillon after their 1930 divorce, and even insisted she quit using his last name. Later she became ill, and she asked Gable for help paying her medical bills. Gable refused. "It went in one big ear and out the other when the girl who had made him what he is today asked for a helping hand. So far as Rhett Butler was concerned, she was 'Gone with the Wind!'" *Confidential* sneered. The article also described Dillon's disgraceful living conditions: "You have to park your illusions with your car when you drive up to 12746 Landale Street in North Hollywood. One glance tells you the building before you is a converted barn . . . paint is peeling from its sides, its roof sags dejectedly. Inside are two large rooms, drafty and cold . . . the furniture is worn and dilapidated. Wherever your eye turns, it picks up the giveaway signs of poverty."[16]

Gable was reportedly unfazed by the story. Wrote columnist Joe Hyams, "Gable rarely reads anything about himself. He has never read a scandal magazine, not even the one which recently blasted him for 'forgetting' his first wife. He pays no attention to the inaccuracies because, he believes, people will form their own opinions of him. "I don't think stories of any kind can change the attitude of my friends towards me. The other people I don't care about."[17]

That summer *Confidential* also exposed June Allyson, voted by fans as the nation's most popular actress. To the public, Allyson was the embodiment of cuteness, perkiness, and spunk. MGM had carefully crafted her screen image as a loyal, steadfast girlfriend and wife with a pageboy haircut and cute dresses with Peter Pan collars. Petite and cheerful, she played wholesome, sugary characters. In 1945 she wed actor Dick Powell, ten years her senior. Their marriage was celebrated as ideal, but it was fraught with conflict.

Earlier that year, Hollywood had buzzed with whispers about their marital troubles. Some said Allyson was having an affair with Alan Ladd and linked her to the breakup of Ladd's marriage. "A good example of rumor-spreading has been in progress here the last few weeks," wrote one columnist in February 1955. "It concerned a reported split between Alan and his wife . . . also a reported tiff between Dick Powell and his wife." But by the middle of the month, columnists were reporting that Powell and Allyson had "ironed out their big difficulty and are off to Sun Valley for a second honeymoon."[18]

"Think June Allyson is too nice to be naughty? Dick's been hitched to her for 10 years but that doesn't keep June from busting out all over," wrote *Confidential* in Jay Breen's article "How Long Can Dick Powell Take It?" Allyson was a "five-foot-one inch petite little blonde who looks nice enough for an angel award. But she is one little book that can't be judged by its cover. . . . June's fans . . . will howl their heads off at the charge that the cutie with the page boy bob and the Peter Pan collar could ever be a hubby-snatcher. Nor can they be blamed, after swallowing years of a publicity build-up typing her as the 'girl next door,' 'cute as a button,' and just too nice to be naughty."

"The one-time Broadway chorus dolly is 31 years old now, a veteran of nearly 10 years of marriage with Powell, and has an uncontrollable itch to push the sugar bowl aside and reach for the spice shelf," *Confidential* reported. "It long ago reached the stage where she was admitting it publicly—although *off* the record." *Confidential* said that she "flipped a pretty finger at the little-girl frock her bosses liked her to wear" and said, "I've had enough of all this. I'd like to land in the middle of a juicy scandal—just to prove I've graduated into a woman."

Every time the studio assigned her to a new leading man in a movie, "her flirtatious ways gave patient Powell something new to sit up nights biting his nails about," *Confidential* wrote. Her favorite "stunt" at Hollywood parties was to "latch onto some handsome actor"—usually years younger than Powell—and "duck into a corner until her glowering husband came to take her home." *Confidential* described how she "cavorted" with Dean Martin and described her latest "caper" with Alan Ladd. "Alan Ladd and his wife separated—after 13 years of marriage, but both carefully refrained from naming the reason. Who was it? None other than that sweet little Allyson lass, who'd been assigned to make a movie with Ladd and—as usual—had gotten ideas that weren't in the script."[19] Powell and Allyson contemplated suing *Confidential* over the article.

German-born Marlene Dietrich, *femme fatale* film star of the 1930s, had passed from the Hollywood scene and was working the nightclub and cabaret circuit. But the public still revered her as Hollywood royalty, and she continued to appear in the news.

Dietrich was famous for her husky voice and her performances in slacks and other masculine attire. But Dietrich was married, and the press portrayed her as heterosexual. In "The Untold Story of Marlene Dietrich," *Confidential* reported, correctly, that Dietrich was bisexual.

"Although she's been married to the same man since she was a girl of 21, Dietrich's never bothered to deny or hush the gossip about herself and her guys," *Confidential* wrote. "It's more likely she wanted it that way—to cover up some sprightlier capers that would have lifted the nation's eyebrows all the way up its forehead. Because in the millions of words that have been written about Dietrich's dalliances, you've never, until now, read that some of them *were not with men*! . . . In the game of amour, she's not only played both sides of the street, but done it on more than one occasion."

Confidential described Dietrich's start in show business in Berlin, singing what it described as a lesbian song, "My Best Girl Friend." "Her very first success on the stage was singing a strange love song—from one girl to another," the magazine reported. "But her boyfriends really flipped when she actually started living up the lyrics!" According to *Confidential*, Dietrich "succumb[ed] to a dame" a year later, when she caught the eye of cabaret singer Claire Waldoff, "notorious for her preference in playmates. It was her view that it was nuts to have a man around the house and she made no secret of it."

After Waldoff, Dietrich "crossed the street"—"back to the boys," with a German comedian. When she came to the United States, she picked up with Mercedes de Acosta, "a writer who favored clothes that seemed to be tailored by Brooks Brothers. . . . Mercedes had been the companion for other Hollywood double-standard dollies and fitted neatly into Marlene's pattern. But this was the U.S.A., where publicity on such capers would have raised a storm, so the girls discreetly limited themselves to quiet get-togethers at each other's home," *Confidential* reported. She then paired up with the Parisian lesbian nightclub owner Frederique "Frede" Baule, and Jo Carstairs, another "mannish maiden."[20]

Dietrich had gone to great lengths to conceal her sexual orientation from the public. The *Confidential* article devastated her. According to columnist Erskine Johnson, "Marlene Dietrich's pals report she was shocked into an emotional tailspin by that article in a current gossip magazine. The wordage hit her harder than anything ever printed about her."[21]

In September 1955, *Confidential* ran one of its biggest, most explosive stories, on the infamous event that would go down in Hollywood history as the Wrong Door Raid. The article implicated Joe DiMaggio and Frank Sinatra in an attempt to break into an apartment where Marilyn Monroe and her lover were having an affair. It would embroil all of the parties involved, including *Confidential*, in legal trouble.

"Exclusive! From a Private Eye's Confidential Report . . . The Real Reason for Marilyn Monroe's Divorce!" screamed the headline. "All the gossip columns called it 'amicable' . . . but why did Joe DiMaggio hire detectives to tail Marilyn?"[22]

After less than a year of marriage, Monroe and DiMaggio broke up. Jealous, possessive, and violent, DiMaggio abused Monroe. In October 1954 she filed for divorce and received an interlocutory decree. Around that time, Monroe had a relationship with her young voice coach, Hal Schaefer, who had arranged her song and dance number in *Gentlemen Prefer Blondes*, "Diamonds Are a Girl's Best Friend," which helped launch her to stardom.

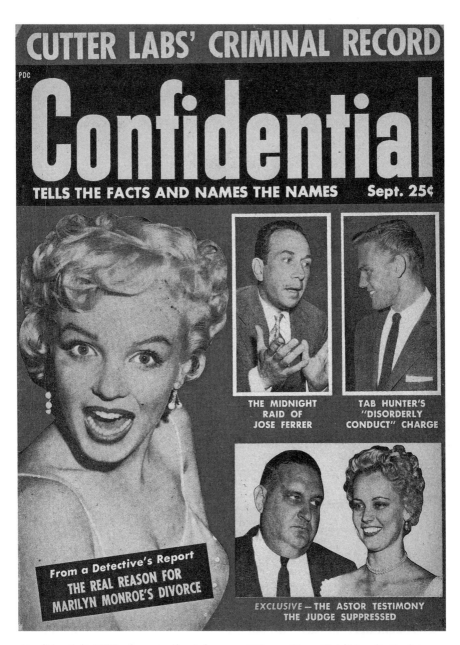

Confidential's 1955 story on the infamous "Wrong Door Raid" implicated Joe DiMaggio and Frank Sinatra in a nefarious apartment break-in. *Photofest*

DiMaggio found out about the relationship. He and Frank Sinatra, his best friend, commiserated about it. Sinatra offered "to take care of it." Sinatra made a few phone calls and was referred to a private detective firm called City Detective and Guard Service, run by Barney Ruditsky. Sinatra told Ruditsky he wanted his agents to trail Monroe and take pictures of her and Schaefer in the act. DiMaggio intended to use the pictures to catch her in an adulterous situation and stop the divorce, to "get that broad back in his life." Ruditsky's detectives bugged Monroe and Schaefer's phones and followed their cars.[23]

In November 1954, one of Ruditsky's associates, twenty-one-year-old Phil Irwin, saw Monroe's Cadillac parked at Kilkea Drive and Waring Avenue in West Hollywood. Monroe was visiting a friend, actress Sheila Stewart. DiMaggio suspected that Stewart, one of Schaefer's students, was letting the couple use her apartment for a tryst.[24]

There were many conflicting versions of what happened next. According to one version, Irwin called Ruditsky, who drove to the apartment, and they spent an hour staking it out. Ruditsky phoned DiMaggio, who was allegedly dining with Sinatra at the Villa Capri restaurant in Hollywood. According to another account, Ruditsky phoned Sinatra at the Villa Capri, during which time DiMaggio, who was circling the block in his car, pulled up behind Ruditsky's car. In another version, Irwin called Sinatra, and an hour later Sinatra, Sinatra's manager Hank Sanicola, Villa Capri owner "Patsy" D'Amore, and the restaurant's maître d' Billy Karen arrived at the apartment together.[25]

Afraid of what would happen if DiMaggio caught Schaefer with Monroe, Ruditsky convinced DiMaggio to let him lead the break-in. Ruditsky approached one of the doors, put his shoulder down and charged the door four or five times. Irwin, Ruditsky, DiMaggio, and Sinatra rushed into the bedroom with a camera. The lights from the flash revealed a thirty-seven-year-old secretary, Florence Kotz, who was fast asleep. They had broken into the wrong apartment. Kotz screamed. "I was terrified. . . . The place was full of men. They were making a lot of noises and lights flashed on," she recalled.[26]

The intruders fled from the building. Kotz filed a police report. The case was thought to be an attempted burglary, but because Kotz could not identify the intruders, it remained unsolved. The LAPD closed the case a year later.[27]

Monroe and Schaefer were in Stewart's apartment at the time. Schaefer recalled, "We were very close to making love; I don't remember the stage we were at, but I would say half-dressed. And all of a sudden for some reason,

Marilyn got these vibrations, and we went over to the window and saw this group standing across the street, one of whom was Joe DiMaggio and another was Frank Sinatra. They all came en masse and broke this door in, demolished it." Monroe and Schaefer scrambled to get out the back door.[28]

Irwin sold the story to HRI, although Irwin claimed Ruditsky gave it to *Confidential*. Harrison confirmed the facts with Ruditsky. Right before the article was to go to press, Harrison called Ruditsky and asked him to fly to New York at Harrison's expense. Harrison showed him the galley proofs of the story. Ruditsky said he recognized the source of the story as one of the private detectives on his staff, and he supplied additional facts.[29]

"Joe still carried a blazing torch for his curvaceous bride of nine months . . . but was Joe's jealousy ridiculous?" asked *Confidential*. "Not by a long shot. His error was in timing—hiring his private eyes too late. . . . Told here, for the first time, are the details Hollywood's reporters either missed or wouldn't print."

Confidential ran a picture of the apartment building with a caption over it: *Joe Staged His Raid Here*. The article described how a "Los Angeles private detective," hired by DiMaggio, had for weeks been tailing "the nation's sexiest blonde," hoping to catch her and Schaefer in the act. Hal had been a "steady visitor" at Sheila Stewart's apartment. "So was Marilyn. And for months Joe had been hearing a steady stream of gossip about his wife and the talented musician-trainer. . . . This was to be a show-down. Neither Joe nor the detective knew whether Hal was inside but they were now only seconds away from finding out."

On the night of November 5, 1954, *Confidential* wrote, DiMaggio waited outside the building where Monroe was having her alleged tryst, while an unnamed detective—Irwin—went up to the building and said, "She's in there again." DiMaggio wanted Irwin to break down the door. Irwin, panicked, called Ruditsky and Sinatra for some "split-second advice." Ruditsky, Sinatra, and the Villa Capri's owner arrived shortly after. Wrote *Confidential*, "What followed would have made topnotch slapstick comedy, had the situation been less grave. After a sidewalk conference, all hands agreed with Joe's original plan of apartment-crashing."

According to *Confidential*, Irwin was ready to go into Stewart's apartment, but Ruditsky, Sinatra and DiMaggio chose a different apartment. "The rest of the raiders outvoted him and picked a different door to attack," *Confidential* reported.

The article went on to describe Monroe's relationship with Schaefer. He carried a torch for her, but he became despondent when she broke off their relationship, and he attempted to commit suicide with pills and typewriter cleaning fluid. He ended up in the Beverly Glen Hospital. Marilyn went to visit him every day. When he left the hospital, she whisked him away to a private home on the beach in Ventura, where she took care of him. But their relationship didn't last; Marilyn was flighty and unstable, and before long she was off to another man.

Asked *Confidential*: "You can hardly blame DiMaggio if he sits alone at night and ponders the jackpot question: What *would* he have found had they kicked in the *right* door?"[30]

12 | HOLLYWOOD

CONFIDENTIAL HIT HOLLYWOOD WHEN it was vulnerable, and it created a panic. In 1956, film attendance was half of what it had been a decade earlier. A Senate committee had begun investigations into the link between motion pictures and juvenile delinquency, and religious organizations like the Catholic Legion of Decency sought to ban films purportedly linked to "indecency," promiscuity, race-mixing, and violence. The Pope declared his "piercing anxiety" over the effects of movies on youth and urged film censorship to "defend the common civil and moral heritage." The film industry continued to battle negative publicity stemming from HUAC's investigations, as well as controversies surrounding the Hollywood blacklist. *Confidential*'s revelations reinforced views of conservative critics that the film industry was a negative influence on morals and a breeding ground of debauchery and sin.[1]

Confidential became the topic of the day in Hollywood, replacing even TV as a subject of conversation. Every time a *Confidential* issue came out, there was "feverish reading and cross-checking," according to *Newsweek*. "We all read it, not because it was any good . . . but to find out if we were in it," remembered Marlene Dietrich. When *Confidential* appeared on newsstands "our stomachs began to turn," recalled George Nader, a closeted gay actor. "Which one of us would be in it?"[2]

The film industry was no stranger to scandal, but *Confidential* threatened damage of epic proportions. Though most stars written up in *Confidential* emerged unscathed, the magazine still wreaked havoc on relationships, reputations, and careers.

Confidential's Ava Gardner–Sammy Davis Jr. story led to a ban on Gardner's films in the South and thousands of nasty letters to MGM. According to one MGM executive, "The things they called her were disgraceful." People all over the country said they would never see her films again. Gardner's hometown of Smithfield, North Carolina, took her name out of its publicity brochure. Shreveport, Louisiana, banned all future Gardner movies from the city. MGM worried about the article for weeks. Although Gardner's career didn't suffer in the long run, "the impact of the article was real for a moment in time and held the potential for a career-rocking scandal," wrote biographer Lee Server.[3]

Lizabeth Scott's career was fatally undermined by *Confidential*. Maureen O'Hara claimed she could no longer get work after *Confidential*'s exposé. Marriages were challenged and sometimes broken by *Confidential*. Several minor up-and-coming actors who were smeared in *Confidential* lost important career opportunities and silently slipped off the radar.[4]

After every *Confidential* blockbuster, studios and fan magazines were swamped with letters from shocked and disappointed fans. "Tell me what I should say to my teenage daughter," one woman wrote to *Photoplay*. "She read your excellent article in *Photoplay* telling about Burt Lancaster's wonderful home life. Now she brings into our house an article that makes Mr. Lancaster appear to be a man of little principle." Even though many readers took *Confidential* with a grain of salt—a 1957 Stanford master's thesis found *Confidential* had "low credibility" among readers—there was still shock, anger, and confusion when a screen idol was publicly disgraced.[5]

Everyone in Hollywood agreed that something had to be done about *Confidential*. The question was *what*. This problem would trouble the industry for the next three years: how to bring down *Confidential* without revealing to the public that many of its stories were actually true.

Hollywood's efforts to fight back against *Confidential* started in 1955 when several stars, burned by *Confidential*, went to the studios seeking help. Surely, they reasoned, the industry would assist its own in taking on the magazine.

To their surprise, they got nothing. Industry leaders feared that openly challenging the scandal magazines would be risky: lawsuits would rehash the scandals, and denials would raise suspicions that the stories were true. They also worried about reprisals from Harrison. "These are individual problems," said an MPAA spokesman. "It is up to the individuals whether they want to take action."[6]

Stars were outraged. "What do they mean by that double talk?" asked Humphrey Bogart. "Actors belong to the movie industry, they're products of the industry, and they should be backed up by the industry. If somebody kept writing that Cadillacs had lousy brakes, wouldn't the Cadillac company take some action? The industry needs some guts."[7]

Disgusted, stars took matters into their own hands. In early 1955, several actors launched a publicity campaign against the scandal magazines. Bogart, who'd been smeared in *Rave*, was one of the leaders, and he denounced the magazines in a series of interviews. "Sex? Yeh, they give you sex by innuendo. They say John was seen going to Mary's hotel room. Is that sex? Maybe, it's gin rummy too. What you find . . . is a jigger of fact and a pitcher of innuendo," he told Jack Olsen of the *Chicago Sun-Times*. "They disgust me. What a lousy reflection on the American taste." He told reporters he'd like to take a "hefty whack" at "those writers who keep earning a dishonest living by running Hollywood down." It was Bogart who famously said about *Confidential*, "Everybody reads it but they say the cook brought it into the house."[8]

Stars denounced *Confidential* in *Newsweek*, one of the first major media outlets to do a story on *Confidential*. "I believe in freedom of the press, but the law should be changed to protect individuals . . . from this type of journalism," said Joan Bennett. "What can you do when a pack of lies appears about your wife?" asked Dick Powell. "This is a job for the government. Maybe once this snowball gets going they'll write about some politicians, and then they'll be in trouble."[9]

At the same time, stars' lawyers and agents worked behind the scenes to kill *Confidential* stories. Attorney Greg Bautzer helped several of his clients stay out of *Confidential*. In 1955, when he was representing Susan Hayward in a child custody battle, she tried to kill herself by overdosing on sleeping pills. *Confidential* planned an article. Bautzer asked notorious Mafia lawyer and Hollywood "fixer" Sidney Korshak for assistance. Korshak worked his magic, and the story disappeared. On November 29 Harrison wrote Korshak, "Dear Sidney, in accordance with your request, we are dropping the Susan Hayward story from the upcoming issue of *Confidential*. Love and Kisses, Bob."[10]

Mamie Van Doren, hired by Universal Studios as a Marilyn Monroe look-alike, heard from publicity director Sam Israel that *Confidential* was going to run a story accusing her and her mother of being prostitutes. "Only the top two men here at the studio and I know about this," Israel said. "I can tell you they are in a panic. You realize what this could mean to the studio if its gets printed?" Van Doren asked if the studio was going to stand behind her or "throw her to the wolves." "We're not going to throw you to the wolves," he said. "We just have to wait and see what happens."[11]

She wasn't willing to wait. Van Doren picked up the phone and called lawyer Jerry Giesler, Hollywood's famous "lawyer to the stars." Giesler told Harrison that he'd better have proof of the story, because if he printed it, "he was going to get an opportunity to use it in court." Giesler promised he'd close *Confidential* down, slapping it with a judgment so large that Van Doren and her mother would be the new owners of *Confidential*. The story never ran.[12]

Jolted into action by *Confidential's* 1955 blockbusters, especially the Wrong Door Raid story, industry leaders finally embarked on a series of covert, disjointed, and ultimately futile efforts to take down *Confidential*.

The campaign began that summer with a secret meeting of studio publicity heads in the Beverly Hills Hotel. After the meeting, publicist Sam Israel was dispatched to New York to convince the scandal magazine editors to focus on politicians, athletes, or socialites—any group other than actors. The editors laughed at him, telling him that attacking politicians would be inviting the loss of mailing privileges. And besides, the public obviously wanted to read about movie stars.[13]

They came up with another scheme. A popular actress with a "spotless reputation" was recruited to plant a phony story with *Confidential*, with the idea of setting Harrison up for a multimillion-dollar libel suit. False affidavits, wiretapped conversations, and bugged phone calls were readied by experts. The story was given to HRI through tipsters. Harrison liked it. Marjorie Meade hired private eyes to check it out; it passed muster and was scheduled for publication. But Marjorie's instincts told her something was wrong. She persuaded Harrison to quash the story.[14]

The next plan was a "secret fund." All six of the studios contributed to a $350,000 "war chest" to fight *Confidential*. A private investigator, William S. Lewis, met with director-producer Mervyn LeRoy regarding a "movie industry organization" to police stars' off-screen activities using a private detective agency made up of former FBI agents. Lewis told the producer it would take $50,000 from each studio and a $50,000 expense fund. According to Lewis, there was "a definite plan of action," and LeRoy contacted Y. Frank Freeman of the MPPA to get his cooperation. The project was dropped when studio heads panicked, fearing that an attack on *Confidential* would "boomerang."[15]

Rushmore and Harrison knew about the fund. DeStefano rejected an editorial by Rushmore titled "Hollywood Against *Confidential*," about the "war chest" to fight *Confidential*. The editorial said, in part, "This is (an) industry . . . where homosexuality is not only condoned but protected." DeStefano advised Harrison and Rushmore not to take on the film industry because it was too powerful. "As big as you are in the publishing business, you are not big enough to fight Hollywood," he told them. "They'll run you out of business."[16]

There was also a plan for a "*Confidential* blacklist." This plot was spearheaded by MGM studio head and former Motion Picture Industry Council leader Dore Schary, a large, flashy man known as the "unofficial spokesman for the motion picture industry" and its most "glib and presentable public relations figure." In the summer of 1955, Schary went before the MPAA with a "blackball" list of writers and tipsters who supplied material to *Confidential*. The *Hollywood Reporter* noted that a group within the industry was planning to release an "authentic documented list" of people "who have received payment from [scandal] magazines for writing articles about Hollywood personalities." Every writer on the list would be "persona non grata both socially and professionally in the industry." The list never materialized; according to journalist James Bacon, Schary got nowhere because some industry leaders got cold feet, and Hollywood "never has been known to stick together on any such action." Even though Rushmore had testified before HUAC and was one of the engineers of the anticommunist blacklist, Rushmore was outraged by the *Confidential* blacklist. According to DeStefano, Rushmore wanted to publish the editorial because he felt it was "discriminatory to prevent people from making a livelihood and to blacklist them for writing for *Confidential*."[17]

Studio heads urged Manhattan district attorney Frank Hogan to investigate charges that *Confidential* was extorting money to kill stories. Nothing came of it. One Hollywood producer who'd been attacked by a scandal magazine had detectives trail the publisher to see what they could uncover. They found out quite a bit that was damaging about the editor, but also found out he had information that was even more damaging to the producer. The investigation was dropped. Harrison accused the studios of trying to sic private detectives on him. "There's a promoter I know out in Hollywood," he said. "He got a selected list of prominent Hollywood people who didn't like me. He got money from each of them to put me out of business. Twenty five thousand bucks. . . . He was going to have private eyes tail me everywhere and dig up a lot of dirt. Well, he got the twenty-five grand and that was the last seen of him. He blew. And his list is whistling for their dough. A cutie, eh?"[18]

That October, Dore Schary told media representatives that it would "bring honor" to the press if it could take down *Confidential*. The film industry's public relations had been made a "shambles," he said. He also chastised Hollywood for not taking action, claiming that the industry encouraged attacks by "sidestepping current ones. "For a mighty, grown-up industry doing close to two billion dollars' worth of business each year all over the world, we often act like the frightened owner of a corner drugstore who is afraid a hoodlum will throw a rock through the window."[19]

Hollywood deplored "the shoddy contents of the magazines" that "live off the sad, tragic mistakes of some, or the indulgences of a maladjusted few," he said. "We deplore the half-truth and the implied slander that avoids the legal or criminal libel. . . . We endure it, and wonder sometimes if you gentlemen cannot evolve a code of practice that would inhibit this kind of journalism."

He added, "I haven't been the victim of an article in *Confidential* magazine. But at this very moment I guess I'm on my way."[20]

———————

Yet at the same time the studios were denouncing *Confidential*, they were feeding Harrison under the table. In a desperate attempt to protect their stars, studios and publicists sometimes gave the scandal magazines gossip in order to kill off more damaging stories. 20th Century Fox traded *Rave* a story about Marilyn Monroe to get the magazine to drop a sensational article about a sex triangle involving a studio executive. To flush out a story about studio boss Harry Cohn, Columbia Pictures gave *Confidential* damning information about Kim Novak.[21]

Busty, blonde Novak was a studio creation, the product of a skillful build-up by the Columbia publicity department. In a 1955 cover story, *Look* called her Hollywood's "sultry new glamour girl," a rising star who was "on her way up." *Look* described Novak as demure and frugal; she got around on a bicycle, put her money into acting lessons, and rented a $19.50 room at the YWCA. *Life* ran a similar story claiming Novak was "discovered" while riding her bike in Hollywood. The bicycle story had been crafted by the studio's head of publicity, George Lait, who had written in a press release that "Kim, who was wearing a perfectly ordinary T-shirt and a pair of sport shorts, and riding a perfectly ordinary bicycle through Beverly Hills, hove into view of talent agent Louis Schurr and created quite an extraordinary impression."[22]

Confidential unmasked the myth. Novak had gotten ahead not on a bicycle, *Confidential* reported, but with the help of a Romanian munitions baron and noted sugar daddy, Edgar Ausnit, who set her up in her own apartment and financed her start in Hollywood. Ausnit rarely visited Novak in her apartment, so she got involved with a part-time actor named Ted Cooper.

"Between the two of them, Ausnit and Cooper had this shapely daughter of a Chicago freight dispatcher busier than a yard switchman," *Confidential* wrote. When the relationship with Cooper broke up, Novak showed up at the apartment with Ausnit and "took good old Edgar up to inspect what he'd been paying for. The check-up took so long, Ausnit didn't totter out of 425 North Oakhurst until after two the next morning." *Confidential* made coy references to Novak's nude photos. Columbia had recently helped Novak buy back some "modeling" photos taken when she was sixteen. Cooper came back a few nights after his rejection and looked through the venetian blinds to reveal Kim in a shocking pose with Ausnit that "even Kim might not have wanted in her scrapbook."[23]

The most famous *Confidential* "trade" involved Rock Hudson, a closeted gay actor who had been voted the nation's most popular male star of 1954. A clumsy truck driver named Roy Scherer Jr., six foot four, handsome, with black hair and rugged features, Hudson had been transformed by the studio machinery into one of Hollywood's leading men. The *Saturday Evening Post* did a lengthy feature on him in 1952, even though he was still playing only minor roles at the time. The *Post* called him the "newest bobby sox idol to be cracked out of the gilded egg" of "the incubation machinery of Universal International." By the end of that year he was the subject of two fan magazine articles a week, was mobbed by swooning teenage autograph seekers, and had just signed a new seven-year contract. Fan magazines showed an athletic Hudson playing charades with friends and grilling steaks at backyard barbecues. One fan magazine described him as "wholesome and pure." Hudson had his first leading role in 1954 in the film *Magnificent Obsession*. In 1955 he starred with Elizabeth Taylor in *Giant*, the most important film of his career.[24]

Hudson's bachelorhood was the subject of curiosity, speculation, and consternation. Fan magazines described the twenty-nine-year-old Hudson as "Hollywood's most eligible bachelor" and wondered when he would settle down. "There is little that love-happy Hollywood follows with more fascination these days than the romantic fortunes of lanky, easy-going Rock Hudson, who would, from all appearances, seem to have been waging a long and frighteningly successful battle to preserve his bachelorhood against a relentless onslaught of irresistible women," wrote *Screenland* in 1955. "Does he have to be brainwashed of bachelor habits before he is ready for wedding bells? Does he fear marriage as a trap that'd rob him of his freedom? . . . Or is he merely waiting for—and willing to let—marriage find him?" In a cover story, "The Simple Life of a Busy Bachelor," *Life* magazine wrote that "fans are urging 29-year-old Hudson to get married—or explain why not."[25]

Hudson was represented by the flamboyant, enormously influential agent Henry Willson. Willson, openly gay, was one of the most important power-brokers of 1950s Hollywood. Willson "discovered, named, represented, promoted, pimped, and protected" a bevy of hunk-like male stars, including Hudson, Guy Madison, Tab Hunter, and Troy Donahue. A "gay Svengali," Willson was notorious for coercing male actors into having sex in return for publicity.[26]

In early 1954, Harrison told his staff that he wanted to do a Hudson expose. Hudson's homosexuality was an open secret in Hollywood, although Hudson was discreet about it; he never allowed himself to be photographed with a man or to be seen on the town with other men. *Confidential* offered Hudson's former lover Bob Preble $10,000 for his story, which Harrison said would be published in the September 1954 issue. Preble refused to talk. *Confidential* also offered Jack Navaar, a former roommate, $10,000 to talk about Hudson. Navaar declined. He called Willson and told him that Harrison was after Hudson. Willson drove frantically around Hollywood looking for news-stands that carried *Confidential*. By then many newsstands had banned it, so it was hard to find a copy. When he found a drugstore that sold the magazine, he bought every copy to see if Hudson was in it.[27]

Willson decided to stave off the impending catastrophe by trading the Hudson story for a story on the long criminal record of Rory Calhoun, another one of his clients. Nicknamed "Smoky" for his smoldering good looks and smoke-gray eyes, Calhoun was a B-list star, a bobby sox hunk of the late 1940s who had been consigned to roles in mediocre Westerns and action films such as *Powder River* (1953), *Four Guns to the Border* (1954), and *River of No Return* (1954).[28]

It's unclear why Harrison accepted the trade. Calhoun was a relatively minor star, nowhere in Hudson's league. Calhoun's criminal record was well-known among Los Angeles reporters, who declined to print it out of respect for Calhoun. The actor had actually registered as an ex-convict with the Beverly Hills police department as far back as September 1944.[29] One reason Harrison took the trade may have been his fear of a studio backlash for a Hudson exposé. In making the deal, Harrison also got leverage with Willson and his stars as potential *Confidential* sources.

Jack Diamond, head of publicity at Universal, gave the story to Howard Rushmore during Rushmore's summer 1954 trip to Los Angeles. When Rushmore got the tip, he called Calhoun to get his side of the story—something

Confidential had never done before. Surprisingly, Calhoun was willing to talk. For over a decade, blackmailers had harassed him, telling him they knew about his past. Calhoun had faced more than thirty extortion attempts. His wife convinced him it would be better if he came out with the truth. Right before Rushmore contacted him, Calhoun had made arrangements with *Redbook* magazine to do a "gentle exposé" of his past. When Rushmore told him *Confidential* had "the story, the pictures, and everything," Calhoun was ready. "Come over tonight," he said to Rushmore. "I'll answer all your questions."[30]

Rushmore was impressed by Calhoun, who had turned himself around with the help of a prison chaplain named Father Don Kanaly. Rushmore decided to run the article not as a smear story, but as a tale of a young man's redemption. He described the story as one of a "young hoodlum [who] had been saved through the intervention of his prison chaplain and had returned to his church and a life of high moral standing."[31] It was one of only a few *Confidential* articles to take a sympathetic approach, and it was the story Rushmore was proudest of.

"Movie Star Rory Calhoun: But for the Grace of God Still a Convict!" appeared in the May 1955 issue. Calhoun's youthful mug shot was emblazoned on the cover. The article recounted Calhoun's impoverished childhood in California and a series of convictions for burglary, car theft, and robbery, which led to time in reformatories. At seventeen Calhoun was convicted of transporting a stolen car across state lines and was sent to the El Reno reformatory in Oklahoma. He was scheduled to go to San Quentin at age twenty-one to serve a twenty-year sentence. During his time at El Reno he made seven escape attempts, which landed him in solitary confinement.

At El Reno, Calhoun met Kanaly. Father Kanaly taught him how to pray, telling him that there was "no escape except through the honesty and grace of God." He demanded Calhoun's promise that he wouldn't attempt to escape again. In a stroke of luck, the charges were dropped, and Calhoun left a free man. Calhoun found a job at an ironworks in California, then went to work in logging camps. During a chance horseback ride he met Alan Ladd, who invited him to Hollywood for a screen test.[32]

Unexpectedly, the *Confidential* story boosted Calhoun's career. He received eight thousand glowing letters from fans inspired by his story. Parties were thrown in Calhoun's honor, and he received more movie offers than he could accept. Rushmore wrote a sanctimonious editorial in *Confidential*'s September 1955 issue. "*Confidential* could have printed nothing more than Calhoun's criminal record, and would have had a world scoop in the field of journalism," Rushmore wrote. "Yet by talking to Calhoun and presenting the entire fact of his spiritual reclamation, we tried to fulfill the function of editors—to get all of the story and to remember that people are human beings."[33]

Harrison was still determined to get Hudson. The magazine articles asking questions about his bachelorhood raised the stakes and made an outing even more tantalizing. To head off rumors about his sexuality, Willson demanded that Hudson get married. In November 1955, Hudson married Phyllis Gates, Willson's secretary.[34]

When Harrison threatened Willson with a Hudson article, the agent bought him off once again, this time with a story about Tab Hunter, who had been one of Willson's clients.[35] Like Hudson, Hunter was a closeted gay man, presented to the public as a heterosexual hunk and heartthrob.

Tab Hunter was a golden boy, a pinup boy, a gorgeous blond twenty-four-year-old with a square jaw and chiseled features, described as the "boy next door" and "The Sigh Guy." He played soldiers, surfers, and other wholesome types. James Dean, quipped the *New Yorker*, was Hunter's mirror image. Hunter, whose real name is Arthur Kelm and later went by the name Arthur Gelien, came to Hollywood in 1952 and had a promising but unremarkable debut. "Right now Tab perches rosily on the doorstep of great expectations in Hollywood," wrote *Modern Screen* in 1953. "He's not rich or really famous yet. He has only three pictures to his . . . name, none of them sensational. But he's swamped with more than 1,000 fan letters a week." Columnists described him as a sweet, shy bachelor devoted to self-improvement, his mother, and his career. Willson planted stories linking Hunter with female stars. In August 1954 *Screenland* ran an article, "There's Nothing Like a

Girl," supposedly written by Hunter, praising "thin girls and voluptuous girls. Plain girls and pretty girls. Short and tall. Bless 'em all!" Columnists needled him about his single status. "Sure I want to get married someday. . . . I will, too," he told *Screenland*. "That's one of my biggest hopes and dreams. But I've got to get straightened around financially first. I want to do a few nice things for my mother."[36]

Hunter was just a boy, struggling to get his bearings in the industry and confused and uncomfortable about his sexuality. Over half a century later, Hunter recalled the difficulty of "living two lives at that time. A private life of my own, which I never discussed, never talked about to anyone. And then my Hollywood life, which was just trying to learn my craft and succeed." "The word 'gay' wasn't even around in those days, and if anyone ever confronted me with it, I'd just kinda freak out. I was in total denial."[37]

When the *Confidential* article came out, Hunter was under contract with the Warner Bros. studio and had just starred in the war film *Battle Cry*, which launched his popularity. Hunter had recently fired Willson, which spurred the vindictive agent to give Harrison the story.

"The Lowdown on that 'Disorderly Conduct' Charge against Tab Hunter," by "Bruce Cory"—Howard Rushmore—appeared in the September 1955 issue of *Confidential*. "The fans who mob this six-footer want to know all about their idol," *Confidential* wrote. "His studio is only too willing to fill the demand with a flood of yarns and pictures—anything the public wants. Anything, that is, except the *real* lowdown on Hunter. That, the build-up boys thought, was safely locked in the records of the Los Angeles County vice squad, confidential file Z-84254. In it is the racy story of a night in October, 1950, when the husky Hunter kid landed in jail, along with some 26 other good-looking young men, after the cops broke up a pajama party they staged—strictly for boys."

That night, said *Confidential*, a vice cop was drifting in and out of Hollywood's "queer bars" "looking and listening for tips on the newest notions of the limp-wristed lads." Pausing for a drink at one "gay joint," he struck up a conversation with "a couple of lispers" who announced that they were going to a pajama party that evening. *Confidential* gave the address—2501 Hope Street in Walnut Park, a suburb of Los Angeles. "Milling around him were two dozen of the gayest guys the vice squad had ever seen. There was one lone pair of women but their mannish attire and baritone voices only added to the novelty of the evening." The whole party was soon under arrest. The guests were booked and went off to the L.A. County Jail.

Most of the partygoers had been extras and bit actors. "But one handsome hunk of man in the crowd seemed to stand out"—"Andrew Arthur Gelien, . . . age 19." A tolerant deputy district attorney dismissed the original charge of lewd conduct and accused him of disturbing the peace. He escaped with a fifty-dollar fine and a suspended sentence of thirty days in jail. "Tab seldom, if ever, goes to pajama parties anymore, but who can blame him? After all, he learned the hard way that you can't tell *who* is wearing that nightshirt next to you. It could be an understanding chap. It could also be a cop!"[38]

Hunter was able to weather the incident because of studio head Jack Warner. Warner's response was to look the other way. Warner put his arm around him and said, "Remember this: today's headlines, tomorrow's toilet paper." Warner didn't panic, didn't force *Confidential* to issue a retraction, or demand that Hunter change his lifestyle. He knew that the number of Americans who read *Confidential* was nothing compared to those who read fan magazines and watched Hunter's films. Right around the time *Confidential* came out, *Photoplay* featured Hunter and Natalie Wood on the cover, identifying them as the year's most popular new stars.[39]

Warner's strategy seemed to work. Even though *Confidential* imitators put out more than a half dozen smear articles in the following months, Hunter's career wasn't affected. He went on to greater screen stardom, and even did a pop record, *Young Love*, that topped charts shortly afterward. His career success, he wrote in his autobiography, was "clear evidence that . . . *Confidential* did not influence the taste and opinions of mainstream America."[40]

Meanwhile, Hollywood confronted *Confidential* in the way it knew best: with cover-ups, media blitzes, and positive spin. Studio publicists worked overtime on damage control, planting stories countering *Confidential*'s accusations with magazines like *Life* and *Look*, major newspapers, Hedda Hopper and Louella Parsons, and the fan magazines.

THE LOWDOWN ON THAT

..."DISORDERLY CHARGE AGAINST TAB

The fans who mob this six-footer want to know all about their idol ... Well, this reporter remembers the night a cop moved in on that limp-wrist pajama party

By BRUCE CORY

FLIP THE PAGES of the movie magazines these days and you'll find him smiling out at you from all of them — Tab Hunter, the crew-cut six-footer who's being touted as the next Gary Cooper or John Wayne.

The bobby-soxers can't get enough of him. They mob him at personal appearances, deluge him with scented love letters and save every word that's printed about him ... where he was born, whether he prefers blondes or brunettes, what he likes to eat, how he sleeps and so on. And his studio is only too willing to fill the demand with a flood of yarns and pictures — anything the public wants.

Anything, that is, except the *real* lowdown on Hunter. That, the build-up boys thought, was safely locked in the records of the Los Angeles County vice squad, confidential file Z-84254. In it is the racy story of a night in October, 1950, when the husky Hunter kid landed in jail, along with some 26 other good-looking young men, after the cops broke up a pajama party they staged — strictly for boys.

Only a year later, Tab had zoomed to where he was being interviewed by front-rank columnists like Earl Wilson,

Case No. C-9848

TRANSCRIPT OF DOCKET (Criminal)

Defendant in Court and having been duly arraigned for judgment and there being no legal cause why sentence should not be pronounced. Whereupon it is so ordered and adjudged by the Court this 2-6-51 that for said offense of Violation of Section 415, Penal Code, the said ARTHUR ANDREW GELIEN be imprisoned in the County Jail of the County of Los Angeles for the term of 30 days and the said defendant be discharged at the expiration of said term.

It is further ordered that the execution of sentence be suspended and that the defendant be placed on summary probation for 1 year subject to the following terms of probation: 1. Pay $50.00 through Court. Stay granted until 2-7-51, 4 PM. 2. Obey all laws for period of probation. See C-8063.

Transcript (above) shows rap given Art Gelien — Tab Hunter to you — after swish party he attended.

18

Confidential's story on Tab Hunter described the actor's presence at a "pajama party ... strictly for boys." *Author's collection*

CONDUCT"
HUNTER !

with whom he blushingly discussed how it feels to kiss Linda Darnell. But he was strictly an unknown on that night of October 14, 1950 — just one more of the scores of overly handsome youths who haunt the studios by day and get their kicks in unusual style after sundown.

There weren't even a dozen people who knew him by his movie monicker. Tab went by his real name, Art Gelien, and he was so far from fame and fortune that the cops found only 20 cents in his pockets when they pinched him.

It all started with a vice cop who was drifting in and out of Hollywood's queer bars on the afternoon of October 14th, looking and listening for tips on the newest notions of the limp-wristed lads.

Vice Cop Picked Up a Hot Tip

Pausing for a Scotch and water in one gay joint, the deputy detective struck up a conversation with a couple of lispers who happily prattled that they were set for a big binge that very evening, at 2501 Hope Street in Walnut Park, a suburb of Los Angeles. One drink led to another and the pair finally invited the snooper to come along. There was only one dashing requirement — bring pajamas.

Since breaking up such queer romps was his business, the detective pretended to fall in with his barroom chums and arranged to accompany them. Between snorts, however, he called the Los Angeles sheriff's office for reinforcements.

The detective and his pals arrived around 10:30 p.m., and one of the couples at the wingding had already changed into pajamas. His escorts gayly informed the cop that he didn't have to hurry about donning his own night togs since the soiree was scheduled to continue through the night and everyone planned to stay until the next morning.

Milling around him were two dozen of the gayest guys the vice squad had ever seen. There was one lone pair of women but their mannish attire and baritone voices only added to the novelty of the evening.

Thirty minutes of watching the strange goings-on was enough for the cop. Walking to a window, he quietly signaled outside and a few minutes later the whole party was under arrest. Off they went to the Firestone Park sheriff's station, where they were booked before being hustled off to the Los Angeles County jail.

There were no big names in the catch, so far as the cops could tell. Students, salesmen, *(Continued on page 60)*

19

Hopper and Parsons took every opportunity to attack *Confidential*. In October 1954, Hopper debunked *Confidential's* report of William Holden's attempted seduction of Grace Kelly, telling her readers Holden thought the story "ridiculous." "I picked Grace up at her apartment. But *Confidential* didn't bother to find out why. I took her to our home for dinner. She dined with Ardis [Holden's wife] and me about four times. I don't understand all this publicity about Grace. I like her, but I don't think she's the femme fatale she's built up to be."[41]

Hopper, Parsons, and the fan magazines tried to soften the impact of the Calhoun revelations. Parsons praised Calhoun as a devout Catholic, committed husband, and contemplative outdoorsman who spent his free time riding horses, hunting, and playing the harmonica. "Since that juvenile delinquency story broke, Rory's become even more popular," Hopper declared. The mainstream press also ran sympathetic stories. "A few of us go wrong but that doesn't make us hopelessly lost souls. All of us should try to help those who, out of ignorance or weakness or an evil impulse, have done wrong," Calhoun was quoted in a syndicated newspaper article, "My Dark Years." "Is Rory Calhoun blue over the stories printed about his juvenile record? Far from it," wrote *Modern Screen*. "He hopes his mistakes will be a lesson for other boys who might be tempted to take the wrong road."[42]

After selling Kim Novak down the river, Columbia came to her defense, planting stories attacking *Confidential's* account of her stardom. "Stabbed by Scandal," in *Photoplay*, was "a plea for people to read the truth about those so-called facts that made Kim another victim of slander." "You might have read a cruel distortion of how she was discovered. But you probably don't know that the author of such a tale hides cowardly behind an anonymous name. Kim has been scandalously painted as an ambition-driven girl who'd let nothing stand in the way of a film career. . . . Has she been wearing a deceitful mask? Or has she become the victim of vicious talk begun by a couple of envious, grasping men after the talent and extraordinary self-discipline she has shown have made her a big star?" Novak was the only star who walked to and from work, wrote *Photoplay*, and she continued to live in the YWCA, which wasn't the most fashionable spot, "but she'd rather go on happily sharing a dormitory setup with ninety-three other girls who don't treat her as a queen, but as one of them."[43]

MGM's publicity department worked hard to protect Clark Gable, maligned in *Confidential's* article "The Wife Clark Gable Forgot." Studio-planted stories appeared in the *Los Angeles Mirror-News* and in *Look* magazine disputing *Confidential's* account that Gable had neglected his elderly ex-wife and left her penniless and sick in a ramshackle Hollywood bungalow. "Clark hadn't read the nasty story about his first wife, Josephine Dillon, in that scandal magazine, but said he, 'She's a very proud, fine woman. She never asked me for alimony, she never asked for anything,'" Hopper reported on May 20, 1955. "Josephine has heard from people all over the world since the article appeared, depicting her as a poverty-stricken, forgotten woman. . . . She is talking a deal with a nationally-known writer to tell her life story and set the record straight about her marriage with Gable."[44]

MGM dispatched publicity head Howard Strickling and Gable's secretary to Josephine Dillon's home. They offered to buy the house from her, remodel it, and give it back to her on a rent-free lease. In August 1955, Gable bought the home for $9,000, painted it, and put in new pipes. This "generous gesture" was written up in the press. Dillon would later reveal in *Confidential* that Gable's act was a cheap publicity stunt. Gable hired the worst plumbers and didn't even paint all four sides of the house, only the sides of the house facing the street.[45]

Photoplay issued indignant editorials. Stars are "being subjected to vicious attacks. *Photoplay* has received hundreds of letters begging to know the truth. In some instances, these stories have dealt with marital difficulties, implying infidelity, in others, the scandal-mongering has implied the worst in human behavior. . . . Much has been written that is pure speculation. Much has been written that has little or no foundation in fact. Even more has been written revealing scandal, dug from the archives of the past, which has no bearing on the person the star has become. If you seek to believe the worst of human beings . . . you can find something bad in everyone. But there is more good than bad in most everyone, and on this truth *Photoplay* stands."[46]

Photoplay was published by Irving Manheimer, who was also president of the Publishers Distributing Corporation, which distributed *Confidential*, *Rave*, and *Whisper*. Publishing *Photoplay* and distributing *Confidential* was "like holding simultaneous general commissions in the Soviet and U.S. armies," quipped *Time*'s Ezra Goodman. Mike Connolly and Hedda Hopper "outed" Manheimer in their columns. "Those horrible stories in *Confidential* magazine are doing our stars more harm than anything that's ever happened to them. Did you know that the magazine is distributed by Irving Manheimer of *Photoplay* magazine?" Hopper wrote on May 7, 1955. Manheimer severed all connections with the distributing company, selling it to Sam Scheff, one of his employees.[47]

Harrison was glib about it all. "Sure, they're scared in Hollywood," he said. "I feel for those guys. You take a producer. He makes a star out of some guy and then he finds out the guy is a [homosexual]. The producer stands to make a million bucks offa this [homosexual]. So why shouldn't he be afraid?" Rushmore added, "Hollywood should be grateful. We're doing the industry a favor, exposing all those perverts and homosexuals. They were giving Hollywood a bad name."[48]

13 | THE CURIOUS CRAZE

IN THE SPRING OF 1955, Harrison took out triumphant ads in newspapers:

> Who are the 3,840,000 people who buy *Confidential* and make it the
> BIGGEST newsstand seller of all time? Everybody reads *Confidential*!
> Latest Audit Bureau of Circulations figures prove conclusively that
> *Confidential* is bought at the newsstands by *more* people per issue
> than *Life, Reader's Digest, Saturday Evening Post, TV Guide, Ladies'
> Home Journal,* or *Look*. . . . Why? Because *Confidential* is *Everybody's*
> magazine!
>
> In *three short years, Confidential* has shattered all-time records for
> single-issue newsstand sales! They love us . . . and they hate us . . . but
> they *READ* us . . .
>
> *Confidential* is the only magazine that Tells the Facts and Names
> the Names.[1]

Between the start of the "hot Hollywood" stories in 1953 and 1955, there
was a massive jump in *Confidential's* readership. Circulation went from
800,000 in mid-1953 to 1,609,000 in November 1954 to more than 3,000,000
in March 1955. In June 1955, circulation had reached 4,040,000. *Confidential's* July 1955 issue, featuring "The Untold Story of Marlene Dietrich," sold
over 3,700,000 copies on newsstands, history's biggest sale of any magazine

issue through newsdealers. Counting so-called pass-along readership—a single issue of *Confidential* was read by an estimated four people—the magazine had around sixteen million readers.[2]

Confidential was the fastest-moving publication on "newsstands," a category that included drugstores, stationery shops, and supermarkets, in addition to corner newsdealers. Although big national magazines like *Life*, *The Saturday Evening Post*, *Reader's Digest*, *Ladies' Home Journal*, *Look*, and *Collier's*, with large subscription lists, topped *Confidential* in overall circulation (*Life*'s weekly circulation was over five million), Harrison outperformed them in newsstand trade. *TV Guide* had an average per-issue newsstand sale of only about 2.4 million. *Life* had a little over nine hundred thousand. *Reader's Digest* sold less than two million per issue, and the *Ladies' Home Journal* one million. While the circulation of major national magazines was declining because of competition from television and increasing postal rates, *Confidential* was booming.[3]

Harrison was making money hand over fist. Shrewdly, he'd set up the magazine so that he only needed to sell 60 percent of his print run to make a profit. Out of the 25-cent price of the magazine, he kept 14½ cents. From that, he paid the Kable Printing Company, which printed the magazine, $100,000 per issue. His other big expense was paper, about $125,000 per issue. Most magazines of the time used a slick grade that cost an average of $190 a ton, but Harrison used a grade called "super newsprint" that sold at only $134 a ton, only slightly better than newsprint. After all expenses except taxes, Harrison made a profit of four to five cents per copy. Most magazines relied on advertising and subscriptions for revenue, but newsstand sales were *Confidential's* main income. *Confidential* had a subscription list of only thirty thousand. Its total ad sales—$55,000 per issue—was the same as the cost of two four-color pages in *Life*. Harrison continued to use the same fly-by-night advertisers for hair-loss creams, diet pills, and male rejuvenation products that he had used in his girlie magazines.[4]

At the height of *Confidential's* popularity, Harrison was earning more than $350,000 per issue. According to *Esquire*, that made him the most successful publisher in American history, "without exception." He moved his operations to a four-thousand-square-foot office at 1697 Broadway, with a gorgeous reception room staffed by a pretty brunette receptionist wearing a low-cut gown. The girlie pictures that once adorned Harrison's office were replaced by Utrillos and a Matisse. Harrison was making a personal income of about $30,000 a week. Sherman Billingsley granted him access to the elite Cub Room at the Stork Club, the "sanctum sanctorum" of the club, dubbed the "snub room." Harrison shut down all his girlie magazines except *Beauty Parade* and *Whisper*. Harrison boasted that *Confidential's* circulation was greater than any publication since the Gutenberg Bible, and that he was thinking of buying another white Cadillac. "With *Confidential*," he announced, "I have finally gone respectable."[5]

Confidential attracted its first national media coverage that spring, rating stories in *Newsweek*, *Time*, a front-page article in the *Wall Street Journal*, and a series in the *Chicago Sun-Times*. It was the first time millions of Americans had heard about *Confidential*, and the publicity, though critical, piqued the public's interest and boosted circulation even further.

"Everyone knows that people enjoy gossip as much as a good dinner," *Newsweek* announced. "But it may come as a surprise that the fastest-selling magazine on American newsstands today is a supercharged gossip journal called *Confidential*. . . . The emphasis is on sin and sex, with a seasoning of right-wing politics." "What our readers want is facts, gossipy facts, and that's what we give them," Harrison told the *Wall Street Journal*.[6]

Time did a scathing piece on *Confidential*, titled "Success in the Sewer," and the *Chicago Sun-Times* ran a five-part series heralded as a "look-see at the masterminds and methods" behind the magazine. "In a little more than two years, a 25 cent magazine called *Confidential*, based on the proposition that millions like to wallow in scurrility, has become the biggest newsstand seller in the US," *Time* reported. "With each bimonthly issue, printed on cheap paper and crammed with splashy pictures, *Confidential's* sales have grown even faster than its journalistic reputation has fallen." *Time* also exposed some of *Confidential's* shadier tactics. "The magazine specializes in finding one black mark in a subject's distant past, and hammering him with it, e.g. Cinemactor Rory Calhoun's youthful prison record."[7] Winchell defended *Confidential* against *Time's* attack. "Time mag., its halo askew, got perturbed about *Confidential* magazine, although that newsweekly often prints gossipy pieces about show folks and celebs," he wrote. "The old-maid animosity towards the expose sheets is more economical than moral: *Confidential* has cut into the sales of many mags and is the biggest US newsstand seller."[8]

It wasn't just *Confidential* that had taken the nation by storm. *Confidential* launched a bastard progeny—a "racy, madcap new family of so-called expose magazines"—that was "making publishing history." There was a "curious craze" for scandal magazines, reported *Newsweek*.[9] In 1955 "scandal mags" emerged as one of the biggest fads of the year.

There were more than fifteen *Confidential* copycats on newsstands, including *Uncensored* ("Lowdown on What's Behind the Headlines"), *Inside Story* ("The Facts Behind the Headlines"), *On the Q.T.* ("Stories the Newspapers Won't Print"), *Behind the Scene, Inside* ("Exposing People and Headlines"), *Hush-Hush* ("What You Don't Know About People You Know"), *Exposed* ("All the Facts, All the Names"), *Private Lives* ("Names the Names and the Facts!"), *Rave, The Lowdown* ("The Facts They Dare Not Tell You"), *Dynamite*, and *Dare* ("The Magazine that Dares Tell the Truth"). Together they had a per-issue sale of about ten million. *Uncensored* had a circulation of eight hundred thousand. Harrison's *Whisper* was in competition with *Confidential*, but it sold only about five hundred thousand copies a month. Three others—*Top Secret*, *Inside Story*, and *Suppressed*—were in the three hundred thousand to five hundred thousand bracket.[10]

All the ripoffs were like *Confidential*, with big pictures, salacious headlines, leering innuendo, and lurid stories about celebrities, vice, and sex. According to one study, there were 194 stories in thirteen different exposé magazines on newsstands in September 1955. Sixty-eight of them were on Hollywood stars, including three "inside stories" on Lana Turner and three each on Mario Lanza, Marlon Brando, Grace Kelly, Ava Gardner, and Marilyn Monroe. Fifty stories were about other famous figures, including three on John Jacob Astor and three on Walter Winchell. There were thirteen pieces on health, five "confessions," and fifty-five general "expose stories" like "Hollywood Stars Fake Their Figures." Many were rewrites of stories that already appeared in *Confidential*.[11]

Lacking Harrison's budget and fact-checking resources, most of the imitators were far less accurate than *Confidential*. The June 1955 issue of *Private Lives* contained a "juicy bit" about actress Maria Montez, who was dead. *The Lowdown* had a story in August 1955 that claimed to "expose" Johnnie Ray as having paid a twenty-five-dollar fine on a morals charge in Detroit. The charge was four years old, so the magazine pegged its story on the title, "*Lowdown* Demands Michigan Governor Pardon . . . ."[12]

Much of the material wasn't "confidential" at all. In August 1956, *Hush-Hush* featured an article titled "Behind Closed Doors: What's Going on in Manhattan's Wee Hour Bottle Clubs." Nothing was, since the clubs were closed four months earlier. Another article was brazenly titled, "General Custer Deserved What He Got!" One technique used by the scandal magazines was to take a "straight" story and give it a "smear" headline. *Hush-Hush* put on its cover, "Exposed: That Strange Perry Como Smear." The article read, "If there's anybody in show business whose reputation has never been besmirched by scandal, it is television's 'Mr. Nice Guy'—Perry Como."[13]

Confidential even spawned a parody—*Cockeyed: Confidential, Top Secret, Makes Up the Facts and Blames the Names*, issued by a subsidiary of Fawcett Publications that put out the men's magazine *True*. It was announced as a quarterly, but only one issue was published. It opened with articles such as:

"Liberace's Wig Maker Tells All!!!"
"Who Slipped a Mickey to Spillane???"
"Mae West EXPOSED as Marilyn Monroe's Grandma!!!"
"Aly Khan to Wed Entire Folies-Bergere Chorus!!!"
"Uncovering Long Island's Amazing Fourth Sex!!!"

The authors were Wolfgang Smutts, Agatha Crisco, Hedda Cabbage, Bernard Macfatty, and C. U. Tamara.[14]

Harrison was unfazed by the competition. "They have not hurt us," he told reporters. "And there's a reason for that. They came in on the backwash of *Confidential*." Former *Whisper* editor George Shute, who went on to become editor of *Uncensored*, told Harrison that "I hope *Confidential* sells 10,000,000 because if you [do] we are going to sell 2,000,000." If anything, Harrison said, the imitators increased demand for *Confidential*. "People buy *Confidential* and they read it. . . . How long does it take? A couple of hours and you're done.

There's a long time to go between months. There's an appetite for this sort of thing, so they want more."[15]

––––––––––––––

Who read *Confidential*? That was the $64,000 question. Just about everyone, it seemed—but almost no one would admit it.

There were millions of casual readers, people intrigued by bright *Confidential* covers at newsstands who bought an issue every now and then. Some read *Confidential* because they'd heard someone talking about it and wanted to know what all the fuss was about. Devotees read each issue religiously. Newsstand owners reported that some customers were reserving copies in advance "so as to be sure to be first in on the dirt."[16]

For many, *Confidential* had become a secret vice. Newspaper publishers "oughta be glad there's a magazine like *Confidential*," quipped the vice president of *Confidential*'s distributor. "It boosts your sales. People go to newsstands to buy *Confidential*. Then they buy a paper. What for? To carry *Confidential* home in; so nobody'll see."

"Riding on a plane one time to the West Coast, I sat by a distinguished gentleman, well-dressed, impeccable in his speech and deportment," Rushmore recalled. "He had refused cocktails . . . and I noticed that in his lapel he wore an emblem indicating his membership in a great religious organization. Yet, snuggled between the covers of a financial magazine, my seatmate had a copy of *Confidential*. He was trying to be anonymous." A Chicago society matron summed up the simultaneous appeal and appall of the magazine: "I've read it from cover to cover, and I think it ought to be thrown out of the house."[17]

Though *Confidential* was originally designed for white working-class men, its appeal crossed racial, ethnic, and cultural boundaries. There were African American readers and female readers. Factory workers, salesmen, and school-teachers read it; so did members of the upper crust. Rushmore was at a dinner party where he met an old friend, a "lady of distinct charm, refinement, and culture." She praised *Confidential*. "I'm glad you like the magazine," he said. "I try to have an article exposing communism in every issue." "Oh pshaw," she said smilingly. "Those articles are all right, Howard, but what I really get a kick out of are those saucy stories on Hollywood. I can't wait until the next issue."[18]

According to *Confidential*'s circulation department, about 75 percent of its readers were female. *Confidential* was replacing the fan magazines, or being read by the same readers as the fan magazines. Harrison had his own theory about *Confidential*'s readership. "Now women for the most part are . . . inhibited . . . so they live in their minds to a great extent," he said. "When they read about other women who are doing the things that they think about, perhaps what they might want to do . . . you know, this is a great excitement to them."[19]

> I talk to educated women who read *Confidential* all the time, and they tell me that they get a tremendous amount of enjoyment out of it because here is freedom that they don't have. Some women have the courage to do the things they want to do. Most women haven't. So in my opinion, that's giving them a certain amount of genuine entertainment. More so than fiction for that matter.[20]

Confidential and the scandal magazines shattered the placid facade of 1950s culture, and their runaway success led Americans to serious doubt and self-questioning. Why were scandal magazines so popular? Why did the public tolerate such sleazy fare? What did the rise of *Confidential* and its imitators say about the nation's values and beliefs?

To some, *Confidential*'s rise was neither notable nor alarming. It was human nature to look for others' failings. Harrison and Rushmore had found a way to profit from people's worst instincts. "Its editors are by no means morons," observed one critic. "One of them is an able ex-communist fired from the Hearst chain; another has been living by his sharp wits for quite some time, capitalizing on the sensational and publishing half a dozen border-line pulps. The success of these men is due in large part to their knowledge of human nature." But Rushmore and Harrison weren't only to blame—*Confidential*'s success was the public's fault. "Blame the [editors] as much as you like, but do not blame them alone," wrote one editor. "Millions of [readers] . . . make those [magazines] possible." "Sad commentary that . . . there is a vast market for this commodity. Gossip magazines exist because people want them."[21]

Some saw *Confidential*'s popularity as a testament to America's unhealthy obsession with movie stars. Stars and their private lives had taken up too much attention, and actors were poor role models for children, they argued. "To the average (or even above-average) teenager . . . the truly important personalities are . . . figures in the entertainment industry," observed newspaper columnist Syd Harris. "If we did not treat our entertainment figures like gods there would be no need, and no excuse, for exposing them as devils." The public was unconsciously resentful of the hold celebrities had over them, and the scandal magazines were its "way of attempting to free itself," opined *Commonweal* magazine. "The expose magazine is the private eye promising liberation from an enchantment that is also an enslavement."[22]

In the vein of influential social critiques like *The Lonely Crowd* (1950) and *White Collar* (1952), others saw *Confidential* as a reflection of alienation and anxiety in an increasingly materialistic, technological, media-driven society, where people were overworked, overwhelmed, and disconnected from meaningful, productive labor. Gregory Zilboorg, a well-known psychiatrist, told *Newsweek*, "Mechanical civilization keeps people busy, and when they stop working there is a pseudo-literary pill they can take for relaxation." To another psychiatrist, *Confidential* was an indication of "widespread emotional and spiritual immaturity." Modern society had yielded men and women who were adults physically but emotionally had "never reached a grown-up level." Scandal magazine readers "prefer the condiment to the meat—the mustard means more than the steak. . . . They have no aspirations, no real hopes." "What used to be champagne from the bottle is now water from the tap as far as they're concerned. . . . They cannot appreciate painting, sculpture, poetry. Something has been left out of modern education."[23]

Perhaps the most trenchant explanation for *Confidential* was the public's growing skepticism, in a communication-saturated culture, toward the constructed nature of media images and media "spin." Newspaper circulation reached historic highs in the 1950s. By the end of the decade, 87 percent of households had at least one television set. The time the average American spent watching television grew from four and a half hours a day in 1950 to more than five hours in 1960. In 1955 there were at least forty-six magazines with circulations of one million or more. Americans were spending $18 billion annually on recreational pursuits, including books, magazines, and newspapers.[24]

"So some people cannot understand the sudden popularity of the new expose magazines. Well I think I know the answer," one critic quipped. "The public has had all the rosy baloney shoved down its throat it can take."[25]

"The US public is the most communication-glutted group of people in world history," observed *Newsweek*. "Daily bombarded by 'facts' which conflict, daily told opposite versions of the same incidents, hopelessly incapable in this complicated world of sorting out the truth, a great many Americans have undoubtedly built a thick shell of skepticism around themselves. Understandably, the shell often hardens into cynicism. Having seen more than his share of legitimate scandals and exposures, the reader begins to think that *every* story must have some kind of a lowdown beneath the surface, some 'uncensored' facts known to only a 'confidential' few."[26]

"This is the age of cynicism," commented Ray Fiore, vice president of the company that distributed *Confidential*.

> Trace it back. Up to 1929 Americans had credulous minds. They believed everything they read in the papers and the magazines. Then came the crash. Then came 12 years of hunger, people selling apples. Then six, seven years of war, and six, seven years of cold war. So pretty soon the people begin to realize that life is tough. And they start not believing what they're told. About two, three years ago they reach a pinnacle of cynicism and doubt. Along comes *Confidential*. It tells the people about crime, filth, vice, and corruption. Just what the people want, just what they suspected was going on.[27]

Others linked *Confidential*, rightly, to America's preoccupation with sex—and its confusion around sex.

Sexual norms were in flux in the 1950s. While the morals preached by society's leaders were conservative, sexual practices were becoming more permissive. With teenage car ownership, more relaxed parenting styles, and disposable income from part-time jobs, teenagers had more freedom than ever. Dating culture revolved around necking and petting, and premarital sex was on the rise. Alfred Kinsey observed that "on doorsteps and on street corners, and on high school and college campuses, petting may be observed in the daytime as well as in the evening hours." Though condemned, same-sex relationships and extramarital affairs were common, as Kinsey's studies revealed. When it came to sex, there was a major gap between private acts and public norms.[28]

Popular culture teemed with contradictory messages. Films, magazines, novels, and advice columns warned girls not to "go all the way" before marriage. At the same time, the media exploded with sex. GIs, exposed to pornographic material overseas, returned with a taste for girlie magazines, which flooded newsstands. Sexual realism pervaded literature; bestselling novels of the decade, including *East of Eden, Ten North Frederick, Island in the Sun, The Deer Park, From Here to Eternity*, and *Peyton Place* frankly discussed abortion, lust, and adultery. The Kinsey reports, with their analyses of sexual prowess, technique, and perversions, became conversation even at suburban dinner parties. Advertisers used the "sexual sell," marketing products using pictures of busty women in tight sweaters and bikinis. Youth subcultures offered beat poetry, jazz, rhythm and blues, and rock and roll, which made their way into mainstream culture.[29]

Confidential played to the fantasies, curiosities, and fears of a nation that was deeply conflicted about sex. It grabbed the attention of a public that was both intrigued by and fearful of sex, that had been taught to shun "deviant" sex but was titillated and fascinated by sexual taboos. With its salacious hush-hush exposés, *Confidential* reinforced the association of sexual desires with the shameful and forbidden. At the same time, it offered Americans an enticing vision of what a less-repressed world might look like. Winking, leering, and snickering, it pushed erotic matters to the forefront of popular consciousness. Exposing the sexual hypocrisy of prominent figures and bringing controversial topics into the spotlight, *Confidential*—however crude and outrageous—became a force of liberation in American culture.

———

Some saw *Confidential* a harmless fad that would die of its own weight. Others viewed it as a major threat. If left unchecked, they feared, it could lead to the nation's downfall—the decline of morals and the corruption of youth.

Although religious and civic groups had long crusaded for "purity" in entertainment, those efforts intensified in the conservative postwar climate. By 1951 racy paperback books, girlie magazines, and other erotic material were "all under fire from advocates of censorship," noted the *New York Times*. As in the years after both the Civil War and World War I, women's clubs, veterans' associations, and religious groups battled fiercely against the public display of sexuality.[30]

The early 1950s saw new awareness of the effects of mass media on attitudes and behaviors, especially youth behavior. The media came to be seen as a pernicious force that stood between parent and child; parents could no longer impress their value systems on children corrupted by pulp novels, television, movies, and girlie magazines. Violent and sexualized entertainment—gangster movies, comic books, and rock and roll—were linked to crime, mental illness, and especially juvenile delinquency. The '50s saw an alleged "epidemic" of delinquency. Although the rise in juvenile crime was statistically slight, delinquency was seen as evidence of a dangerous weakening of home and family that made the nation vulnerable to communist influence.[31]

Legislatures were inundated with demands for laws against violent, "lewd," and "indecent" publications. Lawmaking bodies were "passing censorship laws so fast that it is difficult to make an accurate count." In response to a national crusade against comic books, cities and states passed laws regulating the sale and distribution of violent comics. In some areas, official "review boards" were set up to screen all publications offered for sale and ban those that were deemed "objectionable." Georgia established a state literature commission to study "questionable literature" violating "normal, traditional, and contemporary patterns of decency" and to make reports to the state solicitor general for prosecution for obscenity.[32]

"Citizens' committees" for "decent literature" sprang up across the country. Committees provided lists of "disfavored" publications to police, who warned vendors that material they were selling was "indecent" and must be removed from sale. Certificates were given to newsdealers who complied, and boycotts threatened against those who resisted. In some communities, signs were placed in store windows of retailers who cooperated in "magazine clean-up drives."[33]

Many feared that *Confidential* would attract youth and other "suggestible" people to sin and depravity. "One cannot wonder how much of this sensational junk is taken into US homes by mothers of families," wrote the Catholic magazine *America*.[34] Observed the Tyrone, Pennsylvania *Daily Herald*:

> Teenagers are being subjected to still another demoralizing influence these days: that of the so-called expose magazines. . . . Magazines of this type have all the potentialities of being a . . . potent influence . . . for the simple reason that they do not use fictitious characters. They refer to very real people—celebrities who enjoy great popularity. And they name those famous names. The immoralities attributed to a famous movie or television star could very well be, to the teenagers, a very strong argument for emulating such behavior.[35]

"A monster from the sewers now stands dripping and evil smelling in journalistic circles," wrote one critic. "The monster is the new tell-all magazines. They deal in dirt, sex, sick minds, and lies plus an occasional word of truth buried deep in a dung heap of monthly smear mongering." The *Hartford Courant* described *Confidential* as "nothing but tainted garbage" and a "stench in the nostrils of the nation." The scandal magazines "are dedicated to the glorification of evil. They are slicked-up versions of the cheapest pulp pornography," announced the Tennessee *Church of God Evangel*.[36]

"With the furore over horror and sex comics going on, something new has been added to the newsstands that make the worst of the so-called comic publications look strictly like kid stuff. We refer to the scandal magazines that are flooding the newsstands all over the country," wrote a North Carolina newspaper, the *Gastonia Gazette*. "The censors, in our opinion, should shelve the comic book menace for a season and take a good look at some of the filthy scandal magazines. If they can stand it." "Conscientious people should join together in a fight against these magazines. It is our job to get those magazines off the stands and keep them and others like them off, for good," a woman commented to the *Detroit Free Press*.[37]

By the end of 1955, conservative groups across the country had joined together to bring down *Confidential*. Hollywood had found an unlikely ally.

14 | PUBLIC SERVICE

THOUGH THEY HAD TAKEN a back seat to the Hollywood stories, *Confidential* continued to run articles on the mob and society figures, and its muckraking "public service" articles, revealing purported injustices and frauds that were too "hot" and controversial for the mainstream press.

Harrison remained enormously proud of the "public service" articles. Each issue had at least three or four of them. Those stories, Harrison boasted, made "a definite contribution" to the public's well-being. Harrison went as far as to claim—falsely—that he only published the "hot Hollywood stories" to subsidize the public service stories. "I can tell you this very frankly that if we didn't put our spicy stuff in there no one would ever read [them]. That's the point," he said.[1]

Many of the "public service" pieces were consumer safety articles, such as "Hospital—Enter at Your Own Risk" and "How the Airlines Take Your Life in Their Hands," describing the dangers of airline travel, including "pilot fatigue, brutal schedules, mechanical failure, and death!"[2] "The Criminal Record of Cutter Laboratories" exposed how the lab's polio vaccine, released that year, was tainted.[3] In 1955 wearing a Davy Crockett coonskin cap was a children's fad. Those caps, *Confidential* revealed, were infected with fleas and caused horrific scalp infections.[4]

"Blood for Booze" described alcoholics who were donating blood—"draining their lives away"—to pay for their addiction.[5] "Alimony Jail Is Back," *Confidential* reported in July 1955. "It looks like the little ladies have finally fixed it. The law, already loaded in favor of the gals, has now provided that an alimony judgment in one state can be enforced in nearly all of the other states."[6] "Parole—Freedom on a String" was a bitter critique of the parole system. "What good is a system that censors your job, bars you from women, and puts you back under arrest without cause? Parole can be an engine of torture that succeeds in redoubling hatred of law, cops, and penal 'experts'!"[7]

The magazine's health exposés remained the most interesting and useful of its "public service" stories. "Aspirin—No. 1 Poisoner of Children" reported an increase in deaths from aspirin overdose attributed to a new product: candy-coated children's aspirin.[8] "Danger—Boric Acid Is a Poison!" revealed that the "supposedly harmless ingredient in baby powders, eye ointments, and dusting powders, is a deadly poison!"[9] *Confidential* continued to run antismoking stories, reporting on the tobacco industry's efforts to promote filter cigarettes as safer than unfiltered cigarettes. In "The Big Lie About Filter Cigarettes" *Confidential* wrote, "Tobacco companies will spend more than 52 million dollars this year on advertising. Countless publications . . . will shout the merits of various filter-tip brands. . . . The truth is that some filter cigarettes actually pass on more nicotine than ordinary unfiltered brands. . . . The manufacturers' extravagant claims suggesting that filter-tips are the answer to disease are a *deliberate hoax!*"[10]

Confidential continued to expose high society, and its society stories were as outrageous as its Hollywood articles. In "The Astor Testimony the Judge Suppressed," *Confidential* printed testimony from John Jacob Astor's scandalous divorce proceedings. "The Miami justice was so shocked that . . . he clamped an official blackout on what Astor's third wife . . . had whispered about her pudgy hubby. . . . Here, for the first time, is the sizzling story—the actual testimony—that made [the judge] gasp." Astor's ex-wife testified how "Jakey" wanted movies of them taken in their most intimate moments to amuse him when she wasn't around, and how he enjoyed entertaining call girls in packs of four and five. He ate like a savage, spent hours staring at his fat, naked body in a mirror, and loved to be beaten. During intercourse "he would just lie back and look at me with very blank eyes," she told the judge.[11]

One of *Confidential*'s hottest society exposés was its two-part series outing socialite Walter Chrysler Jr. Chrysler's father had founded the Chrysler corporation in 1925.[12] According to "The Strange Case of Walter Chrysler Jr." by "Brad Shortell"—Howard Rushmore—Chrysler had resigned from the navy in 1944 at the height of hostilities, but all records of the resignation had been purged. *Confidential* sent the Defense Department a letter asking for an explanation of Chrysler's resignation. The reply gave only Chrysler's rank and the date of resignation. *Confidential* came up with its own theory. Chrysler was gay, and "word of the type of parties Chrysler gave for young sailors at his home got to Washington and to Navy intelligence."[13]

When the story generated massive interest, *Confidential* lashed out at Chrysler again a few months later. In an article titled "How the Navy Ousted Its No. 1 Gay Gob," *Confidential* claimed that "hundreds of Navy veterans, mothers of Navy men, and interested readers wrote us asking for the full story of why Chrysler left the Navy. Blocked by all officials, *Confidential* went behind the scenes, sent reporters to Key West and Miami, and came up with the *real reason* why the heir to one of America's greatest fortunes was permitted to resign from the service during wartime. You'll read the authentic story here for the first time—the story the Navy refused to tell."

According to *Confidential*, Navy Intelligence, under suspicion that Chrysler was gay, launched a probe of him in 1943. When Chrysler was stationed in Key West, the navy got an investigator to contact a boy known as "Billy" who had been forced out of the navy for homosexuality. The officer had him attend one of the wild parties Chrysler was giving for enlisted men. Billy told the officer that Chrysler was called "Mary" by other homosexuals.

The navy set up surveillance in Chrysler's home and his phone was tapped. Within days, the intelligence officer reported to his superiors that Chrysler was entertaining enlisted men at his home, and that it was his practice, after the parties, to "bid all but one man goodbye and ask him to spend the night." The next morning Chrysler would drive the man to the base and cover up his absence in the official records. The navy put him under house arrest, and Chrysler offered a $200,000 bribe if the charges were dropped. He then gave a sworn statement in which he admitted he was gay and that his first homosexual experience was at the age of twelve when a teacher at a private school induced him into "unnatural acts."[14] Chrysler threatened to sue *Confidential* for libel but never did.

Rushmore continued to write his anticommunist stories, but they'd declined to a trickle. In January 1955 he attacked *Time* magazine as a "hotbed of communists."[15] There were continuing attacks on Winchell enemies and a few pro-Winchell plugs: "How the Communists Tried to Gag Walter Winchell" (May 1955); "How Walter Winchell Saved a Man from the Commie Kiss of

Death" (July 1955); and "The Truth About the Walter Winchell Retraction" (September 1955). Winchell continued to pump *Confidential* in his column. But by then, *Confidential* didn't need him. It had become bigger than Winchell.

———————

On Friday, July 8, 1955, bold headlines around the world reported that Howard Rushmore had disappeared. Earlier that week, Rushmore had gone to Chicago to work on a story about the death of former Secretary of the Navy James Forrestal, who had reportedly committed suicide in 1949 by jumping from a building. Rushmore said he believed Forrestal's death was connected to William Lazarovich, also known as William Lawrence, a communist party member who had gone underground in 1945. Rushmore believed that the communist official held the key to his theory that Forrestal hadn't actually committed suicide but was murdered by communists.[16]

Rushmore flew to Chicago that Monday. He visited newspaper friends on Tuesday morning, told them about his project, and was given some leads. He went to Chicago police headquarters on Wednesday and got more leads, including the promise of a picture of Lawrence that had been published in the *Daily Worker* in 1945. On Wednesday night he appeared on a TV program, *The Tom Duggan Show*, and said he was looking for a communist party leader. He asked any listener who knew the whereabouts of Lawrence to call him.

When Rushmore returned to his room at the Ambassador East Hotel after the show, he got a message from the desk clerk that a man named "Larry" had called and asked to meet him at 1:15 AM in a "tough neighborhood." Rushmore left his hotel room at 12:55 and never returned. Claiming to be alarmed when he didn't hear from Rushmore, Harrison notified the police.

Police detectives went to Rushmore's hotel room, where they found two suits in the closet, along with two shirts and neckties. His gray straw hat was lying on top of one of the twin beds. Police found the text of a telegram Rushmore sent to Harrison at 10 PM Wednesday night. It read, "Obtain photograf tomorrow. Plan it for layout red story. Howard." The detectives also found return tickets to New York with an unclaimed reservation.[17]

On Saturday, July 9, after a three-day police search, Rushmore was discovered in Butte, Montana.[18] William Touhy, deputy chief of detectives in Butte, got an anonymous call saying Rushmore could be found in the Finland Hotel registered as "H. Roberts." Touhy informed the police chief, who went to the hotel and asked "Roberts" if he was Rushmore. "Yes, my name is Rushmore," he replied. "I registered under the name of Howard Roberts because I didn't want people to know where I was. I'm here on legitimate business. That's the way I operate."[19]

Rushmore said he'd been trailing a "comm" in Chicago when he received a tip that the man was in Butte. He "had to vanish" because "Larry" gave him some "very important information"—that two communists were "strong arm men" in a Butte, Montana, mining union. Rushmore drove to Milwaukee with Larry, bought a sports shirt and a pair of pants and a leather overnight bag, and took a train to Butte.[20] The tip proved groundless.[21] He insisted that the press dispatches about him having gone missing were "all a big mistake" and that the publicity wrecked his chances of getting the story.[22]

An FBI report revealed that Rushmore telephoned the Butte FBI office when he arrived and asked for the special agent in charge, Agent Hosteny. Rushmore told Hosteny he had to meet him urgently to discuss an "important matter." Rushmore went to the FBI building in Butte, talked with Hosteny, and returned to his hotel. During the conversation Rushmore mentioned such big names as Senator McCarthy and Roy Cohn to convince Hosteny he should cooperate with him on a story on communists in the International Union of Mine, Mill, and Smelter Workers. Hosteny told Chicago police about the incident and also reported it to FBI headquarters in Washington. When he heard about it, Associate FBI Director Clyde Tolson commented, "Rushmore must be a nut. We should have nothing to do with him." FBI director Hoover added, "I certainly agree."[23]

Many suspected—rightly—that the whole thing was a stunt. Rushmore denied he'd done anything for publicity, but the event does seem to have been faked.[24] According to the *Chicago Worker*, the *Chicago Tribune*, a "McCarthy-ite paper," helped build the hoax. While the *Tribune* ran a headline, "Editor on Red Hunt Reported Missing," Chicago police began scouring the city. Extra copies of *Confidential* were loaded onto newsstands. The phony story of the disappearance was broken to the press by one of Rushmore's news-paper friends, a *Tribune* copy editor named Stephen Harrison. The William Lawrence story was an obvious fake, said the *Worker*, since Lawrence lived in New York with his two children at the same address where he had lived for ten years.[25] When Rushmore's disappearance made the news, *Confidential*'s sales doubled.[26]

At the same time Rushmore was hoaxing for Harrison, he was getting ready to leave *Confidential*.

Rushmore continued to complain about what he called *Confidential*'s "peep show" stories. Some of the articles, like the Kim Novak piece, he considered outright pornography. Rushmore also resented that Harrison dropped the magazine's focus on communism, and he was constantly battling the lawyers over fact-checking. Rushmore wasn't doing the signed McCarthyite pieces he had done when he first went to *Confidential*, and he felt he wasn't getting the recognition he deserved. These resentments crested when Harrison began approaching prominent writers in other fields, including a few of Rushmore's enemies, to write for *Confidential*.[27]

To dispel charges of *Confidential* being obscenity and smut, Harrison decided to have an important sports story in each issue as well as more articles on political affairs. In the summer of 1955, he set out to find a good sportswriter, as well as a noted writer on political subjects. Harrison got interested in Jimmy Cannon and Murray Kempton of the *New York Post*. In September Harrison dispatched attorney Daniel Ross to *Post* editor James Wechsler to ask permission for Harrison to approach Cannon and Kempton. Wechsler had no objection. When Rushmore found out, he accused Ross of "going around his back" to get other writers.[28]

In late October 1955, columnist Leonard Lyons reported that the "editor of the most notorious of the expose magazines is resigning."[29] Rushmore quit *Confidential*, took his severance pay, bought a plane ticket, and flew to Los Angeles, where he approached lawyer Jerry Giesler, who was in the midst of filing libel suits against *Confidential* on behalf of his movie star clients. Ever the turncoat, Rushmore offered his services to Giesler, telling him he would do anything to help him destroy *Confidential*.[30] It marked the beginning of a new chapter in *Confidential* and a chain of events that would ultimately bring down the magazine.

PART III

15 | LIBEL

FROM THE START, HOLLYWOOD leaders had discouraged libel suits against *Confidential*. Lawsuits would just spur Harrison's wrath, they feared, and would only draw attention to *Confidential*'s accusations. Stars themselves had shunned lawsuits; there was too much potential for disaster. A libel suit would rehash the material, and in attempting to prove the truth of a story, *Confidential* could bring out even more damaging facts in court. There was a legal action for invasion of privacy, but it required admitting that the statements were true.

"Sue 'em and it takes years to get into court. Leave 'em alone and it's forgotten," quipped Gary Cooper, who declined to sue *Confidential* over a story about his affair with Anita Ekberg. "Filing a suit would only give [*Confidential*] the publicity they want," Marlon Brando told the press. "By the time the suit was tried, they'd get more in publicity than the judgment could ever cost them. And maybe I'd get an award of 8 cents." Harvard declined to sue *Confidential* over Howard Rushmore's article "There's Plenty of Red in the Harvard Crimson." Taking *Confidential* to court would just give Rushmore a chance to circulate more nasty rumors about Harvard, the administration reasoned. The university adopted an official policy of ignoring *Confidential*'s stories, concluding that any publicity from a lawsuit would be worse than the article.[1]

MGM's publicity director Howard Strickling counseled Ava Gardner against suing over the Sammy Davis story. "Ava, you don't want to sue this rag," he said. "If you sue you'll get a small apology and no money—but they will get enormous publicity around the world. It'll hurt you, it will hurt the studio." Davis wanted a retraction from *Confidential*. "The best thing to do is forget it," Strickling told him. "By the time they can print your retraction it'll be months from now and it'll be forgotten." "Let it die by itself. Nobody reads retractions."[2]

Stars were also wary of libel suits because there was no guarantee they would win. In California, it was difficult to recover damages in libel cases since plaintiffs had to show economic harm. A star would have to pinpoint exactly how much they lost because of the article, whether in box office returns or career opportunities. That figure was usually impossible to determine. Truth was a defense in libel cases, and much of what *Confidential* printed was true.[3]

In early May 1955, *Chicago Tribune* columnist Herb Lyon asked Rushmore the "perennial question": "How many lawsuits have you had?" "None that count," Rushmore snapped. "Threats, but little actual action."[4] That was about to change. Later that month, Robert Mitchum sued *Confidential* for $1 million, launching a wave of libel suits that would lead to the magazine's swift demise.

––––––––––

"The Nude Who Came to Dinner," in the July 1955 issue, described a wild dinner party thrown by director Charles Laughton and producer Paul Gregory to celebrate the completion of *The Night of the Hunter*, in which Mitchum starred.

> Maybe we'd better prepare you all for this, because it's a pretty crazy story, even for a guy who did time in a Hollywood clink on charges of flying too high with Marijuana Airlines.

Mitchum was late for cocktails—delayed by a bottle of Scotch, said *Confidential*—and arrived at Gregory's Santa Monica home just as the butler was announcing dinner. Mitchum grabbed another bottle, which he nursed as he lurched wildly among the guests. Mitchum, who was married, brought a pretty young "dish" to the party. She steered him into the dining room. Then, "a deathly hush fell over the dinner table." Mitchum had taken off all his clothes down to his socks. He picked up a bottle of catsup from the table and spattered himself with it. "This *is* a masquerade party, isn't it?" he asked guests. "Well, I'm a hamburger—well done."

The hamburger was now dancing around the room, splattering the walls and all who came near. The party was as mixed as a chef's salad by this time and what might have been next on the menu is anyone's guess, had not Bob's babe given him a short order. With the calm authority of a gal who knows her stews, as well as 'burgers, she corralled the good-looking hunk of raw beef and persuaded him to put on his duds. She got Bob out and the guests returned, rather nonchalantly, to the main dish.

"It might have taken *your* appetite away, but in Hollywood they're used to guys fried—not French fried, understand, just plain fried."[5]

———————————

The article wasn't really that shocking; drunken shenanigans were Mitchum's stock in trade. Born in Bridgeport, Connecticut, in 1917, Mitchum had been a prankster since his youth. During the Depression years he lived as a hobo, hitching rides on trains and doing odd jobs. At fourteen he was arrested for vagrancy in Savannah and put on a chain gang. He later made a living writing dirty jokes for nightclub acts and worked as an astrologer's assistant. In 1940 he married his high school sweetheart, Dorothy Spence, and moved to Hollywood, where he was hired as an extra.

In 1944 Mitchum signed a contract with the RKO studio and found himself being groomed for B-grade westerns. Mitchum's big break came in 1945 when he was on loan to United Artists, which cast him in an Academy Award–nominated role as a war-weary officer in *The Story of G.I. Joe*. The rugged, sensual, sleepy-eyed actor achieved tremendous success in the half-decade after the war, when he was renowned for his roles in *films noir*, especially his performance as a hard-boiled, stoic private investigator in *Out of the Past* (1947). RKO wanted to find out what made Mitchum so appealing to fans, so it conducted a poll. The survey revealed that audiences liked Mitchum because he was the "most immoral face we ever saw. . . . He suggested sex in an evil sort of way."[6]

In 1948, in news that made world headlines, Mitchum was arrested in Los Angeles for possession of marijuana. Mitchum was convicted and sentenced to sixty days on an "honor farm." It seemed like the end, not only for Mitchum but for the entire film industry. The studios claimed that Mitchum had been framed, and Dore Schary asked the public not to "indict the entire working personnel of 32,000 well-disciplined and clean-living American citizens" on account of Mitchum. Hedda Hopper wrote articles debunking rumors that Hollywood was a hard-partying community. Stars "seldom drink after dinner for the dread fear of a hangover on the long set day," she wrote. It was "soft drinks, tea, and coffee" for "busy movie makers."[7]

After the arrest, RKO and Mitchum worked overtime to salvage the actor's image. Mitchum appeared in the press and in fan magazines, pleading for forgiveness. The press described the scandal as a "career obituary."[8] But two films released after the arrest were box-office hits. Mitchum's career never suffered because he was able to fold the arrest into his rebellious screen image. His career came back bigger than ever.

Between 1949 and 1954, Mitchum starred in over a dozen films for RKO, many of them mediocre action films in which he played cynical, tough-guy roles. In 1954 he caused a sensation when he agreed to pose with Simone Silva, a busty British actress, at the Cannes Film Festival as a publicity stunt for Silva. She appeared in the photo nude from the waist up. Not long before the *Confidential* article, Mitchum was expelled from the set of *Blood Alley* (1955) for throwing the film's transportation manager into San Francisco Bay during a "horseplay incident." Fan magazines assured readers that though Mitchum might have seemed heartless, "careless, indolent, even dissolute," he had a "soft heart and a genuine concern for acting," and was devoted to his wife, Dorothy, and his three young children. When the *Confidential* article came out, *The Night of the Hunter* was pending release. The film starred Mitchum as a criminal posing as a preacher to find money hidden in the home of his former cellmate. His performance was critically acclaimed and considered the finest in Mitchum's career.[9]

According to Hollywood journalist James Bacon, what appeared in *Confidential* was a watered-down version of the story. In reality Mitchum took his penis out, placed it on a serving plate, poured catsup over it, and turned to Laughton and Gregory, who were gay. "Which one of you wants to eat this first?" he asked. The truth was too raunchy for *Confidential*, so they came up with a funnier story.[10] Right after *Confidential* hit newsstands, Mitchum called up Jerry Giesler, who had represented him in the marijuana case.

———————

Jerry Giesler was a renowned attorney who loved and defended Hollywood. Since the 1920s, he had been "lawyer to the stars." During his career Giesler represented almost every noted film celebrity, including Charlie Chaplin, Errol Flynn, Lana Turner, Marilyn Monroe, Louis B. Mayer, John Barrymore, and Joan Crawford. Giesler rose to fame in 1929 when he got an acquittal for theater magnate Alexander Pantages, who was indicted on charges of statutory rape of a seventeen-year-old showgirl. When the director Busby Berkeley, intoxicated, got into a three-car accident on the Pacific Coast Highway near Malibu, killing three, Giesler got him off the hook. Among his most avidly followed cases were his defense of Errol Flynn against statutory rape charges and the defense of Charlie Chaplin on charges of violating the Mann Act. "Get me Giesler" was a Hollywood cliché—"If you're really in a jam, get Jerry Giesler." Conversely, studio wisecracks quipped, "If you've got Giesler, you must really be in a jam."[11]

A mild-mannered, courtly gentleman, Giesler spoke to juries in a soft, high-pitched, squeaky voice. Short, plump, and balding, Giesler had a solemn, doughy face with perfectly round eyes. Impeccably stylish, Giesler wore double-breasted tailored suits, colorful ties, and gleaming suede shoes with pointed toes. Giesler worked out of a plush Wilshire Boulevard office and was fabulously wealthy. His fees were reportedly among the highest ever collected in criminal cases. Warner Brothers contributed $50,000 to Errol Flynn's defense, since it had $3 million worth of unreleased Flynn movies.[12]

Giesler was famous for his meticulous preparation and uncanny skill in handling juries. The court was a stage for Giesler. Initially he presented himself to jurors as passive and avuncular, asking questions in a timid voice. When he got the answers he wanted, he became a grand orator. Once, demonstrating a murder scene, he lay flat on the courtroom floor and delivered his oration from that position. He broke bones in both hands by thumping them on the counsel table. When Giesler defended stripper Lili St. Cyr on an indecent-exposure charge, he concealed his own chubby frame in the sheer fabric that had allegedly covered his client on the night of the arrest, making the jury chuckle so hard that the case was laughed out of court. He kept St. Cyr's black lace panties in his desk drawer as a trophy.[13]

Giesler warned Mitchum that if he sued *Confidential* he'd be subjecting himself to embarrassment, inconvenience, and name-calling. Those concerns had deterred other stars, he said. Mitchum told Giesler he didn't care about any of those things; he wanted to clear his name and put an end to *Confidential*'s gutter journalism. He was suing in the "interests of justice and fair play."[14]

It was risky for Mitchum to sue *Confidential*, since Harrison could come back with more authentic and damaging stories about Mitchum's real-life antics. A lawsuit would only keep the bizarre accusations in the headlines, spreading them to an audience far greater than *Confidential*'s readers. (The *Los Angeles Herald-Express* ran a headline that read, "Mitchum Denies Nude Hamburger Act, Sues. Ask Million; Didn't Douse with Catsup.") One reason Mitchum sued, according to his biographer, was his concern for his wife and children—"the honor and good name of his family," as Mitchum put it. His son Jim had been recently removed from an elite private school because the principal was repulsed by Mitchum's reputation. "The backwash of these sensational stories about Bob is hurting our children," his wife told a reporter. "Jim idolizes his dad, and the other kids keep ribbing him. He's always getting into fights sticking up for Bob."[15]

Giesler was more than happy to help Mitchum. Giesler, who considered himself part of the film industry, had long believed that *Confidential* posed a dire threat to Hollywood and that studio leaders were making a mistake by not taking more concerted action. "It has always been the industry's weakness that it can only see an inch before its nose," he said. Giesler investigated Mitchum's case and told him it was strong. He commended Mitchum on his "guts" and "gumption." On May 9, 1955, Giesler filed a legal complaint in the Santa Monica Superior Court.[16]

The complaint alleged that the *Confidential* article was "completely untrue" and had been published with an intent to "defame and ridicule" Mitchum. Mitchum claimed damage to his "professional reputation as an actor." He and his family had been subjected to "public scandal, embarrassment, disgrace, contempt, and ridicule." Mitchum named as defendants "Charles Jordan"—Jay Breen's pseudonym—along with Harrison, Breen, Rushmore, Govoni, and the magazine itself. Mitchum told the press, "As a member of a generous and honorable profession, and having been awarded by my colleagues the reputation of high professional standard, I feel in return that my action in exposing the attackers of our structure is my duty."[17]

Hollywood hailed Mitchum as a hero. "Robert Mitchum is suing that scandal magazine that has printed so much filth about so many TV and movie stars and Hollywood is rooting for him, hard," wrote columnist Eve Starr. "Most stars prefer to let such stories just lie there and be forgotten, knowing that to sue means that the whole thing will be spread all over the newspapers. If he wins (and he has Jerry Giesler, one of the country's smartest lawyers, working for him) he might just put the sheet out of business. Which would be good riddance." A few worried that the suit would backfire. "Bob Mitchum's action in suing *Confidential* magazine is not too wise in my opinion. . . . All his move does is create more publicity for the magazine," wrote a columnist for the *Los Angeles Mirror-News*. "Numerous infuriated stars in the past have considered suing the magazine. But wiser heads have prevailed." Harrison told the press smugly that he would "stand on the facts" of the story. "*Confidential* feels Mitchum is entitled to his day in court and will be happy to meet him there," he said. "I think Mitchum will be sorry he ever wanted to see us in court."[18]

On June 8, 1955, *Confidential* sought to quash Mitchum's suit. Harrison's California lawyer H. L. Birnbaum filed a motion for dismissal, saying that *Confidential* had never done business in California and had no property or assets in the state. Harrison, in an affidavit, alleged that he sold his entire print run to a wholesaler, which sold it to newsstands and other distributors, shifting the burden of defense to his California distributors. Giesler described this as a "subterfuge"—"a slick trick of selling the right of distribution in New York and thus claim[ing] immunity in any other state for the widespread publication of the magazine." A few weeks later, Giesler asked Judge Orlando Rhodes for permission to travel to New York to take testimony from Harrison and other *Confidential* staff.[19]

Giesler had just found out that HRI was a branch of *Confidential*. An anonymous caller had tipped him off. Giesler knew that if he could prove HRI was linked to *Confidential* it would force the magazine to trial in California courts. Giesler was determined to bring the suit in California, rather than New York, where court dockets were delayed for more than three years and the law was more favorable to publishers. Giesler didn't get around to making the trip to New York until late January 1956. When Giesler interviewed Harrison, he found him "affable, agreeable, and courteous." Harrison admitted to Giesler that HRI existed and that he bought information from it, but he denied that it had anything to do with *Confidential* or that he owned any part of it.[20]

Mitchum used the lawsuit not only to attack *Confidential* but also to promote his bad-boy image. Publicists helped him, setting up interviews and planting stories. In June 1955, a *New York Times* article brought up "recent news stories [about] Mr. Mitchum bringing suit against a magazine as a result of a story it printed about him." "Look," he said to the *Times* reporter, "I've been in scrapes." *Confidential* could have written about them and "had a germ of the truth, but instead they dreamed up a complete fabrication. No truth whatsoever. Nothing. . . . I've got kids in school. What about them? What am I supposed to do? Just sit still and let these guys kick me in the face?" Later that year a nationally syndicated feature story appeared, titled "This Man Mitchum." Mitchum was quoted in the article as saying that he sued *Confidential* because he felt "so scandalous a publication should be fought by everyone it scandalizes." The article quoted several of Mitchum's friends, who said the *Confidential* suit was evidence of Mitchum's fighting spirit. "Underneath all that toughness he's a crusader—he loves to fight for a principle," said an acquaintance. Mitchum "likes to help people."[21]

Photoplay did a lengthy feature on Mitchum. "For many months, scandal magazines have victimized the top stars of Hollywood. Bob Mitchum believes that the only way to stop this invective is to fight back as he is doing." "I think the general attitude was that most stars preferred to ignore the whole thing rather than get tangled up in a dirty court fight," Mitchum told the magazine. "Some of the stories have been just too ridiculous and far-fetched, and I guess they didn't want to dignify them even to the extent of making a formal denial. . . . But personally . . . I think it's a case of fighting for your honor and good name. . . . They shouldn't be allowed to get away with it. They shouldn't be allowed to get rich by printing lies and smut."

"In the past, you remember, I've had my troubles. I've made my mistakes. . . . The law has made me pay the penalty when I was in the wrong, and that's as it should be. But that was a long time ago. Ever since, I have lived with my family as a decent, moral citizen. And now I expect the law to work both ways. Now I'm on the right side of the fence, and I expect the law to protect me from the wrongs of others."[22]

———————

Mitchum and Giesler opened the floodgates. Stars were emboldened, and a flurry of lawsuits followed.

In June 1955, Errol Flynn sued *Confidential* for libel, asking $1,000,000 in damages.[23] The lawsuit was based on an article alleging that Flynn spent his wedding night with a prostitute. *Confidential* also described a "two-way mirror" in his home that he used at his infamous parties, "dinner parties that Emily Post could chew on for a lifetime. His favorite function of this type spotlighted pressed duck on the table and fresh squabs around it. The duck he presumably got from his butcher. The quails were invariably vice dollies, culled from long lists he kept in an assortment of little black books."

Flynn had a "majestic bedroom" that he loaned out to his friends, including his buddy Bruce Cabot, Francesca De Scaffa's former husband. In it was a massive white bed with red velvet covers, a white marble floor, a grand piano, and tall red candles. Friends who borrowed the bedroom didn't know that directly overhead he had installed a trap door, concealed by a rug. At the push of a button, the door slid away to reveal a two-foot-square slab of trick glass. With the lights out, "it was a plain window through which viewers got 50-yard-line ganders at the sport below." One night Flynn got drunk and told Cabot about it. Enraged, Cabot tricked Flynn into using the bedroom. With a crowd of guests present, he slid back the trap door. "It must have been a whizzer. Some of the ladies present uttered shrill screams after peering through this modern looking-glass for only 30 seconds. Several had to be helped downstairs to the bar for quick restoratives," wrote *Confidential*.[24]

Flynn was mortified. According to his biographer, he "was intentionally made to appear as a scoundrel," and he felt the image upset his children. "Not that I have been a paragon of the conventionalities. I have not, and the world knows it. I acknowledge my own peccadilloes . . . but I resented such a gross mismanipulation of the legend around me," Flynn wrote in his autobiography. In fact, most of the allegations were true, and Flynn contested only the claim that he'd slept with a prostitute on his wedding night.[25]

The other scandal magazines were also hit with libel suits. Humphrey Bogart sued *Rave* magazine for $1 million over an article titled "Pigs in Paris," in which *Rave* had written: "In any competition for superlative swinishness, Mr. Bogart would take the blue ribbon. Bogey has emptied most of the good restaurants in Paris and it would give the proprietors rare satisfaction to hang a placard around the Bogart neck with one word printed on it: Cochon. Cochon means pig." Bogart read it and called his lawyer, Martin Craig. "Bogey, we're rich. We'll sue 'em for nine billion dollars," Craig said. They filed suit but discovered *Rave*'s publisher didn't have any money. They called *Rave*'s editor in New York. Within half an hour he agreed to publish a retraction and to never use Bogart's name again.[26]

James Mason sued *Rave* over "Mr. and Mrs. Mason—Marriage for Three," which alleged that the actor and his wife had a threesome relationship with her ex-husband. *Rave* also went after their six-year-old daughter, calling her one of the "most obnoxious pests ever to roost in Cuckooland," a euphemism for Hollywood. Mason asked for damages of $1,199,000. *Rave* settled, agreeing to print a retraction and a token $1,000 in monthly installments of $100. The publisher couldn't afford any more. "The settlement was not large," Mason's attorney said. "But it represented a tremendous victory for Hollywood people and a sign that the trend toward destroying character must stop."[27]

Instead of suing *Rave*, Grace Kelly's family took more direct action. Its article "She-Wolf Deluxe" listed several actors whose marriages she'd allegedly broken up. When her father, a wealthy Philadelphia contractor, learned that *Rave*'s editor didn't have a dime, he and Grace's brother went to the magazine's office, turned it upside down, and beat up the editor.[28]

———————

The next celebrity to sue *Confidential* wasn't an actor, but a socialite—tobacco heiress Doris Duke, who sued over an article in the May 1955 issue, "Doris Duke and Her African Prince." Represented by Giesler, Duke sought $3 million from *Confidential*.[29]

Duke, known as the "richest woman in the world," had inherited an incredible fortune from her father, Buck Duke, president of the American Tobacco Company. A mainstay of society gossip columns since the 1930s, Doris Duke was an eccentric, often reviled figure whose wealth and lavish lifestyle stood out in stark contrast to poverty and suffering in the Great Depression. Duke married and divorced twice, first to diplomat and politician James Cromwell in 1935 and then to Porfirio Rubirosa, a Dominican playboy and diplomat. Both marriages were short and tumultuous.[30]

Duke spent much of her time travelling internationally and between her many homes, including her palace Shangri La in Honolulu, and Falcon Lair, Rudolph Valentino's former mansion in Hollywood. Like many wealthy Los Angelenos in the early 1950s, Duke became a devotee of Eastern religion. She followed a bearded Hindu yogi name Rao, who ministered to a number of stars. Duke practiced yoga and meditation daily, followed a yogic diet, and even washed dishes in her teacher's tiny Hollywood bungalow apartment. Almost as quickly as he arrived, Rao left the country with several signed blank checks given to him by Duke.

Confidential alleged that Duke had recently gotten hooked on another mystic healer: "Prince David Madupe Mudge Paris, a 54-year-old, five-foot, brown-skinned royalist who claims his right to his title because his father was King of a tribe on Africa's Gold Coast." Madupe had allegedly entered the country illegally by jumping ship in New York. Down on his luck, Madupe was trying to make a living by lecturing on mysticism to women's clubs around Hollywood. Duke sought him out to help her with her insomnia. Although columnists reported that Duke was involved in a tempestuous affair with screen idol Gilbert Roland, in reality she was so unhappy that she was on a steady diet of sleeping pills.[31]

Madupe—known in the press as "Prince Modupe"—was a well-known figure in the entertainment world. A notorious con man who had come to Hollywood in the 1930s, Madupe described himself as a "Nigerian born mission-educated scion of African royalty." Madupe appeared at the Chicago World's Fair in 1933 as a musical performer. He then went to Southern California with a troupe of "drum-beating, chanting Africans," and was hired as a technical advisor for several films on Africa, including *Tarzan Escapes*. By the late 1940s, his expertise was no longer in demand in Hollywood, and he tried out several business schemes, including a food stand called "Prince Modupe's Old Southern Barbecue." Duke got acquainted with Madupe in 1951 when she helped him finance an unsuccessful venture called "Modupe Foods."[32]

"Madupe arrived at Falcon's Lair with his unique prescription for her insomnia," wrote *Confidential*. "He immediately started the tobacco tootsie on a course of involved breathing exercises, broken by sessions in African voodoo dancing." *Confidential* alleged that Madupe was just one of many black men with whom Duke had kept company. "Her real introduction to colored companions dates . . . [back to] 1937 . . . when she took private tap dancing lessons from the late Bill 'Bojangles' Robinson."

"Madupe's training courses were strictly night-time events and the Prince seldom left Duke's Lair before four or five in the morning," *Confidential* explained. "On top of that, Doris apparently valued his soothing touch so much she left standing orders to the help that she was to be awakened by no one but him." The Prince didn't draw a regular paycheck, but was permitted to bring his household bills to Duke. His ready cash "depended on the occasional ten spots Doris slipped him after a particularly rewarding breathing session." Things got ugly when Madupe attempted to extort Duke. "Unlike a gentleman—much less a Prince—he had tape-recorded their fancier ballets and suggested that they might make pretty fancy diversion, if distributed wholesale. Furthermore, he added, he'd kept diaries of his patient's progress and his sprightly treatment, which might be turned into a volume of interest to thousands—including non-medical researchers." Duke promptly contacted her arsenal of private detectives, who lured Madupe to Mexico, where he was denied reentry into the United States. According to biographer Stephanie Mansfield, Duke's friends recalled Duke showing up to social events with Madupe, whom she referred to as "His Highness," and believed the *Confidential* story was true.[33]

Duke's complaint, filed in Santa Monica Superior Court against Harrison, Rushmore, and "Grant Peters," purported author, asserted that the story depicted Duke as "carrying on a relationship with a brown-skinned individual in a manner of intimate relationship" that would imply an "intimacy between the parties" and "indecent conduct." The article was intended to bring her into "public discredit and ridicule and to cause the public to hold [her] in contempt," causing her "mental anguish, shame, and humiliation." Giesler told the press that the purpose of the lawsuit was not only to defend Duke's good name against "ugly, unfounded, and scurrilous attacks made upon her" but also to "discourage this magazine and others of its ilk from making similar unfounded attacks against innocent people." Duke would donate any damages collected to worthy charities.[34]

Duke's lawsuit provoked a strong reaction from columnist Inez Robb of the United Features Syndicate. Described as a "hell-kitten" and "stringent-tongued newspaperwoman" with large "Irish blue eyes," Robb, whose column appeared in 140 papers, was a household name in the 1950s. Robb wrote in her July 22, 1955, column: "Miss Doris Duke, who may or may not be 'the richest girl in the world' . . . has just struck a blow for liberty, freedom and decency by filing a libel action . . . against the most putrid of the so-called 'expose' magazines now defiling the newsstands."

Let us hope she not only collects, but that she is also awarded attorneys' fees and costs in the sum of another million or so. But above all, let us hope that the gutter journalists or hacks responsible draw stiff jail or penitentiary sentences. They are in the same category as the purveyors of pornography via cartoon and comic books.

What is really disturbing is the discovery that [in] the United States of America, despite free public education and a high literacy rate . . . so many morons . . . will support these gamy magazines. No normal person, with a shred of self-respect, would read the slime . . . so the only conclusion possible is that there is either an appalling number of citizens who are either mental defectives, who move their lips when they read, or moral defectives who lick their lips over boudoir revelations.

In a way, I am sorry Miss Duke is suing. I am sorry that, instead, she didn't organize an old-fashioned vigilante party and horsewhip the shabby crew responsible for this verbal assault. A cat-o'-nine tails speaks a powerful language that might even penetrate the elephant hide and conscience of these lice.[35]

Within a week, *Confidential*'s lawyers filed a $9 million libel suit against Robb, the *New York World-Telegram and Sun*, and the United Feature Syndicate. *Confidential* alleged that Robb's column injured it "in the management of its business, in its integrity, credit, and reputation," and the "good name, fame, credit, and reputation" of the magazine and its officials. "Switch: *Confidential* is suing United Features, Inez Robb, and the New York *World Telegram*," Mike Connolly quipped in the *Hollywood Reporter*. *Time* magazine, commenting on the lawsuit, noted that Robb was "properly unworried." "I'm eating and sleeping normally," she said.[36]

16 | FREEDOM OF THE PRESS

THERE WAS ONE MORE libel suit against *Confidential* that summer, brought by actress Lizabeth Scott.

In 1947 Scott had been dubbed the "most promising new face" in Hollywood. A former fashion model and stage actress from Scranton, Pennsylvania, Scott had made her name playing hard-boiled femmes fatale in *films noir*. Scott had a sultry, smoldering look, with green eyes, cascading blonde hair, and a raw, husky voice. Brought to Hollywood by producer Hal Wallis in the early 1940s, Scott made eighteen movies in nine years, four of them in 1947. Among her best-known films were *The Strange Love of Martha Ivers* (1946) and *Dead Reckoning* (1947).

In her first few years in Hollywood, movie columns and fan magazines aggressively promoted her. But by the early 1950s, her career was in steep decline, the result of studio mismanagement and the decline of the *film noir* genre. She was let go from her Paramount contract in 1954.[1]

Confidential pegged Scott as a client of a notorious L.A. prostitution ring. "The vice cops *expected* to find a few big name customers when they grabbed the date book of a trio of Hollywood jezebels," *Confidential* reported in June 1955. "But even *their* cast-iron nerves got a jolt when they got to the 'S's'!"[2]

In "Why Was Lizabeth Scott's Name in the Call Girls' Call Book?" by "Matt Williams"—Howard Rushmore—*Confidential* described a vice raid that started when two detectives broke down the back door of a swanky four-story Los Angeles home. Sandra Ann Betts, Joyce Hicks, and a third woman were arrested for prostitution. "But what many an editor buried on page five or even tossed in his waste basket would have made banner headlines—coast to coast—had the whole story come out," *Confidential* wrote. The detectives found the women's black books, listing their "near, dear, and cash-on-the-line friends." In those pages were a line up of movie luminaries which "would have had even blasé Hollywood gasping," including actors Lou Holtz, George Jessel, and George Raft. "But what stopped men from the vice squad cold was an entry on the 'S' pages . . . Scott, Lizabeth." *Confidential* listed Scott's phone numbers: HO 2-0064, BR 2-6111. According to *Confidential*, the cops didn't believe it until they checked out the phone numbers and found that they really belonged to her.

Scott was a "strange girl, even for Hollywood," *Confidential* wrote. "She never married, never even got close." That alone would have been suspicious, *Confidential* said, but Scott raised speculation even further with an interview she gave to columnist Sidney Skolsky in which she confided that she wore male cologne, slept in men's pajamas, and hated frilly, feminine dresses.

The end of the article went in for the kill. "Liz, according to the grapevine buzz, was taking up almost exclusively with Hollywood's weird society of baritone babes. She was seldom seen in the well-known after dark spots, but those who did catch a glimpse of 'Scotty' . . . reported spotting her from time to time in off-color joints that were favorite hangouts for movieland's twilight set. In recent years, Scotty's almost non-existent screen career has allowed her to roam further afield. . . . On one jaunt to Europe . . . she headed straight for Paris' Left Bank, where she took up with Frede, that city's most notorious Lesbian queen and the operator of a night club devoted exclusively to entertaining deviates like herself.

"Insiders began putting together the pieces of the puzzle that was Lizabeth Scott and it didn't take them long to get the answer. They know the shocking fact that more than one of the screen's top glamour girls are listed in the little black book kept by Hollywood prostitutes. And unlike Los Angeles' vice cops, the insiders don't have to ask what the monickers of such seductive females are doing in such surroundings. They've known for years . . . Now you do, too."[3]

It's unclear whether Scott was actually in the "call girls' call book," but when *Confidential* said she had lesbian relationships, it was probably right.

Scott and her publicists weren't good at concealing her sexual orientation. She often complained to the press about the dresses and hairstyles Paramount made her wear for screen tests, and portrayed herself as an assertive woman who had no time for romance and believed that a woman should "rebel." Fan magazines depicted her as a tomboy, fishing, playing basketball, and wearing slacks. With a wink, perhaps, to the Hollywood insider, Hedda Hopper wrote in 1946 that Scott's "closets are jammed with cotton blouses, checked gingham skirts, straw slippers, bandana scarves—gay, unglamorous rags."[4]

Scott occasionally tried to promote a more feminine image, but her efforts were half-hearted. In 1949, in "Marriage on her Mind," in *Modern Screen*, she dispelled rumors that she was uninterested in men. In a 1953 interview with New York columnist Mel Heimer she talked about her home and said it would be nice to have a husband in the house. She told reporters that she "vetoed" the "mannish style" of French women. "I'll go halfway on the mannish look. If a woman appears mannish below the neck, her face and hair should be feminine. If she wants to wear a short haircut that looks like a man's, her clothes should be feminine."[5]

Scott's career decline was devastating; she was only in her early thirties. She became depressed, anxious, and isolated. A newspaper reported in 1953 that "Lizabeth Scott's pals are worried about her jumpy nerves and her yen for seclusion." Right before the *Confidential* article came out, a columnist noted that "Lizabeth Scott's a puzzlement to friends and former associates. . . . More Garbo-ish for real than any other star in Movietown these days." She was so desperate to keep her career alive that she embarked on obvious publicity stunts, such as constantly changing her hairstyle to attract media attention.[6]

There's no question Scott was outraged by the *Confidential* article, coming at a time when she was already vulnerable. Her anger and humiliation led her to seek out Giesler and file suit. At the same time, Scott also saw a lawsuit as a publicity ploy, a way to keep her name in the papers. That was a mistake.

In July 1955, Scott, represented by Giesler, sued *Confidential* for $2.5 million. Giesler alleged that the article depicted her "in word and in picture" as being guilty of "highly offensive, illegal, and immoral conduct with young women." The story was "willfully, wrongfully, maliciously, and completely without truth." Scott's legal complaint alleged that the article "would have a natural tendency to hold plaintiff up to contempt and ridicule. . . . The viciousness of the completely unfounded and untruthful accusation in [the] article . . . have exposed plaintiff to public scandal, embarrassment, disgrace, contempt, . . . and have caused her to suffer great mental anguish, shame, and humiliation."[7]

It's been said that Scott's career was destroyed by *Confidential*. Film historians and even the *New York Times* in its obituary reported that the *Confidential* story was "ruinous." Although Scott had several roles on TV, she made only three more movies after the *Confidential* article, two in 1957 and one in 1972. While *Confidential* didn't help Scott's career, the allegation that it killed her stardom isn't entirely true. Her career was already on the decline and probably would have failed even if the magazine never targeted her. *Confidential* did, however, put the final nail in the coffin.[8]

The lawsuit didn't have the effect Scott hoped. It kept her name in the papers, but the publicity was of the worst kind. Had she ignored the story, as Marlene Dietrich did, the storm might have blown over. Unlike Mitchum or Doris Duke, who came off as crusaders, Scott wasn't able to spin the attack in her favor. *Confidential*'s accusations were too damaging; Scott hadn't done enough to show the public that the story was false. Millions who never saw *Confidential* opened newspapers to read that Lizabeth Scott had been accused of being a lesbian and was denying it. The reaction was unsympathetic.

In the midst of the libel suits, one lone defender of *Confidential* came out of the woodwork: the American Civil Liberties Union, the nation's foremost civil liberties organization. Since the 1920s, the ACLU had been active in campaigns to expand freedom of speech and the rights of the press. It successfully fought censorship of allegedly obscene books "banned in Boston" in the 1920s, the ban on James Joyce's *Ulysses*, restrictions on birth control literature, and film censorship laws.[9]

With intensified efforts to ban books and films in the 1950s, the national ACLU and its local chapters were involved in a flurry of activity. Along with organizations such as the Authors League of America, the American Newspaper Publishers Association, and the American Library Association, the ACLU denounced the "outbreak of censorship of paper-bound books and other media."[10] The ACLU opposed government bans on literature and film as unconstitutional "prior restraints."

Since the 1930s, it had been a basic principle of constitutional law that the First Amendment prohibits prior restraints. A prior restraint is an official restriction imposed on speech before publication. The rule against prior restraints, derived from William Blackstone's commentaries on the English common law, became a First Amendment requirement in *Near v. Minnesota* (1931). In *Near*, the U.S. Supreme Court struck down a Minnesota law that prohibited the publication of a "malicious, scandalous, and defamatory newspaper, magazine, or other periodical." The law provided that all such "nuisances" could be banned or enjoined from further publication. The majority in *Near* characterized the Minnesota law as a prior restraint, "the essence of censorship." The "chief purpose" of freedom of the press, it declared, is to "prevent previous restraints upon publications."[11]

Prior restraints were different from "subsequent punishments"—criminal or civil penalties imposed on speakers after the fact. The difference between subsequent punishments and prior restraints was that material subject to a prior restraint never reached the public and the "marketplace of ideas." Subsequent punishments were issued after publication, and the speaker had a right to due process and a jury trial. The ACLU wasn't opposed to subsequent punishments, including liability for obscenity and libel, but believed they should be issued narrowly and cautiously. It supported a limited definition of obscenity, and exceptions in libel law for reporting "matters of public concern." The ACLU also opposed what it described as "pressure group censorship"—the efforts of "citizens' committees" and other groups to coerce booksellers and newsdealers to stop selling controversial material.[12]

The ACLU's liberal position was opposed by conservative moralists who sought to stem the tide of "indecent" literature and argued that the First Amendment didn't protect obscenity and "smut." The definition of obscenity, and whether freedom of the press protected obscenity and pornography, were contested issues; the Supreme Court hadn't yet ruled on them. The ACLU's position was left of center, but it was not unpopular. In the wake of Nazi atrocities during the war, and the ongoing repression of free expression in communist countries, much of the public favored strong free speech rights, and there was a liberalizing trend in the courts. Harrison never gave a whit about civil liberties, but with the ACLU's involvement in *Confidential*'s struggles, he became embroiled in the decade's fierce battles over freedom of speech and press.

ACLU leaders made clear that they didn't endorse *Confidential*. At the same time, the methods *Confidential*'s enemies were using to silence the magazine seemed to be egregious violations of free speech principles. Outraged by Inez Robb's endorsement of "horsewhipping" and vigilante action against *Confidential*, ACLU leaders sent an angry letter to Robb's editor at the *New York World-Telegram and Sun*. "We do not take issue with Miss Robb's criticisms of the [*Confidential*] articles, which is not within the scope of a civil liberties organization. . . . However, we . . . are shocked at Miss Robb's position. At the heart of the democratic process lies the fundamental guarantee of free speech. *Confidential* should be able to write what it wishes about an individual. If it is defamatory, then there is a legal weapon to deal with such language—a [defamation] action heard in court. We must not resort to lynch law to curb free speech as Miss Robb suggests. That is the totalitarian way. The democratic way of meeting abusive speech is through the persuasiveness of free speech itself, and not 'horse whipping.'"[13]

The ACLU became even more alarmed when it got word of Giesler's campaign to pass laws against *Confidential*. Knowing the libel suits were unlikely to succeed, Giesler pushed for state and federal laws to ban the scandal magazines. "It is our hope that some government agency will step in and put a stop to the publication and distribution of such scandal sheets," he told the press in July 1955. Giesler lobbied the California legislature for a law that would change jurisdictional rules so that out-of-state defendants like *Confidential* could be sued in California. He also believed the federal government could intervene. In a television interview in Los Angeles that summer, he told host George Putnam, "I am strongly convinced that there should be a change of legislation in this country and it's got to be done and probably only in Washington." He believed that Congress could pass a law prohibiting the interstate passage of "salacious material of that particular type."[14]

In July, Giesler went to Washington to persuade Congress to enact "anti-scandal" legislation to "ban publication of sin and sex expose magazines." Though he realized the difficulty of a legislative ban as a "prior restraint," he urged the formation of a Congressional committee to stop publication of "vicious and slanderous magazines." He said he hoped his intentions to "fight

[*Confidential*] to the limit" would "wake up Hollywood and inspire the film industry to take concerted action to put these magazines out of business."[15]

Shortly after, the conservative, syndicated newspaper columnist and ACLU member Victor Lasky wrote to Patrick Murphy Malin, head of the ACLU, warning him of "recent statements attributed to Jerry Giesler . . . lobbying for federal legislation aimed at banning magazines like *Confidential*." "Giesler is . . . threatening to persuade Congress to enact legislation which would constitute a body blow to the nation's free press," he wrote. He was concerned that "a person of Mr. Giesler's eminence could well persuade Congress to ban publications of the expose variety." "As you and other leaders of the American Civil Liberties Union well know, the defense of civil liberties often requires the defense of persons whose nonconforming activities may not be generally popular."[16]

Lasky was especially disturbed by a conversation he had with Irving Ferman, director of the ACLU's Washington office. Ferman—an avid reader of *Confidential*—tried to buy *Confidential* from his local newsstand and found it was no longer sold there. A "citizens' group" had approached the owner and threatened a boycott if it continued to sell *Confidential*. "As Irving Ferman's experience attests, citizens' groups apparently have begun to exert 'book burning' pressure aimed at preventing sales of *Confidential*," Lasky wrote. "Unlike Irving, I am no devotee of *Confidential*, but like Irving, I am troubled by some of the methods being employed by well-meaning citizens to put *Confidential* out of business. Some of these activities could well do damage to the Constitutional guarantee of freedom of the press. . . . The situation, now developing, is not yet out of hand," he concluded. "However, the American Civil Liberties Union should act to close the stable door, before the horse is stolen." Malin gave the letter to ACLU Assistant Director Alan Reitman and proposed writing an "open letter to Giesler, presenting our view on pressure group censorship and prior restraint."[17]

The libel suits remained an uphill battle. After taking Harrison's depositions and becoming certain about the connection between *Confidential* and HRI, Giesler added the Meades as codefendants in the Scott, Duke, and Mitchum cases. In court, Hollywood attorney Arthur Crowley, representing the Meades, alleged that HRI was completely separate from *Confidential* and that his clients had nothing to do with the stories. *Confidential* was just one of the magazines serviced by HRI, he said, and HRI wasn't the only source of *Confidential*'s material.[18]

In March 1956, Superior Court Judge Leon David quashed Lizabeth Scott's libel suit because *Confidential* had no California representatives. Judge Rhodes granted the motion to quash in the Mitchum case. Giesler dismissed the Mitchum, Scott, and Duke lawsuits and said he would refile them in New York.[19]

As Giesler hoped, his efforts spurred Hollywood to take action against *Confidential*. By the end of 1955, Dore Schary had become vocal about the need for "an open declaration of war." "Short of becoming involved in a conspiracy ourselves, I believe we should take every step toward ending these smears," he told the press. "The trouble up to now . . . was we didn't know what the hell to do. We felt a little lost. Thank God a few courageous individuals have shown us what can be done." Lou Greenspan, executive secretary of the Motion Picture Industry Council, told the press that he was ready for "an open fight with the expose publishers. . . . My organization, 20,000 movie people from laborers to actors, wants the same thing."[20]

"At first Hollywood tried to ignore the problem. We didn't want to compound the publicity. But then we learned that silence isn't golden anymore. Today if you don't answer, you lose by default," Greenspan said. "I'm a Biblical scholar. I have always believed you should turn the other cheek. So we turned the other cheek . . . and what happened? We got pasted right in the face. So now we're back to the Mosaic law—an eye for an eye! That's our stand. From now on we fight."[21]

17 | THE POST OFFICE

STUDIO LEADERS CAME UP with a new strategy to deal with *Confidential.* In August 1955 several studio heads and MPAA head Eric Johnston made "frantic calls" to the postmaster general's office in Washington, DC, asking him to revoke *Confidential's* mailing privileges. For decades, this had been a tried-and-true method for getting controversial publications out of circulation: denying their right to circulate in the mails, or to receive reduced-rate, second-class mailing privileges. "Unless they take away that bastard Harrison's mailing privileges, this industry is done for," one movie producer said to Postmaster General Arthur Summerfield.[1]

Under the Comstock Act of 1873, the postmaster general had the power to prohibit "obscene" or "immoral" publications from the mails. The law was enforced one of two ways, through either criminal sanctions or administrative actions. Under administrative actions, so-called mailability proceedings, the postmaster general had the authority to declare material "nonmailable" and to refuse to deliver it. Criminal prosecution for sending obscene matter, which resulted in fines and jail time, was the "ultimate weapon," reserved for serious offenders and within the discretion of the Department of Justice. The Post Office preferred administrative actions to criminal trials because they were less time consuming and cumbersome. Under a criminal prosecution, a trial took place after distribution of the material, and the publisher

184

had the right to have a jury determine whether the publication was obscene. Under the administrative action, the material was stopped before it was circulated, and only the Post Office authorities could determine whether it was obscene.[2]

When the postmaster general concluded that a publication was obscene, he notified local postmasters not to carry it in the mail. The sender was alerted and given a short time to contact the United States Post Office Department, the predecessor of the current United States Postal Service. If the mailer protested, he was permitted to argue only to the Post Office lawyers who had decided against him in the first place, and there was no appeal to any higher authority.[3]

In 1945 the United States Court of Appeals for the District of Columbia Circuit deemed this practice illegal. The court held that before the mailing privilege was suspended, the Post Office Department had to give the mailer an opportunity to have a formal hearing before an adjudicator who hadn't already decided the case against the mailer. The Post Office ignored the decision. Then, a year later, Congress adopted the Administrative Procedures Act, which required that any agency determination that affected the rights of citizens had to be preceded by a hearing, with notice to the parties and opportunity to present evidence and cross-examine witnesses, and a right to appeal to the courts. The Post Office refused to apply the Act to postal proceedings, claiming that if it applied, every "disappointed purveyor of obscenity" could force them to undergo a time-consuming, expensive hearing, and that if the material could still be mailed while a hearing was under way, the effectiveness of a mail ban would be undercut.[4]

The Comstock Act never specifically defined "obscene" material, and the postmaster general had broad discretion to determine what was obscene or "immoral." In 1925 Postmaster General Harry New reported that the department had applied the postal obscenity statute so strictly that several "erotic and sensational magazines" had been "forced to completely alter the character of their publications." In the 1940s, works suppressed by the Post Office included books by Ernest Hemingway, Margaret Mead, and Sigmund Freud; crime and detective magazines; "magazines for men" such as *Esquire* and *Playboy*; and cheesecake and girlie magazines, including Harrison's magazines.[5]

In the early 1950s, the conservative, hypervigilant postmaster general Arthur Summerfield announced a "clean up the mails" campaign "designed to block a rising tide of obscene books, magazines, and similar material." Summerfield claimed that his staff had been recently confronted by a 73 percent increase in "pornographic magazines and books," and that the Post Office Department was receiving seven hundred letters a day from parents protesting the "corrupting of their children" and demanding that the Post Office take action. Summerfield believed that material should be barred from the mails if it violated the "ordinary standard of common decency of average representative citizens," and that "abysmal ignorance" was displayed by those who cried "censorship" when risqué material was banned from the mail. Summerfield "regarded his fight against obscenity as one of the three most significant efforts of his . . . administration," and viewed obscenity as "one of the most serious moral and social problems in the United States."[6]

On August 27, 1955, Summerfield issued a "withhold from dispatch" order barring the November edition of *Confidential* from the mail. The order instructed the postmaster at Mount Morris, Illinois, where the magazine was printed, to halt distribution and to send copies to the Post Office Department in Washington for examination. The Mount Morris postmaster sent a letter to the head of the Kable Printing Company: "Dear Sir, We have been instructed by the Solicitor not to dispatch any copies of *Confidential* until sample copies have been submitted to that office for examination and advice as to their mailability. Very truly yours, V. F. Shaver, Postmaster."[7]

The Solicitor of the Post Office Department said his office had received hundreds of complaints from the public about *Confidential*—from "concerned citizens" alleging that the magazine was "objectionable," as well as urgent calls from Hollywood executives. The ACLU believed the order was issued "as a result of pressure from the movie capital." No one in the Post Office Department had seen a copy of the November edition before issuing the order. The department made no official announcement of the order and never offered Harrison a hearing to contest it.[8]

As soon as *Confidential* received the letter from the postmaster, the lawyers called the solicitor's office for an explanation. According to the solicitor, the "objectionable" material included "a racy description of a stripteaser's gyrations, and a cheesecake photograph of Hollywood starlet Terry Moore." The Terry Moore photo was in fact quite naughty. When Moore was in Istanbul on a junket put on by Conrad Hilton to celebrate the opening of the Hilton Istanbul Bosphorus, she was photographed for the Turkish daily newspaper *Milliyet*. The photo showed her with her knees drawn up and her skirt awry. It was an "art study" that had been slightly retouched, but not enough to obstruct the view of her crotch. The picture was described in tabloids and newspapers around the world, but "not even the sassiest tabloids allowed their subscribers a peek at the picture," wrote *Confidential*. *Confidential* printed the picture with a panel over her crotch: "This panel covers what Terry's dress didn't."[9]

Several days later, Harrison was advised that the "withhold from dispatch" order was being suspended for the November *Confidential*. Summerfield's order didn't reach Mount Morris until nearly all of the issue had been mailed; only fifteen thousand copies were impounded, but these were later released since the bulk of the November copies were in the mail. The order, however, would remain effective as to all future issues, the Post Office said. No issue of *Confidential* could be sent in the mail unless and until the Post Office Department read it and concluded that it contained nothing "improper."[10]

Harrison called on the famed criminal defense lawyer Edward Bennett Williams. A noted civil libertarian, ACLU member, and defender of free speech, Williams had recently represented Joseph McCarthy in his Senate censure hearings. Described as "one of the brightest and most ingenious legal minds now operative," Williams was on his way to establishing a reputation as the nation's hottest young lawyer. Six foot one and 204 pounds, "blond and looking as innocent as a young Jesuit," Williams wore faultlessly tailored clothes, had wavy brown hair, penetrating gray-green eyes, a "boyishly winning" smile, and an air of confidence and calm. "Even when pacing before a jury box he tends to talk with a disarming and persuasive matter-of-factness," noted *Life* magazine. "Like most good trial lawyers, . . . he has an actor's gift of communicating emotion." In 1953 he conducted the first successful libel action ever brought against political columnist Drew Pearson and got a $50,000 judgment for his client, former Assistant Attorney General Norman Littell. Williams went on to win mobster Frank Costello a twenty-month release from a prison sentence for tax evasion.[11]

Williams and Harrison's lawyer Daniel Ross filed suit against Postmaster General Summerfield in the US District Court for the District of Columbia, claiming the order against *Confidential* was a "clear violation of the Constitution." *Confidential* asked the court to enjoin the postmaster general from continuing his order and that the court enter a declaratory judgment holding the order null and void. They alleged that the order was "arbitrary and capricious" and violated the Administrative Procedures Act. It violated the First Amendment and the Fifth Amendment because it didn't tell *Confidential* it was issuing the order, which was issued after complaints from "anonymous informers," failed to hold hearings, and failed to give grounds for holding up the mailing. The Post Office refused to state the nature of the complaints, and no one from the Post Office had even seen the November issue before it was banned. "Since 1952 *Confidential*'s publisher has expended substantial sums of money in carefully building up among the American public a valuable reputation and goodwill for impartial, objective, and fearless reporting of newsworthy events, all of which constitutes a substantial asset of plaintiff's business," read *Confidential*'s complaint. "There is nothing obscene, indecent, or otherwise objectionable in the magazine."[12]

Williams told Harrison to meet him in the courtroom on the day of the hearing. According to Tom Wadden, Williams's law associate, Harrison had reservations about hiring Williams, who was thirty-five but looked much younger. Harrison traveled from New York to Washington and found his way to the federal courthouse. He went to the courtroom and waited a few minutes, but there was no sign of Williams. Harrison said, "Goddammit, I hired this kid down here. And he's so young and wet behind the ears that he doesn't even know how to find the courtroom." It turned out Harrison was in the wrong courtroom.[13]

"The First Amendment guarantees one thing minimally, and that is freedom from previous restraint, freedom from prior censorship," Williams told the court. "It seemed to me that the action of the Post Office Department constituted a shocking abridgement of freedom of expression . . . one that could set a most dangerous precedent. If the Postmaster General could bar *Confidential* from the mails without notice, without charges, and without a hearing, he could do the same to any periodical." Neither Arthur Summerfield nor anyone else, he said, "was qualified to be the literary dietitian of America."[14]

"The threat of cancellation hovers like a specter over this plaintiff," who faced "corporate execution" and "complete financial destruction" if denied use of the mails, Williams argued. *Confidential* had already spent $300,000 on the issue, and if the magazine wasn't mailed on schedule, Harrison would be liable to the distributor for damages. Harrison alleged in an affidavit that he would be forced to stop publishing *Confidential* if the order remained in effect. Technically this wasn't true, since most *Confidential* issues were delivered by truck to newsstands and less than fifty thousand were sold by mail-order subscription. The Post Office filed a motion to dismiss the suit, saying that a Post Office request to inspect a magazine for objectionable matter was "routine." The lawsuit was a "tempest in a teapot," the department's attorney said, and *Confidential*'s lawyers were "making a mountain out of a molehill."[15]

"I argued as forcefully as I could that the 'withhold from dispatch' order was invalid because it had been issued without giving the publisher a chance to be heard and without specification of charges. I argued, further, that requiring a publisher to submit his publication for approval before distributing it violated the First Amendment guarantees of freedom of the press," Williams recalled in his autobiography. "Since the advent of the Bill of Rights no court had ever countenanced any order or edict which required the censor's stamp of approval on words before they were spoken, printed, or distributed. This was what the courts had characterized as 'unconstitutional prior restraint.'"[16]

The ACLU issued a press release describing the Post Office's action as "unbridled censorship" and a "violation of due process," and sent a letter to Summerfield protesting the order. "We offer no comment on the content of the articles published in *Confidential* or the kind of journalism it reflects. However, as long as the First Amendment is to have meaning and force with respect to the distribution of published material then the Post Office has no right to pre-censor. If a publication has violated the law then it should be properly charged and its case heard in a court of law. Under our democratic system, we do not rely on individual government administrators to decide what material should be read by the public. The protection of the First Amendment applies equally to all magazines and publications, despite the view of government officials as to their contents. . . . The observance of fair procedures is the heart of due process, which characterizes the difference between our democratic society and a totalitarian society."[17]

On October 7, 1955, Judge Luther Youngdahl of the US District Court for the District of Columbia ordered the Post Office to rescind the order. To withhold the magazine from the mails without notice, charges, and a hearing was a violation of due process, he declared. If the Post Office considered any issue nonmailable, it would have to notify the publisher, and an administrative hearing would have to be held before the magazine was denied access to the mails. In order for the Post Office to bar *Confidential* from the mails while the hearing was under way, it would have to obtain an injunction from a court. Voluntarily, *Confidential* agreed to submit two copies of each succeeding issue to the Post Office Department for an informal review within twenty-four hours after printing and binding.[18]

Confidential's lawyers claimed a triumph. "If officials think any particular issue is obscene, they must ask for a hearing and can't interfere with the distribution of that number," Ross told reporters. The decision made clear that the Post Office has "no right to control the contents of magazines."[19]

The victory was short-lived. Harrison had scarcely offered the March issue to the Post Office for review when it declared the issue "obscene, lewd, lascivious, and filthy." William C. O'Brien, the department's assistant solicitor, swore out an affidavit to support a motion for an injunction declaring the issue nonmailable. Among the items O'Brien objected to were "Shh—Have You Heard the Latest About Sammy Davis Jr.?" "Nude Body Found in the Apartment of Will Rogers' Daughter!," "Caught . . . Guy Madison in Barbara Payton's Boudoir!" and "Named . . . The Cutie Who Split Up the John Dereks!" One article really troubled the Post Office—"The Pill that Ends Unwanted Pregnancy," a commentary on a new antileukemia drug, Aminopterin, that was being used by some doctors for therapeutic abortions.[20] A banner headline on that issue's cover read, DON'T BUY THOSE NEW ABORTION PILLS.

"Criminal abortionists have found a new way to practice their bloody profession without the usual risks of being caught," *Confidential* had written. "For the first time in the history of the world, they have a pill that actually works, a pill which can be taken orally in the woman's own home." It denounced "criminal abortionists" as "the biggest group of professional murderers in the world," linking them to the deaths of as many as 7,500 women. "And now the callous racket has sunk to its lowest depth."[21]

Harrison insisted the article wasn't encouraging use of the drug—quite the contrary. He claimed he'd been urged to publish the piece by a public health official, as a "public service." According to the Post Office, the abortion drug story made the issue not only obscene, but unfit for mailing under a law that prohibited from the mails "every paper, writing, advertisement, or representation that any drug, medicine, or thing may, or can be used or applied for producing abortion."[22]

The Post Office went to federal district court and asked for a temporary restraining order barring the issue from the mails. They did this after giving *Confidential* a one-hour notice, despite the fact that Judge Youngdahl ruled that *Confidential* should have "due and proper notice." They also deliberately went to another judge, Edward Tamm, for the order. On December 21, 1955, Tamm issued a temporary restraining order to keep *Confidential* from mailing out the issue. *Confidential* appealed the order; the Court of Appeals refused to stay it. The government came back to the district court seeking to convert its temporary restraining order into a preliminary injunction.[23]

In the hearing before Judge Joseph C. McGarraghy of the US District Court for the District of Columbia, Williams cited the 1931 case *Near v. Minnesota*, which prohibited prior restraints. *Near* stood for the proposition that "the appropriate remedial action is not injunction, but it is subsequent punishment." Williams—who believed the article wasn't obscene—offered to let the government indict Harrison for the crime of publishing obscene material. He challenged Assistant US Attorney William F. Becker to go before a grand jury with charges that the magazine had "stepped into the puddle of obscenity." Becker didn't accept his invitation, but Harrison was terrified at the possibility of indictment.[24]

The magazine wasn't obscene, although it might well have been "coarse," or "vulgar," or "racy," Williams argued. "Maybe this isn't the kind of diet that we live off intellectually. Maybe we don't use it or approve of it, but God forbid that [the government attorneys] or I become the censor of literature in the United States, because the day that comes, the First Amendment will be relegated into the graveyard of oblivion." And if the judge thought that *Confidential* was obscene, he should wait until he saw what "I have here," Williams said. He took out a bagful of men's magazines that went through the mails that had "undressed women and suggestive poses and that are calculated to arouse, maybe in youngsters, libidinous, lustful thoughts. . . . There is a whole bag of this, Your Honor, and I shall be glad to submit them for your consideration . . . to show you what goes through the mails."[25]

In the point that ultimately settled the case, Williams told McGarraghy that the Post Office was trying to ban *Confidential* by filing a motion in a case that had been dismissed three months earlier by Judge Youngdahl. "Your honor, . . . I must bring your attention to the fact that . . . it is basic hornbook law that one cannot use as a vehicle for obtaining injunctive relief a case that has been dismissed from the dockets of the court." McGarraghy turned down the Post Office's motion for a preliminary injunction. The temporary restraining order lapsed, and *Confidential* was mailed on schedule.[26]

Shortly afterward, the Post Office tried to appeal Youngdahl's order, claiming it was inequitable and that the "mailability section of the Post Office cannot live under it." They again asked to be permitted to bar material that they deemed nonmailable without a hearing and a court order. The ACLU sent a letter to postal officials urging them to drop their appeal:

> Under our democratic form of government, censorship and denial of due process of law are abhorrent. In several important cases our courts have flatly ruled that the Post Office Department has no right of prior censorship and it cannot refuse alleged non-mailable material use of the mails without a full and proper hearing. Yet once again, the Post Office is acting as if our courts have never spoken on the issue and given guidance. The reason for the courts' decisions and our repeated protests concerning the Post Office Department's power is the concern that a serious abuse of power, which denies civil liberties, results from the Department's action. . . . Pre-publication censorship is the mark of totalitarianism and our country is vigorously challenging this kind of attack on the press in Iron Curtain countries. Yet should we imitate it in our democracy?[27]

The Post Office didn't drop its case, but Youngdahl refused to revise his order. "I am informed by the Assistant United States Attorney in charge of the *Confidential* case that your release created quite a stir inside the Post Office—all to the good," Williams wrote the ACLU's Alan Reitman.[28]

The *Confidential* decision had impact: in 1959 the Post Office Department issued regulations consistent with Youngdahl's order. The regulations declared that the mailers of allegedly obscene material must receive notice from the Post Office of the charges against them, must have an opportunity to answer the charges, and were entitled to the right to a fair hearing before impartial judges before the mailing was banned.[29]

Despite its millions of readers, "*Confidential* had few friends," observed Edward Bennett Williams.[30] Other than the ACLU, *Confidential* had virtually no allies.

The mainstream press, always a vocal advocate of freedom of the press, had a conflicted relationship with *Confidential*. A few publishers came to *Confidential's* aid in its battles with the Post Office. The postmaster general's order was easy to criticize; a mail ban, a prior restraint, was "censorship" in its purest form. "Can the Post Office Department, without a hearing, bar *Confidential* from the mails?" asked one editor. "If so, couldn't any other publication be similarly barred?" "Precensorship invites arbitrariness and encourages . . . the sort of disregard for due process displayed by Mr. Summerfield in regard to *Confidential.*"[31]

Yet many publishers supported the Post Office. At a time when the mainstream press was under attack, accused of inaccuracy, bias, and sensationalism, journalists sought to distance themselves from Harrison's sleazy operations. Publishers denied that *Confidential* had the same First Amendment rights as newspapers. When it came to scandal magazines, "censorship [was] a benefit rather than a handicap," wrote one editor. "Censorship of publications which thrive on gossip, tearing down reputations and libeling individuals cannot be argued against."[32]

In 1955 the magazine *The Reporter*, known for its liberal, progressive positions, published an editorial in favor of the Post Office ban. "We cannot agree with [those] who, as soon as something like the attempted suppression of *Confidential* occurs, intone the old Voltaire singsong: 'I disapprove of what you say, but I will defend to the death your right to say it.' As a matter of fact, we cannot imagine ourselves dying for *Confidential*." Publications like *Confidential* gave a "bad name to journalism as a profession," and were through their "extreme sensationalism endangering a basic principle of freedom of the press."[33]

The Post Office ban also generated a good deal of public support. "Post-master General Arthur Summerfield may do what four libel suits have failed to accomplish, and that is to modify the journalistic formula of *Confidential* magazine," wrote the reader of a Waukesha, Wisconsin, newspaper. "Its filth laden formula of slime, sin, and sex has finally elicited strong enough protest to cause the postmaster to bar it from the mails. . . . Congratulations to the Post Office for its step in restraining such trash from cluttering the mail and getting to the market."[34]

The Post Office's actions also boosted *Confidential*'s circulation. Many were curious to know what the ban was about and went looking for *Confidential* at newsstands. Quipped a Cincinnati newspaper, the publishers of *Confidential* had been "making capital gain" off the Post Office ban.[35]

18 | THE PEAK

HARRISON'S COURTROOM SUCCESSES EMBOLDENED HIM. The first half of 1956 saw the hardest-hitting, most lurid stories in the magazine's history. *Confidential* was rolling off the presses at the rate of 5,200,000 copies per issue.[1] The magazine had reached its triumphant peak.

What appeared in *Confidential* was dictated largely by its sources. *Confidential* had become a cash cow for a host of fringe elements in Hollywood who sold the magazine tips when they were short on funds.

Fred Otash remained one of *Confidential*'s top tipsters, and he fed Harrison stories about his clients and lovers, including actresses Marie McDonald and Anita Ekberg. There were three *Confidential* stories on Ekberg, a busty blonde from Sweden who was under contract to the Universal studio. Otash dated her for a few months, then gave *Confidential* the details of their liaisons and assigned his men to tail her and take pictures of her with her lovers.

"Gary Cooper's Lost Weekend with Anita Ekberg" appeared in the January 1956 issue. The article was written from the point of view of a private eye who trailed Ekberg and Cooper, a notorious playboy. "Anybody could have collected the lowdown . . . [someone] had only to take up an observation post across the street from Anita's house, 2129½ South Beverly Glen Boulevard in

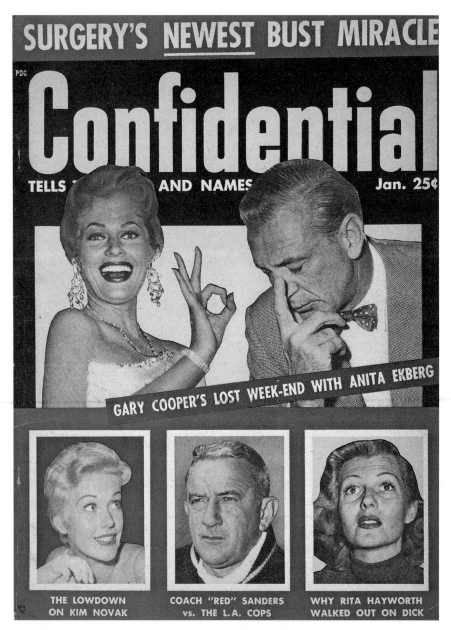

Harrison's courtroom successes emboldened him. By the beginning of 1956, *Confidential*'s articles were increasingly lewd, lurid and explicit. An exposé in the January issue described how Kim Novak purportedly slept her way to stardom. *Photofest*

Beverly Hills, on the afternoon of last August 6th. . . . Did anyone do such a thing?" asked *Confidential.* "Yes indeed."

The detective started at Ekberg's apartment, where Cooper picked her up in his Mercedes-Benz. They drove toward Malibu, stopped to pick up some groceries, then went to a bungalow on the Pacific Coast Highway. At 2:25 AM, *Confidential* reported, the floodlights outside the house flicked off.

> To tell the truth, it was so quiet the whole morning long of Sunday, August 7th that in spite of the fact that Gary's car was still in the garage, he received a mysterious phone call between about two and four in the afternoon. Cooper answered the phone—the number is GLenwood 7-2475, in case you're interested—and drawled his globally famous "Yup?" into the mouthpiece.
>
> That's all the caller wanted to know. There was a soft click on the other end of the line and the world's best-known cowboy could only wonder what it meant. Now he *knows.* He also knows, as of this moment, that there were peeping eyes when he walked out of the house in bathing trunks, shortly after four that lazy Sunday afternoon, and stood—like General Custer—on a bluff overlooking the Pacific. . . . Maybe they do and maybe they don't recall a character scrambling around on the stones well in back of them.
>
> Through the long summer afternoon, "Coop" and the so firm, so fully-packed Ekberg paddled in the surf, smooched in the sand, and otherwise enjoyed their unofficial vacation. . . . As the sun went down they returned to their house, got rid of all that sand, and then drove off to an intimate little beach restaurant for dinner. . . . It took them until 2:30 AM to return to the . . . house.[2]

Cooper was outraged but wouldn't sue. "It's a nope from Mr. Yup on whether he's joining Hollywood's million-dollar lawsuit rush against *Confidential,*" Erskine Johnson reported.[3]

Barbara Payton was another prolific *Confidential* source. A B-actress with a serious alcohol problem and, by 1956, an almost nonexistent career, Payton sold HRI tips. "Caught—Guy Madison in Barbara Payton's Boudoir" described her affair with actor Guy Madison while she was engaged to Franchot Tone, Joan Crawford's ex-husband.[4]

Payton had once been the lover of wealthy Texas oilman Bob Neal, and also Bob Hope. "Have Tux, Will Travel—and That's What Bob Hope Did with That Blonde" described Payton's affair with Hope seven years earlier. "It all goes back to a sunny afternoon in 1949, when our oh-so-fully packed Payton was visiting in Dallas, Texas and happened to run into a millionaire pal, Bob Neal, in the lobby of the popular Baker Hotel." Neal "invited Barbara to a party Hope was giving that night in his own suite at the same hotel. That's the last Neal ever saw of Payton. Barbara came for cocktails and stayed for capers—with Hope. Just like that! They hadn't known each other six hours before they knew each other as well as boy and girl ever can."[5]

Hope nearly had a heart attack when the article came out. Press agents suggested it might be a good opportunity for him to spend time with his wife and family. Hope was livid, but his lawyers dissuaded him from bringing a lawsuit. *That Certain Feeling* was released around the same time, and Paramount executives didn't want to attract more attention to the *Confidential* story.[6]

"Hope's fundamental attitude towards the affair was . . . mixed," writes his biographer. "It had showcased him, however vulgarly, as the Ladykiller Supreme he always longed to come across as." Hope knew his popularity would suffer little from a magazine held in low repute, and he realized that *Confidential* could have come up with worse. His wife, Dolores, was outraged. They almost divorced. Hope turned his wrath on Payton, "putting out the word she was a no-good slut who couldn't be trusted."[7]

———————

An unnamed call girl was the source of "Here's Why Frank Sinatra Is the Tarzan of the Boudoir," which attributed Sinatra's sexual prowess to a hearty breakfast cereal. The article, which ran in the spring of 1956, was written in the format of "An Open Letter to Wheaties."

It may seem brash coming from an outsider, but you've been making a whale of a mistake in the way you plug Wheaties, boys. . . . You've been sitting on a gold mine, fellows, as you'll discover when you've finished reading this story. Then, if you're smart, you'll toddle around to Frank Sinatra's house and get that kid's endorsement on the dotted line.

Frank Sinatra, you say. What's he champ of? Plenty, men. Just ask the babes who know him.

He's had the nation's front-rank playboys dizzy for years trying to discover his secret. Ava Gardner, Lana Turner, Gloria Vanderbilt, Anita Ekberg—how does that skinny little guy do it? . . .

Wheaties! That's the magic, gentlemen. Where other Casanovas wilt under the pressure of a torrid romance, Frankie boy just pours himself a big bowl of crispy, crackly Wheaties and comes back rarin' to go.

Sinatra found himself head over heels in love with a "curvy, dreamy eyed little pigeon," wrote *Confidential*. He took her out for dinner and "dallying," but the woman was unimpressed. "She rated him adequate at that old pajama game but nothing worth bulletins." She changed her mind, though, when Sinatra invited her to spend the weekend with him at his country home in Palm Springs. "The babe hopped at the opportunity—and got practically no sleep at all for the next two days. Why? Frankie was on Wheaties."

At the fashionable Dunes restaurant, Sinatra just "picked and pecked" at his food. "Back at the house, though, he tore into the kitchen, wolfed down a big bowl of those nourishing flakes, and then led her to the boudoir." While the woman tried to catch her breath, "Frankie excused himself and padded back into the kitchen for a refill of that 'Breakfast of Champs.' The girl was still wondering what was going on when he came charging back into the playroom humming 'I'm in the Mood for Love,' and proceeded to prove it."

When Frankie made his *fourth* visit to the Wheaties bin the gal began to cross her fingers. Something, she was sure, was going to explode. Her worries were groundless, though. They cut another caper and she finally nuzzled her weary head into the pillow for some shut-eye— until—she heard a noise. Believe us, General Mills, it was Frankie shuffling into his slippers again. Out to the kitchen he went. Back in her little nook, the unbelieving babe could plainly hear the crunch, crunch, crunch of a man—eating Wheaties.[8]

Al Govoni arranged a supermarket promotion in Los Angeles with Wheaties and *Confidential* stacked side by side. According to Govoni's son Steve, Harrison said the Wheaties story was the best he ever ran—"and I don't know how many times I heard my father, leaning back with cigar and Dewar's, proudly recall that Sinatra had called him personally from Australia to chew him out."[9]

A Los Angeles stripper was the source of "When the Cat's Away, the Mice Will Play, Even with Elizabeth Taylor's Hubby," one of two *Confidential* articles on Elizabeth Taylor. An incomparable beauty, only twenty-three years old, Taylor, one of MGM's most bankable stars, was in the midst of a career upswing. That year she was making *Giant*, one of the most important films of her career. Taylor married British actor Michael Wilding in 1952; he was her second husband and twenty years her senior. She regarded him as a friend and advisor, and the relationship was almost sexless.

Confidential described how Wilding had an affair with a stripper when Taylor was in Texas filming *Giant*. "Around the time Mrs. Wilding's airliner was landing in the Lone Star State, Michael was strolling into a third-rate bag-and-bangle nightery at Western Avenue and Pico Boulevard called Strip City," *Confidential* reported. No one expected to see Wilding there—"To say they were surprised is an understatement. The stripper on stage was so startled when he walked in that she stopped in the middle of a grind and swallowed her gum."[10]

Jennie Lee, nicknamed the "Bazoom Girl" for her forty-two-inch-bust, gave the story to *Confidential*. A twenty-six-year-old from Kansas City, Lee performed five nights a week at a burlesque theater called Strip City. Verena Dale, another stripper, was her close friend. Wilding and his buddies returned to Strip City several times over the next few weeks, and he befriended Lee and Dale. He became especially close to Dale, a "big and buxom bump artist."[11]

"In less time than it takes to knit a G-string, they were holding hands and Wilding was asking her a) whether she was married and b) when she said no, whether he could take her home," wrote *Confidential*. The affair supposedly culminated in a pool party at Wilding's home involving Dale, Lee, and Wilding's friend, rumored to be Hollywood writer James Bacon. The girls swam in the pool; Lee took off soon afterward, leaving Dale at the house. Wrote *Confidential*, "The stripper floated into his arms for a few steps but broke away when the urge overcame her to put on her own specialty. The dance would have brought down the house at Strip City—and attracted the cops as well. For in a hurry to leave the club, she'd forgotten to remove her 'pasties.' Michael and his buddy obligingly plucked them off as Verena glided past them."[12]

Taylor's studio handlers were upset by the *Confidential* story because it undermined their efforts to promote Taylor as a sexy star. "If she couldn't keep her man happy, what woman could?" writes biographer William Mann. Taylor claimed that the article didn't bother her. "Whether it's true or not, you can't let an article like that break up your marriage," she told *Look* magazine. But she was hurt by the story, and tensions in the marriage worsened.[13]

Wilding went off to Europe later that year to appear in *Zarak*, filmed in India, Burma, and Morocco. He invited Taylor to join him. The film's lead was Victor Mature. *Confidential*'s "Hubby Mike Wilding Didn't Knock—That's How He Caught Elizabeth Taylor with Victor Mature" described how Wilding found her in bed with Mature in a Morocco hotel room, "in a scene that would have overheated the cameras."[14]

In October 1956, Taylor announced she was divorcing Wilding. A columnist noted that a major break in their union "came after a scandal magazine published an account of an alleged wild party thrown in the couple's home in Beverly Hills."[15] *Confidential* had damaged another marriage.

Confidential nearly destroyed Jeanne Crain's marriage. Crain, a pretty, svelte star of lightweight romances and comedies, had won acclaim for her Academy Award–nominated performance in the 1949 film *Pinky*. Since 1946, she had been married to former theatrical agent and radio manufacturer, Paul Brinkman. *Confidential* ran an article on Brinkman's alleged philandering titled "Jeanne Crain's Hubby and the Starlet."

"Jeanne's going to be shocked down to her pretty toes when she reads here how at least one of Paul's excursions off the home range" happened "right under her nose," *Confidential* wrote. The article described how one night at a party Brinkman became enchanted with a "well-stacked starlet new to movieland. In spite of the fact that Jeanne was there with him, he managed an introduction and—before his friendship with the strange cutie was 24 hours old—he was dropping around to her apartment as often as an old family friend." The source of the story was the lover herself. Brinkman rejected her, and she took revenge by selling her story to *Confidential*.[16]

Crain filed for divorce in May 1956, shortly after the article came out. She shocked Hollywood with charges that Brinkman beat her, never supported her, and had affairs with other women. She alleged that when he was charged with adultery in *Confidential* he "never denied the charges and his sole reaction has been one of self-pity." According to columnists, "Hollywood was agog with reports—published and whispered—that the climactic fireworks" in the marriage were touched off by the *Confidential* article. Brinkman denied *Confidential*'s accusations, and his lawyer told the press that "a libel suit is very definitely under consideration."[17] The couple reconciled later that year.

According to DeStefano, Harrison never thought *Confidential* was actually hurting anyone. When he found out about Crain's breakup, Harrison broke down in tears. "I've done a horrible thing. I've broken up a home," he lamented. Harrison was surprised when Bob Hope snubbed him in the lobby of the Plaza Hotel. "Bob believed that stories in *Confidential* helped [stars'] careers more often than not," DeStefano recalled.[18]

Harrison was convinced that Sammy Davis Jr. was grateful for publicity in *Confidential*, but Davis apparently felt otherwise. After the Ava Gardner story, the magazine ran another tell-all, "Ssh! Have You Heard the Latest About Sammy Davis Jr.?," falsely describing a tryst with actress Meg Myles. "The lowdown is that, when she wasn't on camera, the fully-packed Miss Myles was steaming it up with Sammy at the Sunset Colonial Hotel on Hollywood's famed Sunset Strip," *Confidential* reported. Later that year Harrison asked Davis to record a new song as a promotion—"Shh—It's Confidential." Davis refused, and Harrison was stunned.[19]

But it wasn't wrong for Harrison to think that *Confidential* was good for some actors. If a star already had a "bad girl" or "bad boy" image, having their skeletons pulled out of the closet could help them, as Mitchum's success revealed. Some press agents, especially for fledgling actors, were selling stories to *Confidential.* Jeanne Carmen's agent wanted to get her affair with Lex Barker into the magazine. The article, "The Gal Who Had Lex Barker Up a Tree," appeared in July 1957. A press agent was fired because he couldn't get his client into *Confidential.* Observed *Esquire,* some publicists were "tumbl[ing] all over themselves in eagerness to co-operate with the expose publishers . . . some of them have leaked scandal when it seems opportune." For an up-and-coming performer, a story in *Confidential* was a sign that one had "arrived."[20]

19 | THE DECLINE

BY 1956 ROBERT HARRISON—son of immigrants, street kid, gutter-mouth, neurotic, publishing pioneer—had achieved his dream of fame, fortune, and "respectable notoriety," as he put it. With a single paragraph, headline, or incriminating photo, he could destroy reputations and careers. Commanding the curiosity and attention of more than sixteen million readers, Harrison had become one of America's most powerful and influential publishers.

But it was the beginning of the end for *Confidential*. By the middle of 1956, *Confidential*'s popularity and readership were declining. The film industry and its allies ramped up their efforts, and public opinion turned against *Confidential*. High on the success of his blockbuster stories and court victories, Harrison began taking things too far. *Confidential* was becoming too nasty, vicious, and crude, and the public started to rebel.

That spring, at the height of his success, Harrison extended *Confidential*'s operations to Europe. He set up the equivalent of HRI in London—a bureau of tipsters, writers, and fact-checkers—and signed a contract to distribute a European edition. *Confidential*'s European bureau was run by Michael Mordaunt-Smith, a thirty-year-old journalist and publicist from an aristocratic family. Harrison asked Mordaunt-Smith "to act as a filter for stories in London, to check on them . . . if necessary, to travel almost anywhere to check out any story or documentation." Mordaunt-Smith went to Morocco, Brussels, Paris, Southern France, and Dublin to verify stories for *Confidential*.[1]

Mordaunt-Smith worked out of a Bond Street office, and his files were said to be a virtual "Who's Who of London Sin." They contained, among items, photographs of a well-known American movie star leaving a London call girl's home, and affidavits concerning a "Hollywood hero" who sent his son to a call girl for "initiation."[2]

Mordaunt-Smith dispatched henchmen to restaurants and nightclubs to spy on foreign royalty, film stars, politicians, and society leaders. They were so pestiferous that a proprietress of a London nightclub employed two wrestlers to sling "*Confidential* people" into the road. His main investigator was thirty-year-old Lee Benson, who visited seedy bars to seek out party girls and help them entrap stars. At one point Benson became disgusted with *Confidential* and divulged the magazine's operations to the London gossip magazine *The Sketch*. Film industry figures, he alleged, had threatened his life if he continued working for *Confidential*.[3]

In March 1956, columnist Earl Wilson noted that newsstand sales of the scandal magazines had declined. "Are scandal magazines slipping?" he asked. One Broadway newsstand returned 500 copies of the 550 it had ordered the previous month.[4]

He was right—the fad was wearing off. Readers had become weary of the screaming headlines and raunchy claims. The market had become saturated; nearly thirty scandal publications were on newsstands.[5] The celebrity lawsuits and the Post Office ban had linked the magazines to debauchery, libel, and obscenity. Already on the edge of public decency, the scandal magazines were going to extremes with increasingly lewd and explicit articles.

Throughout the country, religious and civic groups pressured newsstands to stop selling *Confidential*. Police and prosecutors seized copies of *Confidential* and threatened retailers with obscenity prosecutions if they sold it. A Pennsylvania "Literary Control Board" banned *Confidential* and twenty-seven other "indecent" magazines. In Knoxville, Tennessee, the City Council banned issues of magazines containing "offensive text," including *Confidential*.[6] Vermont considered a law that would impose fines and jail terms for "persons who provide minors with corruptive literature," including *Confidential*. Pasadena police barred an issue of *Confidential* from newsstands for a lurid story about Eddie Fisher and three prostitutes, described in the story as "highly delectable professional pigeons," deeming the article "indecent and immoral."[7]

As the civil rights movement gained momentum, the African American press, which had given *Confidential* some of its earliest media coverage, began to attack *Confidential* for its noxious depictions of interracial relationships. With "snide hints and up-the-sleeve giggles," *Confidential* exploited racial tensions, appealing to "die-hard" racists "who never will admit that harmonious relationships can and do grow out of interracial associations," wrote George Pitts in the *Pittsburgh Courier*. "It seems that wherever persons of different races get together . . . someone tries to link it with scandal. . . . Why should these scandal magazines make such an issue of interracial affairs—why not give them a chance to foster and prove that good race relations can result. Give them a break!"[8]

Even though he was turning a profit, Harrison was hemorrhaging money on legal fees. In early 1956, Harrison made his first out-of-court settlement in a libel suit, paying tabloid publisher Lyle Stuart $9,000. "It was the most businesslike thing to settle," Harrison said. "I didn't want to go to court—what would I have gained? If Errol Flynn wants to take me to court, or Mitchum, or Bogart, I'll run to get there. Even if I lose, look at the publicity! . . . But what would I have got out of a [suit] with Stuart? Who knows him?"[9]

More *Confidential* victims sued or threatened to sue—Dick Powell, George Jessel, Jeanne Crain, Paul Brinkman, Elsa Maxwell, the Vanderbilt family, and professional gambler Nick Dandolos, also known as "Nick the Greek." Dennis Hamilton, the husband of British actress Diana Dors, brought a $1 million libel suit over an article headlined "What Diana Dors Never Knew About Her Ever-Loving Hubby." The National Cancer Hospital sued over an article describing its doctors and treatments as "quacks." Socialite Robert Goelet, grandnephew of Mrs. Cornelius Vanderbilt, sued over a report that he was divorcing his wife to marry "a colored beautician he had found working in a minor Broadway hotel," described as a "tawny temptress" and "Harlem honey."[10]

Former Undersecretary of State Sumner Welles threatened a lawsuit over a vicious article outing him as homosexual. In the 1940s, Welles had been second in command at the State Department and was widely known in inner circles to be gay. The article was a blockbuster for *Confidential*; Harrison had gone to great lengths to get the story. He had a detective travel to Florida, another reported from Washington, DC, and a police investigator went to Cleveland to check the facts.[11]

"We Accuse Sumner Welles" was prefaced by an "Editor's note":

> Authorities tell us homosexuals are security risks in time of war, and the State Department is a prime target for espionage. No government at war could commit greater folly than to retain a confirmed homosexual in its No. 2 Foreign Policy post.
>
> This magazine feels the American people have a pressing right to know that their wartime Under Secretary—SUMNER WELLES—was such a man. Continued suppression of the Welles story can no longer be justified in view of the need of public awareness of this danger and public support of our Federal Security Program. It must not happen again, and an informed citizenry will not let it happen again.

Welles had been undersecretary of state from 1937 to 1943, second only to Secretary of State Cordell Hull. He was "Acting Secretary of State on several occasions and might well have succeeded Hull—if knowledge of his promiscuity with men who were total strangers to him had not rallied opposition among certain apprehensive elements in the Roosevelt coterie," *Confidential* wrote. When Welles resigned in 1943, a "score of newsmen" knew the actual reasons. But no one dared print more than the "reliable report" that Welles was forced to resign by Hull.

Confidential described an incident in 1947 when Welles went to give a lecture in Cleveland, got drunk, and headed out for a night on the town. A detective found him in the Royal Castle hamburger restaurant, "squiring a handsome youth." The boy admitted that an inebriated Welles had given him three fifty-dollar bills to persuade him to come to his hotel suite. The next evening, Welles was caught drunk, trying to get a ride to the Club Vendome, a noted gay club.[12]

Father Divine, the charismatic African American religious leader who preached self-sufficiency, racial equality, and chastity, and also claimed to be God, sued over a May 1956 story, "I Was One of Father Divine's Angels." This wasn't the first time *Confidential* had gone after Father Divine; in April 1953, it described him as "The Greatest Hoax of the Century," alleging that the wealthy cultist operated a string of restaurants, beauty parlors, and other businesses using his followers as "slave labor."[13]

Confidential described how a twenty-one-year-old virgin, one of Divine's disciples, had been subject to a crude "initiation ritual." "It was a hot July night in 1942. Father Divine sent word for me to come to his office from my room upstairs in his Circle Mission church," the woman allegedly told *Confidential*. "Obediently, I slipped out of my dress, took off my shoes, and began pulling off my stockings. Father Divine watched me, then abruptly rose and walked into another room. . . . When he returned, Father Divine—this man I'd thought holy—was wearing only his shoes, socks, and garters. His eyes glistened with lust." He "wrested from me . . . the most precious possession a young girl has." Shortly after the article came out, Divine's lawyers alleged that *Confidential* had made "baseless attacks" on Divine's morals and announced that they were drawing up papers for a $1 million libel suit.[14]

——————————

Harrison and his editors were getting reckless. Many of *Confidential*'s "public service" stories had become downright frightening. "Seduction by Prescription" glorified a date rape drug: "This is no secret aphrodisiac or witches' compound. It's a pill which is being sold by millions in drugstores from coast to coast and all it requires is a doctor's prescription." "Wolves" were putting them in women's drinks, and in "about as much time as it takes to polish off a Martini, the doll finds herself in a languorous, lazy state of relaxation. . . . Before she realizes it, she is heeding the words of an old philosopher who once said, 'When rape is inevitable, relax and enjoy it.'"[15]

There was an outrageous story about actress Marie McDonald, nicknamed "The Body" for her beautiful physique. MacDonald had been recently kidnapped, and the news made front-page headlines. In "Even the Cops Blushed When They Learned Where Marie McDonald Hid That Ring," *Confidential* debunked reports about the kidnapping. The story came from Otash; McDonald was his client. According to the account McDonald told the press, she had been abducted and raped by two Mexicans, who stole her $8,000 diamond ring, "along with her honor." *Confidential* alleged that the ring had never been stolen, but was rather hidden in "The Body": "History tells us that women have often worn gems in the most improbable places. The ancient Egyptian charmers liked to put sparklers in their navels. But hardly anyone . . . has ever gone for interior decoration like Marie's."[16]

HRI scored big scoops on Marilyn Monroe and Elvis Presley. An article in November 1956 reported on Monroe's affair with film director Nicholas Ray.[17] In another article, reporter Bob Slatzer confessed how he had been Monroe's lover and was married to her for a short period of time.[18] In "Elvis Presley and His Doll Point Pen," *Confidential* described how after an "undulating show" outside of Lubbock, Texas, a "pretty young girl" rushed toward Elvis. She pulled down her dress and asked him to autograph her bosom. "With a flourish he hauled out his doll-pointed pen and signed just above the dotted swiss line. Elvis on the righty. Presley on the lefty. . . . You've never read it in your local gazettes but reporters in the know can tell you there are any number of chicks who've sported Presley's print on their superstructure."[19]

In its March 1957 issue, *Confidential* published "When Maureen O'Hara Cuddled in Row 35," describing O'Hara passionately necking with a "Latin lover" in the back of Grauman's Chinese Theatre. A brash, red-headed Irish actress nicknamed "The Queen of Technicolor" for the way her bright hair lit up the screen, O'Hara played feisty, spirited characters in dramas, adventures, and Westerns. Her best-known role was with John Wayne in the 1952 Western *The Quiet Man.* O'Hara's image was one of upright purity; to her fans, she was a "spirited Irish lass." O'Hara lived quietly and wasn't a partier, and she was known in Hollywood for being bossy and prudish. She flew below the radar of Hollywood gossip—until *Confidential.*[20]

> Almost anyone who's ever been to the movies knows about Hollywood's famous Grauman's Chinese Theater. That's where the stars go to get their footprints recorded in cement. . . . But you'd have to be an usher to get the real lowdown on what goes on in this celebrated movie house . . . [b]ecause Grauman's is also the theater where the stars go—not to watch the movie but to bundle in the balcony.

"One November evening not so long ago," the assistant manager of Grauman's "greeted lovely, green-eyed Maureen O'Hara at the head of the main aisle."

Escorted by a tall and handsome Latin American, she looked as dignified as a queen. Politely murmuring that he hoped they enjoyed the picture, the manager turned them over to an usher, who led them to their seats towards the rear of the orchestra.

He'd had his share of over-amorous couples in Grauman's, but such a problem never entered his mind as he watched red-haired Maureen sweep down the aisle into the darkness. O'Hara necking in a public theater? It just couldn't be.

He got the shock of his life an hour later, though, when the usher in charge of aisle "C" came rushing out to report that there was a couple heating up the back of the theater. . . . Easing down the aisle, he saw the entwined twosome. It was Maureen and her south-of-the-border sweetie. . . . Maureen had entered Grauman's wearing a white silk blouse neatly buttoned. Now it wasn't. The guy had come in wearing a spruce blue suit. Now he wasn't. The coat was off, his collar was open, and his tie was hanging limply at half-mast in the steam.

Moreover, Maureen had taken the darndest position to watch a movie in the whole history of the theater. She was spread across three seats—with the happy Latin American in the middle seat.

The usher rushed back to the foyer for a flashlight.

Then . . . he kept flicking the light on the two until Maureen suddenly sat up, snuggled into one seat, and the pair started to watch the movie. . . .

He thought this was the last he'd seen of such goings on . . . but was *he* wrong! So far as Maureen was concerned, this was double feature night and she was giving away more than dishes.

The manager had hardly returned to the candy stand out front before the usher from aisle "C" was on his heels with the breathless announcement, "They're at it again!"

This time, when he went to investigate, he found Maureen occupying one seat—her boy friend's. That is, they were *both* in it, and if she'd come to watch a movie she was wasting a lot of time and money. So was her sweetie. She was sitting on his lap, facing the back of the theater. . . .

The assistant manager turned his flashlight onto them, and they froze. He told them to leave the theater.[21]

Everyone in Hollywood knew who the "Latin lover" was: Enrique Parra, a married Mexico City attorney. Recently divorced and with a young daughter, O'Hara was having a steady, passionate, and open affair with Parra. When the *Confidential* article came out, she was in the middle of a custody battle with her ex-husband, producer Will Price, who alleged she had been "immoral" with Parra.[22]

Harrison was getting so many death threats that he had to have round-the-clock protection. There was a "big rumor" going around that Harrison was "on the other side of three guns." One night he was spotted leaving the Colony nightclub shouting, "A bullet-proof taxi, please!" According to columnist Hy Gardner, Harrison was no longer eligible for life insurance. "Yes that's true Hy," Harrison told him. "Not only have insurance companies refused to sell me any life policies but they've raised the premiums so high for my editors they're practically in the same boat." Harrison tried to peddle his exclusive stories to TV but sponsors rejected him. Chicago radio and TV stations turned him down when he tried to buy airtime for *Confidential*.[23] Sensing that things were slipping, Harrison put on his biggest stunt to date.[24]

In August 1956, DeStefano got an urgent phone call from Harrison saying that he had found out about a "fantastic herb" in the Dominican Republic that men were using for virility. Harrison, DeStefano, Govoni, and Harrison's friend, a busty blonde showgirl named Geene Courtney, took a plane down to Ciudad Trujillo (now Santo Domingo) to research the wonder weed, which they dubbed "Pega Palo." Harrison also planned to relax and to do some hunting with friends, including Dick Weldy, a big-game hunter and a buddy of several Hollywood stars. The virility herb story appeared in *Confidential*'s January 1957 issue as "Pega Palo—the Vine that Makes You Virile."[25]

A few months earlier, *Confidential* had run an article about John Wayne, describing his dalliances with "Latin lassies." Weldy was the source. The article described how Wayne and Weldy had been vacationing in Lima, and Wayne "was in the mood for fillies and fun." Weldy set him up with several women, but they rejected him. "Before he'd finished [his] hectic adventure south of the border, John was forced to cavort with one of those rental wenches—strictly cash in advance. . . . It went on for days that way. Weldy calling babes; Wayne striking out. Aside from being humiliating, it was so darn lonesome. . . . If you can't court 'em, buy 'em."[26] Wayne ended up marrying Weldy's ex-wife, actress Pilar Pallette.

On September 5, 1956, news outlets reported that Harrison had been discovered in the Jarabacoa mountains with a blonde nightclub singer and a bullet wound in his left shoulder. Weldy told officials that Harrison had been accidentally shot when, during a hunting trip, Weldy dropped his gun during an argument and it went off. Weldy said they were arguing over the story about Wayne and Pallette. Harrison and Courtney were said to be stranded in the jungle after the shooting and were found after officials sent out a 5,000 man search party, allegedly including troops, police, and Boy Scouts.[27]

Weldy claimed that he left the scene to seek help but when he reached his car on the highway he couldn't start the engine. Govoni drove to a hotel to call the police, and they arrived soon after. But Govoni was unable to guide them to the spot where he left Harrison. Searchers took more than a day to locate Harrison and Courtney. A spokesperson for *Confidential* said that Harrison was in "serious condition."[28] Newspapers ran photos of Harrison and Courtney in the hospital, bandaged and sedated.

The whole affair was obviously a hoax. Wrote the *Washington Post*, "Just how the night club singer, identified as a Miss Geene Courtney, got into the party is not yet clear, but we only hope that her press agent has plenty of pictures—preferably in extreme décolletage—to make available to the free and fearless American periodical press." The *New York Daily Mirror* noted that the "accident" "accidentally got a great deal of publicity for himself and for *Confidential*, which pleased him and delighted his friends, whoever they are." *Confidential* competitor *On the Q.T.* noted that both Rushmore's "disappearance" the previous year and the Harrison "shooting" happened on the sixth of the month—the same day *Confidential* hit newsstands.[29]

Back in New York, on the WABD *Night Beat* program, Harrison showed host Mike Wallace his "shotgun wounds."

"Why don't you admit it, Harrison . . . the so-called shooting was a fake," said Wallace.

"No one gets shot, Mike, for publicity purposes," Harrison replied. "Would you know a bullet wound if you saw one?" he asked Wallace, and began taking off his shirt.

Harrison later described the incident to journalist Tom Wolfe: "So I start taking off my shirt right there in front of the camera. . . . I have this big mole on my back, a birthmark, and the cameramen are all so excited, they think that's the bullet hole and they put the camera right on that. Well, that mole's the size of a nickel, so on television it looked like I'd been shot clean through with a cannon!"[30]

In October 1956, Harrison and Jay Breen appeared on NBC's *The Tonight Show*, where they were hissed at and heckled by the audience. Host Steve Allen moderated a panel argument on the "Pros and Cons of Expose-Type Magazines." Harrison and Breen defended *Confidential*. The cons were handled by columnists John Crosby of the *New York Herald Tribune* and Max Lerner of the *New York Post*.

Harrison insisted that *Confidential* published nothing but the truth. "No one has ever been harmed by an article in *Confidential*—in fact, I know some who have benefited," he said. Crosby retorted with stories of actor friends who had been devastated emotionally. Breen caused peals of laughter from the audience when he said, "We have a letter from a little old lady," then went on to allege that an eighty-two-year-old woman read only the Bible and *Confidential*.

"You leave no dignity, no shred of privacy in the life of a person," Lerner blasted. Harrison responded, "There are 400 correspondents in Hollywood who would do the same thing but are censored by their own editors who are afraid of losing advertising." Lerner shot back, "That's not true." Crosby rebutted that an "ordinary newspaperman" came across a lot and that he had "the sense of decency and good taste not to print everything." "When a man steps into the limelight he forfeits his privacy," Harrison replied.

When Lerner said that *Confidential* damaged not only celebrities but the youth of America, Breen rejoined: "We have thousands of letters from mothers who say their teenagers read *Confidential*, and it's helpful." The audience gasped with amazement, then booed.[31]

20 | SLANDER

HOLLYWOOD WAS MAKING INROADS with its attack on *Confidential*. Sometime in 1956, Jerry Giesler and several studio executives contacted Attorney General Edmund G. "Pat" Brown and asked him to initiate criminal charges against *Confidential*. It was a plea that the politically savvy, morally conservative prosecutor was happy to entertain.

Brown, former district attorney of San Francisco, was elected the state's Attorney General in 1950 and reelected in 1954. A popular, moderate Democrat, Brown was "not too conservative to frighten California liberals, and not too liberal to frighten the conservatives," as *Newsweek* put it. Brown took liberal positions on many issues; he was known for his support of civil rights and his staunch opposition to the death penalty. At the same time, he was conservative on crime, supporting crackdowns on gambling and corruption. A devout Roman Catholic, Brown was opposed to pornography, and often repeated J. Edgar Hoover's contention that "racy magazines" contributed to crime. As San Francisco's district attorney in the 1940s, he had begun the action that put scandal magazine publisher Jimmy Tarantino behind bars.[1]

A "smooth, bland" man on the stocky side with thin black hair and "horn-rimmed spectacles perched on his square-jowled face," Brown was a consummate politician—prudent, realistic, and extraordinarily ambitious. Brown enjoyed pressing flesh, slapping backs, and making important political connections. He had a ready smile and persuasive way of talking, "a deferentially hearty manner [that] exudes modesty, affability, earnestness, and moderation so pervasively as to make him . . . undislikable," wrote the *New York Times*. As the only Democrat in statewide elective office in 1956, Brown became the party's logical standard bearer for the 1958 gubernatorial election.[2] Brown would formally announce his candidacy in late 1957, at the end of the *Confidential* trial.

Giesler gave Brown information he had collected during his research into his libel cases, including Harrison's deposition and evidence of the connection between *Confidential* and HRI. Brown, whose political ambitions made it prudent to cooperate with one of the state's most powerful industries, and who was morally opposed to *Confidential*, told Giesler he would consider taking action. In the middle of 1955, Brown's office was reportedly investigating possible avenues of prosecution, including an action for criminal libel. Under a California penal statute, any person "knowingly parting with libelous material so others can read it or see it" committed a criminal offense, punishable by one year in county jail and a $5,000 fine.[3]

At the same time, Hollywood was fighting back against *Confidential* with its most powerful weapon: entertainment.

In January 1956 the CBS television series *Studio One* featured an episode titled "A Public Figure." Actor James Daly played a performer who had attained fame as Captain Blake, the hero of a children's show. When a scandal magazine printed that he was an ex-convict, he lost his contract, even though he had lived an upstanding life for twenty years. He went on an interview show to tell his side of the story, and that night he got his contract back.[4]

The show was acclaimed. CBS was reportedly "jammed with phone calls congratulating them on their terrific attack on scandal magazines and the havoc they make in the lives of people." According to one critic, the show had real impact, "thanks to the central theme which considers for the first time on TV one of the most nauseating new phenomena on the contemporary American scene."[5]

Even before the show was aired, producers made offers for writer Harry Junkin's screenplay. Producer Armand Deutsch outbid half a dozen competitors. That spring, Deutsch announced his plans to independently film "a forceful and dramatic attack on the people who have done so much to harm our Hollywood stars." MGM made Deutsch an offer to produce the movie there, and he accepted. MGM wanted to rush the film out, following its usual practice of getting "teaser benefit" out of the TV show by issuing the film quickly.[6]

Other studios jumped on the "hot" scandal magazine theme. In March 1956, the RKO studio filed claims to two titles, *Scandal Incorporated* and *Scandal Magazine*. The production company Filmmakers registered *The Character Assassins, A Public Figure, The Smear Artist, Smeared, Trial by Smear,* and *The Scandal Mongers*. Producer Robert Fellows set an April 10 start date for *Glare*, another scandal magazine film that would star Anita Ekberg.[7]

Columbia Pictures actually planned to do a film about *Confidential*. Columbia executives were said to be working with Harrison on the movie, *The "Confidential" Story*. They submitted a draft script to him, asking for his approval, and assured him that the publicity would make him richer. Noted Erskine Johnson, "The editor of a scandal magazine which has been clobbering film stars is now on Hollywood's payroll—collaborating on a movie about a scandal magazine. It's eyebrow lifting but par for the movietown course." The film was to be shot right in Harrison's office. Quipped one critic, that wasn't the only thing that was going to be shot in Harrison's office.[8] For unknown reasons, the film was never made.

In May 1956, playwright Jerome Weidman finished his screenplay for *Pattern of Malice*, the new title for MGM's "scandal magazine expose," later to be called *Slander*. In June, former *Confidential* victim Van Johnson agreed to star in the film. In July, Ann Blyth, Marjorie Rambeau, and Steve Cochran signed for the three remaining roles. The film would be directed by B-film director Roy Rowland. Johnson would play the children's show hero, and Blyth his wife. Cochran, known for his sleazy, villainous roles, would star as the venal publisher of a magazine called *The Whole Truth*, and Rambeau would play the publisher's mother.[9]

Everyone recognized that the film was an attack on *Confidential*. Wrote columnist James Bacon in August, "Hollywood strikes back at the scandal magazines with its most lethal weapon—the movie expose. MGM is making *Slander* which, if it follows the script, will make the exponents of boudoir and skeleton-in-the-closet journalism the heaviest heavies" of movie history. "The picture, from the studio which has had its greatest success this year in expose movies such as *Blackboard Jungle*, marks a complete reversal of Hollywood policy," Bacon noted. Before, the attitude of the industry toward the scandal magazines was "don't look and it will go away." "The fallacy of that attitude," an MGM executive told him, "is that the magazines now have gotten into the big circulation group."[10]

Released in December 1956, *Slander* told the story of *Real Truth: The Only Magazine That Dares Print All of It!* The magazine's motto was, "The cleaner they are on the surface, the dirtier they are underneath."

Real Truth was run by a slicked-back, fantastically wealthy publisher named H. R. Manley, once a small-time press agent for a string of strip tease artists. The magazine operated out of a well-appointed office in a sleek New York high rise. "We've got tipsters all over the world," boasted Manley. "I specialize in the truth. . . . I'm giving the public not only what they want, but what they need. I'm giving them the truth."

The movie began with an editorial conference for *Real Truth*. Manley and his editors—a flotsam and jetsam crew of barely employable drunks and lowlifes—brainstormed how they could get more sensational stories to boost readership. Circulation was declining, Manley told them. In the past, five million Americans had been willing to buy the magazine. "In the past five or six months, a few less Americans have gone up to their newsstands. Why—because you're all getting fat—you're not getting the dirt."

One reporter discussed doing a story on a Broadway star who had a narcotics conviction back in 1933. Another writer suggested doing a piece on an evangelist who was up on a rape charge, and one on a football coach who was sleeping with a "little Mexican tomato." When the writer said he had pictures of the coach, Manley replied, "You got pictures, but they won't go through the mails."

Manley spotted a sign out the window advertising the actress Mary Sawyer. "In the minds of the American public she is practically a nun, right? . . . There's never been a breath of public scandal about her, right? When we bring in our kind of a story on a Mary Sawyer—that's when we hit the circulation bull's-eye." An editor protested—the only thing he could find out about Sawyer was that she was happily married to a doctor and had a young daughter. Manley replied: "There's something dirty in everyone's past. And Mary Sawyer is no exception. The cleaner they are on the surface the dirtier they are underneath."

The reporters discovered that an up-and-coming actor, Scott Martin, a puppeteer on a popular children's TV show, had been an acquaintance of Sawyer's. Martin grew up in the same neighborhood as Sawyer and knew that she had an illegal abortion as a teenager. They also found out that Martin was an ex-convict who "cut up an innocent man in an attempt to rob him, at 19." They decided to get Martin to squeal on Sawyer by threatening to expose his past. Martin would be smeared in the magazine unless he revealed what he knew about Sawyer.

Martin's wife, played by Ann Blyth, was summoned to the magazine office. Manley showed her a mock-up of the story—"Scott Martin, Ex-Convict"—complete with his mug shot. "If I had children, I wouldn't want them going around thinking that their favorite TV hero is a convicted felon," Manley told her. Martin decided that he couldn't expose Sawyer, even if it meant ruining his own livelihood.

The story was printed in *Real Truth*, and Martin's career was just about over. Then, the unthinkable happened. At school, the boy's friends teased him about the article. Trying to escape his tormenters, he ran into the street and was killed by an oncoming car. His son's death prompted Martin to go on a television talk show to admit the truth of the article and denounce *Real Truth*. "Our son was poisoned," he said. "Every person in America who went to a newsstand and put down 25 cents for a copy of the latest issue helped spread the poison that killed my boy. . . . I hope the next person you help to kill won't be someone you love." Manley was thrilled by the publicity, telling editors that the boy's death was the "biggest publicity coup we've ever had." He ordered his staff to load more copies of the magazine onto newsstands. His aged mother, disgusted by the monster her son had become, took a gun and killed him.

H. R. Manley was far more heartless and venal than Harrison, not to mention more groomed, elite, and waspish. But on the whole, the film described *Confidential*'s operations with surprising accuracy. The movie tipped off the public to *Confidential*'s workings and set the stage for California's investigations of *Confidential* the following year.

Reviewers praised MGM for taking a stand against *Confidential*. "It's about time that someone did some hitting back against the vicious gutter mags catering to the public's thirst for sensationalism and operating just on the brink of the libel laws," wrote *Variety*. "Metro's 'Scandal' tackles the job of exposing the exposure racket and in the doing achieves that difficult blend of message and entertainment that is vital if a story such as this is to be put over. . . . In exposing the ugliness of the men and the thinking that goes into the gutter mags—and in making it plain that the public must share part of the responsibility—it deserves wide attention." The *Detroit Free Press* urged readers to "give Hollywood credit for registering a film protest against the scandal magazines."[11]

But the story was crude and contrived, and the plot and acting were panned. *Newsweek* described *Slander* as "a sentimental chronicle of a broken home."[12] The *New York Times* called it "cliché" and "mawkish. . . . It makes scandalmongering the menace of free enterprise, parental love, and the American home. . . . Slender is the word for this film."[13] "It reeks with the motion picture industry's long-pent-up sense of vengeance," noted the *Amarillo Globe-Times*. "Another one of those low-budgeted MGM pictures that thrives on single-thought development."[14] The film was a box office flop; MGM lost half a million dollars on it.[15]

Harrison came back with an amazing—and characteristic—retort. He hired five beautiful, scantily clad young women to picket the movie in front of the Loew's State Theatre on Broadway. The women paraded in front of the theater on one of the coldest days of the year. The models carried signs saying *Slander* was "unfair to *Confidential*."[16]

PART IV

21 | THE KRAFT COMMITTEE

IN EARLY 1957 a war on *Confidential* was under way in California. Prodded by the studios, Pat Brown's office was looking into criminal libel charges. A grand jury was investigating the Wrong Door Raid. A special Senate committee was going after the private detectives who sold information to *Confidential*.

Hollywood leaders denied they had anything to do with the investigations. Actor George Murphy, head of the Motion Picture Industry Council and a "public relations man" for the industry, told reporters, "I've never heard of any movie studio or any of the guilds or unions pouring money into the Attorney General's office for that purpose . . . the Attorney General's office has been operating completely on its own and without any suggestion or help from the motion picture producers."[1] The next nine months would test the limits of Robert Harrison and the boundaries of freedom of the press.

California's attack on *Confidential* began in January 1957 with the formation of the Senate Interim Committee on Collection Agencies, known as the Kraft committee, after its chairman Fred Kraft, a Republican from San Diego. The committee, formed to look into allegations of misconduct by private detectives, was an attempt to undermine *Confidential* by going after its newsgathering methods. The committee knew that private eyes were selling information to *Confidential* and claimed that the practice was compromising the state's detective industry.[2]

"The scandal magazines and the unscrupulous collection agencies both employ professional goons who will stop at nothing—even to the breaking of an arm or a leg—to collect an unpaid debt from a working man," Kraft said. "Our investigators have found that these same floaters, all ex-convicts and known hoodlums, also work at gathering material for the scandal magazines." Senator Lloyd Harris, the committee's chief investigator, claimed his staff discovered that private detectives, call girls, "party girls," bit actors and actresses, and other "fringe elements of Hollywood" were operating as a "tip service" for *Confidential*. The Kraft investigation was the result of film industry pressure. Stars and executives had lobbied state officials, hoping that a public airing of how the scandal magazines got their stories would undermine their popular appeal.[3]

The investigation focused on the Wrong Door Raid. On February 18, 1957, the committee subpoenaed Frank Sinatra to appear at a hearing later that month. The subpoena was served on Sinatra by two plainclothes policemen and a female police officer named Glory Dawson, described by newspapers as a "pretty policewoman." Dawson knocked at the front door of Sinatra's Palm Springs home, calling out "daddy," "darling," "lover boy," and "Frankie" to get him out of bed. When she failed to stir him, the plainclothesmen entered the house with a key they found sticking in the door. One shined a flashlight in Sinatra's eyes and shook him awake while the other read the subpoena aloud. Sinatra uttered profanities.[4]

Sinatra tried to have the service quashed. His lawyer, Martin Gang, claimed that the process servers had violated his privacy. Sinatra brought a lawsuit against the LAPD, ultimately unsuccessful, claiming an invasion of his constitutional rights. Kraft accused Sinatra of "an apparent effort to get additional publicity."[5]

Kraft invited DiMaggio, who was in Miami Beach, to appear before the committee voluntarily. DiMaggio sent the committee a letter saying he couldn't attend because of "pressing business." Ruditsky was also in Miami Beach, but the committee didn't summon him. According to Harris, Ruditsky didn't have a private detective's license but was working under the license of a private detective named Jack Stambler, who was also a deputy county marshal. "That's one of the evils of the system the committee wants to correct," Harris told the press. "A license can be issued to one man and he can hire any number he wants but they won't have to be licensed."[6]

Shortly afterward, Brown announced that his office planned to take action against the scandal magazines. "We may have grounds for prosecution for circulation of libelous, lewd, and lascivious material," he said. The Kraft committee coordinated its efforts with Brown's office. Los Angeles District Attorney William McKesson also promised to cooperate with Kraft; Kraft was to pass along any "evidence of a criminal nature" to McKesson if it came up. The Meades were subpoenaed to appear before the committee but the subpoena was dropped when Brown worried that an appearance might make them immune to prosecution.[7]

At the same time, the L.A. District Attorney's Office was conducting its own investigation into *Confidential*. Newspapers reported that the DA's office interviewed a witness with information about *Confidential* so vital that he "might be killed if his identity were known." The witness was Howard Rushmore. The "mystery witness . . . was closeted with three investigators for more than an hour and then spirited out of the Hall of Justice," the *Los Angeles Times* reported. The Kraft committee also interviewed the "hot" new witness.[8]

The county grand jury, with the help of the Los Angeles Police Department, was launching two "fact finding forays" into *Confidential*'s activities, one on alleged extortion and the other on the Wrong Door Raid. Los Angeles police had been investigating the recent kidnapping of Marie McDonald. They found that the "inside story" of the kidnapping had been offered by private investigators to the highest bidder among the scandal magazines. Police Lieutenant Frank Cunningham was scheduled to go before the county grand jury's criminal complaints committee to discuss extortion indictments in the McDonald case. The grand jury was also considering conspiracy indictments for the Wrong Door Raid.[9]

Amidst a fanfare of publicity, on February 27, 1957, the Kraft committee began its hearings. Heralded with a big buildup in the press, it was a media spectacle with cameramen and reporters, much like the Kefauver hearings six years earlier. "The sets are in place and the lighting is ready for the opening scene of the State Senate interim committee investigation. . . . Waiting to walk on is a cast of an estimated 30 to 40 witnesses with Crooner Sinatra as the not-overjoyed star," reported the *Los Angeles Times*.[10]

One by one, private detectives lined up before the committee and testified that they sold information to *Confidential*. Twenty-two-year-old Fred Redke confessed that he dug up facts on UCLA football coach Red Sanders and strip-teaser Lili St. Cyr that he turned over to Barney Ruditsky, who passed them to *Confidential*. Allen Amadril, an employee of Fred Otash, told the committee about spying on Anita Ekberg.[11] Phil Irwin, who previously worked for Ruditsky, confessed his involvement in the Wrong Door Raid.

Irwin blamed Ruditsky for selling the Wrong Door Raid story to *Confidential*. DiMaggio never got around to paying for the investigations, he said; Ruditsky threatened DiMaggio that he would tell the story to *Confidential* if he didn't get paid. "There were only four people alive who knew all the details about the raid that appeared in *Confidential*," Irwin said. "That was me, Ruditsky, Sinatra, and DiMaggio. I didn't tell and Sinatra and DiMaggio wouldn't. That leaves Ruditsky." Irwin said he went to see Sinatra after the story to "clear himself," explaining to Sinatra that he hadn't sold the story to *Confidential*. They talked, and according to Irwin, Sinatra suggested that if there were any questions about what happened that night they should say they were at a party at Sinatra's place. Irwin, who was then working for Hollywood detective Clyde Duber, claimed that after he quit Ruditsky and sued for back salary, he was beaten up by "some hoods" in Highland Park. He suspected the attack was connected to the *Confidential* story—that Sinatra had arranged for him to be beaten.[12]

Looking jaunty and dapper in a black knit tie and black hat, Sinatra openly lied before the committee. He claimed that he drove DiMaggio to Sheila Stewart's apartment but that he waited in his car while DiMaggio disappeared around the corner with Ruditsky and another man carrying a camera. He said he drove DiMaggio back to the Villa Capri without knowing what happened. Throughout his questioning, the press reported, "Sinatra was alternately flippant and serious."[13]

Irwin denounced Sinatra, claiming that Sinatra followed Ruditsky into Florence Kotz's apartment. "Sinatra was wrong. Almost all of his statements were false," Irwin told the press. Sinatra didn't hear Irwin's testimony at the time, but later did and snapped, "Who are you going to believe—me or a guy who makes his living kicking down bedroom doors?" Sinatra said he hadn't read the *Confidential* story because "I don't have enough time to read that type of trash." He admitted, though, that a man he had never seen before approached him at the MGM studio on the set of his film *The Tender Trap* and told him he heard that the people "who handled the DiMaggio case" had made a deal to sell the story to *Confidential*. After hearing the conflicting testimony, committee members cried perjury. One senator announced that the transcript of the hearings would be certified to the district attorney for "whatever action he deems necessary." He added: "there is perjury apparent here."[14]

Other witnesses confirmed that DiMaggio and Sinatra were at the apartment that night. Building owner Virginia Blasgen said she saw two men, a tall one and a short one, walking around the apartment before the commotion. "The tall one was mad and was walking up and down. The little one was jumping up and down and looking at me, smiling." At about 11 PM she heard a terrible noise, and she went to call the police. She ran out of her apartment and saw the silhouettes of four men running from the building. Sheila Stewart testified that she saw three of the four men filing into the car and identified two of them as Sinatra and DiMaggio.[15]

———

Fred Otash appeared before the committee with his attorney, Arthur Crowley, a slick, well-dressed Hollywood divorce attorney who would represent the Meades in the *Confidential* trial. The press was fascinated with the smug, smirking, "black haired and manicured" Otash, who insisted that he never gave the scandal magazines stories from his files. Otash admitted, though, that he checked out stories for HRI, which he described as a "literary agency" selling information to "all sorts of publications," including *Confidential*.[16]

Otash detailed a "hypothetical case" of how he did investigations for *Confidential*. "Say that movie star X has committed adultery with some little girl. I am given a memo as to what phases of the story they (*Confidential*) want checked. Say that movie star X drove a white Jaguar and was working on a movie at MGM and his wife, who is also a movie star, is on location in Tucson. Say he went to this girl's apartment and they saw the landlady on the way in. I will be told to check whether he has a white Jaguar and whether he was working at MGM, and whether his wife is in Tucson and if the landlady saw the couple in question. That's how it works." He testified that he made a yearly retainer of $7,500 plus extra fees charged for stories "depending on how long it takes to check them."[17]

Testifying at the Kraft hearings in February 1957, private eye Fred Otash insisted that he never gave *Confidential* material from his files. *Photofest*

Otash was threatened with a contempt citation when he refused to disclose the details of his investigation of Anita Ekberg. He finally admitted that he assigned his men to spy on Ekberg. One photograph was taken at a beach where "my man hid behind a hill and shot movies of her coming out of a beach house. He had a telephoto lens," Otash said. He described his agency's wireless listening device and said he used a panel truck that had one-way mirrors so that "pictures can be shot from the inside to the outside." Otash claimed he hadn't been hired by *Confidential* at the time of the Wrong Door Raid, but admitted investigating people involved in it, including Monroe, DiMaggio, and Sinatra. Otash said he turned down appeals from movie stars who were going to be written up in *Confidential* and wanted him to "save them." "If you're scheduled to appear, you'll appear and no amount of money can keep you out and no detective can keep you out because that's the way it is," he told them.[18]

In one of the most sensational moments of the hearings, detective William Lewis described the plan by producer Mervyn LeRoy to launch a "movie industry-wide assault" on the scandal magazines. Lewis recalled how he consulted with LeRoy after being contacted by the security officer of a major studio; he told LeRoy it would take $50,000 from each big film company and a $50,000 expense fund to make an investigation aimed at scuttling *Confidential*. Otash admitted he'd been approached by a detective working on behalf of Hollywood leaders and offered $100,000 to help them shut down the scandal magazines.[19]

The only way to do away with scandal magazines, Otash told the committee, was to do away with scandal. If "communists and sex deviates" were ousted from the movie industry—if male movie stars stayed with their wives and female movie stars stayed with their husbands—"you'll have no scandal--and no scandal magazines."[20]

The Kraft committee hearings made national headlines and revealed *Confidential*'s seedy workings to a fascinated and horrified public. But Hollywood was far from overjoyed—the state's investigation was backfiring. As witnesses brought up stars like Sinatra and Monroe, those names were smeared all over again.

The Kraft hearings fueled the attack on "Hollywood morals." "The hearing in California . . . has underlined the general unhealthy climate which settles over handsome men and beautiful women who provide our motion picture films with . . . human characters," wrote *The Bee* of Danville, Virginia. Quipped the Estherville, Iowa, *Estherville Daily News*, "It took a detective to figure out what's wrong with Hollywood. It isn't the scandal magazines; it's the amoral characters in the bright-light town who prefer other persons' spouses to their own and don't hesitate a moment to exercise those preferences."[21]

At the same time, the state's actions were praised. Many hoped that California's tactics could be adopted in other states, or that if Harrison stopped doing business in California, *Confidential* would be forced to shut its doors. "Action has been instigated in the California courts that might very well be repeated in every state in the nation," cheered the Tyrone, Pennsylvania, *Daily Herald*.

> We welcome California's actions. . . . Go to news stands and drug stores . . . take a good look at the reading material being sold. Ask the various dealers' cooperation in cutting down on the most objectionable types. And back any move made in Pennsylvania to follow California's lead in attempting to ban the scandal magazines completely. You—and more important, your children—will benefit by it!"[22]

The hearings adjourned after three days. "A definite tieup between some private detective agencies and the scandal and expose magazines does exist," the committee concluded. "To spy on Hollywood celebrities in an arbitrary manner for the express purpose of furnishing material and photographs for scandal magazines is an abuse of the privilege to hold an investigator's license." It recommended that the state legislature consider a new law making it unlawful "for any licensee to accept employment for verifying, or the sale of, information of a scandalous nature to such magazines." However sensational, the hearings were inconclusive. As the *New York Times* reported correctly, they not only failed to turn up any concrete suggestions for stopping the scandal magazines but also demonstrated that *Confidential* was diligent in checking out and documenting its scandalous reports.[23]

Kraft said he would ask the California legislature for support to "dig below the surface" of *Confidential*'s operations. His committee had been given $5,000; Kraft said he would seek $10,000 more. He told the press, "We are being flooded with mail and phone calls from motion picture, television, and business figures who say they hope and pray we will get to the bottom and put an end to what is going on."[24]

Less than a week after the Kraft hearings, *Confidential* was indicted on federal criminal charges. In Illinois, a six-count indictment was filed in federal district court charging Confidential, Inc., and the Kable Printing Company with violating federal law by mailing "obscene or crime-inciting" material. The indictment was based on the article, "The Pill That Ends Unwanted Pregnancy." The government charged that the pill was described "in a manner calculated to lead another to use or apply it for producing an abortion." *Confidential*'s attorney described the article as a warning against the use of the pill, but the indictment said the story gave information about how abortions could be produced. The obscenity charges "typify those that people of conscience have wished on the magazine for years," noted the *Hartford Courant*.[25]

Shortly after, California Governor Goodwin Knight called for an "all-out war" on scandal magazines. The magazines "are obviously a menace and gain widespread notoriety. If people can be protected from this sort of thing by law, this legislature should do it," he said. Pat Brown then announced that his office was about to take action against *Confidential* and "maybe others of that type." He made the announcement upon his return from a trip to Washington and New York, where he had conferred with state and federal officials. Brown, who was planning a broader attack on "pornographic literature" in the state, met with New York County District Attorney Frank Hogan to discuss "some phases of the *Confidential* magazine investigation." Hogan agreed to help Brown, since there were New York angles to the inquiry.[26]

Meanwhile, the county grand jury was making plans for the hearing on the Wrong Door Raid. The grand jury was looking into conspiracy and extortion charges and also perjury charges against Sinatra. Ultimately the perjury charges were dropped; District Attorney McKesson admitted that there was conflict between Sinatra's and Irwin's testimonies but thought it fell short of showing the complete elements of perjury.[27]

In March, the grand jury heard more testimony from Sinatra. Sinatra again insisted that he hadn't been involved in the raid and that he only went along with DiMaggio for the ride. After two days, the grand jury adjourned. The jurors concluded that there was no basis for conspiracy and extortion charges and dumped the Wrong Door Raid back into the lap of the L.A. Police Department.[28]

At the end of March 1957, Brown announced that he was ready to move against the "agents, printers, and guys behind" *Confidential.* Brown's chief assistant, Clarence Linn, flew to Los Angeles to confer with District Attorney McKesson. "We want to put a crimp in the operation of *Confidential* and its breed in California and we're going to try every way we can," Linn said. After huddling with McKesson for an hour, he formally announced a joint effort between the attorney general's office and the Los Angeles County District Attorney's Office to prosecute *Confidential.* Linn cited three possible charges—conspiracy to commit criminal libel, conspiracy to extort or the commission of extortion, and violation of the state's laws against the publication of obscene material.[29]

The state senate authorized the renewal of Kraft's committee and $5,000 for continued investigations. The same day, Kraft's wife filed for divorce, charging the senator with adultery, beating her, and threatening her life. The allegations made salacious headlines across the state. Kraft alleged his wife was being used as a "dupe" by foes of his probe into *Confidential.*[30]

22 | CRIMINAL LIBEL

AFTER THE KRAFT HEARINGS, DeStefano told Harrison and the Meades that the "handwriting was on the wall" and that they should shut down their Hollywood gossip operations. HRI closed its doors, and the Meades flew back to New York.[1]

California's actions against *Confidential* emboldened stars to bring more lawsuits. In March 1957, Dorothy Dandridge sued *Confidential*, seeking $2 million in damages. A talented, elegant actress and nightclub singer, Dandridge had recently starred in the lead role in the musical *Carmen Jones*, which had made her one of Hollywood's first African American sex symbols. She had just been nominated for a Best Actress Academy Award, was the first African American woman featured on the cover of *Life*, and had signed a three-movie deal with 20th Century Fox.

Dandridge charged that the article "Only the Birds and the Bees Saw What Dorothy Dandridge Did in the Woods" was "completely false" and caused her "embarrassment, humiliation, and mental anguish," as well as put her career and potential income of more than $250,000 a year in jeopardy. The article was published with "evil motive and malice," and with intent to "injure, disgrace, and defame her" by imputing to her "a laxity of moral character," she claimed.[2] The story, describing a purported sexual liaison with a white man in Lake Tahoe—later revealed as bandleader Dan Terry—was only two pages long.

Up at Tahoe Village in Lake Tahoe where Dorothy played an engagement some time ago, the playboys spent most of their time plotting how to get a warm tumble from the sensuous singer. They tried all the tricks the wolf uses to snare the rich prize, but their message wasn't getting through to Dorothy.

Then one brisk afternoon on a wooded mountain top, a guy with a little ingenuity and a lot of patience discovered that no matter how glamorous a chick is, she can be a pushover for the simple things in life.

Terry was out in the woods trying to get a tan when he saw Dandridge go by, and he convinced her to go for a hike.

After 10 minutes of hiking, Dorothy sat down on a rock to rest and the guy, breathless with anticipation, got down beside her. . . . "Would she in the woods?" he wondered. There was nothing like finding out. He let one arm snake around the famous Dandridge hips and pretty soon they were going through some very passionate preliminaries, but then old Mother Nature cued them into the main event. The birds were doing it and the bees were doing it, so why shouldn't they?

The tender grass might have been a far cry from the man-made comforts of a fancy boudoir and a downy bed, but let's face it—the green grass was good enough long before beds were invented.[3]

The article was based on an affidavit Terry had given to HRI. Fred Meade had a complete background check made on Terry and got confirmation that he'd performed in Tahoe when Dandridge was there.[4]

This wasn't the first time Dandridge had sued a scandal magazine. In January 1957, an article appeared in *Hep*, a scandal magazine aimed at African American audiences, titled "Dorothy Dandridge—Her 10,000 Lovers." It was a false account of the men in her life, including several white men. Dandridge was outraged, and she consulted her friend's husband, a young attorney named Leo Branton Jr. Branton brought suit against *Hep* for $2 million. Shortly afterward another African American magazine, *Sepia*, published an article titled "Why Dorothy Dandridge Is Afraid of Marriage," which also deeply upset her. The magazine said she had been warned by colleagues that marriage to a white man could wreck her career.[5]

According to her friend Geri Branton, Dandridge was "highly, highly incensed" by the *Confidential* article. The article depicted her as a loose woman; it also suggested that a black woman was always sexually available to a white man. "She was not interested in money from a [lawsuit]," Branton recalled. "She was interested in correcting a wrong. She really was strong in that respect." Dandridge feared the press reaction to another interracial sex story, and the article seemed to add to the view that she wasn't attracted to black males. Other magazines linked her with white actors and socialites, including Tyrone Power, Otto Preminger, Michael Rennie, Farley Granger, and Arthur Loew Jr.[6]

Dandridge's lawsuit differed from any other libel suit filed against *Confidential*. She sued Harrison, Govoni, Hollywood Research Inc., and one thousand "John Does," dealers who sold the magazine. Branton had figured out a way to get at *Confidential* in California: filing suit against the in-state news vendors.[7]

In early April, Brown's office moved forward with criminal charges. Clarence Linn went to Los Angeles to push "investigations into scandal magazines." His first stop was the county jail, where he interviewed Ronnie Quillan. Quillan had been imprisoned for smashing her mother-in-law's window in a nasty dispute over a TV set. Quillan had recently married twenty-year-old Daniel O'Reilly. O'Reilly was petitioning for an annulment, claiming that Quillan concealed that she "was not a chaste woman" and was addicted to drugs, and that she threatened to stab him with a knife.[8]

At the end of the month, Brown's office announced that it was ready to go before a grand jury to seek an indictment against *Confidential* for charges of criminal libel and obscenity. Every issue of the magazine contained "an example of libel," Clarence Linn said. "In a criminal libel action it is up to the magazine to prove the stories it printed were true. I do not think it can do so." He claimed that California did have jurisdiction over *Confidential*; *Confidential* had a corporate presence in California through HRI, which he intended to prove was a branch of *Confidential*.[9] A grand jury hearing was set for mid-May.

Brown, who considered himself a civil libertarian, assured the press that criminal charges were not "censorship." He denied that the film industry pressured him, claiming he'd been motivated by "the effect of such publications on children." Brown claimed to know of cases where blackmailers had shaken down stars on the threat of "telling *Confidential*." In an interview many years later, Brown also said "it was a . . . personal thing. Dorothy Dandridge came to Sacramento for a benefit and told me that a story about her in *Confidential* came from a God-damned liar. I was so outraged that I turned the matter over to one of my deputies."[10]

In early May, Linn left on a ten-day trip for New York and Washington to interview potential witnesses. He promised that no Hollywood stars would be called to testify and that the proceedings would be tame compared with Kraft's recent hearings. "We will go into just about everything in the magazine printed during 1956, on the grounds that it was filth and served no legitimate purpose," he told the press. "Right now we are amassing the only complete file of *Confidential*, going back over four years, available on this coast. We want it for background."[11]

"Confidentially, it looks as if the scandal magazine . . . might be close to the end of the road," columnist Drew Pearson reported a few days later. "It might be a good idea to hold on to any copies of *Confidential* magazine you might have. There may be some very drastic editorial policy changes coming up—or else a magazine going down."[12]

Liberace then announced that he planned to sue over an article outing him as homosexual. As the world would discover after his death from AIDS in 1987, the flamboyant pianist was gay, but he never confirmed it his entire life. Revealing his sexual orientation, he felt, would destroy the "perfect son" image that made him so popular with elderly women.[13]

With his wild sequined costumes and gregarious style, Liberace was one of the most popular entertainers of the 1950s. Since 1952, he had been the star of television's *The Liberace Show*. By 1955 he was making $50,000 per week at the Riviera Hotel in Las Vegas, in addition to millions from other public appearances. He had fan clubs with a quarter of a million members and appeared regularly on the covers of magazines. Liberace sought $20 million in damages, more than six times greater than any previous claim against *Confidential*.

"Why Liberace's Theme Song Should Be 'Mad About the Boy'" described how a New York publicity agent had flown from Manhattan to Akron, Ohio, to promote a Fourth of July celebration featuring Liberace. After a huge welcoming ceremony at the airport, the young man accompanied Liberace back to his hotel.

> There are few show business personalities today with a gaudier sense of theater than the Kandelabra Kid himself . . . but the pudgy pianist's many faithful fans would have popped their girdles if they had witnessed their idol in action last year in an *offstage* production that saw old Kittenish on the Keys play one sour note after another in his clumsy efforts to make beautiful music with a handsome but highly reluctant young publicity man.

According to *Confidential*, Liberace wasted no time in persuading the press agent to join him in his suite for a drink. He "had no idea that in a few short minutes he would be fighting for his honor." Innocently, he told Liberace, "whatever you want—I'm your boy." Liberace went to sit on his lap, and a scuffle ensued.

The press agent needed to obtain a legal release from Liberace, and he flew to Los Angeles to get his signature. There, another round of harassment ensued. Later the publicist, still in pursuit of releases, went to see Liberace in Dallas, and there was another incident.[14]

Like Dandridge, Liberace was a familiar figure in the scandal magazines. A September 1954 article in *Rave*, "Don't Call Him Miss," implied a bathroom pickup in a public lavatory and claimed he had given his phone number to a bodybuilder. There were similar stories in *Inside Story*, *Private Lives*, and *Uncensored*. Liberace had recently sued London's tabloid the *Daily Mirror* over a story describing him as "the summit of sex—the pinnacle of masculine, feminine, and neuter. Everything that he, she, and it can ever want . . . a deadly winking, sniggering, snuggling, chromium-plated, scent-impregnated, luminous, quivering, giggling, fruit-flavored, mincing, ice-covered heap of mother love."[15]

Liberace was determined to destroy *Confidential*. In a telephone interview with KTTV newscaster George Putnam, he declared, "George, this story is a damn lie and I'm damned mad. If it takes every nickel I've got I'll guarantee it will never happen to anyone else as long as I live. . . . It's real heartbreak to see your life's work destroyed so viciously by a magazine in an article of this kind. It's a lie. It's trash."[16]

Liberace's complaint alleged that the article was "malicious, false, defamatory, [and] degrading," and subjected him to "public contempt" and ridicule. The story would cause the public to believe that he was a person of "immoral character who performs immoral acts and conducts himself in shocking disregard of public morals and conventions." Liberace claimed he suffered great financial loss because the article caused "unfavorable public comment and opinion toward him and reduced his popularity with the public."[17] He insisted that he could prove he was somewhere else on the nights of the alleged incidents.

Not long before Liberace filed his lawsuit, a Union County, New Jersey, grand jury indicted *Confidential* and several men's magazines on charges of conspiring to sell indecent literature in the county. The county prosecutor said *Confidential* wasn't technically obscene but "went beyond the limits of common decency." The true bills handed down by the grand jury followed complaints from the mother of a nine-year-old boy, who said she was shocked and disgusted when her son brought the magazines home.[18]

On the eve of the grand jury hearing, one of *Confidential*'s California attorneys called up Brown, panicked, and offered him a deal. *Confidential* would cut out "sex and scandal" and revamp its makeup in return for dropping the prosecution. If the deal weren't accepted, he threatened, *Confidential* would subpoena "big names" in Hollywood to prove the truth of its stories. The lawyer, Adolph Alexander, told Brown and McKesson that the "American public has the right to know when the stars of the motion picture, radio, and TV world do not lead moral lives," and that *Confidential*'s exposés were "an influence for good." A criminal libel trial against *Confidential* would be "the dirtiest in history." Brown rejected the proposal, insisting that a criminal trial and conviction was the only effective way of stopping *Confidential*.[19]

Even though Brown promised that the hearings would be "without fireworks," they became a star-studded spectacle thanks to two surprise guests: Maureen O'Hara and Liberace, who appeared voluntarily as witnesses.[20]

The grand jury hearing in May 1957 became a star-studded spectacle thanks to Maureen O'Hara and Liberace, who appeared voluntarily as witnesses.
Photofest

Marching into the grand jury room wearing a flared print skirt, white linen jacket, and gold earrings, O'Hara denounced the *Confidential* article as a "complete lie." "It damaged me personally and professionally," she said.[21] In reality, the Grauman's episode may well have happened. The article contradicted O'Hara's prim and upright image, and she felt that the only way to redeem herself was to deny the charges.

O'Hara testified that the *Confidential* article came to her attention when a schoolteacher friend confiscated the magazine from one of her pupils. "And, as the mother of a twelve-year-old daughter, faced with the same fears of mothers all over the world, I find it shocking that this type of literature is available to children on the newsstands of the United States. . . . I don't think we can measure the damage to the minds and morals of young children by magazines like that," she said briskly.[22]

Liberace, looking sober and conservative in a black suit, decried *Confidential*'s article as "completely false." His "sole purpose" in appearing before the grand jury, he said, was to help the state bring indictments against *Confidential* and the individuals who "publish this obscene tripe." Later that day he issued a statement: "I am going to use the full extent of the law and I am going to attempt in my own humble way to see that these malicious lies and character assassinations will never again happen to another entertainer or American if I can prevent it."[23]

Howard Rushmore appeared before the grand jury, and he was the most damning witness of all. Rushmore, who was working for *Confidential* competitors *Uncensored* and *Tip Off*, alleged that *Confidential*'s elimination would be a "service to American journalism." "We pay a hell of a price for a free press in America when we must have such magazines as *Confidential* and the *Daily Worker*," he said. He described the magazine as "the lowest of the low" and claimed that he quit *Confidential* because he couldn't go along with its policy. He said—falsely—that he never wrote any stories with a "sex angle."[24]

Rushmore revealed *Confidential*'s tipster network—how Harrison "paid for information [from] call girls, private eyes, [and] the bed partners of stars." He gave the grand jury a list of *Confidential*'s Hollywood sources, including Ronnie Quillan and Francesca De Scaffa. De Scaffa received $30,000 for thirty stories over a two-year period, including the Doris Duke, Errol Flynn, and Mitchum stories, Rushmore said. He claimed that the Wrong Door Raid story had come from "an operative"—Irwin—and that Ruditsky provided additional facts. Rushmore denounced Harrison as money-hungry and reckless: "Some of the stories are true, and some have nothing to back them up at all. Harrison many times overruled his libel attorneys and went ahead on something." Despite knowing that Quillan and De Scaffa were unreliable, Harrison took tips from them anyway.[25]

Ronnie Quillan, her bronze hair flowing, appeared in a low-cut brown dress and gold ankle-tied shoes. She admitted that she was one of *Confidential*'s sources, and that the magazine used "call girls" and "private eyes" to get "bedroom gossip." Other witnesses included Samuel Scheff, president of the Publishers Distributing Corporation; Albert Borchard, an official from the General Trucking Company, which transported the magazines; and Arthur Kates, manager of a local distributor of *Confidential*. A member of the state division of corporations outlined HRI's corporate setup. He presented HRI's incorporation applications that revealed it as nothing more than a hollow shell.[26]

———————

On May 16, 1957, Whisper Inc., Confidential Inc. Hollywood Research Inc., Publishers Distributing Corporation, the Kable Printing Company, and eleven individuals, including Helen Studin, Daniel Studin, Fred Meade, Marjorie Meade, Francesca De Scaffa, Michael Tobias, Edith Tobias, Al Govoni, and Richard W. Cox and Robert R. Kable of the Kable Printing Company were indicted for the charge of conspiracy to:

> —circulate material pertaining to abortion (to write, compose, and publish notices and advertisements of medicines or means for procuring and facilitating a miscarriage or abortion and for the prevention of conception);
> —circulate material pertaining to "lost manhood" (to exhibit and distribute advertising and other printed matter concerning lost manhood, lost vitality and impotency, and call attention to medicines, devices, compounds, treatments, and preparations that may be used therefore);
> —circulate "obscene and indecent" material
> —commit criminal libel (to write, print, and by signs and pictures, and the like matter, to impeach the honesty, integrity, virtue, and reputation of living persons and thereby expose such persons to public hatred, contempt, and ridicule)[27]

The state described the entire May 1955, May 1956, and September 1956 issues as "lewd and obscene." "Pega Palo—The Vine That Makes You Virile" was the state's evidence of conspiracy to circulate material pertaining to "male rejuvenation." "The Pill That Ends Unwanted Pregnancy" was evidence of a conspiracy to "circulate material pertaining to abortion." Eight articles—on Mae West, Robert Mitchum, Dorothy Dandridge, and Maureen O'Hara, among others—were the basis of the criminal libel charge. The indictment was returned in the court of Superior Judge Louis Burke, who set bail on Harrison at $25,000 and the others at $10,000 each.[28]

To be clear: *Confidential* was charged with a single crime—*conspiracy* to commit obscenity, criminal libel, and the other two offenses—not obscenity and criminal libel, as often reported in newspapers. The crime of conspiracy is defined as "entering into an agreement with another person to commit a crime." The reason the state brought conspiracy charges, rather than criminal libel and obscenity charges, was that conspiracy was a felony; libel and obscenity were misdemeanors, as was the "lost manhood" charge. Conspiracy to commit a misdemeanor was a felony, carrying imprisonment up to three years or a $5,000 fine.[29] A misdemeanor was not an extraditable offense, but a felony was, which would potentially permit California to summon Harrison from New York.

Under the penal code's section on obscenity, every person who "willfully or lewdly" "writes, composes, stereotypes, prints, publishes, sells, distributes, keeps for sale, or exhibits any obscene or indecent writing, paper, or book" was guilty of a misdemeanor. The law did not specify what "obscenity" was. As in most states, the definition of obscenity used by the California courts was vague—a book was obscene "if it had a substantial tendency to deprave or corrupt its readers by inciting lascivious thoughts or arousing lustful desires."[30]

Under Section 248 of the California Penal Code, criminal libel was the publication of defamatory matter with malicious intent. A defamatory publication was assumed to be false unless the publisher could prove it true, and presumed to be malicious if no "justifiable motive" for publishing it could be shown. A justifiable motive included publishing "matters of legitimate public interest," such as "matters of public health, safety, and security, and all facts pertaining to them, as causes of epidemics, . . . and the news of crime waves." Criminal libel differed from civil libel in that in civil libel cases truth was a complete defense. Criminal libel defendants had the additional burden of showing that the material was published with "good motives and justifiable ends."[31]

The criminal libel charge was unusual, since the crime of libel was practically defunct by the 1950s. Criminal libel laws had originated in the sixteenth century with the English Star Chamber; criminal libel statutes were adopted in the American colonies and remained on the books in most states into the twentieth century. The premise of criminal libel was that, in an age when dueling was used to resolve disputes over reputation, libels caused violence and could therefore be punished by the state: "libels, regardless of what actual damage results to the reputation of the defamed, may be penalized by the state because they tend to create breaches of the peace when the defamed or his friends undertake to revenge themselves on the defamer." While the action for civil libel was based upon the damage done to an individual, the basis for criminal libel was the injury done to society. A criminally libelous publication need not actually result in a breach of the peace; it could be criminal if it had a "tendency" to cause the person or group libeled to breach the peace.[32]

One reason for the decline of criminal libel was that civil actions had largely replaced physical violence as a remedy for defamation.[33] Criminal libel was also disfavored as officials recognized its potential conflict with freedom of the press. As Harvard Law School professor Zechariah Chafee wrote in 1947, criminal libel was a "pretty loose kind of crime." Observed one constitutional law scholar, "A publisher never knows when the law may be applied to him; arbitrary and discriminatory prosecutions are encouraged by such an unclear . . . rule." A 1956 study in the *Texas Law Review* found that most criminal libel cases since the 1920s involved "political controversies" and were used by in-groups to punish their enemies.[34]

Confidential became the first national publication in history to be put on trial for conspiracy to commit criminal libel. Brown told the press that California was reviving criminal libel, "pioneering new fields in the prosecution of criminal libel." *Confidential*, Drew Pearson noted, was "faced with one of the toughest criminal suits in the history of American magazines."[35]

The state's actions were cheered. Brown's office received congratulatory letters, including several from film industry figures. "We want to congratulate you on the fine stand you are taking regarding *Confidential*," producer Walter Wanger wrote. "More power to you." "Let me take this opportunity to wish you and your office well in your fight against a national disgrace like *Confidential* magazine," wrote one constituent. "If you succeed in doing away with this form of criminal invasion of privacy and blackmail you will deserve the thanks of the nation."[36]

The ACLU was silent. It was hard to disapprove of what the state had done; California had moved against *Confidential* not with a "prior restraint" or outright ban on the magazine, but a "subsequent punishment" affording due process and a jury trial.

Harrison's lawyers insisted that *Confidential* couldn't be indicted; only HRI was a California corporation, they maintained, and HRI had no connection to *Confidential*. Harrison and his staff stayed in New York and fought extradition, while Fred and Marjorie, California residents, flew back to Los Angeles and surrendered.[37]

The Meades arrived in the courtroom of Judge Louis H. Burke with their lawyer Arthur Crowley. A well-known Hollywood divorce lawyer who was just thirty-two, Crowley was a fastidious and fashionable dresser who enjoyed big-game hunting and ballroom dancing. Crowley told reporters that the Meades considered the charges "quite ridiculous and are anxious to prove their innocence—to vindicate themselves."[38]

"We've come back voluntarily at our own expense. We've committed no crime whatsoever," Fred Meade told the *Los Angeles Times*. Marjorie, wearing a fur scarf and a five-karat diamond ring, asked coyly, "Don't you think this whole thing has a little to do with the destruction of freedom of the press?" Although bail had been set for $10,000 each, Burke was swayed by the Meades' voluntary surrender and reduced the sum by half. The Meades presented a certified check and were freed. In early July, they returned to court to plead not guilty. The trial was scheduled for the end of July.[39]

The state sought the return of Francesca De Scaffa, who had moved to Mexico after marrying Mexican bullfighter Jaime Bravo. She claimed she was a Mexican citizen and filed for an injunction against her arrest and deportation. After the grand jury hearings implicated her as a *Confidential* informant, she attempted suicide by taking an overdose of sleeping pills and slashing her wrists with a razor blade. Bravo said that the Mexican press was treating her very cruelly, branding her a "pornographer."[40]

Harrison's extradition hearing was held in July in Albany. Milton Pollack, Harrison's lawyer, told the governor's chief legal advisor that extradition would "open the floodgates to wholesale reprisal" against *Confidential* in other states. The charges against Harrison, he said, had been inspired by "certain elements of Hollywood that were made uncomfortable by disclosures of the magazine." To permit extradition would encourage other states to act against New York editors who published material that was "not to their liking."[41] The decision was to be made in October. In the end, Harrison and his staff were never extradited; Fred and Marjorie were the only *Confidential* defendants to stand trial.

———————

The day after the Meades' surrender, *Confidential* settled with Dorothy Dandridge for $10,000 and an apology.[42]

Harrison was determined to fight the lawsuit but gave up because it involved the magazine's Los Angeles distributors and threatened to spread to every newsstand that handled *Confidential*. Harrison's lawyers told him, "Miss Dandridge is a consummate actress. She could come into court and shed a few tears" and win. Harrison agreed to publish an apology but not a retraction. The apology read, "In the May 1957 edition there appeared an article concerning you. You have advised us that this article is completely untrue, and without foundation in fact. We accept your statement without equivocation. The publishers and staff of *Confidential* magazine extend you our deepest apology for the story and all its implications. We hope that this will in some measure ameliorate the humiliation and embarrassment you have suffered."[43]

Confidential later tried to revoke the settlement when it claimed Dandridge misrepresented it. It demanded its money back because Dandridge and her attorney declared at news conferences that the settlement proved that the story was false. Harrison sent a letter to Dandridge: "As you well know, *Confidential* magazine has never admitted this story is false . . . in our opinion the story is unquestionably true and we could prove it."[44] *Confidential*'s lawyers wanted to weasel out of the settlement because of the grand jury indictment; the lawyers knew the settlement could be used against them. Dandridge went ahead and cashed the check.

Not long after, Maureen O'Hara sued *Confidential* and its Southern California news vendors for libel, asking for $1 million in damages. She alleged that the article was "false and untrue, libelous and defamatory, and . . . caused the public to hold [her] in contempt and ridicule, injuring her in her employment, [and] her profession." As a result of the article, she said, she was subjected to "contempt and ridicule" by "friends, acquaintances, motion picture fans, the general public, as well as members of her own family, including her daughter in elementary school, a nephew in Canada, a sister in West Virginia, and further including a sister who is a nun in Ireland."[45]

Liberace's libel suit survived attempts by *Confidential*'s lawyers to quash the complaint. They offered several defenses: that the allegations were true, that the statements were opinion and not actionable, and that the article contained newsworthy "matters of public concern." *Confidential*'s lawyers also claimed the allegations weren't defamatory. "The article does not reflect adversely upon the plaintiff's abilities or reputation as an entertainer or pianist. Plaintiff's argument is groundless as would be the assertion that people do not listen to the music of Tchaikovsky or Wagner because of the known facts concerning their private lives."[46]

Liberace's lawyers retorted, "*Confidential* magazine, the so-called Grand-father Stink Pot of the scandal magazines, 20th century purveyors of literary filth and trash, selects well known Hollywood celebrities as its favorite hunting ground for alleged inside stories of private escapades in the field of sex. The owners of the magazine now come into court to ask that its vicious stories be given an innocent meaning. . . . Scandal publications are neither educational, informative, nor newsworthy. . . . The scandal magazine deliberately fashions outrageous falsehoods to commercially exploit the needs of the prurient. The product is not news." Judge Leon David overruled the motion to dismiss the case, concluding that "the court is satisfied that the article complained of is libelous."[47]

Several hours after Liberace gave his deposition, his sixty-five-year-old mother was brutally beaten. As she was going into the garage to take out her trash, she saw two men in business suits, their faces covered by black hoods. The men caught her on the porch and kicked her. One of them said, "Kick her again so we will have something to laugh about later." Her heavy corset saved her from being injured. A family spokesman told reporters, "I feel this whole thing is connected with the *Confidential* suit. Somebody is trying to frighten us."[48]

In Illinois, *Confidential* and the Kable Printing Company pleaded not guilty to federal charges of mailing obscene material. *Confidential*'s lawyers waived a jury and asked for a speedy trial. The Kable Printing Company's attorney asked for a dismissal of the indictment, saying that it didn't state specific charges and violated the First Amendment.[49]

Judge Joseph Sam Perry of the US District Court for the Northern District of Illinois described *Confidential* as "a magazine that is a purveyor of social sewage." It is "like a bad boy and ought to be whipped for that." He proceeded to find *Confidential* not technically obscene, and dismissed the indictment. *Confidential's* attorney hailed the ruling as a victory for freedom of the press.[50]

In June, Brown's office ordered Harrison to hold back a new issue of *Whisper*, telling him that distribution of the magazine would be considered another violation of the law. Clarence Linn had gotten a copy of the latest issue and declared it libelous and obscene. Linn said that if *Whisper* were put on sale in California, he would seek indictments against the Publishers Distributing Corporation and its officers, as well as wholesalers of the magazine in California. Harrison promised to ship one hundred thousand copies back to New York. "I don't think *Confidential* will ever be on sale in this state again," Linn said. "Ultimately, it won't go anyplace. Other states will see that we've been able to run it out and they will do the same."[51]

Harrison's lawyers proceeded to file two lawsuits against Brown and Linn, seeking damages of over $3 million as well as a restraining order. US district court judge Harry Westover dismissed the suits, ruling that Brown and Linn were within their authority in warning distributors that prosecution would follow sale of the magazines. "In the present case," said the judge, "all the Attorney General has said is, 'If you violate the law, we will prosecute you.' . . . One of the attorney general's duties is to warn possible law violators. I can't see anything wrong with that."[52]

Meanwhile, Crowley told Otash to serve subpoenas on over one hundred stars to appear as witnesses in the trial. Linn called the move "a reign of terror." Stars frantically met with their attorneys to figure out if they'd actually be called to the stand. Dozens fled Hollywood to avoid the process servers. "Most of my colleagues decided that [it] was the perfect time to take that long delayed Mexican vacation," Tab Hunter recalled. Crowley described the flight from Hollywood as like the "exodus from Egypt." Dan Dailey managed to avoid detectives at the Hollywood Bowl, where he was appearing in a concert. Otash posted detectives with subpoenas all at the stage door exits. At the end of the concert, Dailey took a bow, then "vaulted over the footlights when the curtain fell." He wound his way through the aisles, got into a friend's car, and sped away. In the end, 117 subpoenas were served.[53]

The prospect of stars being forced to divulge their private lives in court created a panic among Hollywood leaders. In their zeal to go after *Confidential*, they had overlooked the possibility that stars could be forced to testify about whether *Confidential*'s stories were true. "Hollywood's jitters have mounted toward hysteria," noted the *New York Daily News*. One executive at a major studio was reportedly working full-time to prevent stars from being called to the witness stand.[54]

Fearing that the exposure would be even worse than the continued publication of *Confidential*, industry representatives made a desperate effort to get the state to drop the case. George Murphy met with Clarence Linn, who conferred with Arthur Crowley. Linn and Crowley reached a compromise and presented it to the judge on the first morning of the trial. *Confidential* and *Whisper* would stop printing smear articles about celebrities and would announce the change in newspaper ads. The guilt or innocence of Confidential Inc., Hollywood Research Inc., and the Publishers Distributing Corporation would be decided by the judge based on the transcript of the grand jury hearing. Charges against Fred and Marjorie would be dismissed.[55]

"I want to make it clear that the reputations of many persons will suffer if this case goes on trial, because we are going to offer the truth as a defense against the libel charges," Crowley threatened Judge Herbert V. Walker. He predicted that the trial would drag out for six months, and "a lot of reputations would be endangered—which no one wants to do." Linn told the judge that the compromise was satisfactory: "We'll obtain suppression of the magazines in their present form. Everything will have been accomplished except a jail term for the Meades." "We will have put out of business . . . the two magazines involved, and we believe this action will lead their imitators to desist from publication."[56]

Walker rejected the deal. A serious, stern, bushy browed former L.A. County district attorney appointed to the bench in 1953, Walker said he could not in good conscience accept the proposed disposition of the case. "I don't think a good reason has been given here for the dismissal of the indictments," he said. The trial would proceed on schedule.[57]

Right before the trial was to open, Harrison made his last gutsy move. The September 1957 issue of *Confidential*, appearing on newsstands in July 1957, ran a two-page editorial titled "Hollywood v. Confidential." Labeled "A Publisher's Statement," it was the only *Confidential* article ever signed by Harrison.

> That this magazine is under assault in the California courts is, we assume, a fact known to most of our nine million readers. . . . A California Assistant Attorney General has stated to the press, "In my opinion, *Confidential* is finished."
>
> This is a determined effort, initiated by a segment of the motion picture industry, to "get" this magazine.
>
> We hold no secrets from our readers. In our first issue, nearly five years ago, we promised to "publish the facts" and "name the names." We have kept that promise, and our readers have made us successful. We have *the world's largest newsstand sale*. . .
>
> WE ARE *NOT GUILTY* OF "CONSPIRACY TO PUBLISH CRIMINAL LIBEL."
>
> A precious and historic American principle is this: truth may be distasteful but truth can *never* be libelous. . . .
>
> In an American courtroom, under the Stars-and-Stripes, thank God, truth stands as the unassailable shield against charges of libel. . . .
>
> "Hollywood" is in the business of lying. Falsehood is a stock in trade. They use vast press-agent organizations and advertising expenditures to "build up" their "stars." They "glamorize" and distribute detailed—and often deliberately false—information about their private lives. Because of advertising money, in these "build-ups" they have the cooperation of large segments of the daily press, many magazines, columnists, radio, and TV. They have the cooperation of practically every medium *except Confidential*. . . . They can't "influence" us, so they want to "get" us.
>
> We do not underestimate this effort to "get" us. We concede that those who want to "finish" us are powerful and resourceful. They have

some tricky arguments; they are artists in the old three-shell game. But we expect to survive. For we believe that even those Americans who may not like what we say will, nevertheless defend our right to say it.

We doubt that the time has arrived when Americans can be "gotten" for the crime of telling the truth.[58]

23 | THE TRIAL

ON FRIDAY, AUGUST 2, 1957, 135 film stars jammed the courtroom of Judge Herbert Walker, trailed by a mob of unruly onlookers. Walker's courtroom was on the eighth floor of the Hall of Justice, one of the older buildings in Los Angeles's Civic Center, with a granite-clad exterior and an opulent grand lobby with ionic marble columns. The courtroom had a high, ornate gilt ceiling and the walls featured dozens of panels with paintings of the state seals. It was stiflingly hot, and large portable air conditioners whirred heavily in the windows.[1]

Scores of fans, mostly housewives and teenage girls, thronged the hallways hoping to get seats in the two rows open to the public. A necktie salesman hawked his wares outside from an open suitcase. Sheriff's deputies wrestled with hundreds of gawkers. Tempest Storm, a stripper known as the "Queen of Exotic Dancers," created a stir when she showed up in an ice-blue high-collared dress. Dozens of reporters sat in the press box taking notes on notepads and clacking manual typewriters. A screenwriter was in court daily to record the proceedings for a planned movie about *Confidential.* Fred and Marjorie were in court every day, impeccably dressed; the press lavished attention on Marjorie's pretty, demure frocks and described her as "red haired" and "sloe-eyed." Judge Walker allowed photographers to take pictures when court was not in session, and "photographers did not use the opportunity to display their good manners," recalled a law student who sat in on the trial.[2]

"Don't you think this whole thing has a little to do with the destruction of freedom of the press?" Marjorie Meade asked. *Photofest*

The spectacle, one of the biggest news events of the summer, became an airing of dirty linen on an epic scale. *Confidential* was being put on trial, but so was Hollywood. After the trial and its sordid revelations, it was no longer possible to completely buy into the movie star fantasy. The illusion was shattered, and there was no going back.

As it stood on the eve of the trial, the main issues in the trial were whether the *Confidential* defendants intended and conspired to publish obscene material, to violate the abortion-promotion and "lost manhood" provisions in the penal code, and to commit criminal libel, based on eight *Confidential* articles. Defeating the criminal libel charge required showing that the articles were true, and that they were published "with good motives and for justifiable ends." Proving the truth of the articles would likely require testimony from the stars. The other big issue was whether *Confidential* was actually on trial. The state said that *Confidential* had a California presence through HRI, but Crowley insisted that *Confidential* and HRI were separate. Crowley would try to convince the jury that *Confidential* and HRI had no official connection.

Corinne Calvet, Gary Cooper, Walter Pidgeon, Scott Brady, Rory Calhoun, Sonny Tufts, Lana Turner, Paul Gregory, Tom Neal, Buddy Baer, Allan Nixon, and Tab Hunter were among those who showed up to testify on the first day. Hunter, who had just come back from an expensive European vacation, couldn't afford to flee town and remained in Hollywood as "a sitting duck," he recalled. Hunter was terrified at the prospect of being called to testify about the "gay pajama party": "I'd have to admit that it was indeed true, and the story would run in a million mainstream papers—ruining my career for sure."[3]

Hunter appealed to the court to release him from his subpoena. His attorney argued that the testimony would be worthless since Hunter wasn't described in any of the *Confidential* stories at issue in the trial. It resulted in a "chest-to-chest," "baseball umpire type" argument with Crowley. Walker rejected the appeal. The judge said he couldn't foresee the defense's argument and rule on the relevancy of evidence in advance. Walker implied that he would allow the defense to call any star named in any *Confidential* article, not just those in the eight articles cited by the prosecution.[4] It was an important ruling, and it caused a good deal of panic in Hollywood.

Rory Calhoun's lawyers also tried to suppress his subpoena, claiming that his testimony could "serve no purpose" and that the subpoena had been issued to "harass" him. Walker denied the motion and said he would send uniformed officers to haul into court any of the stars who failed to appear as witnesses. "I'll send the law after them," he threatened.[5]

The state's two prosecutors were Assistant Attorney General Clarence Linn and Los Angeles Deputy District Attorney William Ritzi. A graduate of the University of Southern California Gould School of Law, Ritzi had been an Assistant US Attorney and was appointed Los Angeles County Deputy District Attorney in 1953. Dogged and boyish, a soft-spoken, contemplative man in his early forties who had an "almost constant mien of dead-earnestness" about him, Ritzi was the father of two young children. An acquaintance described him as "a sweetheart . . . one of the kindest, most wonderful men you could ever hope to encounter." A quiet-voiced, barrel-chested man with short pepper-gray hair, enormous eyebrows, and a bulldog look about him, Linn also worked as a Sunday School teacher in San Francisco.[6]

Jury selection started the first day. Crowley asked every prospective juror whether they had read *Confidential*. Of the first twenty-five examined, only four said yes—women who flipped through the magazine at the beauty parlor. Crowley warned potential jurors that they would have to listen to testimony that was "distasteful and repugnant." Several begged off because they didn't think they could be unbiased. One woman was dismissed when she professed "vehement dislike" for *Confidential*. A nurse was challenged by the defense because she might be prejudiced about abortions. Others said the trial's length—several weeks up to several months—made it impossible to serve. A "shock-proof" jury of seven men and five women was seated on August 7. Only two were under forty; most described themselves as retired or housewives married to retired men.[7]

Linn told the jury he would prove that *Confidential* "operated through private eyes and women of the night to make contacts with prominent people around Hollywood and create situations." The magazine "specialized in embarrassing situations which depict the lewdest sort of thing," he alleged. *Confidential* "maliciously dredged up from forgotten gutters a slip from the straight and narrow path by a prominent individual and depicted it as the individual's way of life."[8]

Crowley insisted that *Confidential* was totally innocent and "clean." For the last two years the Post Office had examined every issue and all passed scrutiny. A New York law firm vetted every word to make sure nothing was defamatory or obscene. "Private detectives are employed to verify the information," Crowley explained. Far from seeking to exaggerate celebrities' sins, *Confidential* tried to conceal their more sordid escapades. "The real stories behind the stories printed in *Confidential* are far worse than the actual stories in the magazine and the evidence will show it," he told the jury. Crowley pointed out that there had only been 110 criminal libel cases in the United States since 1920, and more than fifty of them were "politically inspired." *Confidential* had "made powerful enemies in Hollywood because we name names."[9]

The state's first witnesses, two Beverly Hills bank clerks, confirmed the existence of cashed checks and bank records connecting HRI to *Confidential*. Jack Stern, an investigator for the state Division of Corporations, presented HRI's incorporation papers. An employee of the Pacific Telephone and Telegraph Company showed records of calls between the Meades' office and *Confidential*'s New York headquarters. As the Meades left the courtroom on the first day, they were handed a subpoena to testify in Maureen O'Hara's lawsuit.[10]

Sharply dressed in crisp suits and expensive ties, Howard Rushmore—described by the press as "lanky [and] balding"—was the prosecution's major witness. For three hours Rushmore bitterly described his time at *Confidential* and the magazine's seedy workings. The press called it the "first lively testimony."[11] Rushmore's testimony was by far the most damaging in the case against *Confidential*.

Rushmore recalled *Confidential*'s origins, how he started working for Harrison, and how Harrison started the "hot Hollywood stories" policy. He told the jury that Harrison dispatched him to Hollywood to dig up informants, including "madams, procurers, call girls, [and] private detectives" and how the Meades set up HRI and the tipster network. Rushmore recalled hiring Francesca De Scaffa and named her as a key source: "She told us she had access to practically every home in Hollywood . . . that she knew all the secrets and could get the stories we wanted," even if it involved sleeping with someone. "I told Mr. Harrison that we had to be very careful with De Scaffa as I considered her dangerous and emotionally unstable," Rushmore said.[12]

The names began dropping. Rushmore revealed that De Scaffa supplied facts for the story on Josephine Dillon, which she got by having sex with Clark Gable. Stunned reporters contacted Gable, vacationing on Maui; he feigned ignorance and denied everything. Rushmore rattled off the names of dozens of others who supplied tips, including Florabel Muir, H. L. von Wittenberg, Agnes Underwood, Mike Connolly, and Barney Ruditsky.[13]

Harrison's "main object was to sell magazines. And it wasn't within our province to determine whether it hurts people. He told me . . . that if the truth hurts, that's it," Rushmore said. According to Rushmore, Harrison often overrode his lawyers, telling them, "I'd go out of business if I printed the kind of stuff you want." When Crowley asked Rushmore if he'd ever written a story just to hurt someone, he replied, "I certainly did!" That answer, one newspaper reported, "knocked the wind out of the ordinarily suave Crowley."[14]

Tired and haggard, wearing a tight, sleeveless white knit dress, Ronnie Quillan—described by the press as a "Hollywood sex spy"—took the stand for the prosecution. When asked her occupation, she confessed she had been a prostitute.[15]

Quillan described meeting Harrison in Beverly Hills, and how he asked her to report "activities of celebrities in Hollywood." "He wanted stories primarily dealing with the sexual activities of celebrities in the movie colony, the more lewd and lascivious those stories were, the more colorful the magazine," she said. Quillan testified that she fed Harrison news about an "incident" involving Desi Arnaz back in 1944. Reporters called Arnaz for his reaction. "I don't remember meeting the lady and I guess I'm being kind in calling her a lady," he replied. The *Confidential* article "was a lot of baloney. . . . I've never seen her before in my life. And I don't think it's right to let an admitted prostitute get up on the witness stand and say anything she likes about anybody."[16]

Frank Goldberg, a freelance writer, confessed that he volunteered embarrassing facts about actor Sonny Tufts. Reporter Jerry McCarthy said he worked for *Confidential* briefly but quit because he felt it was "digging too far in a lot of dirt." A former prostitute, Gloria Wellman, admitted that she was paid $650 for three stories, including one about a "naked pool party" at the home of actor John Carroll. Detective H. L. von Wittenberg testified that he met Harrison in Hollywood, and that Harrison gave him business cards giving the detective's office as a *Confidential* address. He worked for *Confidential* for a few days, then quit because he thought the whole thing "stank."[17]

The prosecution had introduced thirteen allegedly libelous and obscene articles into evidence but asked that jurors read them themselves. Walker told Ritzi that copies of the magazines hadn't been given to the court and that the articles would have to be read aloud to the jury, word for lurid word.

Smiling wanly as the bailiff fetched him a glass of water, Ritzi reluctantly approached the witness chair. Peeling back the red-and-yellow cover of a *Confidential*, with a microphone in his hand, he read the articles slowly and hesitantly, with the inflection of a father reading bedtime stories to his children. When the jurors began to titter during the reading of the first article, Walker, famous for his strict courtroom decorum, reprimanded them sternly. The entire reading took more than two days. Newspapers reprinted excerpts of the articles, exposing millions of Americans, for the first time, to *Confidential*'s tawdry accusations about Mae West, Frank Sinatra, Eddie Fisher, Elvis Presley, Anita Ekberg, Dick Powell, June Allyson, and Dorothy Dandridge.[18]

Crowley made two motions to dismiss the charges. Jurisdiction over *Confidential*'s actions lay with New York rather than California, he argued; if a conspiracy had been committed, the charges should have been brought where the magazine was published. Walker retorted, "If your view were correct, I could set up a place downtown and advertise that I would murder anyone outside the state of California and be safe as far as conspiracy was concerned." Crowley also challenged the libel section of the indictment because it cited only a section of the state penal code defining libel, and not the next section, which prescribed punishment for "willfully and maliciously" committing libel. Walker rejected the challenge. He also declined to rule on a prosecution motion to deny Crowley the right to call the 117 stars under subpoena. Linn and Ritzi argued that only the stars mentioned in the articles entered into evidence could be called. The judge said Crowley could call anyone he wanted to the stand and the court would rule case by case whether the witness could testify.[19]

Studio leaders continued to try to get the state to drop the prosecution, or to have the case settled out of court—"or at least conducted without the lid being ripped off Hollywood boudoirs," Aline Mosby reported for the United Press. District Attorney William McKesson denied rumors of a studio-inspired deal between the prosecution and defense. "Hollywood does not control justice in California," he insisted.[20]

The prosecution's final witness was Paul Gregory, the celebrated producer of *The Night of the Hunter* and *The Naked and the Dead*. Gregory had been the subject of a brutal *Confidential* exposé, "The Lowdown on Paul Gregory Himself." The article described how Gregory, back in 1944, had been hauled into a Los Angeles courtroom and ordered to "return to a plump, gray-haired widow of 61 several thousands of dollars which he had bamboozled from her."

The woman had just become a widow and took Gregory in as one of her boarders. According to *Confidential*, Gregory pretended to be romantically interested in her and proposed marriage. He also proposed some lucrative business deals. The woman loaned him money, and she had her lawyer draw up papers making Gregory the joint owner of her home and the four lots it stood on. No sooner was she business partners with Gregory than "they became less and less partners in amour," *Confidential* wrote. When she filed a lawsuit to get her property back, he started abusing her. A judge concluded that Gregory's proposal had been false and ordered Gregory to relinquish his claims to her property.[21]

Gregory testified that *Confidential* tried to extort him—to commit "character assassination and blackmail." In 1955, he said, he had gotten a call from Marjorie Meade, describing herself as "Miss Dee." In a meeting at Sherry's Restaurant, she told him that a "derogatory article" about him could be kept out of *Confidential* if he paid $800. The story involved a "wild filmland party" attended by Gregory, Charles Laughton, Robert Mitchum, and Elsa Lanchester. He also testified that his secretary had been harassed by calls from a "Miss Ann Smith" who warned him "something terrible was going to happen to my business associates if I didn't do certain things."[22]

Gregory clearly lied on the stand. Crowley proved that Sherry's wasn't even around at the time and brought up a witness who showed that Marjorie was out of town visiting a friend that day. As Gregory spoke, Marjorie broke down sobbing and had to be examined by a physician. Fred walked over to the prosecution counsel table and banged his fist. "You must want to win this case pretty bad by putting that lying character on the stand," he shouted.[23]

Ritzi was unamused. "She says she feels real bad, and that this is hurting her character. I wonder how Maureen O'Hara feels today and some of the other people that they have pilloried," he said.[24]

The trial was a massive media circus. It made the front pages of newspapers around the country nearly every day during August and September 1957, rating top headlines along with other major world events. Every big American newspaper and news organization had reporters in the courtroom. The *New*

York Daily News had two correspondents, the *New York Times* had one, and the *Chicago Tribune* and *Kansas City Star* each had one. There were nine reporters from Los Angeles newspapers. ABC and CBS had radio reporters and CBS also had TV reporters in the courtroom. Almost one fourth of the press section was occupied by the foreign press. The foreign reporters looked on with astonishment at the spectacle that only celebrity-obsessed America could deliver. Radio Moscow informed listeners that it provided "an excellent illustration" of those "morals about which American political figures so dearly love to pontificate."[25]

Several outlets covered the trial conservatively. The *New York Times* instructed its West Coast reporter to "write this one for your Aunt Minnie" and put the stories in its back pages under tame titles like "Magazine's Plea Denied by Court." The *Chicago Evening American* tucked the coverage of the trial on its inside pages. Some papers ignored it altogether. *The San Diego Union* told its readers it considered the story too tawdry for a family newspaper. In the South and Midwest, stories about the trial were censored or banned altogether. In Detroit, Hearst's *Detroit Times* was the only paper to cover it on the front page.[26]

Other papers ran riot with it. The New York tabloids ran lurid headlines like "14 Stars Shine in Hollywood Bedtime Story," "Elvis Wriggled on Mag's Hook," "V-Girl Tells of Desi Smear," and "Clark Gable Linked to Vice Mag Party Girls." Sales of newspapers—and *Confidential*—skyrocketed during the trial. Even in small towns, *Confidential* was flying off newsstands. The residents of Pottstown, Pennsylvania, were said to be buying "expose magazines" at the rate of almost five thousand a week.[27]

Critics blasted the sensational coverage as just more "smut." "The large newspapers who make such a fetish of building up our democracy should be great-hearted enough to pass up a few extra sales to the sensation-minded segment of the public and leave such trashy subjects in the gutter where they belong. To print scandal unnecessarily in order to sell papers is wrong. Confidentially, it stinks," said Father Denis Dougherty, writing in the *Catholic Advance*. The Vatican's official organ complained that newspapers were giving the *Confidential* trial the same space they would give news on the subject of "disarmament or the Russian missile or the Middle East situation." In a public address, preacher Billy Graham lamented that "our papers are taken up with news about Maureen O'Hara, not the awesome fact the Russians have an intercontinental missile." He begged Americans to forget about the *Confidential* trial. "It's time for us to wake up."[28]

At long last, as the lurid facts rolled out of the courtroom, the film industry organized to fight. In late August, George Murphy put together a Hollywood "vigilante committee" to fight back against the scandal magazines. The group was formed at a closed meeting of the Motion Picture Industry Council at the Beverly Hilton. It promised to immediately "take steps to safeguard the entire industry against present and future attacks by scandal publications." "Because of the great damage to our industry and to the reputation and standing of all who work in it, a permanent committee has been appointed to protect the welfare of our entire industry," Murphy announced. Nine organizations joined, including the Association of Motion Picture Producers, the Independent Motion Picture Producers Association, the Screen Actors Guild, and the Screen Producers Guild. The committee proposed the establishment of a "permanent organization with the best legal advisers, the purposes of which will be to curtail the activities of smut gatherers preying on the people in our industry," as well as an educational campaign "formed to combat lies with the facts and truth." "We've got to set up the machinery to prevent such a thing as this *Confidential* trial from ever happening again," Murphy said.[29]

Throughout the trial, stars blasted *Confidential* and denounced prosecution witnesses' testimony. Every time a witness dropped a prominent name, reporters called the star to get his or her reaction. Mae West called *Confidential*'s story about her affair with Chalky Wright an "outright lie." Dick Powell denied that June Allyson had carried on with Alan Ladd. Josephine Dillon told the press that *Confidential*'s allegations about Clark Gable were "completely impossible." Several stars boasted that they would be happy to testify. Corinne Calvet said *Confidential* was a "malignant growth" and that she would gladly testify if it would put an end to the magazine. Errol Flynn also offered his services. "I think it is about time someone stepped forward to unsully the fair name of we thespians," he said. "The fact that this magazine is getting away with a pack of lies is an outrage against civil liberties and leaves a bad odor where it is not deserved."[30] Crowley dared them to come to court and swear under oath that *Confidential*'s stories were false.

Panicked and desperate, Harrison watched the proceedings unfold from the safety of his New York office. In September the *New York Daily Mirror* and the *New York Post* each did multipart series on Harrison. The *Post*'s "The Man Behind *Confidential*" portrayed Harrison as deflated and defeated, stripped of his trademark swagger and bravado. He paced "continually from wall to wall of the room" and complained that he was being treated unfairly. Since *Confidential*, publications of all kinds, even respected magazines, had started publishing star exposés. "What about *Look*? . . . What about the *Saturday Evening Post*?" he asked. "What about your paper? . . . Why do they pick on me? No one speaks of the good we've done. Is this the price of success?"[31]

Two weeks into the trial, the defense opened its stunning presentation. Crowley told the press that his opening witness would be a bombshell, a "complete surprise to the prosecution."[32]

That witness was James Craig, an Irish film producer living in London, who had previously been assistant manager of Grauman's Chinese Theatre. Craig had given *Confidential* the story about Maureen O'Hara. In a crisp, clipped accent, the neat, bespectacled Craig testified that he saw O'Hara and an "unidentified male" embracing in the theater in November 1953. Craig had met O'Hara in Ireland and recognized her immediately when she entered Grauman's. Ritzi cross-examined him for a half an hour.

Craig's account of the incident was identical to what appeared in *Confidential*. "An hour after they were seated, I found the gentleman was seated facing the screen, but Miss O'Hara was laying across his lap. . . . She looked very disheveled and very untidy." "When I observed what was going on, I coughed," he said. "But they did nothing at all." Craig returned with a flashlight and played the beam across their bodies to get them stop. Startled, they both sat up.[33]

Craig continued, "Later I found the gentleman sitting on the seat and Miss O'Hara sitting on his lap. I asked them to leave." Craig said he told *Confidential* about the incident because he "did not think such behavior should be permitted in a public theater, even in Hollywood." Ritzi thundered, "And you thought you would set yourself up as God to judge the public?"[34]

On cross-examination, Ritzi took out a blackboard and asked Craig to diagram the positions of O'Hara and her escort. He drew the outlines of three seats and two people in them. Craig and Ritzi jostled back and forth in an effort to place each arm, leg, trunk, and foot in its proper place. At one point, an exasperated Ritzi blurted out, "To put it bluntly, where was her rear end?" Craig replied solemnly, "Her rear end was on the edge of seat number 2." Walker asked Craig and a blonde female reporter, Lee Belser of the International News Service, to act out the scene, and laughter swept the courtroom. "This is not amusing. It may affect the lives of many people," Walker said sternly.[35]

O'Hara denounced Craig's testimony. "In an effort to be charitable to Mr. Craig, I can only say that he is entirely mistaken either in his identity of me or in his testimony," she told the press. O'Hara claimed that during November 1953, when the alleged incident took place, she was overseas making a movie. She showed reporters her passport to prove that she left the United States in early fall and went to Ireland, Paris, and then to Spain to film *Fire Over Africa*, returning in January 1954. O'Hara's attorney told her to boost her $1 million libel suit to $5 million because of Craig's testimony—based on the "additional publicity given this ridiculous article." The following morning she appeared at the attorney's office and signed an amended complaint.[36]

Michael Mordaunt-Smith, who had also flown in from London, described *Confidential*'s European operations. He claimed he documented the O'Hara story for *Confidential*, including going to Ireland to get information. As Craig and Mordaunt-Smith walked from the courtroom, both were handed subpoenas to appear as witnesses in O'Hara's libel suit. The day Mordaunt-Smith testified, thugs broke into his London office. Twenty-eight files were stolen, including affidavits about stars' activities with call girls, and "the story of a recently-married society girl and a wealthy prince from India." The thieves smashed cabinets and overturned furniture. Police suspected a "blackmail gang" was involved.[37]

There were other shady incidents involving *Confidential* witnesses. Polly Gould, an investigator who once worked for *Confidential*, was found dead in her Hollywood apartment. The coroner listed her death as "natural, or possibly accidental due to an overdose of narcotics." She was reportedly helping the state and was on the list of possible rebuttal witnesses for the prosecution. Gould's death followed less than a week after the death of Chalky Wright, subpoenaed by the defense. Wright was found drowned in his bathtub. Gertrude Arnold, Wright's former wife, had gotten an anonymous telephone call: "Gert, you better clam up if you know what's good for you."[38]

On August 19, Judge Walker issued his most important ruling in the trial. Walker limited testimony to the stars specifically mentioned in the articles introduced by the prosecution. The decision came when a tall, twenty-two-year-old showgirl named Mylee Andreason was called to testify about the story she'd given *Confidential* about a "casting couch" incident with actor Mark Stevens. Ritzi complained that the story hadn't been admitted into evidence and that her testimony was inadmissible. Ritzi hailed the ruling as a blow to Crowley's "reign of terror." Crowley threatened, "This is all out war. From now on, there will be no holds barred."[39]

Shortly after, attorney Daniel Ross took the witness stand for the defense. The suave, dapper attorney put on and took off his horn-rimmed glasses repeatedly and seemed "mildly amused" by the proceedings. Ross explained how Harrison paid his firm $100,000 a year for "consultations aimed at excluding libelous or obscene material." Ross said the only reason he had Harrison set up HRI was for tax purposes.[40]

Ross described his meticulous checks of *Confidential*'s articles and insisted that the O'Hara story wasn't obscene. "If you read the whole story and if you read the current state of the law as enunciated by the Supreme Court, you will know that obscenity and sex are wholly unrelated," he said, referring to the Supreme Court's landmark decision in *Roth v. United States*, the Court's first ruling on obscenity, handed down just a few weeks earlier.[41]

Samuel Roth, a renegade publisher notorious for erotica, had been convicted under a federal statute criminalizing the sending of "obscene, lewd, lascivious, or filthy" material through the mail. The Court upheld the conviction but made an important ruling on the definition of obscenity. In an opinion by Justice William J. Brennan Jr., the Court said that the First Amendment protected the communication of all ideas having "the slightest redeeming social importance," but implicit in the history of the First Amendment was the rejection of obscenity as "utterly without redeeming social importance." *Roth* set out a constitutional criterion for obscenity: "Whether to the average person, applying contemporary standards, the dominant theme of the material taken as a whole appeals to prurient interest." The "prurient interest" requirement came from the Model Penal Code: "A thing is obscene if, considered as a whole, its predominant appeal is to prurient interest—i.e., a shameful or morbid interest in nudity, sex, or excretion, and if it goes substantially beyond customary limits of candor in description or representation of such matters."[42] *Roth* was a victory for both conservative reformers and free speech advocates. The decision reaffirmed obscenity as a category of speech without constitutional protection yet at the same time narrowed the definition of obscenity.

An obscene matter is one that "arouses prurient interests as defined in the most recent Supreme Court cases," Ross asserted. "You've got to get an itchy mental reaction which gives the reader an uncontrollable desire to commit lewd and lascivious acts." Creatively stretching the *Roth* opinion, he said *Confidential*'s stories couldn't be obscene because they were humorous. Something couldn't be "prurient" and laughable at the same time.[43]

The O'Hara story was a watered-down version of what actually happened and was "mildly funny," Ross said. The "Tarzan of the Boudoir" article was "a humorous story and very entertaining story." In comparison to racy paperback novels and girlie magazines, *Confidential*'s articles were no more harmful than *Grimm's Fairy Tales*, Ross insisted. Crowley offered a flood of literature into evidence to show that *Confidential* was no more obscene than bestsellers *Peyton Place, East of Eden, Ten North Frederick, Island in the Sun,* and *The Naked and the Dead*.[44]

With his sleek suits and slicked-back hair, Fred Meade, called by the defense, alleged that HRI was an "independent research agency" offering services to magazines throughout the country. Meade denied that HRI hired prostitutes and described HRI's meticulous efforts to verify *Confidential* stories. During his testimony, he rattled off dozens of *Confidential* informants by name. Ralph Cercy, a Texas radio station executive, was paid for tips about Elvis Presley. A Los Angeles police officer and former roommate of Fred Otash was paid several hundred dollars. A freelance publicist provided a "very amusing story" about Joan Crawford for $100. Bruce Jones, a "public relations man," was paid $500 for a story on one of his clients who wanted publicity in *Confidential*.[45]

In one of his most stunning disclosures, Meade revealed that he once persuaded director Mike Todd to give a tip to *Confidential*. The March 1957 article, "How Mike Todd Made a Chump of a Movie Mogul," described how Todd, to help an actress named Marion Hill, phoned producer Harry Cohn and said he wanted to borrow her for a film he was planning. Cohn didn't have her under contract but quickly arranged for it. After he signed her at $150 for twenty weeks, with the intent of loaning her to Todd at $500 a week, Todd told him he'd decided not to make the movie. The story came out around the time of Todd's film *Around the World in 80 Days*. He gave *Confidential* the story because he felt it would help the movie. Todd provided photos for the story and even wrote the article's last line. Todd denied Meade's testimony, saying he wouldn't know Meade "if I fell over him, and I aim to keep it that way."[46]

Meade's testimony, according to Ritzi, "opened the door wide open." It showed a definite relationship between *Confidential* and HRI; Ritzi promised to "tie the knot even tighter." Ritzi tried to show that *Confidential* and HRI were "co-conspirators" in a plot to publish obscene and libelous material. Meade acknowledged that *Confidential* paid HRI $150,000 during the year and a half the agency was in business.[47]

Toward the close of Ritzi's cross-examination, Meade revealed that he and Marjorie gave up their scandal-buying business because "we learned the movie studios were pouring money into the state attorney general's office with orders to 'get' the magazine at all costs." Ritzi bristled.

> Q: All right sir, how much have I been paid?
> A: You are not in the attorney general's office.
> Q: How much do you think was paid Clarence Linn sitting here?
> A: I don't know.
> Q: You don't blame the movie companies for being a little perturbed do you?
> A: I certainly do. If the movie companies would exercise the morality clauses in their contracts there would be no need for anything like this. No star has been injured by a *Confidential* story.[48]

An actor who was a convicted narcotics user and who was on the Georgia chain gang—Robert Mitchum—had his earnings go up by five times after *Con-*

fidential's story, Meade asserted. Another actress was "openly consorting with a married man in Mexico and took her child along"—Maureen O'Hara. "How could she be injured by a story about her necking in a theater? . . . Take yet another actress whose name has been synonymous with sex since I was a little boy," Meade said, referring to Mae West. "Could we have injured her? . . . None of these people have been hurt."[49]

"Are you setting yourself up as a censor of the movie industry?" demanded Ritzi. "No, sir," Meade replied. "But the movie industry is always the first to scream about censorship. It should keep itself cleaned up."[50]

On August 30, Crowley rested his case without having called a single star to testify. He told the press, "I don't want to call [the stars] because then I couldn't cross examine them." If Crowley were to call them himself, he would be bound by their answers. If the state called them, he could attack their stories on cross-examination. If he were to ask a star if he was guilty of adultery and the witness answered "No," Crowley could question them no further.[51]

After the Labor Day weekend, the trial shifted to Hollywood's iconic Grauman's Chinese Theatre. Taken by bus to the theater on Hollywood Boulevard, the jurors were shown the spot of the alleged Maureen O'Hara episode. Although the article and testimony had put it in Row 35, described as the last row, the theater actually had forty rows.[52]

Juror LaGuerre Drouet, a short, fat, bushy-haired fifty-year-old postal worker who wore a moustache waxed and uptwisted, requested the theater visit. Drouet would become one of the stars of the trial; the press described him as a "complete extrovert" and "the personality juror of all time." Throughout the trial, Drouet made many loud requests to Judge Walker for explanations of legal points. At Grauman's, Drouet asked if he could sit in one of the seats. Walker said yes, and he sprawled in the seat with his arms outstretched, mimicking O'Hara's embrace. For several moments, he turned and tried various poses as he recalled the defense testimony about what allegedly happened. He got stuck in the seat and had to be dug out by one of the bailiffs.[53]

Shortly after the jurors returned to the courtroom, there was a stir at the door. Maureen O'Hara stormed in, clad in a striped dress and white hat and gloves, flanked by her brothers Charles and James Fitzsimons. O'Hara was appearing as a prosecution rebuttal witness to attack defense allegations that the article was true. It was the trial's most dramatic moment—photographers literally fell over each other. "I'm delighted I've been called to testify and I'm not the least bit afraid of Mr. Crowley's questions," she said to the press. She announced that she would "tell all." Off the stand, she told reporters that she hadn't had a work offer since the article appeared, and that *Confidential* was to blame. Her daughter had been so upset by the story that she sobbed herself to sleep each night.[54]

Composed and deliberate, speaking in an Irish brogue, O'Hara admitted that she dated Parra but denied the Grauman's episode.

Ritzi asked:

Q: Miss O'Hara, during 1953 of 1954 were you at Grauman's Chinese Theatre?
A: I was once in September of 1953. I went to see the premiere of the picture *The Robe*, accompanied by my brother.
Q: Have you been in Grauman's Chinese Theatre since that period of time? . . .
A: In 1953 or 1954, other than that one date, I have never been in Grauman's Chinese.[55]

Crowley rigorously cross-examined. O'Hara delivered her answers sharply, clipping her words and glaring intently at Crowley as she spoke.

Crowley: You were dating a Mexican in February 1954, isn't that true? . . .
A: I have very many friends that are Mexicans. . . .
Q: Would you answer my question, were you dating a Mexican during February of 1954?
A: I don't know what you mean by dating.
Q: Going out socially with a gentleman is what I am referring to. . . .
A: I'm trying to think of the correct and proper answer to your question. Yes, I have gone out socially with a Mexican. . . .

Q: What was that gentleman's name? . . .

A: The name of the gentleman is Enrique Parra.[56]

O'Hara gave Crowley her passport. Stamps showed that she left for Europe on October 6, 1953 and returned in January 1954. Crowley insisted that the necking incident really happened, though admitted that Craig might have been wrong in setting the date as November 1953.[57]

Wearing an elegant beige suit, white shoes, and pearl earrings, Dorothy Dandridge walked in after O'Hara.[58] Her half-hour testimony received less coverage than O'Hara's, but it was far more powerful. Staring somberly at the judge, Dandridge denounced the *Confidential* story and at the same time delivered a forceful attack on racism. During her visits to Tahoe, she said, she was prohibited from socializing with whites because of racial prejudice.

Q: Did you ever walk in the woods? . . .

A: I wouldn't have done it alone. . . . Lake Tahoe at that time was very prejudiced, as you know, and I don't think I would have wanted to walk around. Negroes [were] not permitted that kind of freedom in Lake Tahoe at the time.

Q: Where did you spend your time while you were working up there?

A: Unfortunately I had not much of a choice. I just stayed in my suite most of the time . . . there's really no place to go there. . . .

Q: Do you remember taking a ride with Mr. Terry?

A: I did not take a ride with Mr. Terry because I didn't know him, and I would not have been seen with Mr. Terry . . . at a prejudiced place like Tahoe.[59]

"With the 'Sunday punch' of race prejudice, Dorothy Dandridge knocked out *Confidential* magazine's efforts to prove that its scandalous article [was true] . . . taking even the prosecution unaware," wrote the *Baltimore Afro-American*. "In a few brief brushstrokes, the star painted a picture of denial of normal human activity endured by colored performers who must appear in such places as Tahoe to make a living. The tiny star's blast at American standards . . . visibly impressed the jury, the judge, the prosecution, and took the wind out of the defense's sails. . . . The pretty brownskinned star rared back and let the courtroom, made up entirely of whites, have it right in the solar plexus."[60]

After more than a month of lurid testimony, on September 6, the trial went into its closing arguments. That morning a crowd of sixty spectators waited outside the courtroom; only twenty of them got past the ropes.[61]

Sweaty and exhausted, his mop of dark hair hanging limply over his forehead, Ritzi spoke to the jury first. Addressing them in a homespun style, he called them "you folks" and "just folks." The press described his presentation as a "sermon." Ritzi told the jurors that it would be up to them—like biblical elders—to right the wrongs inflicted by *Confidential*.[62]

Ritzi brought in stacks of charts and giant photographs of Grauman's Chinese Theatre. Bailiffs hauled in artists' easels to prop up the pictures at the front of the courtroom. One chart was a "family tree" depicting the relatives involved in *Confidential*, showing Harrison as the "father." The defense's contention that there was no collusion between HRI and *Confidential* was laughable, Ritzi said.[63]

Harrison sought lurid material about stars, and it belied the contention that *Confidential* was a "public service." "Illicit conduct" was they key to the magazine's operations, Ritzi charged. "Human conduct—proper or improper—is a matter of individual conscience, not a matter for Fred and Marjorie Meade and Robert Harrison to sit in judgment on," he said.[64]

"Look at them!" Ritzi shouted, pointing and waving a finger at Fred and Marjorie. "They were sewering this smut to *Confidential*. . . . They are the self-appointed purveyors of filth and gossip in the United States. . . . They got [gossip] by having Fred Meade spread money among every shadowy tipster he could possibly get. Picture in your mind, folks, the miserable figures—the scurvy informers—who gave stories on Dorothy Dandridge and Maureen O' Hara. . . . Folks, you have been asked to believe a defense that is utterly ridiculous. You have been asked to believe that *Confidential* never struck terror into the heart of anyone. You have been asked to believe that these people performed a public service by 'smashing false idols.'"[65]

The trial wasn't just about *Confidential*, Crowley told the jury—at stake was nothing less than freedom of the press. "If this magazine can be suppressed, so can other magazines and newspapers." "I ask you to remember that if you find my clients guilty you will be taking a precious piece of liberty from the constitutions of the United States and California."[66]

The state's actions were "censorship," no different from the book burnings and witch hunts of history, he told the jury. "The prosecution wants to indulge in censorship . . . to do your thinking for you, to satisfy a certain political segment," Crowley said. "They're trying to put the largest newsstand-selling magazine in the world out of business. Who is the prosecutor and who is the attorney general to tell you what you can and can't read?"[67]

Crowley took out several racy magazines containing seminude pictures of actresses and models to show that *Confidential* was no more obscene than other periodicals. Hollywood was out to "get" *Confidential* but didn't object to those magazines. "Here's Jane Russell . . . look at this. Do you ever see any nude or semi-nude or scantily-clad girls in pictures in *Confidential*?" Crowley asked. LaGuerre Drouet nearly lost his balance as he reached over the rail and grabbed the magazines. The lawyer handed them to him and Drouet leered at the pictures, making notes on a yellow tablet.[68]

"Why haven't Mr. Ritzi and Mr. Linn prosecuted the publishers of these magazines?" asked Crowley. "Why do they pick on the largest selling magazine on the newsstands in the United States? For political reasons? For Hollywood reasons? These magazines are accepted by the community. They are sold over the counter, not under the counter." He told the jury not to be swayed by O'Hara and Dandridge because they were celebrities. "Miss O'Hara has an ax to grind," he said. "She has a 5 million dollar suit against *Confidential*. Miss Dandridge also has an ax to grind. She filed suit against *Confidential* to harass and annoy news dealers."[69]

The charges were a "conspiracy" by the industry to cover up the "immoral activities of people who are idols to millions of teenagers," Crowley concluded. "Does Mr. Ritzi think it is a public service to sacrifice freedom of the press on the altar of expediency to cover up people in this town who walk around like they wear the purple of ancient Rome?" The "war chest" could have been better used to "clean out the homosexuals, nymphomaniacs, and dope addicts from their ranks," he asserted. "*Confidential* incurred the wrath of the movie industry because it dared to publicize the immoral activities of film idols."[70]

––––––––––––

The following Monday the case went to the jury. Judge Walker told the jurors to pack overnight bags with toothbrushes, toothpaste, and a supply of aspirin. Confronting the panel were eight hundred thousand words of testimony that filled sixteen inch-thick volumes, along with 139 exhibits placed in evidence.[71]

In his instructions to the jury, Walker explained that criminal libel is "malicious defamation," and "truth alone is not a defense against criminal libel." "There must be good motives and a justifiable purpose. . . . Without justifiable motive, the law presumes there is malice," he said, adding that making money was not considered a justifiable end. He told the jury that the "right of freedom of the press does not extend to obscenity," and, contradicting *Confidential*'s lawyers, insisted that "the fact that something is humorous does not affect its obscenity to any degree."[72]

The jurors were confused by the complicated legal issues, and not long after they left the courtroom they went back in with questions for the judge: "What is a conspiracy? Is hatred necessary for malice? What is criminal libel? What is an injurious publication?" "A conspiracy is an agreement or understanding between two or more persons to commit an unlawful act," Walker said. "In my opinion, hatred is not an essential ingredient to malice." Walker explained that criminal libel existed when a publication exposed persons to "public hatred, ridicule, and contempt without any justifiable motive."[73]

The jurors were no longer smiling. "There was no laughing as in the past, and it was obvious to observers that the earlier harmony had gone," noted a reporter on the third day of deliberations. The *Los Angeles Times* described "discord and confusion." Three of the jurors went back to Walker with more questions about conspiracy, intent, obscenity, and criminal libel.[74]

After four days, the jury, locked up incommunicado in the Mayfair Hotel, was reportedly split nine to three in favor of conviction. By the end of the week, the jury was showing more signs of wrangling and being nowhere near a verdict. A few days later, courtroom observers were predicting a hung jury. One report said that the jurors were split eleven to one in favor of returning a guilty verdict with a "lone holdout relentlessly keeping others on edge." Ritzi promised that, in the event of a hung jury, "we will try them again and again and again until we convict them."[75]

As the jurors went into their second week, the defense asked for a mistrial. Crowley claimed that the jury was confused about the judge's instructions and that the panel had deliberated too long. Crowley charged that the nine-day lockup of the jury amounted to a "form of coercion." Walker denied the motion. By the end of the week, the jurors were still debating. At thirteen days it marked a milestone in Los Angeles county criminal cases for the longest jury deliberations on record.[76]

24 | THE END AND THE AFTERMATH

AFTER A RECORD FOURTEEN days of jury deliberation, on October 1, 1957, the trial finally came to a close. The jury was split seven to five on the criminal libel part of the conspiracy charge, and eight to four on the obscenity part of the charge. Judge Walker declared a mistrial. "Naturally the case will be retried. But I am very disappointed with the result of this trial," Ritzi told the press. "I feel very good about it," Crowley announced. "After the prosecution tried everything in the book, they couldn't get a conviction."[1]

What happened?

The jury is a "black box," and its deliberations are secret. What is known is that not all the jurors were convinced that the articles were false, malicious, and lewd enough to justify a conviction. Some might have found the prosecution witnesses unpersuasive; some might have been swayed by Crowley's stirring arguments. The majority of jurors thought *Confidential* was obscene, but four weren't convinced that *Confidential*'s stories actually rose to the level of obscenity. Given the animus against *Confidential* and the massive buildup around the trial, the outcome was surprising—it was a coup for *Confidential*, and in many ways the entire principle of freedom of the press.

According to LaGuerre Drouet, most of the jurors had been dead set on conviction. "I thought we were supposed to be impartial, but some of the others seemed to feel the defendants were guilty from the start," he said. "We had a big fight over reading the books." Some of the jurors objected to him reading aloud passages from the racy novels and magazines. There was "a lot of table-

273

pounding." "Things became acrimonious," he said. The "freedom of the press" argument, he explained, was the deciding factor in his vote for *Confidential*.[2]

While the jurors were unable to arrive on a verdict, all agreed they'd been traumatized by having to decide the case. "I don't expect to go to purgatory after I die. I've had it," said one juror. "I am mentally, emotionally, and physically exhausted, mostly because of him," remarked another, referring to Drouet. Drouet provoked fights, asked endless questions, and at one point came into the courtroom without a shirt and socks. "They told me to bring my toothbrush," he explained. "That's what I brought. So naturally, when it dragged . . . I had to wash my clothing at night."[3]

Harrison celebrated the mistrial as a victory for publishing freedom. "The fact that reasonable people of good will could differ so strongly is proof that there was no basis for a criminal prosecution," read his statement to the press. "I feel that the 12 ladies and gentlemen of the jury are to be congratulated for refusing to be swayed by a hostile atmosphere and appeals to prejudice, from their sworn duties as jurors to base their decision on the evidence." The trial's result, he believed, "constitutes a vindication and reaffirmation of our basic constitutional guarantees of freedom of speech and freedom of the press—not only the freedom of a publisher to publish, but equally, if not more important, the freedom of the public to read."[4]

The public was outraged at the state's failure to convict *Confidential*. "*Confidential* Trial Lays Egg," announced a newspaper headline. "No verdict, nothing . . . Nobody goes to jail, . . . *Confidential* is still in business." "After all the time, trouble, and money spent in the California libel trial of *Confidential* magazine, it is a little short of tragic that the jury could not agree," wrote one editorial. Some were optimistic that despite the courtroom loss, the state could still put *Confidential* out of business. "The long, costly, and sensational trial of *Confidential* . . . was not wasted effort," observed the *Redlands Daily Facts*. "It is . . . handwriting on the wall for others to read." "Men who hope to make a fat living by publishing scandal are put on notice that they may be subject to costly lawsuits."[5]

Film industry leaders hoped that the courtroom revelations would gut the magazine's readership. At the same time, those revelations threatened stars' images, and at the end of the trial, Hollywood announced more fervent efforts at damage control. The MPIC launched a campaign to disclose the identity of "journalistic parasites" who fed the scandal magazines information. "We will organize effective opposition to fight these peephole writers, and we will seek to gather conclusive proof of the identity of these performers," said executive director Lou Greenspan. "Those who have criticized the industry . . . will have cause to change their mind." Hollywood leaders also promised a "crackdown" on the immoral behavior of stars, threatening that "wrongdoers" would be permanently shut out of the industry.[6]

Pat Brown told the press he would ask for a retrial—"as soon as the courts will allow. . . . We hope for a better case in the next trial and a much shorter one." Yet just days later, he ordered Clarence Linn, in a private letter, to "confidentially and without publicity attempt to settle the *Confidential* . . . case on terms not less than those approved by me prior to the first trial." Brown had been pressured by the studios to avoid another name-dropping spree. On October 22, Linn and Brown approached Judge Walker with a deal. If *Confidential* and *Whisper* agreed go out of the gossip business immediately, charges against the Meades would be dismissed, and the charges against *Confidential* and *Whisper* would be reduced to a single charge, conspiring to publish obscenity. Brown said that attempts to extradite Harrison had failed and that trying the case again without him would be difficult. "To play this record a second time is repugnant to me," he told Walker.[7]

Harrison, who was exhausted from the ongoing litigation and spent more than $400,000 on the case, was open to the compromise. "We had three sets of lawyers. Oh, the lawyers! We flew witnesses from Europe. We cabled, we telephoned, we hired more lawyers," he complained to columnist Earl Wilson. Harrison also worried about the possibility of a conviction and jail time for Fred and Marjorie. Walker turned down the proposal, saying it "was not in the interests of justice," but claimed he would be open to a different compromise. A week later, Brown announced he was running for governor.[8]

An agreement was reached on November 12. *Confidential* would stop publishing star exposés, and Harrison would publish ads announcing the magazine's change of heart. The state's original charges would be narrowed down to a token charge of conspiring to publish obscenity, which would be judged on the grand jury transcript. "November 12, 1957, marked the end of a terrifying era for actors," reported *Daily Variety*.[9]

Shortly after, *Confidential* took out newspaper ads promising to "eliminate expose stories" on celebrities beginning with the March 1958 issue. The announcement, signed by Harrison, added, "While we have never felt that such stories violated any laws, in a spirit of cooperation with Edmund G.

Brown . . . and William B. McKesson . . . we have agreed with them to so change our format. We are confident that our millions of readers will find the new format interesting and exciting." Harrison refused to reveal *Confidential*'s new look. Al Govoni told *Newsweek*, "Inasmuch as we gave birth to a whole new industry, we don't want to give our ideas [for a new format] away."[10]

For a while, the spotlight turned on Pat Brown. After Brown made his decision not to seek a retrial, members of the county grand jury said they felt they'd been "misused" by Brown in being induced to return indictments against *Confidential*. They ordered researchers to check newspaper libraries for Brown's statements leading to the indictment in May. Brown first issued sweeping statements about the importance of prosecuting *Confidential*, then changed his mind after the trial. Some suspected that politics were at play— that Brown had a deal with Hollywood, and that he'd been paid off to avoid another trial. Brown recently told the press that he needed $500,000 for his campaign.[11]

"We were faced with the problem of trying the case again. This meant the continuing dissemination of this type of scandalous testimony," Brown explained. "No one in the film industry had initiated the plan for dismissal of the indictments. I initiated it myself. . . . No money was paid to the state or county for this prosecution. There was no slush fund. No one made any campaign contributions to me." The grand jury concluded that Brown was telling the truth and that politics weren't involved.[12]

On December 18, after brief oral arguments, Judge H. Burton Noble found *Confidential* and *Whisper* guilty of conspiring to publish obscenity and fined each $5,000. He gave Harrison until January 15 to pay the fines. The case was officially closed on January 15, 1958. Later that year, Maureen O'Hara dropped her libel suit and Errol Flynn settled. The terms of both settlements were undisclosed. In July 1958 Liberace accepted a $40,000 settlement, saying that it constituted a "complete vindication and apology." "Thank God," he told the press. "Now, perhaps 99 percent of the entertainment industry, among the finest people and families I have ever known, can live in peace and enjoy a normal life, without being constantly attacked by vicious untruths."[13]

In the spring of 1958, *Confidential* announced its new look:

> Pardon us while we take a bow.
>
> It's a proud bow.
>
> We're proud because we like our new look which begins with this issue.
>
> If *Confidential* seems changed . . . if you've noticed a new complexion, it's because we've broadened our outlook.
>
> We're quitting the area of private affairs for the arena of public affairs. . . . Where we pried and peeked, now we'll probe, and occasionally we'll take a poke. . . . If wiseacres say that we've retreated from the bedroom, we'll say yes, that's true. From now on we'll search and survey the thoroughfares of the globe for stories of public interest that are uncensored and off the record. . . . It's a big world, a foolish world, a crazy world . . . and we'll be taking you on an inside tour, telling the facts and naming the names.[14]

The new *Confidential*, featuring stories like "What's Wrong with the Oil Burner in the White House Basement?" and "Penicillin Can Save Your Life!" was tepid and tame. The magazine's transformation was stunning to millions of Americans who had gotten used to *Confidential*'s bimonthly punch of sex and sin. "My, how *Confidential* magazine has changed!" quipped a columnist for the *Los Angeles Times*. "Filled with innocuous generalities, the latest issue is prefaced with a report from Publisher Robert Harrison . . . so instead of Maureen O'Hara and Marilyn Monroe the magazine is full of exciting stuff about opium smoking in China and door-to-door salesmen's rackets." Newsstand sales of *Confidential* plummeted to one million in May.[15]

After only three issues of the new formula, Harrison announced he was getting out of publishing. Faced with the impossibility of putting out an interesting magazine under the state's requirements, Harrison sold the rights to *Confidential* to thirty-six-year-old publisher Hy Steirman. "I've had six years of real rip-roaring experience and time. And now I'm going into the next phase of my life," Harrison told the press. "I have no regrets. These six years will always live with me and contrary to what many people think I think we did a lot of good." The last issue under Harrison's ownership came out June 17, and Steirman's version hit newsstands in August.[16]

The former publisher, Bob Harrison, in six stormy years, built a magazine that skyrocketed into the largest-selling newsstand magazine in the world. Its impact was felt by every person, newspaper, and magazine in the country. It answered a need—for no magazine could sell over 4,000,000 copies per issue without reflecting what the public demanded.

Phase one of the magazine is over.

This is phase two of *Confidential*—with a new staff, two-fisted ideas, and a renewed enthusiasm.

Confidential will be a journalistic gadfly! . . .

Confidential will continue telling the truth. It will be positive in its approach. It will be a sensational magazine that reflects the best traditions of Joseph Pulitzer and William Randolph Hearst. . . .

Our motto will be, "We will respect the respectable, love the lovable—but detest the detestable."[17]

The new *Confidential* bombed. The first issue offered articles like "The Great Filter Tip Swindle," "The Big Shame of the Nobel Prize," "Terror on the School Bus," and "The Truth About Poisons in Our Food." In December 1959 the Dear Abby column noted that *Confidential*, with its new policy of "letting sleeping stars lie," had been reduced to sending out free copies to drum up interest, along with a weekly teaser called the "Confidential Memo." The magazine had become "about as racy as racing programs," wrote *Time* in 1963. That year, newsstand sales dropped to 510,000.[18]

In the end, Harrison's *Confidential* had been "censored," though not exactly as its opponents planned. *Confidential* wasn't banned by the government; no one was thrown in jail, there were no massive libel judgments, and the fines it paid were minimal. Instead, it was killed by a thousand cuts—the burden of defending itself against an onslaught of criminal and civil lawsuits.

"For the first time in our history, governmental power has been used to alter the editorial content of a national magazine whose circulation is in excess of 4,000,000," observed Maurice Zolotow, one of the most thoughtful commentators on the *Confidential* saga.

It has been shown that the cost of defending such a charge is so expensive that by merely threatening an indefinite series of prosecutions any publication can be put to death. Regardless of one's personal opinion of *Confidential*, . . . many may regard the use of the judicial power to muzzle a magazine—any magazine—as an act discouraging freedom and controversy.[19]

This kind of "censorship" was entirely within the bounds of the First Amendment.

There was one final chapter to the *Confidential* story.

On January 3, 1958, a taxi driver was cruising at Madison Avenue and 97th Street in New York when he was hailed by an arguing couple. The woman jumped in the cab and tried to stop the man from getting in. He forced his way in, telling the driver, "I'm her husband. Don't worry about it." The woman, panicked, asked to be taken to the police station, and the cabbie sped toward the precinct station on E. 104th Street.[20]

The couple continued to argue. Then the woman screamed, "Oh My God." The driver heard two pistol shots. He turned around to see the woman on the seat in a pool of blood. The man had the gun to his temple. There was another flash. The man fell over.[21]

Howard Rushmore had shot his wife, Frances, then himself. Frances had been shot in the right side of the neck and in the head. Rushmore had one bullet in his temple. Another bullet had been fired through the roof of the cab. A commando knife with a seven-inch blade was tucked in Rushmore's waistband. The bodies of the couple, slumped together in the back seat, were identified by neighbors and two of Rushmore's coworkers.[22] Pictures of the bloodied bodies appeared in newspapers around the world.

Their marriage had been deeply troubled. In September 1955, police pulled Frances from the East River. "I didn't fall and I wasn't pushed," she told them. "I jumped." Rushmore threatened to kill her. Two days before Christmas 1957, he chased her out of their apartment with a shotgun. On the night of the murder-suicide, she had arranged to see him in a desperate effort to patch up their problems.[23]

Since he left *Confidential*, Rushmore had spiraled into penury and depression. His career had been destroyed by *Confidential*, and even his allies in

Hollywood turned on him for his vicious, attention-grabbing trial testimony. By the end of 1957 he was broke and contemplating suicide. Clarence Linn recalled, "I saw Rushmore last a few months ago in New York, when I came to ask him about testifying at the retrial of *Confidential*. He came to my hotel and told me he had no permanent position and that the magazine he had been working for had folded. . . . At that time, he seemed to be laboring under the idea that he and even his wife were being boycotted everywhere. He told me he thought he had been ruined by his activities in the *Confidential* trial." An editor of the tawdry *Police Gazette* said Rushmore had recently come to his office asking for a writing job. His last known position was as an outdoor editor for *True War*, a pulp men's magazine.[24]

Rushmore's body lay unclaimed in Bellevue Hospital for several days. His adopted daughters wanted nothing to do with him. His first wife finally claimed the body, and it was cremated. Harrison found out about the death in a taxi on the way to Idlewild Airport (now John F. Kennedy International Airport). "The publisher of *Confidential* magazine," the driver told him, "just shot himself in the back of a cab."[25]

Not long before he died, Rushmore wrote a tell-all article, "I Worked for *Confidential*," which ran in the magazine *Christian Herald*. It was his last attempt to pursue his vendetta against Harrison. "The former editor of America's most notorious magazine tells why he took the job, why he quit, what 'Peeping Tom journalism' is doing to life and morals," read the subhead.[26]

The article portrayed *Confidential* as a pernicious toxin infecting American society, and Harrison as lewd, greedy, and callous. Harrison had only one aim, said Rushmore: to grab power, fame, and money, even if he had to destroy lives in the process. "I am not proud of the two years I spent at *Confidential*. I was an adult man, an experienced writer, a professional reporter, and I should have known better," he wrote. "To *Confidential*'s millions of readers, I say this: 'My conscience is clear. I am out. Are you?'"[27]

25 | CONCLUSION

HARRISON'S *CONFIDENTIAL* PASSED AWAY, but its legacy lives on. Its impact on American culture was nothing short of revolutionary. *Confidential* redefined celebrity and the public's relationship to stars. It took movie stars off their pedestals, making them flawed, human, and real. It redrew the boundaries between public and private life and the limits of sexual expression. It transformed celebrity journalism from an exercise in fiction and make-believe to an enterprise that was more honest, blunt, and true.

Confidential pulled back the blinders, took off the blindfolds, and introduced a new cynicism toward public figures into American culture. It precipitated a historic shift in American life, fostering the jadedness, skepticism, and loss of innocence that would increasingly define the world in the 1960s and beyond. *Confidential* didn't do this alone—it pushed the nation down a path it was already taking. But it was a tremendous push.

Confidential shattered the romantic, larger-than-life image of movie stars. After *Confidential*, Americans no longer expected stars to "regularly pay off the mortgage, teach Sunday School, and retire by 10 at night," quipped Jerry Giesler. "When I was a boy . . . fan magazines were filled with chocolate marshmallow sauce," recalled one columnist. "Joan Crawford was shown in her kitchen, dicing carrots, and spouting wholesome thoughts about motherhood, the sanctity of marriage, and the intrinsic goodness of God. . . . Then *Confidential* magazine came along. . . . Overnight our movie stars became extreme practitioners of the more extreme forms of sexual license, committing incest for breakfast."[1]

Nowhere was that transformation more visible than in the fan magazines. After *Confidential*, the sickly sweet fan mags were forced to change their tune. "When a magazine like *Confidential* ran a story about Melody Myopic, the Hollywood personality, shacking up with every male in sight, the fan magazines were left out on a journalistic limb," remarked columnist and critic Ezra Goodman. "They could not . . . keep running articles about how sweet, snow-white, wholesome—and unhappy—this same Melody Myopic was, because, after all, the youngsters who read the fan magazines also saw *Confidential*."[2] The fan magazines picked up elements of *Confidential*'s style, with lurid articles, sensational quotes, and screaming headlines. The fan magazines became so salacious that they faced *Confidential*-style lawsuits. In 1960 Liz Taylor and Eddie Fisher filed seven libel suits against fan magazines over stories like "Eddie Flees to Debby: We Dare to Print Facts," "Trouble Between Liz and Eddie," and "Liz Taylor's Hidden Love Life."[3]

It wasn't just fan magazines that changed; *Confidential* revolutionized all media coverage of celebrities. The press began to defy Hollywood's line, and there was little to stop them. By 1960 studios no longer had many stars under contract. When publicists threatened to bar writers from their lots, the writers shrugged. Jealous of *Confidential*'s massive, glory-days readership, mainstream magazines like the *Saturday Evening Post, Life, Look,* and *Ladies' Home Journal* began mimicking *Confidential*. In 1958 *Variety* described a new "slick mag neo-*Confidential*" genre, citing a *Saturday Evening Post* article revealing George Raft as the "gun-toting consort" of underworld big shots, a feature in *Look* describing Frank Sinatra's suicide attempts, and a "psychoanalytic" investigation of Jackie Gleason in the *Saturday Evening Post*. Quipped one editor not long after the *Confidential* settlement, "A leading 'expose' magazine says it is going to change its policy and material, so that in a few months it will be 'similar to the *Saturday Evening Post*.'. . . Confused readers may wonder who is really changing policy and who isn't."[4]

Some of these exposés came from investigative reporting, but many were offered by the stars themselves. "Telling all" had become "one of Hollywood's favorite pastimes," columnist Erskine Johnson observed in 1958. There was a "confess-all binge" in Hollywood. Stars were "literally tumbling over each other to tell it all" in autobiographies and "slick-paper magazines." Recent celebrity biographies were "nothing more [than] . . . *Confidential* between hard covers," noted *Variety*, citing works by Diana Barrymore, Eartha Kitt, and Errol Flynn in which they frankly revealed sexual liaisons. "It's getting rougher for the [gossip] columnists when celebs peddle the lowdown on themselves that they threaten to sue about," Walter Winchell joked.[5]

The new tell-all genre was a testament to the profound change in the public's attitudes toward movie stars. *Confidential* left Americans more realistic, open-eyed, and jaded about celebrities, yet at the same time more accepting and forgiving. While *Confidential*'s stories shocked readers early on, by the end of its run many *expected* stars to have flaws and rough edges. Being less than perfect made them seem exciting, relatable, and real.

"Movie stars raised in the glossy, fictionized, Never-Never Land of yesterday's protective studio publicity now feel it is better box office to be known as 'real' persons rather than as 'to-the-glamour-born,'" Erskine Johnson noted. Even older stars wanted "to let it be known that they have had a fling or two themselves."[6] The celebrity confessional genre was born. *Confidential*, inadvertently, launched a new trend in celebrity culture, one marked by personal revelations, public transgressions, and massive self-disclosure.

The year 1958 saw the end of Harrison's *Confidential* and the end of an era. Thanks in part to *Confidential*, the age of *hush hush* was over.

The 1960s witnessed a massive cultural upheaval, and at the heart of it was a revolution in sex. By the end of the decade, sexual desire was no longer seen as shameful, but as something normal and natural, and worthy of expression. In the age of the pill, feminism, and hippies, premarital sex was normalized, and erotic images and themes permeated popular culture. Public discussion of sexual matters was no longer off-limits. Though there were still culture wars around sex, the intense "purity movements" of the 1950s had subsided. *Playboy* magazine, the 1964 bestseller *Sex and the Single Girl*, and the wave of erotic and pornographic publications that flooded the nation in the 1960s owed their success, in part, to *Confidential*. After *Confidential*, and because of *Confidential*, "books, magazines, and newspapers now print, without even the raising of eyebrows, material that 25 years ago would have shocked the country," Maurice Zolotow observed in 1958. Even by the end of *Confidential*'s reign, the shift toward greater sexual candor had begun. Only a decade before *Confidential*, sordid episodes described in detail would have caused the "downfall of any public figure," Zolotow noted. It was once a given that "involvement in scandal could kill . . . careers."[7]

Confidential pushed the press to greater frankness, not only in its reporting on sexual affairs and its celebrity coverage, but its treatment of public affairs and news. By showing that people were interested in other people, especially their personal lives, the scandal magazines led the mainstream media to more realistic depictions of subjects. By the end of the 1960s, "human interest," going "behind the scenes," and a focus on private lives were conventions of respectable journalism. The public had come to expect the "lowdown" behind every story, and the press delivered. Media scandals proliferated in the post-*Confidential* decade, from the quiz show scandal of the late 1950s, revealing the rigging of popular game shows, to the "payola" scandal, disclosing payoffs to disc jockeys for song promotions, to political sex scandals like the Walter Jenkins scandal of 1964, implicating an LBJ aide in a bathroom sexual encounter. There was a boom in investigative journalism fueled by the public's thirst for the "real story," and also by the decade's turbulent events—the Kennedy assassination, Vietnam, and in the early 1970s, Watergate. Seeing the "real truth" became a motif of the era as Americans questioned established authorities and assumptions, including "truths" like white superiority, male supremacy, and the normalcy of heterosexuality.[8]

The new cultural climate led to legal changes, and changes in the law encouraged openness. Within a few years of the *Confidential* trial, government restraints on publishing had declined, and freedom of the press was revolutionized. *Confidential*'s trial was a milestone in the law—it marked the last gasp of an old order in which officials had overt authority to quash speech that offended or criticized them. The systematic use of "lists" by policemen and prosecutors to threaten dealers of "objectionable material" almost disappeared by the early 1960s. Literature "review boards" were dismantled and bans on books were removed. Obscenity law was liberalized by several Supreme Court decisions, including a 1966 decision that defined obscenity as material "utterly without redeeming social value." A leading publishers' attorney called the era the "end of obscenity" and the end of censorship.[9]

In 1964 the Supreme Court's decision in *New York Times Co. v. Sullivan* imposed constitutional restrictions on the civil action for libel. Public figures suing for libel would have to demonstrate the falsity of the defamatory statement, and that the publisher had issued it with "reckless disregard" of the truth. Criminal libel was all but eliminated. The Supreme Court, in *Garrison v. Louisiana* (1964), recognized the fading need for criminal libel statutes: "Changing mores and the virtual disappearance of criminal libel prosecutions lend support to the observation that . . . 'under modern conditions, when the rule of law is generally accepted as a substitute for private physical measures, it can hardly be urged that the maintenance of the peace requires a criminal prosecution for private defamation.'" Several states, including California, declared their criminal libel laws unconstitutional and repealed them.[10]

Confidential tarnished the public's image of scandal magazines, and for a while, they practically disappeared. Most of the exposé publications folded shortly after the *Confidential* trial. Even the gossip column was in decline. The *New York Times* reported in 1967 that the rise of television, growing sophistication among newspaper readers, and changing sexual norms led to the shutdown of gossip columns at many urban newspapers. "People are still interested in scandal, but certainly not to the extent that they once were," a press agent told the *Times*. "Look, you have glamorous stars now openly living with each other. You get people going on TV and talking about the most intimate things. You get magazine articles that are incredibly blunt. Everything's changed. No one's shocked any more."[11]

In the late 1960s, publisher Generoso Pope Jr. spurred the resurgence of celebrity gossip with his infamous *National Enquirer*. In 1952 Pope had purchased a failing Sunday afternoon broadsheet, the *New York Enquirer*, which he transformed into a successful tabloid, renamed the *National Enquirer*. Initially the *Enquirer*'s focus was "gore and guts," with stories like "Mom Uses Son's Face for an Ashtray" and "Madman Cut Up His Date and Put Her Body in His Freezer." Following a dip in sales in the mid-1960s, Pope transformed the tabloid's image. The new *Enquirer* turned to celebrity stories, with articles like "Why Hollywood Never Quite Got to Me" by Katharine Hepburn, and

Zsa Zsa Gabor describing "My Biggest Break." By 1969 the *Enquirer* sold 1.2 million copies per week. By 1975 it was the nation's top-selling newspaper.[12]

The *Enquirer*'s success was the prelude to a celebrity gossip explosion. In 1974 *People* magazine, published by Time Inc., featured stories about stars, written in an airy, human-interest style. *People's* first issues offered articles like "Gloria Vanderbilt: A Fourth Marriage That Really Works," "Burt Reynolds & Dinah Shore: The Superstar She Said No To," and "James Cagney Hoofer or Thug, Always the Star." With toned-down stories and the imprimatur of a respectable publisher, gossip went upscale. In less than a year *People's* circulation hit one million and it reached two million within three years.[13]

People's success led to the creation of literally dozens of magazines, newspapers, tabloids, and television shows devoted to gossip and "personality" stories about entertainment stars and public figures. Within three years after *People* was founded, virtually every publisher in the country entered the field. In 1974 Rupert Murdoch began publishing *Star* and soon had a circulation base of three million. The *New York Daily News* and the *New York Times* began "people" sections and *Celebrity*, *In the Know*, and *Us Weekly* debuted. By the end of the 1970s, tabloids included the *Globe*, *National Examiner*, *Sun*, and *Star*, in addition to the *Enquirer*. Traditional news outlets also moved into "personality journalism." With Watergate whetting appetites for scandal and personal revelations, "the public seems more fascinated than ever by behind-the-scenes glimpses, by now-it-can-be-told revelations, and by private details," *Newsweek* observed in 1976.[14]

To keep up with the competition, the gossip publications became more salacious, especially the *Enquirer*. By the 1970s, *Enquirer* stories spotlighted celebrities' arrests, affairs, and misfortunes. Stories described Steve McQueen's agonized death from lung cancer and blamed Mary Tyler Moore for her son committing suicide. The *Enquirer* gained fame for its scoops on the deaths of Elvis Presley, Princess Grace, and Natalie Wood, and its exclusives on Rock Hudson and Liberace dying of AIDS. It was offensive, lurid, and in bad taste—and wildly fascinating. Pundits observed a "red-faced syndrome": "shoppers, mostly women, snatched the *Enquirer* from the checkout racks, buried it in their grocery bags, and took it home." It was "literary contraband, to be secretly circulated among friends."[15]

All the new gossip publications were indebted to *Confidential*. Almost all duplicated *Confidential's* setup, with legal vetting, fact checks, top-notch writers, and networks of well-paid tipsters. The *Enquirer* was most like *Confidential*.

Like Harrison, Pope paid handsomely for ideas, tips, and finished articles. At the tabloid's peak in the 1980s, Pope offered some of the highest salaries in American journalism, and many of the nation's most distinguished journalists worked for him pseudonymously. *Enquirer* reporters were famously deceptive. One reporter tried to disguise herself as a tourist with a broken-down car when she went to see Warren Beatty, in an effort to uncover whether he was going to marry Diane Keaton. Another pretended to be insane to gain access to a mental hospital.[16]

The *Enquirer*'s vast tipster network comprised over five thousand "correspondents." Pope set up a Los Angeles research bureau and relied on personal trainers, hotel doormen, maids, butlers, limousine drivers, pizza delivery boys, valet car parkers, gardeners, publicists, mistresses, and ex-mistresses. The *Enquirer* became notorious for its use of hidden cameras. At Elvis Presley's funeral, only family members and friends were to view him. The tabloid bribed a relative to take a picture with a miniature camera of Elvis in his coffin. The issue with the photo on the cover sold more than six million copies.[17]

Pope hired a former Time Inc. employee named Ruth Annan to lead a twenty-six-person fact-checking team. Gossip items required two independent sources, and all interviews had to be tape-recorded so that quotes could be verified. The *Enquirer* boasted that it was the most accurate paper in America—it spent $2 million a year to verify articles. "Gossip is so documented now it's not even gossip anymore," complained a celebrity columnist for the *Enquirer*. "I know of people in hospitals dying of complications from face lifts, but I can't print it unless I know the name of the doctor, the time of the operation, the room number in the hospital, and have two eyewitnesses." The law firm Rogers & Wells handled prepublication review for the *Enquirer*. "We can't afford to touch an iffy story," said Dick Allison, Pope's assistant. "If it doesn't pass the lawyers, we don't run it."[18]

The *Enquirer* counted on the likelihood that stars wouldn't sue for libel, especially after the *New York Times Co. v. Sullivan* decision. Yet by the end of the 1970s, celebrity animus against the tabloids was brewing, and there were rumors of a campaign to bring down the *Enquirer*. Actor Larry Hagman, outraged by a story reporting that as a child he shot birds and tore up his brother's photo album, encouraged his fellow stars to fund a "war chest" to force the tabloid into bankruptcy.[19]

In 1976 Carol Burnett disputed an *Enquirer* article that described her arguing with Henry Kissinger in a Washington restaurant, then giggling when she knocked a glass of wine over another diner. She claimed the story was false. The article, which implied she'd been drinking, was painful to Burnett because her parents died of complications related to alcoholism. She sued for libel and the results were bad for the *Enquirer*. In a deposition, a reporter testified that he tried to fact-check the story right before the deadline and failed. The restaurant's employees said they had disclosed to the *Enquirer*'s reporters that Burnett hadn't been drunk. In the middle of the trial, Johnny Carson rallied the entire country against the *Enquirer*. "It's based on innuendo, it's based on gossip, it's based on half-truths, it's based on speculation," he said.[20]

In 1983 Burnett won a $1.6 million judgment against the *Enquirer*. Just as it abandoned *Confidential*, the mainstream press lauded the outcome and blasted the *Enquirer*. Three dozen celebrities subsequently sued the *Enquirer*, and there was talk that it was headed for the same fate as *Confidential*. But many of the libel suits were dismissed, and even Burnett's award was cut in half by the judge and settled. After the Burnett suit, the *Enquirer* retained former *Confidential* defender Edward Bennett Williams, and they set up an even more elaborate legal screening process. Burnett's suit opened the floodgates to more celebrity lawsuits. "The era of tabloid litigation—the extreme sport of First Amendment law"—had begun.[21]

Harrison's insight that "people will always want the lowdown"—that sex sold, and that there's always a market for scandal—was truly vindicated in the 1990s, dubbed the "Tabloid Decade." Celebrity gossip dominated the media, from the thriving tabloids to slick celebrity magazines like *People* and *Vanity Fair*, to entertainment and gossip TV shows like *Entertainment Tonight* and *Lifestyles of the Rich and Famous*, to news shows like *A Current Affair* and *Hard Copy*. Tabloidism was overtaking journalism. With increasing competition from tabloids and cable TV, traditional news outlets faced more pressure to take on tawdry subjects and deploy tactics used by gossip publications.[22]

Events of the 1990s were practically made for the tabloid genre: the car-crash death of Princess Diana, the Clarence Thomas hearings, President Clinton and Monica Lewinsky, and a parade of celebrity sex scandals involving Hugh Grant, George Michael, Paul Ruben, and Michael Jackson, among others. In 1995 the O. J. Simpson trial marked the triumph of the tabloids. The *Enquirer* broke the stories that Simpson had bought a knife just before his wife was murdered, that Kato Kaelin had received death threats, and that DA Marcia Clark had been battered by her first husband. All the *Enquirer*'s stories were picked up by the national press, something that would never have happened in the *Confidential* era. By the end of the decade, mainstream media had so thoroughly adopted tabloid styles that they were actually putting the tabloids out of business.[23] There was a race to the bottom as cable networks, broadcast news, slick magazines, and newspaper publishers all sought to capture the attention of an increasingly jaded, media-savvy public. Then a new medium came along that upped the game even further.

The rise of the internet put the *Confidential* formula into overdrive. The competition became fierce. Not only had the number of information channels exploded, but gossip could now travel to a global audience practically at the speed of light, putting pressure on outlets to scoop, publish, and outdo the competition with more sensational revelations. Shocking, unposed paparazzi pictures of celebrities, which could instantaneously cut through internet noise, took on importance in the new gossip game. The rise of social media like Facebook led to a massive change in the tone of public discourse. With civility eroding, the public's appetite for lurid material increased, and websites delivered.

TMZ.com, one of the most notorious, cynical, and successful of the celebrity gossip sites, debuted in 2005. Of all the gossip websites, it most closely resembles *Confidential*. A blog, it lacks the literary pizazz and long-form writing of Harrison's magazine. It publishes scoops almost instantaneously and has broken some of the biggest celebrity stories of the past decade. It also distinguishes itself with its images, something *Confidential* was never heavy on—candid videos of stars doing anything from going to the gym or the store without makeup to swearing and fighting drunkenly with paparazzi. But in its mission to unmask celebrities, its legal savvy, contemptuous tone, and tipster network, it is the modern-day *Confidential*.

TMZ was launched by Harvey Levin, a former law professor and longtime host of the TV show *The People's Court*. Promising that it wasn't content to "wait on the red carpet for photo ops," it pledged to deliver "every celebrity meltdown and wig-out." "You make them stars. But TMZ makes them real," is its motto. TMZ crushed its competitors by being first on breaking news, reporting, among other scoops, Mel Gibson's drunken anti-Semitic rant, Tiger Woods's extramarital indiscretions, and Michael Jackson's death. It posted a picture of Anna Nicole Smith's refrigerator filled with methadone and SlimFast, an audio recording of Los Angeles Clippers owner Donald Sterling making racist remarks, and a video showing NFL player Ray Rice knocking out his fiancée in an elevator. Like *Confidential*, TMZ sports an aggressive aesthetic and style, with a bold font and red, black, and yellow color scheme. Levin—deeply tanned, dapper, and assertive—boasts of TMZ's accuracy: "Our accuracy record is probably better than anyone in the media right now. TMZ is a better news operation in the celeb world than any news operation out there in the country, by far. It's not even close." The *New York Times* described Levin as a "feared figure in Hollywood," likening his power that of the "1940s and '50s gossip columnists like Walter Winchell." By 2008 the site had ten million unique viewers each month.[24]

In a bombshell article in 2016, the *New Yorker* claimed to expose TMZ's inner workings. What it revealed is that TMZ uses the same methods that *Confidential* pioneered sixty years ago. Levin cultivated an extensive network of tipsters, including entertainment lawyers, reality-television stars, adult-film brokers, court officials, beauty salon workers, valets, and waiters. TMZ pays informants at a celebrity limousine service to provide lists of customers, their routes, and license plates, so paparazzi can stalk them. An employee of Delta Air Lines gives TMZ the itineraries of celebrity passengers going through Los Angeles and New York. TMZ operates a telephone line and receives more than a hundred tips through it each day. "Everybody rats everybody else out," said a former cameraman for the site. "That's the beauty of TMZ."[25]

Levin has been described as the "high prince of sleaze." It's his personal belief that celebrity is fake and that it's his job to expose it. Yet he draws lines around what can be published, and often more conservatively than *Confidential* did. He declines articles on minors, or stories that would police "bedroom affairs." He once rejected a salacious story on Michael Jackson because it was based on what he thought were stolen documents. Levin, who is openly gay, also draws a line at outing. In 2012 Ellen DeGeneres, whose show is produced by Telepictures, a subsidiary of Warner Bros. Television (which owns TMZ), implied that the site outed homosexuals. Levin said to a Telepictures executive, "She's ruining the brand!"[26]

TMZ's restraint stands in contrast to the former website Gawker. Founded in 2002 by Nick Denton, a British-born journalist and entrepreneur who was educated at the University of Oxford and wrote for the *Financial Times*, Gawker was notorious for its snarky and vicious tone, no-holds-barred approach to gossip, and crude voyeurism. Denton defined "public interest" as "the right to know everything about a public figure," and a "public figure" as "anyone with an unlocked Facebook account." Gawker's purported "ethics philosophy," Denton often said, was to "publish the real story, the one that so-called . . . journalists have spent their careers avoiding."[27]

Gawker made waves in 2008 with an article about Tom Cruise's role in the Church of Scientology. It printed screenshots of vice presidential candidate Sarah Palin's hacked personal emails, and in 2013 published a video of former Toronto mayor Rob Ford smoking crack. Despite having taken many years to come out himself, Denton was fine with outing others. In July 2015, Gawker ran a story about Condé Nast CFO David Geithner picking up a male escort, which was criticized for gay-shaming and outing a man in a heterosexual marriage. At one point, it published videos of a college student being raped in a bathroom for apparently no point other than to attract clicks and ad revenue.[28]

In 2016 Gawker was forced to shut down after a massive lawsuit. Former pro wrestler Hulk Hogan sued Gawker for invasion of privacy when it published a graphic sex tape of him. The lawsuit was funded by Peter Thiel, a Silicon Valley billionaire and founder of PayPal who was upset that Gawker had outed him. The Hogan suit resulted in a $140 million judgment, the biggest invasion of privacy award of all time. Gawker was forced into bankruptcy, and it ceased publishing in August 2016.[29] Unlike *Confidential*, Gawker wasn't quashed by the government. But its demise shows how free speech is not an absolute; the law can still take down publications that push boundaries and upset the powers that be.

———————

There is a lot to dislike about *Confidential*. It reinforced the worst aspects of America in the 1950s—its paranoia and intolerance, its homophobia, misogyny, and racism. It's unclear whether *Confidential* "corrupted" anyone, but there is no doubt that the magazine inflicted a good deal of harm. *Confidential* invaded privacy. It broke homes and upset lives. Sometimes intentionally, sometimes unintentionally, it created strife, shame, and hardship.

At the same time, however unsavory, *Confidential* did much that was noteworthy. Compared to the writing that would come out of later tabloids, *Confidential*'s prose, though often corny, could also be witty, sophisticated, and imaginative. Some of its public service stories were genuinely enlightening. However raunchy and crude, *Confidential* pushed the boundaries of public discourse around sex and paved the way for greater openness and tolerance in later decades.

And there's no question that *Confidential* accomplished what it set out to do: exposing the truth—the sometimes ugly, sometimes funny, and often-shocking truth—behind stars' images. *Confidential* whetted the public's appetite for reality, spurring deeper journalistic digs and more aggressive reporting on public figures and public issues, both for good and for ill. As Ezra Goodman noted in 1961, it was easy to attack *Confidential*, but the magazine, in its own way, was groundbreaking. What the magazine "proved was that there was too much pallid, punches-pulled reporting elsewhere and that the average, untutored reader was probably wise to it and instinctively knew that he was being hornswoggled. He undoubtedly realized that *Confidential*, in its own way, was giving him a glimmer of the truth."[30]

The trial killed *Confidential*, but it didn't break Harrison. The publisher, whose personal fortunes remained intact, maintained his flamboyant lifestyle and not long after the trial was reportedly going around town in a white Lincoln Continental Mark III. He lived in the Hotel Madison on East 58th Street, an upscale, conservative old building full of big cooperative apartments and a lobby with plum and umber walls, where he lived under an assumed name with his sister Helen and his new girlfriend, a blond showgirl named Reggie Ruta.[31]

After selling *Confidential*, Harrison became an investor and allegedly made more than a million dollars on the stock market. He continued doing what he loved best—publishing pictures of half-naked women and sleazy magazines. In 1959 he began publishing a short-lived magazine called *New York Confidential*. The magazine—claiming to be "New—Uncensored—Unafraid," offering "The Lowdown on the Big Town"—roared with headlines like "Broadway—the Hardened Artery," "Harlem—Three Square Miles of TNT," and "Chinatown—Is It True What They Say?" When *New York Confidential* folded, Harrison put out several "one-shot" magazines, part of a series titled *U.S.A. Inside Report*. One was called "Menace of the Sex Deviate."[32]

In 1961 Harrison published *Naked New York*, a purported expose of the "seamier side of the big town." The cover read, "The chippies, the chiselers, and cheats still rule the roost, but the gimmicks are all new. This is how New York takes, and is taken." Despite its salacious promises, the book, consisting largely of excerpted stories from *Confidential*, was tame and boring. Wrote one reviewer, "Except for the lewd leers that he pops out on every page, his modest little work is about as racy as the 'Golden Book of Favorite Songs.'"[33]

Perhaps Harrison's biggest post-*Confidential* triumph was a little-known, poorly circulated but surprisingly long-lived supermarket tabloid called *Inside News* ("the lowdown around the world"), which he started in 1963. "This is going to be bigger than *Confidential*," he told Tom Wolfe, who was writing a feature on Harrison for *Esquire* magazine. "The keyhole stuff is dead. The big thing now is getting behind the news."[34]

Inside News was covered with half-naked women and outrageous headlines, like "I was Raped in the Tunnel of Love," "Warning: Your Toothbrush Can Give You Cancer," "Mom and Two Daughters Share Lover," and "Cops Arrest Queen of Homo Orgies." Harrison bought hundreds of head and body shots cheaply from Europe and pasted unrelated parts together, giving the tabloid a bizarre, unworldly feel. Harrison published *Inside News* up until his death in 1978. In January 1978, gossip columnist Liz Smith reported that Harrison was preparing a comeback with a new paperback book company. Harrison died in his Manhattan office a few months later at the age of seventy-three.[35]

To the end, Harrison remained enormously proud of *Confidential*. The magazine was beautiful, he insisted. It brought a smile to readers—and no one had been harmed. "Some of these people we wrote about would be very indignant at first, but I knew goddamned well it was a beautiful act. What they really wanted was another story in *Confidential*. It was great publicity for them," he said.

"You couldn't put out a magazine like *Confidential* again," Harrison told Wolfe. "You know why? Because movie stars have started writing books about themselves! . . . They tell all. No magazine can compete with that."[36]

Harrison had one regret: never writing his own story. He would have called it, "Now It Can Be Told—'Inside' *Confidential*."[37]

NOTES

Introduction

1. Brad Shortell, "Does Desi Really Love Lucy?" *Confidential*, January 1955, 23.
2. Horton Streete, "What Makes Ava Run for Sammy Davis Jr.?," *Confidential*, March 1955, 12.
3. Matt Williams, "Why Was Lizabeth Scott's Name in the Call Girls' Call Book?" *Confidential*, September 1955, 50; "Why Liberace's Theme Song Should Be 'Mad About the Boy,'" *Confidential*, July 1957, 16.
4. Richard Gehman, "Confidential File on Confidential," *Esquire*, November 1956, 144.
5. "The Curious Craze for Confidential Magazines," *Newsweek*, July 11, 1955, 50.
6. Transcript of Record, *California v. Meade* (Cal. Super. Ct. L.A. County, August 21, 1957), 1043 (hereafter cited as TR).
7. Bowling Green State University Popular Culture Library, Bowling Green, Ohio.
8. Since the 1950s, *Confidential* has been the subject of numerous magazine and newspaper articles, as well as dissertations, book chapters, and two full-length books. None offer a complete history of the magazine, especially its legal travails. For books on *Confidential*, see Henry E. Scott, *Shocking True Story: The Rise and Fall of Confidential, "America's Most Scandalous Scandal Magazine"* (New York: Pantheon Books, 2010); and Samuel Bernstein, *Mr. Confidential: The Man, the Magazine, and the Movieland Massacre That Changed Hollywood Forever* (London: Walford, 2006). Significant magazine pieces include Neal Gabler, "*Confidential's* Reign of Terror: Inside the Magazine that Catalyzed the Celebrity Tabloid Culture," *Vanity Fair*, April 2003, 190; and Sam Kashner, "Confidential," *GQ: Gentleman's Quarterly*, March 2000, 212. Chapters in books on gossip and Hollywood history offer broad overviews of *Confidential*, including Sam Kashner and Jennifer MacNair, *The Bad and the Beautiful: Hollywood in the Fifties* (New York: W.W. Norton, 2003), and Jeannette Walls, *Dish: How Gossip Became the News and the News Became Just Another Show* (New York: Perennial, 2001). Film studies profes-

sor Mary Desjardins has offered a more scholarly treatment of the trial in *Recycled Stars: Female Film Stardom in the Age of Television and Video* (Duke University Press, 2015), and "Systematizing Scandal: *Confidential* Magazine, Stardom, and the State of California," in *Headline Hollywood: A Century of Film Scandal*, ed. Adrienne L. McLean and David A. Cook (New Brunswick, NJ: Rutgers University Press, 2001). See also Anne Helen Petersen, "The Gossip Industry: Producing and Distributing Star Images, Celebrity Gossip and Entertainment News 1910–2010" (PhD diss., University of Texas, 2011).

9. Thomas K. Wolfe, "Public Lives: Confidential Magazine," *Esquire*, April 1964, 87.

Chapter 1: The Education of a Publisher

1. United States Census, 1900, 1910, 1930.
2. United States Census, 1900, 1910, 1920; New York State Census, 1915.
3. David Gelman and Edward Katcher, "The Man Behind *Confidential*," Part I, *New York Post*, September 3, 1957, M2.
4. David Nasaw, *Children of the City: At Work and at Play* (Garden City, NY: Anchor/Doubleday, 1985), 55.
5. Gelman and Katcher, "Man Behind *Confidential*," Part I.
6. Gelman and Katcher, "Man Behind *Confidential*," Part I; "Fair Game: Interview with Robert Harrison," *Writers' Yearbook*, 1956, 15–16.
7. Gelman and Katcher, "Man Behind *Confidential*," Part I.
8. Ibid.
9. Martin Weyrauch, "The Why of the Tabloids," *Forum*, April 1927, 492, 500; Neal Gabler, *Winchell: Gossip, Power, and the Culture of Celebrity* (New York: Knopf, 1994), 73–75.
10. Matthew Huttner, "The Police Gazette," *American Mercury*, July 1948, 15–23.
11. George H. Douglas, *The Golden Age of the Newspaper* (Westport, CT: Greenwood, 1999), 229. On MacFadden, see William R. Hunt, *Body Love: The Amazing Career of Bernarr Macfadden* (Bowling Green, OH: Bowling Green State University Press, 1989), 80–89; Samuel Fuller, Christa Fuller, and Jerome Rudes, *A Third Face: My Tale of Writing, Fighting, and Filmmaking* (New York: Alfred A. Knopf, 2002), 40.
12. Hunt, *Body Love*, 137–138.
13. Samuel Taylor Morse, "Those Terrible Tabloids," *Independent*, March 6, 1926, 264–266; "A Tabloid a Day," *Forum*, March 1927, 379; Gabler, *Winchell*, 72.
14. "Chorines Posed for Composograph of Famous Siamese Twins," *Editor and Publisher*, August 18, 1928, 19; John Spivak, "The Rise and Fall of a Tabloid," *American Mercury*, July 1934, 311; Simon Bessie, *Jazz Journalism: The Story of Tabloid Newspapers* (New York: Russell & Russell, 1969), 197; "Tabloid Poison," *Saturday*

Review of Literature, February 19, 1927, 589; Bruce Bliven, "Graphic Realist," *New Republic*, December 29, 1926, 167–169.

15. Bessie, *Jazz Journalism*, 205; John Stevens, *Sensationalism and the New York Press* (New York: Columbia University Press, 2011), 143.

16. Gehman, "Confidential File," 144.

17. Wolfe, "Public Lives," 90.

18. United States Census, 1930; Gelman and Katcher, "Man Behind *Confidential*," Part I; "Fair Game," 17.

19. Thomas Patrick Doherty, *Hollywood's Censor: Joseph I. Breen and the Production Code Administration* (New York: Columbia University Press, 2007), 25; "Censorship of Motion Pictures," *Yale Law Journal* 1939, 103.

20. Gelman and Katcher, "Man Behind *Confidential*," Part I; "Fair Game," 16.

21. "Fair Game," 17.

22. Theodore Peterson, *Magazines in the Twentieth Century* (Urbana: University of Illinois Press, 1964), 307–309.

23. Douglas Ellis, *Uncovered: The Hidden Art of Girlie Pulps* (Silver Spring, MD: Adventure House, 2003), 60; "Vice Foes Ask War on Sex Magazines," *New York Times*, August 31, 1937, 11.

24. Leonard Lyons, "The Lyons Den," *Detroit Free Press*, July 25, 1941, 24; Jack Devlin, "Painting Nifty Calendar Girls Calls for Some Lily Gilding," *Alton (IL) Evening Telegraph*, December 16, 1941, 11; Louis Sobol, "New York Cavalcade," *Harrisburg (PA) Evening News*, August 18, 1941, 10.

25. Richard Foster, *The Real Bettie Page: The Truth About the Queen of the Pinups* (Secaucus, NJ: Carol, 1997), 52–53; *Bettie Page Reveals All*, directed by Mark Mori (New York: Single Spark Pictures, 2012).

26. David Felts, "Second Thoughts," *Decatur (IL) Herald*, December 6, 1945, 6; "Fair Game," 18.

27. "Fair Game," 18; "Politics and Peek a Boo," *New York Post*, September 17, 1953, 28.

28. Alan Betrock, *Unseen America: The Greatest Cult Exploitation Magazines, 1950–1966* (Brooklyn, NY: Shake Books, 1990); "Politics and Peek a Boo"; Gelman and Katcher, "The Man Behind *Confidential*," *New York Post*, Part II, September 4, 1957.

29. Excerpts of Harrison's magazines are reprinted in Harald Hellman and Burkhard Riemschneider, *1000 Pin-Up Girls* (London: Taschen, 2008).

30. Gelman and Katcher, "Man Behind *Confidential*," Part II.

31. Alvin Davis, "*Confidential's* Wrongoes," *New York Post*, September 17, 1953; "How *Confidential* Does It: Tricks with Words and Pictures," *New York Post*, September 15, 1953, 4.

32. Dan Walker, "Along Broadway," *Massilon (OH) Evening Independent*, June 24, 1946, 4; D. A. Munro, "Magazine Ferment," *New Republic*, April 15, 1946, 500–502.

33. "Fair Game," 18; "Titans of Trash: Doctored Photos Attract Readers," *Miami News*, November 14, 1955, 4.

34. "Politics and Peek a Boo," 28; Gelman and Katcher, "Man Behind *Confidential*," Part III, *New York Post*, September 5, 1957.

35. Steve Govoni, in discussion with the author, May 2016; Gelman and Katcher, "Man Behind *Confidential*," Parts II, III.

36. Saul Pett, "Cheesecake Triumphant in Return to Normalcy," *Bridgeport (CT) Telegram*, September 29, 1947, 46; Gelman and Katcher, "Man Behind *Confidential*," Part II.

37. Gelman and Katcher, "Man Behind *Confidential*," Part III; Scott, *Shocking True Story*, 134; *Real Bettie Page*, 53.

38. "Vermont, St. Albans Canadian Border Crossings, 1895–1954," *FamilySearch*, June 14, 2016, https://www.familysearch.org/search/collection/2185163, citing NARA microfilm publications M1461, M1463, M1464, and M1465 (Washington, DC: National Archives and Records Administration, n.d); Gelman and Katcher, "Man Behind *Confidential*," Part III; Earl Wilson, "It Happened Last Night," *Uniontown (PA) Morning Herald*, September 18, 1947, 16.

39. "Smut and Smear, the Story of *Confidential*," *New York Post*, September 14, 1953; Maurice Zolotow, "Scandal Magazines and How They Work," *Indianapolis Star*, November 2, 1955, 21; Gehman, "Confidential File," 143.

40. Wolfe, "Public Lives," 152.

41. Naomi Barko, "A Woman Looks at Men's Magazines," *The Reporter*, July 1953, 29–32.

42. "Cleveland Bans Sexy Magazines," *Logan (OH) Daily News*, October 14, 1949, 2; "The Confidential Story: How Dirty Can You Get?" *New York Post*, September 17, 1953.

43. "Local Dealers Agree Not to Sell Books Banned by Pittsfield Chief," *North Adams (MA) Transcript*, January 31, 1949, 2; Harold Liston, "15 Magazines Fade from Local Stands," *Bloomington (IL) Pantagraph*, April 10, 1950, 3; "Magistrate Labels Cheesecake Magazines 'Criminally Indecent,'" *Brooklyn Daily Eagle*, May 8, 1952, 19; "Confidential Story, How Dirty."

44. "Confidential Story: How Dirty."

45. Lucille Cromer, "Harlemites Sue for Scandalous Article," *New York Age*, October 7, 1950, 19.

46. Ibid.

Chapter 2: The Age

1. Douglas T. Miller and Marion Nowak, *The Fifties: The Way We Really Were* (Garden City, NY: Doubleday, 1977), 22–23.
2. Ibid., 29.
3. Wini Breines, *Young, White, and Miserable: Growing Up Female in the Fifties* (Boston: Beacon, 1992), 3; David Halberstam, *The Fifties* (New York: Random House, 1993), 587.
4. Halberstam, *Fifties*, 590; Daniel Horowitz, *Betty Friedan and the Making of "The Feminine Mystique": The American Left, the Cold War, and Modern Feminism* (Amherst: University of Massachusetts Press, 1998), 3.
5. John D'Emilio and Estelle B. Freedman, *Intimate Matters: A History of Sexuality in America* (New York: Harper & Row, 1988), 262–263.
6. Miller and Nowak, *Fifties*, 10.
7. On the effects of the containment ideal on family life, see Elaine Tyler May, *Homeward Bound: American Families in the Cold War Era* (New York: Basic Books, 2008), 16–36.
8. See generally N. Megan Kelley, *Projections of Passing: Postwar Anxieties and Hollywood Films, 1947-1960* (Jackson: University Press of Mississippi, 2016).
9. Samantha Barbas, *Laws of Image: Privacy and Publicity in America* (Stanford, CA: Stanford University Press, 2015), 155.

Chapter 3: *Confidential*

1. James Ciment, "American Mafia," in *Postwar America: An Encyclopedia of Social, Political, Cultural, and Economic History*, ed. James Ciment (New York: Routledge, 2015), 335.
2. Halberstam, *Fifties*, 190; Lee Bernstein, *The Greatest Menace: Organized Crime in Cold War America* (Amherst: University of Massachusetts Press, 2009), 72–83.
3. Gilbert King, "The Senator and the Gangsters," Smithsonian.com, April 18, 2012.
4. Ibid.; Harold H. Martin, "Mystery of Kefauver," *Saturday Evening Post*, June 2, 1956, 89; Gus Russo, *The Outfit* (New York: Bloomsbury, 2003), 267.
5. William Howard Moore, *The Kefauver Committee and the Politics of Crime, 1950-1952* (Columbia: University of Missouri Press, 1974),184; "The US Gets a Close Look at Crime," *Life*, March 26, 1951, 33.
6. "Confidential: Between You and Me and the Bedpost," *Fortnight*, July 5, 1955, 25; "Fair Game," 19.
7. TR, 125; "Confidential: Between You and Me," 179.

8. K. A. Cuordileone, *Manhood and American Political Culture* (New York: Routledge, 2004), 73–74.

9. "Jack Lait, 71, Dies; Editor of Mirror," *New York Times*, April 2, 1954, 27; Jon Lewis, *Hard-Boiled Hollywood: Crime and Punishment in Postwar Los Angeles* (Berkeley: University of California Press, 2017), 32.

10. "Confidential Book Spotlights New York Intimacies, Foibles," *Cumberland Evening Times*, August 24, 1948, 14; Advertisement, "Chicago Confidential," *Chicago Tribune*, March 5, 1950, 7.

11. See David K. Johnson, *The Lavender Scare: The Cold War Persecution of Gays and Lesbians in the Federal Government* (Chicago: University of Chicago Press, 2004), 92–93.

12. Jack Lait and Lee Mortimer, *U.S.A. Confidential* (New York: Crown, 1952), x.

13. John P. Mallan, "U.S.A. Confidential: Voyeurism in Politics," *New Republic*, April 28, 1952, 15–16.

14. D'Emilio and Freedman, *Intimate Matters*, 291; "Medicine: The Abnormal," *Time*, April 17, 1950, 86.

15. Ralph H. Major, "New Moral Menace to Our Youth," *Coronet*, September 1950, 101, 106.

16. Jennifer Terry, *An American Obsession: Science, Medicine, and Homosexuality in Modern Society* (Chicago: University of Chicago Press, 1999), 335, 341.

17. Lait and Mortimer, *U.S.A. Confidential*, 44–45.

18. John H. Summers, "What Happened to Sex Scandals? Politics and Peccadilloes, Jefferson to Kennedy," *Journal of American History* 87 (2000), 847; Lait and Mortimer, *U.S.A. Confidential*, 43.

19. Mallan, "U.S.A. Confidential," 16.

20. David Gelman and Edward Katcher, "The Man Behind *Confidential*," *New York Post*, Part IV, September 6, 1957, M2.

21. Steve Govoni, in discussion with the author, May 2016.

22. "Confidentially Speaking," *Confidential*, December 1952, 4.

23. Hugh V. Haddock, "Hoodlums' Paradise," *Confidential*, December 1952, 8–9; Jack Watson, "What Virginia Hill Didn't Tell Kefauver," *Confidential*, April 1953, 28; Carlton Mitchell, "Monte Carlo of the Air," *Confidential*, December 1952, 30; Wolfe, "Public Lives," 156.

24. A. P. Govoni, "Highway Larceny," *Confidential*, December 1952, 42; George Drexel, "I Was Tortured on a Chain Gang!," *Confidential*, December 1952, 14; A. P. Govoni, "Devil's Island for Boys," *Confidential*, April 1953, 24.

25. "They Pass for White," *Confidential*, December 1952, 35; J. Morgan Haskell, "Let's Abolish Common Law Marriage," *Confidential*, April 1953, 40.

26. "World's Queerest Wedding," *Confidential*, December 1952, 37–38.

27. Jay Williams, "Is It True What They Say About Johnnie Ray?," *Confidential*, April 1953, 37–39, 63.

28. Michael S. Sherry, *Gay Artists in Modern American Culture: An Imagined Conspiracy* (Chapel Hill: University of North Carolina Press, 2007), 30.

29. Wolfe, "Public Lives," 87.

30. "Confidentially Speaking"; Gehman, "Confidential File," 140; "How *Confidential* Does It," 4; Jack Olsen, "Titans of Trash: Inside Look at Dreamed-Up Story Factory," *Pittsburgh Press*, November 3, 1955, 21.

31. "Confidential: Between You and Me," 24; Morton Dahlgren, "Gangster Ghouls," *Confidential*, August 1953, 16.

32. Greg Young, "The Mob Moves in on Show Business," *Confidential*, April 1953, 34–35.

33. "*Confidential* Backs Down," *New York Post*, September 16, 1953, 60; "When We Make a Mistake," *Confidential*, July 1953, 56.

34. Jack Olsen, "Titans of Trash: Publisher Boasts of Past Fakeries," *Miami Daily News*, November 16, 1955, 30.

Chapter 4: Winchell and Rushmore

1. J. Howard Rutledge, "Gossipy Private Peeks," *Wall Street Journal*, July 5, 1955, 1; Peterson, *Magazines in the Twentieth Century*, 64; Huttner, "Police Gazette," 15–23; "Curious Craze," 11; "Sin, Sex and Sales," *Newsweek*, March 14, 1955, 88.

2. Jack Olsen, "Titans of Trash: Magazine Lured Winchell Plugs," *Miami Daily News*, November 15, 1955, 15.

3. "Walter Winchell's Big Ear Hears All Broadway's Gossip and Slang," *Editor and Publisher*, March 17, 1928, 20; Charles W. Wilcox, "Winchell of Broadway," *Scribner's Magazine*, February 1931, 199–202; Harry Saltpeter, "Town Gossip," *Outlook*, July 10, 1929, 413.

4. Ernest Cuneo, "Walter Winchell: The Greatest of the Great Gossips," *Saturday Evening Post*, September 1976, 32; "The Press: Newspaperman," *Time*, July 11, 1938, 33.

5. Stanley Walker, *The Night Club Era* (Baltimore: Johns Hopkins University Press, 1999), 130.

6. St. Clair McKelway and Margaret Case Harriman, "Gossip Writer," *New Yorker*, June 15, 1940, 30; "Gossip Writer," *New Yorker*, July 20, 1940, 30; Herman Klurfeld, *Winchell, His Life and Times* (New York: Praeger, 1976), 93; Cuneo, "Walter Winchell," 32.

7. Dickson Hartwell, "Walter Winchell, An American Phenomenon," *Collier's*, February 28, 1948, 12–13; Gabler, *Winchell*, 355–356; Marilyn Nissenson, *The Lady Upstairs: Dorothy Schiff and the New York Post* (New York: St. Martin's, 2007), 159.

8. Tim Brooks and Earle Marsh, *The Complete Directory to Prime Time Network and Cable TV Shows, 1946–Present* (New York: Ballantine Books, 1995), 1483.

9. Olsen, "Titans of Trash: Magazine Lured Winchell Plugs," 15.

10. Gabler, *Winchell*, 406–410; "Winchell v. Baker," *Time*, November 12, 1951, 47–49.

11. Gabler, *Winchell*, 423; "The Biggest Success Story," *Time*, January 21, 1952, 76; "Feud Days," *Time*, December 8, 1952, 44.

12. Edward H. Gray, "Winchell Was Right About Josephine Baker," *Confidential*, April 1953, 33.

13. "Broadway and Elsewhere," *Logansport (IN) Pharos-Tribune*, February 16, 1953, 4; "Broadway and Elsewhere," *Stroudsburg (PA) Pocono Record*, January 31, 1953, 4; Wolfe, "Public Lives," 155; "Literati," *Variety*, February, 11 1953, 61.

14. Wolfe, "Public Lives," 155.

15. Edward Horace Weiner, *Let's Go to Press; A Biography of Walter Winchell* (New York: Putnam, 1955), 223; Gabler, *Winchell*, 468.

16. "Broadway and Elsewhere," *Logansport (IN) Pharos-Tribune*, April 2, 1953, 4; "On Broadway," *Terre Haute (IN) Tribune*, June 16, 1953, 4; "Broadway and Elsewhere," *Logansport (IN) Pharos-Tribune*, September 18, 1953, 4; "Walter Winchell of New York," *Burlington (NC) Daily Times-News*, September 18, 1953, 2.

17. Howard Rushmore, "The Rebirth of an American," *American Magazine*, April 1940, 18, 157–158.

18. Theo Wilson, "Confidentially Rushmore," *New York Daily News*, January 6, 1958, 2; D. M. Ladd to A. H. Belmont, 14 April 1953, Howard Rushmore FBI Records, Marquette University Raynor Memorial Libraries Archives, Milwaukee; Rushmore, "Rebirth," 158–159.

19. Rushmore, "Rebirth," 161.

20. George Sokolsky, "The Ex-Communists Are Very Unhappy Crew," *Traverse City (MI) Record-Eagle*, January 9, 1958, 4; William Carr, "Rushmore: The Last Contradiction," *New York Post*, January 1, 1958, 3.

21. Howard Rushmore Testimony, July 26, 1948, Howard Rushmore FBI Records; Kashner and MacNair, *Bad and the Beautiful*, 27.

22. D. M. Ladd to A. H. Belmont, 14 April 1953, Howard Rushmore FBI Records; Kashner and MacNair, *Bad and the Beautiful*, 28.

23. Howard Rushmore, "I Worked for Confidential," *Christian Herald*, January 1958, 32–38; TR, 110.

24. TR, 119.

25. TR, 118, 195; Gabler, *Winchell*, 440–441; Rushmore, "I Worked."

26. Howard Rushmore, "Controversy of the Year: The People vs. Wechsler of the New York *Post*," *Confidential*, August 1953, 34–35, 54; "Walter Winchell of New York," *Burlington (NC) Daily Times-News*, May 5, 1953, 4; "Walter Winchell on Broadway," *Zanesville (OH) Times Recorder*, June 12, 1953, 4.

27. Kashner and MacNair, *Bad and the Beautiful*, 29.

28. "Smut and Smear"; TR, 230.

29. "They Exposed the Cancer Chiselers," *Confidential*, January 1954, 34; "America, On Guard!," *Confidential*, January 1954, 12.

30. "The Strange Death of J. Robert Oppenheimer's RED Sweetheart," *Confidential*, November 1954, 8; "There's Plenty of Red in the Harvard Crimson," *Confidential*, May 1954, 16; "Broadway and Elsewhere," *Indianapolis Star*, March 19, 1954, 13.

31. "Star Crossed," *Newsweek*, January 1958, 19–20; William Carr, "Rushmore: The Last Contradiction," *New York Post*, January 1, 1958, 3; "New York Confidential by Lee Mortimer," *Eureka (CA) Times-Standard*, September 4, 1954, 4.

32. "The Press: Rushmore v. Cohn," *Time*, November 1, 1954, 52; Kashner and Mac-Nair, *Bad and the Beautiful*, 60.

33. Rushmore, "I Worked for Confidential."

Chapter 5: Asbestos

1. Wolfe, "Public Lives," 90.

2. Kenneth Nichols, "The Town Crier," *Akron (OH) Beacon Journal*, June 23, 1953, 26.

3. Jay Breen, "Scandal at the Waldorf," *Confidential*, November 1954, 10; J. Shirley Frew, "Tip Off on Hat Check Girls," *Confidential*, July 1954, 38; Walter Barnes, "Operation Diaper: Call 'Em Daddy," *Confidential*, September 1954, 4, 10.

4. Renee Christine Romano, *Race Mixing: Black-White Marriage in Postwar America* (Cambridge, MA: Harvard University Press, 2009), 45.

5. Roger Thomas, "Pearl Bailey and the Drummer Boy," *Confidential*, July 1953, 41.

6. Mrs. Billy Daniels, "White Women Broke Up My Marriage to Billy Daniels," *Confidential*, May 1954, 26, 63.

7. "Martha Tells on Billy!," *Pittsburgh Courier*, March 13, 1954, 13.

8. Bruce Cory, "Elliott Roosevelt: Blondes, Brunettes, and Bankruptcies," *Confidential*, July 1953, 22; "Why Bobo Flew the Rockefeller Coop," *Confidential*, August 1953, 13; "Walter Winchell in New York," *Muncie (IN) Star Press*, July 3, 1953, 8.

9. Hewitt Van Horn, "Jimmy Donahue's Hush-Hush Secret," *Confidential*, July 1954, 10.

10. Jim Johnston, "Nation's Biggest Showplace: Nation's Biggest Sweatshop," *Confidential*, August 1953, 20; Robin Sharry, "The Red Cross—How Sweet Is Its Charity,"

Confidential, November 1954, 10; Homer Shannon, "Alcoholics Anonymous," *Confidential*, September 1954, 34; "Why Work—Know a Politician!," *Confidential*, August 1953, 12; Al Govoni, "The Perfect Tax Swindle," *Confidential*, November 1954, 34; A. P. Govoni, "How They Tap Your Phone," *Confidential*, August 1953, 44.

11. A. P. Govoni, "Poison on Your Plate," *Confidential*, March 1954, 45; "Pills That Kill the Smoking Habit," *Confidential*, May 1954, 12.

12. D'Emilio and Freedman, *Intimate Matters*, 293–294; Terry, *American Obsession*, 323.

13. Brooks Martin, "The Lavender Skeletons in TV's Closet," *Confidential*, July 1953, 34.

14. Juan Morales, "Hollywood, Where Men are Men—and Women Too!," *Confidential*, January 1954, 28–29.

15. Gene Huffman, "Bad Boys of Tennis," *Confidential*, July 1953, 45.

16. Joseph M. Porter, "How That Stevenson Rumor Started," *Confidential*, August 1953, 41, 60.

17. Gail Collins, *Scorpion Tongues: Gossip, Celebrity, and American Politics* (New York: William Morrow, 1998), 106; Jean H. Baker, *The Stevensons: A Biography of an American Family* (New York: W.W. Norton, 1996), 328–330.

18. Porter, "Stevenson Rumor," 41.

19. "*Confidential* Backs Down."

20. Davis, "Confidential's Wrongoes"; "Smut and Smear."

21. Walter Winchell, "Broadway Lights," *Terre Haute (IN) Tribune*, September 21, 1953, 4; Robert M. Grannis, "Wishful Thinking, Kenny, and a Crusade," *Brooklyn Daily Eagle*, September 21, 1953, 8.

22. Gehman, "Confidential File," 141.

23. Bob Farrell, "New York At Night," *Brooklyn Daily Eagle*, August 26, 1953, 11.

24. "Literati," *Variety*, October 7, 1953, 77; "Ciggies—More 'Guilty' than You Think," *Top Secret*, spring 1954, 21; Walter Winchell, "Broadway and Elsewhere," *Logansport (IN) Pharos-Tribune*, January 14, 1954, 4.

Chapter 6: The Dream Factory

1. "Hollywood's Press: Why the Stars Are in Your Eyes," *Newsweek*, February 22, 1954, 62.

2. On the rise of the star system, see generally Richard DeCordova, *Picture Personalities: The Emergence of the Star System in America* (Urbana: University of Illinois Press, 1990); Samantha Barbas, *Movie Crazy: Fans, Stars, and the Cult of Celebrity*

(New York: Palgrave, 2001); Lucy Fisher, *American Cinema of the 1920s: Themes and Variations* (New Brunswick, NJ: Rutgers University Press, 2009), 15, 26.

3. Michelle Pautz, "The Decline in Average Weekly Cinema Attendance: 1930-2000," *Issues in Political Economy* 11 (2002): 54–65; Samantha Barbas, *The First Lady of Hollywood: A Biography of Louella Parsons* (Berkeley: University of California Press, 2005), 194.

4. On the studios' manipulation of star images, see generally Jeanine Basinger, *The Star Machine* (New York: A.A. Knopf, 2007); Ronald L. Davis, *The Glamour Factory: Inside Hollywood's Big Studio System* (Dallas: Southern Methodist University Press, 1993); Joseph Wechsberg, "They Make the Stars Glitter," *Reader's Digest*, February 1947, 179.

5. Barbas, *First Lady*, 140; Scott Eyman, *Lion of Hollywood: The Life and Legend of Louis B. Mayer* (New York: Simon & Schuster, 2005), 4.

6. On the history of film censorship see generally Laura Wittern-Keller, *Freedom of the Screen: Legal Challenges to State Film Censorship, 1915-1981* (Lexington: University Press of Kentucky, 2008); Samantha Barbas, "How the Movies Became Speech," *Rutgers Law Review* 64 (3): 665–745.

7. Leonard J. Leff and Jerold Simmons, *The Dame in the Kimono: Hollywood, Censorship, and the Production Code* (Lexington: University Press of Kentucky, 2001), 5.

8. Eyman, *Lion of Hollywood*, 216; Bernard F. Dick, *Hollywood Madonna: Loretta Young* (Jackson: University Press of Mississippi, 2011), 76–82.

9. Eyman, *Lion of Hollywood*, 215, 216; Axel Madsen, *Stanwyck: A Biography* (New York: Open Road Distribution, 2015), 117.

10. William J. Mann, *Wisecracker: The Life and Times of William Haines, Hollywood's First Openly Gay Star* (New York: Viking, 1998), 228, 236; Eyman, *Lion of Hollywood*, 211; Axel Madsen, *The Sewing Circle: Sappho's Leading Ladies* (New York: Kensington Books, 2002), 110; Christopher Finch and Linda Rosenkrantz, *Gone Hollywood* (London: Weidenfeld and Nicolson, 1980), 163, 288.

11. Anthony Slide, *Inside the Hollywood Fan Magazine: A History of Star Makers, Fabricators, and Gossip Mongers* (Jackson: University Press of Mississippi, 2010), 3; Ezra Goodman, *The Fifty-Year Decline and Fall of Hollywood* (New York: Simon & Schuster, 1961), 76; Carl F. Cotter, "The Forty Hacks of the Fan Magazines," *The Coast* (February 1939): 2.

12. "Hollywood's Press," 63.

13. Cotter, "Forty Hacks," 1, 21; See also Gordon Kahn, "The Gospel According to Hollywood," *Atlantic Monthly*, May 1947, 101; Mary Desjardins, "Fan Magazine Trouble: The AMPP, Studio Publicity Directors, and the Hollywood Press, 1945–

1952," *Film History: An International Journal* 26 (2014): 29–56; Goodman, *Fifty-Year Decline*, 46.

14. Paul McDonald, *The Star System* (New York: Columbia University Press, 2000), 68; Tino Balio, *Hollywood in the Age of Television* (New York: Routledge, 1990), 3, 187; Mark Shiel, *Hollywood Cinema and the Real Los Angeles* (London: Reaktion Books, 2012), 211; Bureau of Economic and Business Research, "Theaters Coming Back," *Illinois Business Review* 22 (1965): 3.

15. Jennifer Frost, *Hedda Hopper's Hollywood: Celebrity Gossip and American Conservatism* (New York: New York University Press, 2011), 125.

16. Gregory D. Black, *The Catholic Crusade Against the Movies, 1940–1975* (Cambridge: Cambridge University Press, 1997), 4.

17. "New Film Council Plans War on Hollywood Immorality," *Pittsfield (MA) Berkshire Eagle*, October 15, 1949, 18.

18. Thomas Schatz, *The Genius of the System: Hollywood Filmmaking in the Studio Era* (New York: Pantheon Books, 1988), 435.

19. Barbas, *First Lady*, 308; Christopher Anderson, *Hollywood TV: The Studio System in the Fifties* (Austin: University of Texas, 1994), 41; Leo Rosten, "Hollywood Revisited," *Look*, January 10, 1956, 25–26.

20. Crowther, "Picture of Hollywood," SM17.

21. "Hollywood's Press," 64–65; Irving Shulman, *"Jackie"! The Exploitation of the First Lady* (New York: Trident, 1970), 71–72.

Chapter 7: Hot Hollywood Stories

1. Jacques DuBec, "Howard Hughes, Public Wolf No. 1," *Confidential*, April 1953, 8.

2. Peter H. Brown and Pat H. Broeske, *Howard Hughes: The Untold Story* (New York: Dutton, 1996), 274; "Literati," *Variety*, February 11, 1953, 61.

3. "Sinatra and Ava Split After Spectacular Row," *Akron Beacon Journal*, October 21, 1952, 4; Kitty Kelley, *His Way: The Unauthorized Biography of Frank Sinatra* (New York: Bantam Books, 1986), 205; "Sinatra Ava Boudoir Row Story Buzzes," *L.A. Times*, October 21, 1952, 29.

4. John B. Swift, "Why Sinatra Kicked Lana and Ava Out of the House," *Confidential*, July 1953, 24–25, 52.

5. Earl Wilson, "Earl Gets Undie-Cover Facts on Marilyn Monroe," *Winona (MN) Republican-Herald*, August 26, 1952, 4.

6. Barbara Leaming, *Marilyn Monroe* (New York: Crown Publishers, 1998), 64; Louella Parsons, "In Hollywood," *Cherry Hill (NJ) Courier-Post*, February 12, 1953, 16; Dorothy Kilgallen, "Voice of Broadway," *Shamokin (PA) News-Dispatch*, February 20, 1953, 4.

7. Harrison L. Roberts, "Why Joe DiMaggio Is Striking Out with Marilyn Monroe," *Confidential*, August 1953, 18–19.

8. Ibid.

9. Anthony Summers, *Goddess: The Secret Lives of Marilyn Monroe* (New York: Macmillan, 1985), 52; Leaming, *Marilyn Monroe*, 14–17, 25.

10. "Jimmie Fidler: In Hollywood," *Monroe (LA) News-Star*, July 1, 1953, 14.

11. Ibid.

12. Peter James, "The Sleeping Habits of the Stars," *Confidential*, May 1954, 36; Audrey Minor, "Operation Hollywood: Custom-Tailored Bosoms," *Confidential*, July 1954, 13–14.

13. "Behind the Scenes: Eartha Kitt," *Look*, October 6, 1953, 72–73; John L. Williams, *America's Mistress: The Life and Times of Eartha Kitt* (London: Quercus, 2012), 86; Aldo Cellucci, "Why Orson Bit the Lip of Eartha Kitt," *Confidential*, March 1954, 41–42, 60, 62.

14. Gigi Durand, "Lana Turner, Why They Love Her and Leave Her," *Confidential*, March 1954, 27–29.

15. Aldo Cellucci, "Why the Rossellini and Bergman Volcano Is Blowing Up," *Confidential*, January 1954, 20–21.

16. "Mario Lanza, Fired by MGM, Vows to Fight," *Akron Beacon Journal*, April 11, 1953, 12; Sam Munsey Jr., "Is Mario Lanza Looney," *Confidential*, January 1954, 36, 48.

17. Louis Reid, "The Confused Mr. Skelton," *Screenland*, June 1953, 42, 66; "Skelton 'Dood It'," *Decatur (IL) Daily Review*, January 25, 1954, 18; Alfred Garvey, "The Skeletons in Red Skelton's Closet," *Confidential*, July 1954, 20–21.

18. "The Inside Story," *Modern Screen*, May 1953, 4.

19. Slide, *Inside the Hollywood Fan Magazine*, 180; Hedda Hopper, "Why Dan Dailey's Marriage Failed," *Modern Screen*, September 1949, 39; Everett Aaker, *Encyclopedia of Early Television Crime Fighters: All Regular Cast Members in American Crime and Mystery Series, 1948–1959* (Jefferson, NC: McFarland, 2006), 168; Dan Dailey, "To All as to Myself," *Modern Screen*, November 1953, 49.

20. Dorothy Kilgallen, "Dorothy Kilgallen's Exclusive Movie Gossip," *Screenland*, November 1953, 23.

21. Alfred Garvey, "Why Dan Dailey Is Too Hot for the Gossip Columns," *Confidential*, March 1954, 18–19, 54–55.

22. André Previn, *No Minor Chords: My Days in Hollywood* (New York: Doubleday, 1991), 64.

23. William J. Mann, *Behind the Screen: How Gays and Lesbians Shaped Hollywood, 1910–1969* (New York: Viking, 2001), 315; Erskine Johnson, "Man-About Hollywood," *Mattoon (IL) Journal Gazette*, March 5, 1954, 3.

24. Ronald L. Davis, *Van Johnson: MGM's Golden Boy* (Jackson: University Press of Mississippi, 2001), 152; Steve Cronin, "I'm Not Afraid Any More," *Modern Screen*, August 1953, 42; Aljean Harmetz, "Van Johnson, Film Actor, is Dead at 92," *New York Times*, December 13, 2008.

25. Eyman, *Lion of Hollywood*, 5.

26. Ibid.

27. Bruce Cory, "The Untold Story of Van Johnson," *Confidential*, September 1954, 14–15.

28. Barbara Leaming, *If This Was Happiness: A Biography of Rita Hayworth* (New York: Viking, 1989), 260.

29. "Judge Says Rita 'Devoted Mother'," *Asheville (NC) Citizen-Times*, April 27, 1954, 1.

30. Dorothy Kilgallen, "Schine Has Lady Fan," *Dover (OH) Daily Reporter*, May 8, 1954, 9.

31. Jay Breen, "How Rita Hayworth's Children Were Neglected," *Confidential*, September 1954, 41–43, 46–48.

32. Dorothy Kilgallen, "Bette Davis in Trouble," *Daily Reporter*, July 8, 1954, 6.

33. TR, 212; Rushmore, "I Worked for Confidential."

Chapter 8: Hollywood Research Incorporated

1. Goodman, *Fifty-Year Decline*, 51.

2. TR, 256; Goodman, *Fifty-Year Decline*, 25.

3. TR, 1522; "Hollywood's Press," 63–64; Val Holley, *Mike Connolly and the Manly Art of Hollywood Gossip* (Jefferson, NC: McFarland, 2003), 30.

4. TR, 1521; Gehman, "Confidential File," 139.

5. Maurice Zolotow, "Here's How 'Confidential' Mag Digs Up All Its Erotic Pay Dirt," *Daily Plainsman*, November 21, 1955, 4.

6. "Confidential: Between You and Me," 24.

7. TR, 149.

8. TR, 160.

9. TR, 137.

10. "Onetime Actress Is Held on Vice Count," *Lubbock (TX) Morning Avalanche*, April 15, 1955, 28.

11. "Dancer, Charging Mate Hit Her, Wins Divorce Decree," *L.A. Times*, July 1, 1943, 3; "Fur Robbery Suspect Shot and Two Seized," *L.A. Times*, February 6, 1944, 18.

12. "Actress Hurt In Razor Fight," *Arizona Republic*, October 11, 1949, 19; "Billy Daniels Slashed, To Sue Movie Actress," *Chicago Defender*, December 16, 1950, 1; "Actress Slashes Night Club Singer," *Philadelphia Inquirer*, December 8, 1950,

15; "Fed Up with Set Up, Red-Head Slashes Singer in 3 a.m. Brawl," *Blytheville (AR) Courier News*, December 8, 1950, 22.

13. TR, 373, 372, 517.

14. TR, 375, 376.

15. Louella Parsons, "Keeping Up with Hollywood," *Cumberland News*, September 16, 1950, 12; Emily Belser, "Sultry Actress Embarks on Career Predicted By Gandhi," *Lubbock (TX) Evening Journal*, January 6, 1954, 11; "Clark Gable 'Affair' Outlined by Magazine Trial Witness," *Klamath Falls (OR) Herald and News*, August 13, 1957, 2.

16. "Name Former Wife of Star As 'Confidential' Source," *Mt. Vernon Register-News*, August 10, 1957, 1; "Actress Named Scandal Source," *San Mateo (CA) Times*, May 28, 1957, 20; "Miss De Scaffa Sets Libel Suits," *Bend Bulletin*, September 28, 1957, 5.

17. TR, 154, 383, 387, 238.

18. Gehman, "Confidential File,"140.

19. TR, 150.

20. Rushmore, "I Worked for Confidential," 32–38; Holley, *Mike Connolly*, 20.

21. Rushmore, "I Worked for Confidential," 32–38.

22. "Shock Gone, Just Numb, Says Marjorie Meade," *Ogden (UT) Standard-Examiner*, August 21, 1957, 4.

23. TR, 1557.

24. TR, 1557, 1219, 1225, 1233.

25. TR, 1518.

26. TR, 1104.

27. TR, 1096.

28. TR, 1101.

29. TR, 177, 1112.

30. Gehman, "Confidential File," 143; "Curious Craze," 51; TR, Vol. 12.

31. TR, 140; Harold Conrad, *Dear Muffo: 35 Years in the Fast Lane* (New York: Stein and Day, 1982), 98–99; "Fair Game," 23.

32. TR, 1130–1131.

33. TR, 1132–1134.

34. Harry McCarthy, "Mae West's Open-Door Policy," *Confidential*, November 1955, 18; Emily Wortis Leider, *Becoming Mae West* (New York: Farrar, Straus and Giroux, 1997) 8, 350.

35. "Film Stars May Get the Last Laugh," *Daily Defender*, February 26, 1957; Dorothy Kilgallen, "Gossip a la Gotham," *Greenville (PA) Record-Argus*, May 28, 1956, 4; TR, Vol. 10–12.

36. TR, 1292.

37. "Light Shed on McCarthy Accuser," *Cincinnati Enquirer*, July 22, 1957, 8; William Howard Moore, "Barney Ruditsky," American National Biography, Oxford University Press, www.anb.org/view/10.1093/anb/9780198606697.001.0001 /anb-9780198606697-e-2000888.

38. James Ellroy, *L.A. Confidential* (New York: Mysterious, 1990); "Death: Obituary of Fred Otash," *Guardian*, October 20, 1992, 22; "Mr. O: Legend With Nothing More To Prove," *L.A. Times*, January 9, 1983, 69.

39. David Ehrenstein, *Open Secret: Gay Hollywood, 1928–1998* (New York: William Morrow, 1998), 103; Fred Otash, *Investigation Hollywood* (Chicago: H. Regnery, 1976), 7, 13; "Shooting Ruffles Calm of Square," *Arizona Republic*, December 29, 1946, 1; "Fred Otash," *L.A. Times*, October 17, 1971, 611; Fred Otash, interview by Mike Wallace, *The Mike Wallace Interview*, August 25, 1957.

40. Otash, *Investigation Hollywood*, 1–2.

41. Otash, *Investigation Hollywood*, 10; *Mike Wallace Interview;* "Challenge Parker Right to Control Off-Duty Police Jobs," *Lebanon (NH) Valley News*, October 6, 1954, 25.

42. Ehrenstein, *Open Secret*, 103; "Investigator Hired," *Lubbock (TX) Morning Avalanche*, May 17, 1955, 8; TR, 1147.

43. "A Current Affair—Hollywood Confidential," YouTube video, 16:43, posted by "Sherlock G.," July 25, 2013, www.youtube.com/watch?v=OY4?7iDM384.

44. Ibid.

Chapter 9: Gossip

1. "Smashing the Broadway Blackmailers," *Palm Beach Post*, June 15, 1924, 41; Will Straw, "Traffic in Scandal: The Story of Broadway Brevities," *University of Toronto Quarterly* 73 (Fall 2004): 947–971.

2. "Show Girl Paid $150 for Silence," *New York Times*, January 22, 1925, 21; "Clow Called Her 'Ungrateful Rat,' Mrs. Bobe Swears," *Brooklyn Daily Eagle*, January 26, 1925, 2.

3. "Charge Blackmail in Broadway Paper," *New York Times*, April 10, 1924, 8; Straw, "Traffic in Scandal," 952–4; "Publisher of Broadway Brevities," *St. Louis Post-Dispatch*, February 1, 1925, 1.

4. Will Straw, "United States: Broadway Brevities (1930–1935)," Will Straw website, https://willstraw.com/united-states-broadway-brevities-1930–1935/; "Traffic In Scandal," 958.

5. David Stenn, *Clara Bow: Runnin' Wild* (New York: Cooper Square, 2000), 228.

6. "Blackmailers Find Mecca in Hollywood," *Des Moines (IA) Register*, June 2, 1931, 8.

7. Tere Tereba, *Mickey Cohen: The Life and Crimes of L.A.'s Notorious Mobster* (Toronto: ECW, 2013), 103; Tom Kuntz and Phil Kuntz, *The Sinatra Files: The Secret FBI Dossier* (New York: Three Rivers, 2000), 105; Tab Hunter and Eddie Muller, *Tab Hunter Confidential: The Making of a Movie Star* (Chapel Hill, NC: Algonquin Books, 2006), 117; also see FBI records, "The Vault," Frank Sinatra File.

8. Gerald Clarke, *Get Happy: The Life of Judy Garland* (New York: Random House, 2005), 257; "Editor Promises to Rid Hollywood of Addicts," *Salt Lake Tribune*, December 27, 1948, 11.

9. "Former Nixon Aide Will Testify in Tarantino Probe," *Fresno (CA) Bee*, February 5, 1953, 50; "Tarantino Mag Sold For Dollar," *San Mateo (CA) Times*, December 11, 1953, 6.

Chapter 10: The Legal Department

1. Gelman and Katcher, "Man Behind *Confidential*," Part II.

2. TR 1781, 1680.

3. TR, 1573; James B. Stewart, "The Twelfth Annual Albert A. Destefano Lecture," *Fordham Journal of Corporate and Financial Law* 18 (2012):1–18; Bernstein, *Mr. Confidential*, 44.

4. TR, 831; "News Stories Read Into Libel Trial," *Oakland Tribune*, August 20, 1957, 1.

5. TR, 832.

6. "Curious Craze," 50; J. Howard Rutledge, "Sin and Sex," *Wall Street Journal*, July 5, 1955, 1.

7. William Blake Odgers and Melville Madison Bigelow, *A Digest of the Law of Libel and Slander* (Boston: Little, Brown, 1881), 32.

8. Stanley Walker, *City Editor* (Baltimore: Johns Hopkins University Press, 1999), 186; Nancy Barr Mavity, *The Modern Newspaper* (New York: H. Holt, 1930), 161.

9. Leonore Bistry, "They Pay to Wear the Pants," *Confidential*, July 1953, 50; "On Broadway," *Pittsburgh Post-Gazette*, April 28, 1953, 27; "The Press: Ssh!," *Time*, April 2, 1956, 88.

10. "Publishers' Corner," *Saturday Review of Literature*, July 15, 1950, 26.

11. TR, 281; "Scandal Magazines and How They Work," *Indianapolis Star*, November 2, 1955, 21.

12. "Fair Game," 23.

13. "Success in the Sewer," *Time*, July 11, 1955, 90; Conrad, *Dear Muffo*, 99.

14. Scott, *Shocking True Story*, 40.

15. Brad Shortell, "Does Desi Really Love Lucy?" *Confidential*, January 1955, 25.

16. Wolfe, "Public Lives," 87.

17. "Rave Mag," *Variety*, July 20, 1955, 4; Rutledge, "Sin and Sex," 1.

18. TR, 1000.

19. TR, 836.

20. TR, 1693.

21. TR, 292, 1593; "The Town Crier," *Detroit Free Press*, May 5, 1955, 44.

22. TR, 838.

23. Conrad, *Dear Muffo*, 100; TR, 838.

24. "Giesler Heads Committee to Protect Stars," *San Bernardino County Sun*, April 19, 1957, 8.

Chapter 11: 1955

1. Museum of Broadcasting, *Lucille Ball, First Lady of Comedy* (New York: Museum of Broadcasting, 1984), 1914.

2. Grady Johnson, "What's the Secret of 'I Love Lucy'?" *Coronet*, July 1953, 42; Arthur L. Charles, "Now We Have Everything," *Modern Screen*, April 1953, 84.

3. Constance White, "Hollywood's Bachelor Husbands," *Screenland*, August 1954, 60; Lucille Ball, "Lucille Ball Finds Grace Key to Lasting Marriage," *Kokomo (IN) Tribune*, February 28, 1955, 2.

4. Shortell, "Does Desi Really Love Lucy?" 22, 23–24, 46.

5. Scott, *Shocking True Story*, 55.

6. Kathleen Brady, *Lucille: The Life of Lucille Ball* (New York: Hyperion, 1994), 227.

7. Ibid.

8. Ibid.

9. Lee Server, *Ava Gardner: Love Is Nothing* (London: Bloomsbury, 2010), 304.

10. Streete, "What Makes Ava Run?," 12, 15.

11. Server, *Ava Gardner*, 304.

12. Ibid.

13. Gary Fishgall, *Gonna Do Great Things: The Life of Sammy Davis, Jr.* (New York: Scribner, 2003), 87.

14. Charles A. Wright, "The Secret's Out About Burt Lancaster," *Confidential*, May 1955, 11, 48.

15. Kate Buford, *Burt Lancaster: An American Life* (New York: Knopf, 2000), 156; "'Scandal Sheet' Lifts the Lid on Lurid Tabloids," *Akron (OH) Beacon Journal*, January 8, 1985, 72.

16. Alfred Garvey, "The Wife Clark Gable Forgot," *Confidential*, July 1955, 14.

17. "The Great Gable: King of them All," *St. Louis Post-Dispatch*, December 2, 1956, 263.

18. "Fidler . . . In Hollywood," *Nevada State Journal*, February 9, 1955, 4; "Dorothy Kilgallen: Gal About Gotham," *Cincinnati Enquirer*, February 22, 1955, 15.

19. D. Loring Taylor, "How Long Can Dick Powell Take It?" *Confidential*, July 1955, 34–35, 58–59.

20. Kenneth G. McLain, "The Untold Story of Marlene Dietrich," *Confidential*, July 1955, 22–25, 56.

21. "Erskine Johnson," *Indiana Gazette*, June 15, 1955, 10.

22. J. E. Leclair, "The Real Reason for Marilyn Monroe's Divorce," *Confidential*, September 1955, 22–23.

23. J. Randy Taraborrelli, *The Secret Life of Marilyn Monroe* (New York: Grand Central, 2009), 254.

24. Ted Schwarz, *Marilyn Revealed: The Ambitious Life of an American Icon* (Lanham, MD: Taylor Trade Publishing, 2009), 461–462.

25. Taraborelli, *Secret Life*, 261; Schwarz, *Marilyn Revealed*, 464–466; "Sinatra Story," *L.A. Times*, February 28, 1957, 18; "DiMaggio Backs Up Sinatra," *Van Nuys (CA) Valley News*, March 14, 1957, 63.

26. "Victim Tells Jury of Raid at Wrong Place," *Muncie (IN) Evening Press*, March 20, 1957, 22.

27. "L.A. Then and Now," *L.A. Times*, June 5, 2011, 22; James Kaplan, *Sinatra: The Chairman* (New York: Doubleday, 2015), 26; "Sinatra Story," 18.

28. Bruce Weber, "Hal Schaefer, Jazz Pianist and Marilyn Monroe Friend, Dies at 87," *New York Times*, December 12, 2012, 36.

29. TR, 173.

30. Leclair, "Real Reason," 22–23, 55–56, 58.

Chapter 12: Hollywood

1. "Pope Asks Movie Men to Ban Corrupt Films," *St. Petersburg (FL) Evening Independent*, June 21, 1955, 10; Drew Casper, *Postwar Hollywood, 1946–1962* (Malden, MA: Blackwell, 2007), 43; "Senate Juvenile Delinquency Hearing Preparing TV Rebuke," *Paris (TX) News*, February 10, 1955, 6.

2. "Curious Craze," 50; Goodman, *Fifty-Year Decline*, 50; Kashner and MacNair, *Bad and the Beautiful*, 149.

3. Server, *Ava Gardner*, 305, 306.

4. Gehman, "Confidential File," 67.

5. "Scandal in Hollywood," *Photoplay*, July 1955, 29. See Jerome Michael Kelly, *The Credibility of Confidential Magazine and the Newspaper Compared* (unpublished masters' thesis, Stanford University, 1957).

6. Bob Thomas, "Hollywood Has Been Fair Game for all Scandalmongers Since 1920 Scandals," *Kingsport (TN) News*, September 30, 1957, 8.

7. Jack Olsen, "Titans of Trash: Doris Duke, Lizabeth Scott Sue Magazines," *Pittsburgh Press,* November 5, 1955, 9; Shulman, *"Jackie"!,* 75.

8. "The Crusade Against Titans of Trash," *Provo (UT) Sunday Herald,* December 4, 1955, 108; "Whatever It Is That Bogart Has," *Louisville (KY) Courier-Journal,* November 6, 1955, 92; "Success in the Sewer," 90.

9. "Curious Craze," 50.

10. Gus Russo, *Supermob: How Sidney Korshak and His Criminal Associates Became America's Hidden Power Brokers* (New York: Bloomsbury, 2006), 126.

11. Mamie Van Doren and Art Aveilhe, *Playing the Field: My Story* (New York: Putnam's, 1987), 112.

12. Ibid.

13. "Crusade Against Titans," 108.

14. "Hollywood Pulls Cloak Dagger Trick on Scandal Magazine," *L.A. Mirror,* February 21, 1957, 12; TR, 1652.

15. "Perjury Action Possible," *L.A. Times,* March 1, 1957, 1; "Scandal Mag Probers to View Nude Photos of Anita Ekberg," *Bridgeport (CT) Post,* March 1, 1957, 47; "Cary Grant Defends Babs, Movie Crowds Applaud Him," *Raleigh (NC) Register,* September 1, 1955, 9; "Detective Tells of Secret Pictures of Anita Ekberg," *L.A. Times,* March 1, 1957, 2.

16. TR, 299, 300.

17. "Dore Schary," *Theater Arts,* May 1952, 43; "Hollywood Hits Back," *Lansing (MI) State Journal,* August 30, 1956, 24; "Rambling Reporter," *Hollywood Reporter,* July 10, 1955, 2; TR, 1783.

18. Gabler, "*Confidential's* Reign of Terror," 190; Goodman, *Fifty-Year Decline,* 51; "Confidential: Between You and Me," 26.

19. "Dore Schary Lashes Confidential Mag," *Variety,* October 24, 1955, 4.

20. "Movie Head is Not for 'Dirty Gossip,'" *Neosho (MO) Daily News,* October 21, 1955, 3; "Hits 'Expose' Magazine," *Indianapolis Star,* October 23, 1955, 2.

21. Goodman, *Fifty-Year Decline,* 51.

22. "On Her Way Up," *Look,* May 31, 1955, 62–64; "Kim Novak Moves Uncertainly in New World of Movie Fame," *Life,* March 5, 1956, 149–156; "She Started at the Top and Is Still Soaring," *Long Beach (CA) Independent Press-Telegram,* November 28, 1954, 163.

23. Robin Sharry, "What They 'Forgot' to Say About Kim Novak," *Confidential,* January 1956, 31–33, 60–61.

24. Richard G. Hubler, "How to Create a Movie Star," *Saturday Evening Post,* September 27, 1952, 26.

25. Paul Benedict, "Rock Hudson: Scared of Marriage?" *Screenland,* March 1955, 22, 26; "The Simple Life of a Busy Bachelor," *Life,* October 3, 1955, 129.

26. See generally Robert Hofler, *The Man Who Invented Rock Hudson: The Pretty Boys and Dirty Deals of Henry Willson* (New York: Carroll & Graf, 2005); Scott Feinberg, "SXSW: Tab Hunter Opens Up About Life as a Closeted Gay Star During Hollywood's Golden Age," *Hollywood Reporter.com*, March 13, 2015.

27. Rock Hudson and Sara Davidson, *Rock Hudson: His Story* (New York: Morrow, 1986), 49; Hofler, *Man Who Invented Rock Hudson,* 241.

28. Hudson and Davidson, *Rock Hudson,* 49; Goodman, *Fifty-Year Decline,* 52.

29. "Blackmail Is Ending for Hollywood Stars," *St. Louis Post-Dispatch*, August 5, 1956, 128.

30. James Bawden and Ron Miller, *Conversations with Classic Film Stars: Interviews from Hollywood's Golden Era* (Lexington: University Press of Kentucky, 2016), 46; Rory Calhoun, "My Dark Years," *American Weekly*, August 28, 1955, 138.

31. Howard Rushmore, "Movie Star Rory Calhoun: But for the Grace of God, Still a Convict!" *Confidential*, May 1955, 21–25, 51–52.

32. Ibid.

33. "An Editorial," *Confidential*, September 1955, 35.

34. Kashner and MacNair, *Bad and the Beautiful*, 150; Hudson and Davidson, *Rock Hudson*, 61–62.

35. Lillian Faderman and Stuart Timmons, *Gay L.A.: A History of Sexual Outlaws, Power Politics, and Lipstick Lesbians* (New York: Basic Books, 2006), 68.

36. Michael Schulman, "Tab Hunter's Secrets," *New Yorker*, October 16, 2015; Kirtley Baskette, "A Pocketful of Dreams," *Modern Screen*, July 16, 1953, 60; Tab Hunter, "There's Nothing Like a Girl," *Screenland*, August 1954, 35.

37. Tim Parks, "The Many Lives of Tab Hunter," *The Gay and Lesbian Times*, December 5, 2005, 52.

38. Bruce Cory, "The Lowdown on that 'Disorderly Conduct' Charge Against Tab Hunter," *Confidential*, September 1955, 18–19, 60.

39. Ehrenstein, *Open Secret*, 93–94; Hunter and Muller, *Tab Hunter Confidential*, 122.

40. Hunter and Muller, *Tab Hunter Confidential*, 3.

41. "Gorgeous Gina Scheduled to Make U.S. Film in Europe," *Detroit Free Press*, October 3, 1954, 15.

42. "Filmtown Backs Up Rory after Unfavorable Magazine Article," *Lubbock (TX) Avalanche-Journal*, August 7, 1955, 72; "Drama: Todd Sets Film Deals Here and in England," *L.A. Times*, March 31, 1955, 10; Rory Calhoun, "My Dark Years," 138; Louella Parsons, "The Letter Box," *Modern Screen*, November 1955, 16.

43. Tex Maddox, "Kim Novak—Stabbed by Scandal," *Photoplay*, February 1956, 54.

44. "Clark Gable's Happy to Be 'Rediscovered,'" *L.A. Times*, May 20, 1955, 70.

45. Sheila Graham, "From Hollywood Current Movie Chatter," *St. Louis Post-Dispatch*, August 28, 1955, 84; "Names in the News," *Akron (OH) Beacon Journal*, September 4, 1955, 7; Josephine Dillon, "Clark Gable's First Wife Talks Back," *Confidential*, March 1956, 35, 50.

46. "Scandal in Hollywood," *Photoplay*, July 1955, 29.

47. "Brando, Paramount Discuss Film Deal," *L.A. Times*, May 7, 1955, 14; "Rambling Reporter," *Hollywood Reporter*, May 23, 1955, 2; "Just For Variety," *Variety*, October 19, 1955, 2.

48. "Crusade Against Titans," 108.

Chapter 13: The Curious Craze

1. Advertisement for *Confidential*, *Indianapolis Star*, November 16, 1955, 30.

2. Rutledge, "Sin and Sex," 1; "Walter Winchell on Broadway," *Terre Haute (IN) Tribune*, June 28, 1955, 14; TR, 1043.

3. Rutledge, "Sin and Sex," 1; David Abrahamson and Carol Polsgrove, "The Right Niche: Consumer Magazines and Advertisers," in *A History of the Book in America*, ed. D. P. Nord et al. (Chapel Hill: University of North Carolina Press, 2015), 107; "Sin, Sex and Sales," 88.

4. See transcript, *Confidential, Inc. v. Summerfield* (Civil No. 3982—55, October 7, 1955); Rutledge, "Sin and Sex," 1; Gehman, "Confidential File," 67.

5. Gehman, "Confidential File," 143; Jack Olsen, "Titans of Trash: Do Magazines Print Uncensored Truth?" *Pittsburgh Press*, October 31, 1955, 21; "Confidential Story, How Dirty"; Gelman and Katcher, "Man Behind *Confidential*," Part IV.

6. "Sin, Sex and Sales," 88; Rutledge, "Sin and Sex," 1.

7. "Success in the Sewer," 90.

8. "The Broadway Lights," *Chicago Daily Herald*, July 10, 1955, 25.

9. Rutledge, "Sin and Sex," 1; "Curious Craze," 50.

10. Rutledge, "Sin and Sex," 1; Jack Olsen, "Titans of Trash: Facts Some Magazines Dare Not Tell You," *Pittsburgh Press*, November 4, 1955, 21.

11. Olsen, "Titans of Trash: Do Magazines Print Uncensored Truth," 21.

12. Olsen, "Titans of Trash: Facts Some Magazines Dare Not Tell You," 21.

13. Gehman, "Confidential File," 141.

14. "Curious Craze," 52; "Trenchant," *La Grande (OR) Observer*, July 18, 1955, 7.

15. "Fair Game," 22.

16. Rutledge, "Sin and Sex," 1.

17. Olsen, "Titans of Trash: Do Magazines Print Uncensored Truth," 21; Rushmore, "I Worked for Confidential"; "The Press: Success in the Sewer," 90.

18. Rushmore, "I Worked for Confidential."

19. "Fair Game," 21.

20. "Fair Game," 22.

21. "Putting the Blame Where It Belongs," *Catholic Advance*, September 16, 1955, 13; "Editorials: The Problem Is Social and Legal," *Progress-Index*, October 24, 1955, 6.

22. Sydney J. Harris, "Strictly Personal: Smut Sheets Responding to Demand," *Des Moines (IA) Register*, September 30, 1955, 20; John P. Sisk, "Exposé Magazines," *Commonweal*, June 1, 1955, 223–225.

23. "Curious Craze," 50; Edith Roosevelt, "Depicted By Psychiatrists as Cultural Bankrupts," *Muncie (IN) Star Press*, January 5, 1958, 3.

24. Peterson, *Magazines in the Twentieth Century*, 41; Barbas, *Laws of Image*, 160.

25. Clara Jordan, "So That's It!" *Detroit Free Press*, August 12, 1955, 8.

26. "Curious Craze," 50–51.

27. Olsen, "Titans of Trash: Do Magazines Print Uncensored Truth," 21.

28. D'Emilio and Freedman, *Intimate Matters*, 261.

29. Terrence J. Murphy, *Censorship: Government and Obscenity* (Baltimore: Helicon, 1963), 86.

30. Murray Schumach, "Censorship Fight Waged on a Nation-Wide Front," *New York Times*, November 1, 1953, E7.

31. James Burkhart Gilbert, *A Cycle of Outrage: America's Reaction to the Juvenile Delinquent in the 1950s* (New York: Oxford University Press, 1986), 66; James P. Wesberry, "Georgia Scrubs Its Newsstands," *Christian Century*, December 23, 1953, 1498.

32. Henry E. Schultz, "Censorship or Self Regulation?" *Journal of Educational Sociology* 215 (1949): 217; Lewis Smith, "The Truth Beaten Down," *College Composition and Communication* 139 (December 1953): 138–144; "Indiana Governor Backs Smut Drive," *New York Times*, August 30, 1959, 45; Wesberry, "Georgia Scrubs Its Newsstands," 1498–1499.

33. William J. Hempel and Patrick M. Wall, "Extralegal Censorship of Literature," *New York University Law Review* 33 (1958): 992; Robert W. Haney, *Comstockery in America: Patterns of Censorship and Control* (Boston: Beacon, 1960), 87; William B. Lockhart and Robert C. McClure, "Literature, the Law of Obscenity, and the Constitution," *Minnesota Law Review* 38 (1954): 310n93.

34. "Women Are Expose Fans," *America*, February 11, 1956, 520.

35. "Those 'Tell-All' Magazines," *Tyrone (PA) Daily Herald*, June 28, 1955, 4.

36. "What Other Papers Say," *Sikeston (MO) Daily Standard*, November 4, 1955, 2; "Federal Court Bears Down on Confidential," *Hartford Courant*, March 9, 1957, 8; "Says Obscene Literature is Flooding Newsstands," *Greenville (SC) News*, July 5, 1957, 14.

37. "Comic Books?—Kid Stuff," *Gastonia (NC) Gazette*, June 9, 1955, 2; Ruth Adamites, "Trash and Filth," *Detroit Free Press*, July 30, 1955, 6; "Slugging the Exposé Magazines," *Newsweek*, August 1, 1955, 75.

Chapter 14: Public Service

1. "Fair Game," 21.
2. Henry X. Sperry, "How the Airlines Take Your Life in Their Hands," *Confidential*, January 1955, 20.
3. Ernest Stevens, "The Criminal Record of Cutter Laboratories," *Confidential*, September 1955, 16.
4. Armand Hartley, "Beware the Davy Crockett Skin Game," *Confidential*, September 1955, 40.
5. Robin Sharry, "Blood for Booze," *Confidential*, January 1955, 34.
6. Charles A. Wright, "Alimony Jail Is Back," *Confidential*, July 1955, 44.
7. Edward Gregory, "Parole—Freedom on a String," *Confidential*, January 1955, 44.
8. Morton Sandler, "Aspirin—No. 1 Poisoner of Children," *Confidential*, March 1955, 16.
9. John Griffith, "Danger—Boric Acid Is a Poison!" *Confidential*, July 1955, 20.
10. John Griffith, "The Big Lie About Filter Cigarettes," *Confidential*, March 1955, 32.
11. Horton Streete, "The Astor Testimony the Judge Suppressed," *Confidential*, September 1955, 10, 62.
12. Peggy Earle, *Legacy: Walter Chrysler Jr. and the Untold Story of Norfolk's Chrysler Museum of Art* (Charlottesville: University of Virginia Press, 2008), 34, 40. Chrysler's sexual orientation was widely known in society circles.
13. Brad Shortell, "The Strange Case of Walter Chrysler Jr," *Confidential*, July 1955, 31.
14. "How the Navy Ousted Its No. 1 Gay Gob," *Confidential*, January 1956, 10–13, 64.
15. "What Time Won't Tell," *Confidential*, January 1955, 30.
16. "Leaves Hotel Here to Keep Appointment," *Chicago Tribune*, July 9, 1955, 1; "Rushmore Missing on Red Hunt," *Chicago American*, July 9, 1955, 3.
17. "Editor on Red Hunt Reported Missing Here," *Chicago Tribune*, July 9, 1955, 6.
18. "Lost Editor in Montana," *Chicago American*, July 10, 1955, 13.
19. Kashner and MacNair, *Bad and the Beautiful*, 35.
20. "Editor Tells Why He Had to Vanish," *Chicago American*, July 11, 1955, 9.
21. "Magazine Editor Found in Montana," *Albuquerque Journal*, July 10, 1955, 1.
22. "Missing Magazine Editor Found in Hotel at Butte," *Great Falls Tribune*, July 10, 1955, 1.
23. Untitled document, Howard Rushmore FBI Records, July 10, 1955; Clyde Tolson to L.B. Nichols, 12 July 1955; A. H. Belmont to L. V. Boardman, July 11, 1955.

24. "Rushmore Denies Publicity Stunt," *Mattoon (IL) Journal Gazette*, July 10, 1955, 1.

25. Carl Hirsch, "The Lost Weekend of Howard Rushmore," *The Worker*, July 24, 1955, Howard Rushmore FBI Records.

26. Ibid.

27. TR, 1595.

28. TR, 1400.

29. Leonard Lyons, "The Lyons Den," *Pittsburgh Press*, October 24, 1955, 14.

30. Theo Wilson, "Failed in His Biggest Role: Turncoat of Many Colors," *New York Daily News*, January 5, 1958, I6.

Chapter 15: Libel

1. "Hollywood Today," *Ironwood (MI) Daily Globe*, December 8, 1955, 7; "Brando Ignores Scandal Mags," *Tucson (AZ) Daily Citizen*, July 20, 1957, 10; J. Anthony Luk, "Harvard Confidential: The Fourth Estate," *Harvard Crimson*, March 11, 1954.

2. Peter Evans and Ava Gardner, *Ava Gardner: The Secret Conversations* (New York: Simon & Schuster, 2013), 239; Sammy Davis, Jane Boyar, and Burt Boyar, *Sammy: An Autobiography* (New York: Farrar, Straus and Giroux, 2000), 166.

3. Irwin O. Spiegel, "Defamation by Implication—In the Confidential Manner," *Southern California Law Review* 29 (1956): 316–318.

4. Herb Lyon, "Tower Ticker," *Chicago Daily Tribune*, May 4, 1955, D2.

5. "Robert Mitchum . . . The Nude Who Came to Dinner!" *Confidential*, July 1955, 18–19.

6. Cameron Shipp, "Robert Mitchum: Movie Menace," *Colliers'*, February 1948, 59.

7. "Pocketbook Morality," *Indianapolis Star*, September 5, 1948, 16; Hedda Hopper, "The Ten Great Myths of Hollywood," *Modern Screen*, January 1949, 28.

8. "Career Obituary," *Huron (SD) Daily Plainsman*, September 12, 1948, 14.

9. Lee Server, *Robert Mitchum: "Baby, I Don't Care"* (New York: St. Martin's, 2001), 257; Sam O'Steen and Bobbie O'Steen, *Cut to the Chase: Forty-Five Years of Editing America's Favorite Movies* (Studio City, CA: Michael Wiese Productions, 2001), 11; Louis Pollock, "This Is a Monster," *Modern Screen*, December 1953, 40.

10. James Bacon, *Made in Hollywood* (Chicago: Contemporary Books, 1977), 79–80.

11. "Jerry Giesler, Lawyer Is Dead," *New York Times*, January 2, 1962, 29; on Giesler's life, see generally Jerry Giesler and Pete Martin, *Hollywood Lawyer: The Jerry Giesler Story* (New York: Permabooks, 1962); "Jerry Giesler: The Smartest Criminal Lawyer On West Coast," *Life*, May 1, 1944, 53.

12. "Hollywood: The Ambivalence Chaser," *Time*, January 12, 1962, 118; Tony Thomas, Rudy Behlmer, and Clifford McCarty, *The Films of Errol Flynn* (New York: Citadel Press, 1969), 42.

13. "The Jerry Giesler Story," *Saturday Evening Post*, November 21, 1959, 40; "Hollywood: The Ambivalence Chaser," 118.

14. "Mitchum Files Suit for Libel," *Longview (WA) Daily News*, May 10, 1955, 5.

15. "Mitchum Denies Nude Hamburger Act, Sues. Ask Million; Didn't Douse with Catsup," *L.A. Herald Express*, May 9, 1955,1; David Albright, "Robert Mitchum: The Man Who Dared to Sue," *Photoplay*, January 1956, 36; Server, *Robert Mitchum*, 288.

16. Albright, "Robert Mitchum," 36.

17. "'Nude Who Came to Dinner' Label Brings Libel Action," *Sioux Falls (SD) Argus-Leader*, May 10, 1955, 73.

18. "Phony Awards Becoming a Racket," *Rochester (NY) Democrat and Chronicle*, May 16, 1955, 28; Untitled, *Los Angeles Mirror-News*, May 11, 1956; "Confidential: Between You and Me," 25;"Mitchum Denies Magazine Story, Sues for Million," *Indianapolis Star*, May 10, 1955, 22.

19. Giesler to Orlando H. Rhodes, Mitchum v. Confidential, June 27, 1955; "Davis Jr. Sues Hush Hush Mag for Defaming Him," *Variety*, July 22, 1955, 10.

20. "Film Biz Giving Only Lip Service in Fight Against Smear Mags," *Variety*, April 19, 1957, 3.

21. "Mitchum," *New York Times*, June 12, 1955, X5; "This Man Mitchum," *American Weekly*, October 30, 1955, 8.

22. "Robert Mitchum: The Man Who Dared To Sue," *Photoplay*, January 1956, 76.

23. *Flynn v. Confidential, Inc.*, 286 A.D. 1068 (N.Y. App. Div. 1955).

24. Greg Martin, "Errol Flynn's Two-Way Mirror," *Confidential*, March 1955, 34, 51–52.

25. Errol Flynn, *My Wicked, Wicked Ways* (New York: Cooper Square, 2003), 434; Thomas McNulty, *Errol Flynn: The Life and Career* (Jefferson, NC: McFarland, 2004), 262.

26. "Walter Winchell: On Broadway," *Eureka (CA) Times Standard*, July 1, 1955, 4; Olsen, "Titans of Trash: Doris Duke, Lizabeth Scott Sue Magazines," 9.

27. "Home Life of Actor Is Subject of Story," *Lubbock (TX) Morning Avalanche*, June 29, 1955, 2; "Rave Mag in Poverty Plea," *Variety*, July 20, 1955, 4; "Actor Mason Wins Libel Payment," *Long Beach (CA) Independent*, July 20, 1955, 19.

28. Donald Spoto, *High Society: The Life of Grace Kelly* (New York: Harmony Books, 2009), 206–207; "Sewer Trouble," *Time*, August 1, 1955, 48.

29. "Heiress Sues for 3 Million Dollars," *Fairbanks (AK) Daily News-Miner*, July 18, 1955, 2.

30. "Doris Duke, Tobacco Heiress, at 80," *Asbury Park (NJ) Press*, October 29, 1993, 10.

31. Grant Peters, "Doris Duke and Her African Prince," *Confidential*, May 1955, 12, 14–15, 54.

32. "Hollywood Film Shop," *Dunkirk (NY) Evening Observer*, October 1, 1940, 14; Karin Patterson, "Prince Modupe: An African in Early Hollywood," *Black Music Research Journal* 31 (2011): 29–44; "King Racket Is Shot, So Why Plug Princes?" *Louisville Courier-Journal*, March 25, 1954, 7; See Doris Duke papers, Box 4, Folder 10, Duke University, Durham, NC.

33. Stephanie Mansfield, *The Richest Girl in the World: The Extravagant Life and Fast Times of Doris Duke* (New York: G.P. Putnam's Sons, 1992), 221.

34. "Heiress Doris Duke Files $3,000,000 Suit Against Confidential Magazine," *L.A. Times*, July 19, 1955, 1; "Doris Duke Files $3 Million Suit Against Magazine," *Dover (OH) Daily Reporter*, July 19, 1955, 10; "Mitchum Denies Magazine Story," 22.

35. Inez Robb, "Blow Struck for Decency," *Detroit Free Press*, July 23, 1955, 7; "Hurrah for Doris!" *Syracuse (NY) Post-Standard*, July 22, 1955, 17.

36. "Confidential Sues for $9,000,000," *Akron (OH) Beacon Journal*, August 2, 1955, 4; "Rambling Reporter," *Hollywood Reporter*, August 2, 1955; "Cat-o'-Nine-Tale," *Time*, August 8, 1955, 68.

Chapter 16: Freedom of the Press

1. Erskine Johnson, "In Hollywood," *Portsmouth (NH) Herald*, February 17, 1954, 11.

2. Matt Williams, "Why Was Lizabeth Scott's Name in the Call Girls' Call Book?" *Confidential*, September 1955, 32.

3. Ibid., 50.

4. "Hollywood Film Shop," *Shamokin (PA) News-Dispatch*, July 9, 1953, 14; Hedda Hopper, "Watch Lizabeth Scott!," *Modern Screen*, May 1946, 126.

5. "Marriage on Her Mind," *Modern Screen*, September 1949, 32; Mel Heimer, "My New York: House in Hollywood," *White Plains (NY) Journal News*, July 15, 1953, 4; "Lizabeth Scott Vetoes French Mannish Styles," *Winona (MN) Republican-Herald*, January 19, 1954, 4.

6. "In Hollywood," *Dixon (IL) Evening Telegraph*, February 23, 1953, 4; "Hollywood Today," *Franklin (PA) News-Herald*, June 18, 1955, 14.

7. Complaint for Libel, Lizabeth Scott v. Confidential, Superior Court of Los Angeles County, July 25, 1955; "Giesler Declares War on Slander Magazines," *L.A. Times*, July 17, 1955, 15; "Actress Sues Magazine for $2,500,000," *Shreveport (LA) Times*, July 26, 1955, 11.

8. See Robert D. McFadden, "Lizabeth Scott, Film Noir Siren, Dies at 92," *New York Times*, February 7, 2015, D7.

9. On the ACLU, see generally Samuel Walker, *In Defense of American Liberties: A History of the ACLU* (New York: Oxford University Press, 1990).

10. "Censorship Called Threat," *New York Times*, March 15, 1953, 54.

11. Thomas I. Emerson, "The Doctrine of Prior Restraint," *Law and Contemporary Problems* 20 (1955): 648, 649; *Near v. Minnesota*, 283 U.S. 697 (1931).

12. Walker, *In Defense of American Liberties*, 234.

13. Patrick Murphy Malin (executive director, ACLU) to Lee B. Wood (editor, *N.Y. World Telegram and Sun*), 1 September 1955, ACLU Papers, Princeton University, Princeton, NJ.

14. "Actress Sues Beleaguered Magazine for $2,500,000," *Indianapolis Star*, July 26, 1955, 5; "Giesler May Be Called in Scandal Hearings," *L.A. Times*, February 2, 1957, 8; "Hollywood," *Detroit Free Press*, October 6, 1957, 80.

15. "Giesler Declares War," 15.

16. Victor Lasky to Patrick Murphy Malin, 5 August 1955.

17. Patrick Murphy Malin to Alan Reitman, 9 August 1955.

18. "Codefendants' Part in Libel Suits Denied," *L.A. Times*, February 1, 1956, 7.

19. "Actress' Libel Suit Quashed," *San Bernardino County (CA) Sun*, March 10, 1956, 5; "Jerry Giesler Heads Fight Against Scandal Magazines," *Van Nuys (CA) Valley News*, April 23, 1957, 7.

20. Olsen, "Titans of Trash: Doris Duke, Lizabeth Scott Sue Magazines," 9.

21. Ibid.

Chapter 17: The Post Office

1. Gehman, "Confidential File," 146.

2. James C. N. Paul and Murray L. Schwartz, *Federal Censorship: Obscenity in the Mail* (Westport, CT: Greenwood, 1977), 17–18; Fred S. Siebert, *The Rights and Privileges of the Press* (New York: D. Appleton-Century, 1970), 247.

3. Edward de Grazia, "Obscenity and the Mail," *Law and Contemporary Problems* 20 (1955): 608–609; Harvey Lyle Zuckerman, "Obscenity in the Mails," *California Law Review* 33 (1960): 177; James C. N. Paul and Murray L. Schwartz, "Obscenity in the Mails: A Comment on Some Problems of Federal Censorship," *University of Pennsylvania Law Review* 106 (1957): 222; Paul & Schwartz, *Federal Censorship*, 92–94.

4. De Grazia, "Obscenity and the Mail," 610; Paul & Schwartz, *Federal Censorship*, 96.

5. Paul Boyer, *Purity in Print: Book Censorship in America from the Gilded Age to the Computer Age* (Madison: University of Wisconsin Press, 2002), 157.

6. "Spread of Smut," *Newsweek*, April 27, 1959, 41–42; "Public Help Sought in Clean Mail Drive," *Bridgeport (CT) Post*, March 17, 1955, 6; Murphy, *Censorship*, 189.

7. "Confidential Fights Order Barring Mails to Magazine," *Hartford (CT) Courant*, September 10, 1955, 8; Edward Bennett Williams, *One Man's Freedom* (New York: Atheneum, 1962), 265.

8. Gehman, "Confidential File," 146; Marty Mechlin, "When Terry Moore Became a Turkish Delight," *Confidential*, November 1955, 32; Williams, *One Man's Freedom*, 265; "Magazine's Suit Seeks to Block Postal Ban," *Washington Post*, September 10, 1955, 40.

9. "The Press: Lid on the Sewer," *Time*, September 19, 1955, 76; Mechlin, "When Terry Moore," 32.

10. Williams, *One Man's Freedom*, 265–266; "Confidential Fights Order," 8.

11. "Star Attorney," *Life*, June 22, 1959, 111.

12. See documents, *Confidential, Inc. v. Summerfield* (Civil No. 3982—55, October 7, 1955), National Archives and Records Administration; "Confidential Fights Order," 8; "Magazine's Suit Seeks to Block Postal Ban," 40.

13. Robert Pack, *Edward Bennett Williams for the Defense* (Bethesda, MD: National Press Books, 1988), 56.

14. Williams, *One Man's Freedom*, 266.

15. "Magazine Fights Post Office Ban," *New York Times*, September 10, 1955, 15; "Post Office Asks Dismissed of Suit," *Washington Post*, September 24, 1955, 32; "Confidential, Post Office Both Gain Point in Fight," *Washington Post*, October 8, 1955, 23.

16. Williams, *One Man's Freedom*, 267.

17. ACLU News Release, September 26, 1955, ACLU Papers, Princeton University, Princeton, NJ; "Liberties Union Protests Mailing Ban on Magazine," *Washington Post*, September 26, 1955, 19.

18. Andrew W. Bingham, "Inside Confidential," *Harvard Crimson*, October 27, 1955; "Confidential Wins a Round," *Time*, October 17, 1955, 91; TR, 874.

19. Bingham, "Inside Confidential."

20. Pack, *Edward Bennett Williams*, 57.

21. "The Pill that Ends Unwanted Pregnancy," *Confidential*, March 1956, 26.

22. TR, 857; "Magazine Wins Round with PO On Obscenity," *Washington Post*, January 5, 1956, 21.

23. *Confidential Case*, February 17, 1956, ACLU Papers, Princeton University, Princeton, NJ.

24. "Magazine Ahead in Legal Fight," *Hartford (CT) Courant*, October 8, 1955, 26; Pack, *Edward Bennett Williams*, 58.

25. Pack, *Edward Bennett Williams*, 58.

26. Pack, *Edward Bennett Williams*, 59; "Another Attempt to Bar Magazine Is Refused," *Hartford (CT) Courant*, January 5, 1956, 4B, 4C; "Magazine Wins Round with PO on Obscenity," *Washington Post*, January 5, 1956, 21; *Confidential Case*; Edward Bennett Williams to Alan Reitman, 1 March 1956, ACLU Papers, Princeton University, Princeton, NJ.

27. Press Release, February 24, 1956, ACLU Papers, Princeton University, Princeton, NJ.

28. Williams to Reitman, 1 March 1956.

29. Zuckman, "Obscenity in the Mails," 178; 39 CFR 203.2–14 (Supp. 1959).

30. Williams, *One Man's Freedom*, 264.

31. "Confidential Case Arouses Some Editors," *Corpus Christi (TX) Caller Times*, October 22, 1955, 3; *Washington Post*, quoted in Williams, *One Man's Freedom*, 270; "War on Slander," *Greenville (MS) Delta Democrat-Times*, June 2, 1957, 4.

32. "A Perspectus of Publications," *Chapel Hill (NC) Daily Tar Heel*, May 15, 1957, 2.

33. Press release, February 27, 1956, ACLU Papers, Princeton University, Princeton, NJ; "War on Slander," 4; "Confidentially," *The Reporter*, November 3, 1955, 11.

34. "From the Editor's Mail," *Waukesha (WI) Daily Freeman*, September 23, 1955, 6.

35. Mildred Miller, "Talk About Women," *Cincinnati Enquirer*, January 16, 1956, 15.

Chapter 18: The Peak

1. Gehman, "Confidential File," 67.

2. "Gary Cooper's Lost Weekend with Anita Ekberg," *Confidential*, January 1956, 23, 63.

3. Erskine Johnson, "Cooper Says Lawsuits Make Public Remember," *Gastonia (NC) Gazette*, December 12, 1955, 16.

4. "Caught Guy Madison in Barbara Payton's Boudoir," *Confidential*, March 1956, 23.

5. Horton Streete, "Have Tux, Will Travel and That's What Bob Hope Did with That Blonde," *Confidential*, July 1956, 11.

6. Lawrence J. Quirk, *Bob Hope: The Road Well-Traveled* (Thorndike, ME: Thorndike, 2001), 236–237.

7. Ibid.

8. "Here's Why Frank Sinatra Is the Tarzan of the Boudoir," *Confidential*, May 1956, 22–23.

9. Steve Govoni, "Now It Can Be Told," *American Film*, February 1990, 32.

10. Fred Wilson, "When the Cat's Away, the Mice Will Play, Even with Elizabeth Taylor's Hubby," *Confidential*, November 1955, 12–15.

11. William J. Mann, *How to Be a Movie Star: Elizabeth Taylor in Hollywood* (London: Faber and Faber, 2011), 150; Wilson, "When the Cat's Away," 14.

12. Wilson, "When the Cat's Away," 15.

13. Mann, *How to Be a Movie Star*, 155.

14. George Pace, "Hubby Mike Wilding Didn't Knock—That's How He Caught Elizabeth Taylor with Victor Mature," *Confidential*, July 1956, 21–23.

15. "Liz to Shed Mike; for Another Mike?" *Cincinnati Enquirer*, October 4, 1956, 1.

16. L. J. Kearns, "Jeanne Crain's Hubby and the Starlet," *Confidential*, May 1956, 10–11, 46; Walter Winchell, "Hollywood Fixing Up Law for Those Mags," *Jackson (MS) Clarion Ledger*, March 6, 1957, 8.

17. "2 Film Beauties Claim Their Husbands Beat Them," *Munster (IN) Times*, May 18, 1956, 23; Mark Dayton, "The Story That Rocked Hollywood," *Screenland*, July 1956, 18. See also Herb Lyon, "Tower Ticker," *Chicago Tribune*, April 2, 1956, 46; "Jeanne Crain Reconciled with Manufacturer Mate," *Arizona Republic*, January 2, 1957, 21.

18. Susan Schrenk, "Confidential: The Demise of a 1950s Scandal Magazine" (master's thesis, University of Washington, 2000), 41.

19. Matt Williams, "Ssh! Have You Heard The Latest About Sammy Davis Jr.?," *Confidential*, March 1956, 14; "Theatrical Whirl," *Afro American*, May 19, 1956, 12.

20. Brandon James, *Jeanne Carmen: My Wild, Wild Life as a New York Pin Up Queen, Trick Shot Golfer and Hollywood Actress* (Bloomington, IN: iUniverse, 2008), 500; L. Masco Young, "The Low Down," *Atlanta Daily World*, February 1, 1956; Gehman, "Confidential File," 146.

Chapter 19: The Decline

1. Earl Wilson, "It Happened Last Night," *Camden (NJ) Courier-Post*, June 20, 1956, 22; Earl Wilson, "England Invaded by the Yankees," *Hammond (IN) Times*, June 22, 1956, 31; TR, 313.

2. "Thieves Take 'Confidential' London Files," *San Mateo (CA) Times*, August 17, 1957, 3.

3. Victor Davis, "The Father of Scandal," *British Journalism Review* 13 (2002), 74–80.

4. Earl Wilson, "Bing Croons by Long Distance," *Zanesville (OH) Times Recorder*, March 1, 1956, 4.

5. Walter Winchell, "Along Broadway," *Zanesville (OH) Times Recorder*, February 2, 1956, 4.

6. "City Bans Six Mags to Keep Knox 'Pure'," *Kingsport (TN) Times*, February 6, 1957, 15.

7. See "Slugging the Exposé Magazines," 75; "Burlington Eases Ban on Magazine If It Toes Line," *Bristol (PA) Daily Courier*, March 27, 1957, 1; "Sale of Corruptive Literature to Minors Now Illegal," *Bennington (VT) Banner*, July 23, 1957, 1; "Eddie Fisher and the Three Chippies," *Confidential*, September 1956, 11–13; Erskine Johnson, "Hollywood Today," *Corpus Christi (TX) Caller-Times*, August 8, 1956, 27.

8. See Al Monroe, "Romance or Admiration?," *Chicago Defender*, January 21, 1956, 14; George G. Pitts, "Scandal Magazines Getting Fat off Interracial Affairs," *Pittsburgh Courier*, June 4, 1955, 23.

9. "Ssh!," *Time*, April 2, 1956, 88; Gehman, "Confidential File," 142.

10. "Briton Suing the Magazine," *L.A. Times*, August 20, 1957, L53; *National Cancer Hospital of America v. Confidential, Inc.*, 151 N.Y.S.2d 443 (N.Y. Sup. Ct. 1956); "Defense Blasts Gregory Charges," *L.A. Times*, August 28, 1957, 45; *Goelet v. Confidential, Inc.*, 5 A.D.2d 226 (N.Y. App. Div. 1958).

11. TR, 1641.

12. Truxton Decatur, "We Accuse Sumner Welles," *Confidential*, May 1956, 12–15, 62.

13. D. Alfred Simms, "Father Divine: The Greatest Hoax of the Century," *Confidential*, April 1953, 16.

14. Carol Sweet Hunt, "I Was One of Father Divine's Angels," *Confidential*, May 1956, 34–35; "Father Divine Planning Suit for $1 Million," *Norfolk (VA) New Journal and Guide*, July 21, 1956.

15. "Seduction by Prescription," *Confidential*, May 1957, 12.

16. Michael Nixon, "Even the Cops Blushed When They Learned Where Marie McDonald Hid That Ring," *Confidential*, May 1957, 28–29.

17. J. E. Leclair, "That Blonde Sharing Nick Ray's Pillow Was Marilyn Monroe," *Confidential*, November 1956, 13.

18. Tom Wallace, "He Was an Ordinary Little Guy, But He Sure Made Time on That Couch with Marilyn Monroe," *Confidential*, May 1957, 20.

19. Lou Anderson, "Elvis Presley and His Doll Point Pen," *Confidential*, January 1957, 14.

20. Aubrey Malone, *Maureen O'Hara: The Biography* (Lexington: University Press of Kentucky, 2013), 137–138; also see Mary Desjardins, *Recycled Stars: Female Film Stardom in the Age of Television and Video* (Durham, NC: Duke University Press, 2015).

21. R. E. McDonald, "When Maureen O'Hara Cuddled in Row 35," *Confidential*, March 1957, 11, 46.

22. Maureen O'Hara and John Nicoletti, *'Tis Herself: An Autobiography* (New York: Simon & Schuster, 2005), 210–222; "Maureen O'Hara Heard in Custody Litigation," *L.A. Times*, June 25, 1955, 3.

23. "Walter Winchell on Broadway," *Eureka (CA) Times-Standard*, June 1, 1956, 4; Earl Wilson, "Billy Won't Tell Joyce," *Palm Springs (CA) Desert Sun*, May 1, 1956, 4; "Big-Time Beat: Hy Gardner Says . . . ," *Amarillo (TX) Globe-Times*, May 28, 1956, 26.

24. Jack Eigen, "Hittin' on the Keys," *Chicago Tribune*, August 4, 1956, C2.

25. TR, 1582; "Hunter Held After Publisher Wounded," *Medford (OR) Mail Tribune*, September 5, 1956, 20; "Pega Palo—the Vine That Makes You Virile," *Confidential*, January 1957, 18.

26. Miguel Negri, "Why John Wayne Was the Topic of the Tropics," *Confidential*, November 1956, 18–19, 50.

27. "Shooting of Publisher Brings Query," *Green Bay (WI) Press-Gazette*, September 6, 1956, 47; "Shooting Accident, Says Confidential Publisher," *L.A. Times*, September 7, 1956, 2.

28. "Big Game Hunter Says He 'Accidentally' Shot 'Confidential' Publisher," *San Bernardino County (CA) Sun*, September 6, 1956, 2.

29. "Publisher Harrison: Now for Some Shocking Facts," *Decatur (IL) Herald*, September 13, 1956, 6; "The Great Harrison Hoax," *On the QT*, March 1957.

30. Wolfe, "Public Lives," 157.

31. "Studio Audience Boos," *Variety*, October 5, 1956, 12.

Chapter 20: Slander

1. "This Week's Newsmaker," *Newsweek*, June 16, 1958, 31; on Brown's life and career, see generally Ethan Rarick, *California Rising: The Life and Times of Pat Brown* (Berkeley: University of California Press, 2005).

2. "This Week's Newsmaker," 31; Gladwin Hill, "That Dark Horse Named Brown," *New York Times Magazine*, December 6, 1959, SM38.

3. See Jerry Giesler to Pat Brown, 17 May 1957, Pat Brown Papers, Bancroft Library, University of California, Berkeley; "Possible Action Against Gossip Magazines Studied," *San Bernardino County (CA) Sun*, August 6, 1955, 24; "Brown Will Act on Scandal Mags," *Eureka (CA) Times-Standard*, February 20, 1957, 5.

4. Eve Starr, "'Studio One' Blasts Smear Magazines," *Rochester (NY) Democrat and Chronicle*, January 30, 1956, 5.

5. Hedda Hopper, "Looking at Hollywood," *Chicago Tribune*, February 1, 1956, 6; "The Best on TV Today," *Des Moines (IA) Register*, January 23, 1956, 18.

6. Hedda Hopper, "Armand Deutsch Will Film 'Public Figure'," *L.A. Times*, February 1, 1956, 18; Hedda Hopper, "Gracie Fields' Life Story to Be Filmed," *L.A. Times*, February 20, 1956, 68.

7. "RKO and Filmmakers," *Variety*, February 27, 1956, 1.

8. "Just For Variety," *Variety*, June 6, 1956, 2; Earl Wilson, "Big-Time Beat," *Amarillo (TX) Globe-Times*, May 31, 1956, 27; Erskine Johnson, "Hollywood Today: Abbott, Costello to End Slapstick," *Nashville Tennesseean*, June 26, 1956, 49.

9. Oscar Godbout, "Diana Dors Signs Pact with R.K.O.," *New York Times*, July 12, 1956, 31; Hedda Hopper, "Susan Hayward Will Star in 'Wayward Bus'," *L.A. Times*, May 26, 1956, 22.

10. James Bacon, "Hollywood to Strike Back at Scandals," *Green Bay (WI) Press Gazette*, August 30, 1956, 27.

11. "Slander," *Variety*, December 17, 1956, 3; Helen Bower, "Star Gazing: Hollywood Hits Back," *Detroit Free Press*, March 30, 1957, 4.

12. "Slander," *Newsweek*, February 1957, 91.

13. Bosley Crowther, "Screen: Scandal Is Their Business," *New York Times*, January 17, 1957, 32.

14. "'Slander' Gushes Vengeance," *Amarillo (TX) Globe-Times*, May 29, 1957, 13.

15. *The E. J. Mannix Ledger* (Los Angeles: Margaret Herrick Library, 1962), Vol. 1956–1957, 2.

16. "Confidential Mag Hires Gals," *Variety*, January 23, 1957, 8.

Chapter 21: The Kraft Committee

1. Bob Thomas, "Meade Claims Todd Confirmed Some Material in Confidential," *San Bernardino County (CA) Sun*, August 27, 1957, 2.

2. *Report of the Senate Interim Committee on Collection Agencies, Private Detectives, and Debt Liquidators* (Sacramento: Senate of the State of California, 1957).

3. James Bacon, "State Starts Probe of Scandal Mags," *San Rafael (CA) Daily Independent Journal*, February 27, 1957, 7; James Bacon, "Heat's on for Scandal Magazines," *San Mateo (CA) Times*, February 27, 1957, 28.

4. "Policewoman Tells of Call on Sinatra," *Odessa (TX) American*, March 8, 1957, 3.

5. James Kaplan, *Sinatra: The Chairman* (New York: Anchor Books, 2016), 138; "Kraft Tells of Goons Who Collect Debt By Force," *San Bernardino County (CA) Sun*, February 22, 1957, 4.

6. Seymour Korman, "Probers Turn Fire on Scandal Magazines," *Chicago Daily Tribune*, February 19, 1957, 5.

7. Korman, "Probers Turn Fire," 5; Aline Mosby, "Sinatra's Story of Raid Disputed," *L.A. Times*, February 28, 1957, 18.

8. "Hearing Threatens to Shake Up Movie Colony," *Mansfield (OH) News Journal*, February 22, 1957, 23; "Grand Jury Ready to Open Scandal Magazine Inquiry," *L.A. Times*, February 21, 1957, 2.

9. "Grand Jury Ready," 2; "Private Eye Eyed: 'Peep and Sell' Operators Under Investigation," *Carbondale Southern Illinoisan*, February 28, 1957, 16; "Police Chief, Aides Ordered to Talk in Row with Sinatra," *Lebanon (NH) Valley News*, February 24, 1957, 34.

10. "Grand Jury May Call Marilyn in 'Raid' Inquiry," *L.A. Times*, February 27, 1957, 1.

11. "Private Eye Admits Trickery," *Albuquerque Journal*, February 23, 1957, 23; "Crowd Jams Hollywood Private Eye Hearing," *Redlands (CA) Daily Facts*, March 1, 1957, 1.

12. Mosby, "Sinatra's Story," 18; "Magazine Inquiry," *L.A. Times*, February 21, 1957, 2; Schwarz, *Marilyn Revealed*, 469.

13. Mosby, "Sinatra's Story," 18; "Sinatra's Story of Raid," *L.A. Times*, March 13, 1957, 1.

14. Ibid.; James Bacon, "Sinatra Behind Raid," *Janesville (WI) Daily Gazette*, February 28, 1957, 8; "Raid Designed to 'Catch' Marilyn, Detective Says," *Shreveport (LA) Times*, February 28, 1957, 1; "Singer Flatly Denies Taking Part as DA Office Action Looms," *L.A. Times*, February 28, 1957, 1.

15. "Apartment Raid," *L.A. Times*, February 28, 1957, 19; "Sinatra's Story on Wrong Door Raid Disputed," *St. Louis Post-Dispatch*, February 28, 1957, 1.

16. "End Scandal to Clean Up Magazines, Says Detective," *San Mateo (CA) Times*, March 1, 1957, 2; "Eye Relates Spicy Story Workings," *Long Beach (CA) Independent*, February 21, 1957, 1.

17. "Eye Relates Spicy Story," 1; "Senators Probe Scandal Magazines," *Redlands (CA) Daily Facts*, February 28, 1957, 1.

18. "How Stories Are Gathered for Scandal Rags," *Mt. Vernon (IL) Register-News*, March 1, 1957, 2; "Detective Tells of Secret Pictures of Anita Ekberg," *L.A. Times*, March 1, 1957, 2.

19. "Magazine Quiz," *L.A. Times*, March 1, 1957, 6.

20. "Anita Ekberg Friend Sold Her Photos," *Petaluma (CA) Argus-Courier*, March 1, 1957, 1.

21. "America's Gutter Press," *Danville (VA) Bee*, March 4, 1957, 4; "Editorial: Right of Public to Know," *Estherville (IA) Daily News*, March 7, 1957, 4.

22. "Get Rid of Those 'Scandal' Magazines," *Tyrone (PA) Daily Herald*, February 19, 1957, 4.

23. *Report of the Senate Interim Committee*; Gladwin Hill, "Scandal Inquiry Finds No Answer," *New York Times*, March 2, 1957, 19.

24. "Senators May Extend Scandal Magazines Probe," *Redlands (CA) Daily Facts*, March 2, 1957, 1; "Private Eye Probe Pushed," *Petaluma (CA) Argus-Courier*, March 20, 1957, 6.

25. "Indict 2 Firms for Article on Abortion Pill," *Chicago Daily Tribune*, March 8, 1957, 9; *United States v. Confidential* (N.D. Ill. June 6, 1957); "Confidential Publishers Plead Innocent Friday," *Freeport (IL) Daily Journal*, May 25, 1957, 2; "A Federal Court Bears Down on Confidential," *Hartford (CT) Courant*, March 9, 1957, 8.

26. "Knight Urges War on Exposé Magazines," *L.A. Times*, March 13, 1957, 1; "Brown in New York for Conference on Smut," *Redlands (CA) Daily Facts*, March 11, 1957, 1; "Scandal Magazines Labelled Menace," *Reno (NV) Gazette-Journal*, March 13, 1957, 13; "Action Due on Confidential, Brown Says," *L.A. Times*, March 13, 1957, 17.

27. Schwarz, *Marilyn Revealed*, 472; "DiMaggio Story," *L.A. Times*, March 13, 1957, 17.

28. "DiMaggio Backs Up Sinatra Story on 'Wrong Door' Raid," *Van Nuys (CA) Valley News*, March 14, 1957, 63; "Grand Jurors Rebuke Police on Wrong-Door Episode," *L.A. Times*, April 3, 1957, 2.

29. "Grand Jury Looming Over Scandal Magazines," *L.A. Times*, March 28, 1957, 44.

30. "Lack of Funds May End Magazine Quiz," *L.A. Times*, March 27, 1957, 37; "Kraft Declares Wife May Be Dupe of Foes," *San Bernardino (CA) County Sun*, March 28, 1957, 50.

Chapter 22: Criminal Libel

1. TR, 1654.

2. "Dorothy Dandridge Files $2,000,000 Suit Against Confidential Magazine," *L.A. Times*, March 27, 1957, 37.

3. "Only the Birds and the Bees Saw What Dorothy Dandridge Did in the Woods," *Confidential*, May 1957, 10.

4. TR, 1123.

5. Donald Bogle, *Dorothy Dandridge: A Biography* (New York: Boulevard Books, 1998), 372–373.

6. Ibid., 373–75.

7. "Dandridge to Take Stand and Defy Confidential," *New York Amsterdam News*, September 7, 1957.

8. "New Grand Jury Inquiry on Scandal Magazines Likely," *L.A. Times*, April 2, 1957, 2; "Ronnie Quillan Jailed and Sued for Divorce," *L.A. Times*, February 26, 1957, 5.

9. "Confidential, 6 Other Publishers Indicted," *L.A. Times*, April 30, 1957, 7; "Scandal Magazines Face Trouble in the Courts," *New York Times*, May 5, 1957, 208.

10. "Brown Outlines Steps to Halt Crime Rise," *L.A. Times*, June 20, 1957, 53; Drew Pearson, "Scandal Magazine Faces Showdown on West Coast," *Greenville (MS) Delta Democrat-Times*, May 3, 1957, 4; Govoni, "Now It Can Be Told," 32; Desjardins, "Systematizing Scandal," 130.

11. Wilson, "It Happened Last Night," *Nashville Tennessean*, May 3, 1957, 23; "20 Called in Quiz on Confidential," *L.A. Times*, May 2, 1957, 2; "Scandal Mag Faces Charges," *Petaluma (CA) Argus-Courier*, April 30, 1957, 8.

12. Drew Pearson, "Washington Merry Go Round," *Anderson (IN) Herald*, May 3, 1957, 4; Ray Wight, "Views and News," *Ogden (UT) Standard-Examiner*, May 15, 1957, 6.

13. "Liberace Sues Scandal Magazine," *Redlands (CA) Daily Facts*, May 14, 1957, 1; Darden Asbury Pyron, *Liberace: An American Boy* (Chicago: University of Chicago Press, 2013), 207.

14. "Why Liberace's Theme Song Should Be 'Mad About the Boy,'" *Confidential*, July 1957, 16, 18–21, 59, 60–61; Pyron, *Liberace*, 221–222.

15. Pyron, *Liberace*, 225.

16. "Lee to Sue Scandal Mag for $20 Million," *L.A. Mirror*, May 8, 1957.

17. Complaint for Libel, Liberace v. Confidential, May 14, 1957, Los Angeles County Superior Court, 5.

18. "7 Magazines Face Charges of Indecency," *Bristol (TN) Kingsport Times*, April 30, 1957, 1.

19. "L.A. Grand Jury Probes Stories," *Redlands (CA) Daily Facts*, May 14, 1957, 1; "State Rejects Confidential's Offer to Hush Up Inquiry," *L.A. Times*, May 14, 1957, 41.

20. "Maureen O'Hara, Liberace Hit Lies," *L.A. Times*, May 15, 1957, 1.

21. Ibid.

22. Ibid.

23. "L.A. Grand Jury Probes Stories," *Redlands (CA) Daily Facts*, May 14, 1957, 1; "Jury Told Scandal Magazine Uses Call Girls, Detectives," *Lubbock (TX) Evening Journal*, May 15, 1957, 11.

24. "Ex-Editor Relates 'Bedroom Sources,'" *Long Beach (CA) Independent*, May 15, 1957, 1, 4.

25. "Ex-Editor Relates 'Bedroom Sources,'" 1; "Maureen O'Hara, Liberace Hit 'Lies,'" *L.A. Times*, May 15, 1957, 1.

26. "Call Girls Dug Up Information, Ronnie Says," *Phoenix Arizona Republic*, May 15, 1957, 3; See Indictment, *People of the State of California v. Harrison*, et. al.; see also "Confidential," *L.A. Times*, May 15, 1957, 12.

27. Indictment, *People of the State of California v. Harrison*, et. al.

28. "Magazine Publisher, Five Corporations Reported Accused," *L.A. Times*, May 16, 1957, 1.

29. Ibid.

30. Cal. Penal Code § 311; Hunter Wilson, "California's New Obscenity Statute," *Southern California Law Review* 36 (1963): 513.

31. Cal. Penal Code. § 248; Alvin Glick, "Group Libel and Criminal Libel," *Buffalo Law Review* 1 (1951): 260–361.

32. William Reed Arthur and Ralph L. Crosman, *The Law of Newspapers: A Text and Case Book for Use in Schools of Journalism and a Desk-Book for Newspaper Workers* (Buffalo, NY: HeinOnline, 1940), 220–221; David Riesman, "Democracy and Defamation, Control of Group Libel," *Columbia Law Review* 42 (1942): 747–748; "Constitutionality of the Law of Criminal Libel," *Columbia Law Review* 52 (1952): 521–534.

33. John Kelly, "Criminal Libel and Free Speech," *University of Kansas Law Review* 6 (1958): 317.

34. Zechariah Chafee, *Government and Mass Communications* (Chicago: University of Chicago Press, 1947), 115; Robert Leflar, "Social Utility of the Criminal Law of Defamation," *Texas Law Review* 34 (1956): 984; Kelly, "Criminal Libel," 320.

35. "Brown Outlines Steps to Halt Crime Rise," *L.A. Times*, June 20, 1957, 53; Drew Pearson, "Washington Merry-Go-Round," *Oxnard (CA) Press-Courier*, May 13, 1957, 16.

36. Walter Wanger to Pat Brown, 15 May 1957, Pat Brown Papers.

37. "Confidential Publisher to Fight Extradition to L.A.," *L.A. Times*, June 12, 1957, 2.

38. "The Remarkable Life and Quiet Death of Hollywood's Forgotten Superlawyer," *Hollywood Reporter*, March 24, 2011; "Confidential," *L.A. Times*, May 17, 1957, 16.

39. "2 Surrender on Criminal Libel Counts," *San Mateo (CA) Times*, May 21, 1957, 8; "'Confidential' Couple Fly Back to L.A.," *L.A. Times*, May 21, 1957, 2.

40. "De Scaffa Return Sought in Confidential Case," *L.A. Times*, May 18, 1957, 4; "Indicted Actress Attempts Suicide," *Albany (OR) Democrat-Herald*, May 20, 1957, 1; "Actress Attempts Suicide After Confidential Charge," *Oxnard (CA) Press-Courier*, May 20, 1957, 2.

41. "Magazine Publisher Fights Extradition," *Bridgewater (NJ) Courier-News*, July 24, 1957, 2.

42. "Confidential Pays $10,000," *New York Times*, May 23, 1957, 39.

43. Harrison agreed to settle "only to prevent expensive litigation and a possible involvement of newsstands which sell the magazines," Al DeStefano said. "Dorothy Dandridge Files $2,000,000 Suit Against Confidential Magazine," *L.A. Times*, March 27, 1957, 37; "Dandridge in Second Suit for $2 Million," *Los Angeles Sentinel*, March 28, 1957, A1; "Confidential Backs Off Dotty Dandridge," *Los Angeles Sentinel*, May 23, 1957, A2; "Confidential Settles With Miss Dandrige For 5 Figures," *L.A. Times*, May 22, 1957, 3; "Star List Cut to 26 By Court," *Long Beach (CA) Independent*, August 20, 1957, A1.

44. "Saying It Has Facts, Magazine Tells Dottie, Sue Us Again," *Norfolk (VA) New Journal and Guide*, September 7, 1957.

45. Complaint for Libel, Maureen Fitzsimmons v. Confidential, Los Angeles County Superior Court, July 9, 1957.

46. Birnbaum & Hemmerling (law firm) to Judge Leon David, July 2, 1957, Liberace v. Confidential.

47. Points and Authorities in Opposition to Demurrer, Liberace v. Confidential, June 26, 1957, 1–2.

48. "Liberace's Mom Beaten Up," *L.A. Mirror*, July 19, 1957, 5; "Force of Armed Guards to Protect Liberace Families," *L.A. Times*, July 21, 1957, 58.

49. "California Seeks 2 of Illinois Firm," *Edwardsville (IL) Intelligencer*, July 18, 1957, 6.

50. "Find Confidential 'Not Guilty' of Obscenity Charge," *Anderson (IN) Herald*, June 7, 1957, 25; *U.S. v. Confidential*, N.D. Ill., June 6, 1957. "Magazine Not Obscene," *Mt. Vernon (IL) Register-News*, June 7, 1957, 1.

51. "Brown Not Scared by 'Whisper'," *Long Beach (CA) Independent*, June 4, 1957, 2; "New Confidential Issue Won't Be Sold in State," *L.A. Times*, July 2, 1957, 37.

52. "Magazine," *L.A. Times*, July 2, 1957, 45; "Confidential Loses Two More Rounds of Battle," *L.A. Times*, July 9, 1957, 17.

53. See Jeannette Walls, *Dish: The Inside Story on the World of Gossip* (New York: Perennial, 2000), 21; "Defense Subpoenas 117 Celebrities: Bombshells Readied in Libel Trial," *Delaware County Daily Times*, August 16, 1957, 1; Gabler, "*Confidential's* Reign of Terror," 190; Hunter and Muller, *Tab Hunter Confidential*, 183.

54. Walls, *Dish*, 21.

55. "Judge Rejects Compromise on Confidential," *San Bernardino County (CA) Sun*, July 30, 1957, 1.

56. "Judge Won't Approve Deal to Avoid Confidential Trial," *L.A. Times*, July 30, 1957, 2; "Judge Refuses Deal to Halt Scandal Trial," *Santa Fe New Mexican*, July 30, 1957, 34.

57. "Reputations Threatened in Libel Suit," *Petaluma (CA) Argus-Courier*, July 30, 1957, 13; "Judge Won't Approve Deal," 2.

58. "Hollywood v. Confidential," *Confidential*, September 1957, 22–23.

Chapter 23: The Trial

1. "Bigger Courtroom Needed in Spicy Confidential Trial," *Bend (OR) Bulletin*, August 2, 1957, 5.

2. "Confidential," *L.A. Times*, August 3, 1957, 26; Theo Wilson, *Headline Justice: Inside the Courtroom: The Country's Most Controversial Trials* (New York: Thunder's Mouth, 1996), 56; Maurice Oppenheim, "Shall We Have Cameras in Our Courtrooms," *Student Lawyer Journal* 19, no. 4 (1958): 42.

3. "Confidential Pair Call Top Film Stars," *L.A. Times*, July 26, 1957, 39; Hunter and Muller, *Tab Hunter Confidential*, 183.

4. "Attorneys Mix in Confidential Court Action," *Bend (OR) Bulletin*, August 9, 1957, 1.

5. "First Shot Fired in 'Confidential' Magazine Trial," *Kingsport (TN) Times*, August 7, 1957, 8.

6. Bob Houser, "Scandal Trial Circus Without Laughs," *Long Beach (CA) Independent Press-Telegram*, August 25, 1957, 24; "Confidential Case," *L.A. Times*, August 8, 1957, 29; Roger M. Grace, "Office of District Attorney Shines During Evelle Younger Years," *Los Angeles Metropolitan News-Enterprise*, August 6, 2008, 7.

7.   "Stars Warned to Obey Writs in Scandal Trial," *Philadelphia Inquirer*, August 6, 1957, 1; "Jury Selection Resumes Today in Filmland Trial," *Shreveport (LA) Times*, August 5, 1957, 7; "'Shock-Proof' Jury Selected to Hear Scandal Trials," *Tyrone (PA) Daily Herald*, August 7, 1957, 1; "Confidential Trial Jury Being Picked," *Galveston (TX) Daily News*, August 6, 1957, 8.

8.   "Battle Lines Are Drawn for Confidential," *Asheville (NC) Citizen-Times*, August 8, 1957, 9; Gladwin Hill, "Magazine Draws Scorn," *New York Times*, August 8, 1957, 16.

9.   "Defense Claims Confidential Published Toned Down Stories on Hollywood Stars," *Wilmington (DE) Morning News*, August 8, 1957, 17; "Confidential Rests Case at Criminal Libel Trial," *Albany (OR) Democrat-Herald*, August 30, 1957, 1.

10. "Confidential Case," *L.A. Times*, August 8, 1957, 29.

11. "Editor Says Actress Offered Hot Stories," *Nashville Tennessean*, August 10, 1957, 11.

12. "Actress' Offer to Confidential," *San Bernardino County (CA) Sun*, August 10, 1957, 1; "State Ready to Blow Lid Off Confidential," *Camden (NJ) Courier-News*, August 10, 1957, 1.

13. "Clark Gable's Name Figures at Trial of Confidential," *Baltimore Sun*, August 13, 1957, 7.

14. "Filmland Visions Only Black Eyes," *Nashville Tennessean*, August 11, 1957, 33.

15. "Hollywood Sex Spy," *Long Beach (CA) Independent*, August 14, 1957, 4.

16. TR, Vol. 4; "Scandal Jury Hears Lurid Tale on Maureen O'Hara," *Tucson (AZ) Daily Citizen*, August 14, 1957, 2.

17. "'Lot of Baloney' Says Desi of Scandal Story," *Ogden (UT) Standard-Examiner*, 2; "Confidential Trial Turns to TV Show," *Santa Rosa (CA) Press Democrat*, August 21, 1957, 12.

18. "Snickers Ruled Out by Judge," *Long Beach (CA) Independent*, August 15, 1957, 1.

19. "Stars Will Have 'Day' in Court," *Long Beach (CA) Independent*, August 16, 1957, 1; "Confidential Loses Bid to Drop Charges," *Washington Post*, August 16, 1957, A16.

20. Aline Mosby, "Film Colony Works to Prevent Libel Trial from Producing Huge Scandal," *Provo (UT) Daily Herald*, August 9, 1957, 16; "Lucy's Arnaz Denies Ronnie Tryst," *Long Beach (CA) Independent*, August 14, 1957, 4.

21. "The Lowdown on Paul Gregory Himself," *Confidential*, May 1956, 40, 49.

22. TR, 565.

23. TR, 600; "Scandal Magazine Agent Accused of Blackmail by Producer," *San Mateo (CA) Times*, August 16, 1957, 1.

24. Ibid.

25. Houser, "Scandal Trial Circus Without Laughs"; untitled article, *Medford (OR) Daily Tribune*, August 25, 1957, 32.

26. "Clean—and Otherwise," *Newsweek*, August 16, 1957, 60–61; "Putting the Papers to Bed," *Time*, August 26, 1957.

27. Walls, *Dish: Inside Story*, 25; "Lurid Love Echoes of Libel Lawsuit Whet Local Appetite for Smut Tales," *Pottstown (PA) Mercury*, August 22, 1957, 1.

28. Denis Dougherty, "Confidentially," *Catholic Daily Advance*, September 13, 1957, 4; "Confidential Case Scored by Vatican Paper," *San Bernardino County (CA) Sun*, August 29, 1957, 1; "Graham Urges Us 'To Wake Up,'" *Eureka (CA) Times-Standard*, August 31, 1957, 19.

29. "Drive on 'Smut Gatherers' Set," *Palm Beach (FL) Post*, August 19, 1957, 7; Vernon Scott, "Murphy Heading Fight Against Scandal Sheets," *Pittsburgh Press*, August 25, 1957, 93.

30. "Mae West Says Confidential Done Her Wrong in Story," *Pampa (TX) Daily News*, August 30, 1957, 3; "Confidential Subjects Deny Scandal Stories," *Tuscon Arizona Daily Star*, August 23, 1957, 7; "Corinne Calvet May Appear in Magazine Trial," *Port Huron (MI) Times Herald*, August 22, 1957, 13; "Errol Flynn Offers to Testify at Confidential Trial," *Opelousas (LA) Daily World*, August 19, 1957, 6.

31. Gelman and Katcher, "Man Behind *Confidential*," Part IV.

32. "Scandal Mag Agent Accused of Blackmail by Producer," *San Mateo (CA) Times*, August 16, 1957, 1.

33. "Film Stars Have Little Hope of Escaping Confidential Publicity," *Sayre (PA) Evening Times*, August 18, 1957, 5; "Witness Tells of 'Cuddling' By Irish Star," *Montgomery (AL) Advertiser*, August 17, 1957, 6.

34. "Movie Manager Tells Court of Love Scene," *Philadelphia Inquirer*, August 17, 1957, 1.

35. "Theater Scene Enacted in Court," *L.A. Times*, August 17, 1957, 6; "Movie Manager Tells Court," 1.

36. "Maureen Says She Was in Europe," *Fort Myers (FL) News-Press*, August 18, 1957, 15; "Judge Rules on Evidence," *Baltimore Sun*, August 20, 1957, 5.

37. "Confidential," *L.A. Times*, August 20, 1957, 10; "Magazine's Defense Cites O'Hara Story," *St. Louis Post-Dispatch*, August 18, 1957, 7.

38. "Scandal Mag Trial Figure Found Dead," *Tyrone (PA) Daily Herald*, August 9, 1957, 1; "Chalky Wright, Ex-Featherweight King, Dies in Accidental Drowning," *L.A. Times*, August 13, 1957, 41; "Libel Witness Receives Threat," *Albany (OR) Democrat-Herald*, August 23, 1957, 1.

39. "Confidential," *L.A. Times*, August 20, 1957, 2; "Key Confidential Witness Found Dead in Apartment," *New Castle (PA) News*, August 19, 1957, 17.

40. "Magazine Trial," *L.A. Times*, August 21, 1957, 18.

41. TR, 1014.

42. Roth v. U.S., 354 U.S. 476, 489 (1957); 354 U.S. at 487 n.20, quoting American Law Institute, Model Penal Code, SS207.10(2) (Tent. Draft No. 6, 1957).

43. TR, 1710.

44. Index, TR.

45. TR, Vol. 9.

46. Conrad, *Dear Muffo*, 103–105; "Todd Denies He Gave Secrets to Confidential," *St. Cloud (MN) Times*, August 27, 1957, 11; "Witness Says Mike Todd Gave Confidential Yarn," *Greeley (CO) Daily Tribune*, August 29, 1957, 29.

47. "Meade Gives Names of 10 Informants," *San Bernardino County (CA) Sun*, August 24, 1957, 2.

48. "Scandal Trial Defense," *Chicago Tribune*, August 27, 1957, 12.

49. Ibid.

50. Ibid.

51. "Magazine Ends Defense," *Allentown (PA) Morning Call*, August 31, 1957, 27.

52. "That Seat in Row 35," *Sydney (Australia) Morning Herald*, September 8, 1957, 29.

53. Ibid.

54. Ibid.

55. TR, 1881.

56. TR, 1870–1872.

57. TR, 1860.

58. "Actress Takes Witness Chair in Libel Trial," *Wellsville (NY) Daily Reporter*, September 4, 1957, 1.

59. TR, 1906–1909.

60. "No Walk in Woods—Dottie," *Baltimore Afro-American*, September 14, 1957, 1.

61. Vernon Scott, "Smog Brings Tears to Eyes of Jurors in Libel Trial," *Bend (OR) Bulletin*, September 6, 1957, 1.

62. "Scandal Trial Juror Faints in L.A. Smog," *San Mateo (CA) Times*, September 6, 1957, 1; "Prosecutor Rips Pair For Supplying Smut," *Santa Rosa (CA) Press Democrat*, September 10, 1957, 10.

63. "Jury Told Family Ran Confidential," *New York Times*, September 11, 1957, 30.

64. "Confidential Case Defense Pleads Freedom of Press," *L.A. Times*, September 12, 1957, 44.

65. "Defense Arguments Opened in Exposé Magazine Trial," *Palm Beach (FL) Post*, September 12, 1957, 2; "Confidential," *L.A. Times*, September 12, 1957, 73.

66. "Counsel Ends Confidential's Plea to Jury," *Oxnard (CA) Press-Courier*, September 14, 1957, 2.

67. "Confidential Case Defense Pleads Freedom of the Press," *L.A. Times*, September 12, 1957, 44.

68. "Press Freedom at Stake Jury Told," *Las Vegas Daily Optic*, September 14, 1957, 1; "Juror Nearly Tumbles for 'Girlie' Photos," *Chicago Daily Tribune*, September 14, 1957, 16.

69. "Expose Attorney Makes Final Appeal to Jury," *Honolulu Advertiser*, September 14, 1957, 2; "Nude Pictures Shown to Confidential Jury," *Nashville Tennessean*, September 14, 1957, 7.

70. "Gregory Lied, Confidential Lawyer Says," *Chicago Daily Tribune*, September 13, 1957, 24.

71. "Jury Awaits Scandal Case," *San Rafael (CA) Daily Independent Journal*, September 16, 1957, 7; "Confidential Jury Still in Session," *San Mateo (CA) Times*, September 17, 1957, 16.

72. "Discord and Confusion Snag Confidential Trial," *L.A. Times*, September 21, 1957, 4.

73. "Confidential Jury Reported Split," *New Philadelphia (OH) Daily Times*, September 20, 1957, 12.

74. "Verdict Not Near on Confidential," *Sioux-Falls (SD) Argus-Leader*, September 20, 1957, 1; "Judge Deluged by Questions," *Long Beach (CA) Independent*, September 21, 1957, 1; "Discord and Confusion," 4.

75. "Confidential Jury Reported Split," 12; "Verdict Not Near," 1; "Judge Deluged," 1; "Ritzi Sees More Trials if Jury Hung," *Tucson (AZ) Daily Citizen*, September 23, 1957, 2.

76. "Long Delay of Scandal Jury Hit," *L.A. Times*, September 27, 1957, 35; "Record for Criminal Case," *L.A. Times*, October 1, 1957, 2.

Chapter 24: The End and the Aftermath

1. The vote was seven to five against Publishers' Distributing Corp. and six to six on Fred and Marjorie Meade. "The Exhausting Juror," *Newsweek*, October 14, 1957, 74; "Mistrial Verdict for Confidential," *New York Times*, October 2, 1957, 18; "Mistrial Ends 'Confidential' Libel Case," *Blair County (PA) Altoona Tribune*, October 2, 1957, 1; "Confidential Jury Can't Agree; Case Is Mistrial," *Chicago Daily Tribune*, October 2, 1957, 3.

2. "Jurors Discount Rumor That One Had Been Bribed," *L.A. Times*, October 2, 1957, 8; "Mistrial Ordered on Scandal Mag," *Long Beach (CA) Independent*, October 2, 1957, 1; "Confidential Mistrial Called; Jury Stymied," *San Rafael (CA) Daily Independent-Journal*, October 2, 1957, 24.

3. "Jurors Discount Rumor," 8; "Exhausting Juror," 74.

4. "Confidential Case Retrial to Be Asked," *L.A. Times*, October 3, 1957, 44.

5. "'Confidential' Trials Lays Egg," *Canonsburg (PA) Daily Notes*, October 2, 1957, 8; "Views on the Day's News," *Pittsburgh Press*, October 4, 1957, 26; "War Against Filth," *Camden (NJ) Courier-Post*, October 4, 1957, 6; "Confidential Prosecution Reached Its Goal," *Redlands (CA) Daily Facts*, November 9, 1957, 8.

6. "MPIC Intensified Campaign," *Variety*, October 17, 1957, 3; "Confidential Trial Is Ended but the Story Lingers On," *Anderson (IN) Herald*, September 29, 1957, 37.

7. "Libel Jury Bribe Talk Investigated," *Long Beach (CA) Independent*, October 3, 1957, 8; Pat Brown to Clarence Linn, 9 October 1957, Pat Brown Papers; "Move to Avert Public Retrial of Case Denied," *Petersburg (VA) Progress-Index*, October 23, 1957, 1.

8. Earl Wilson, *The Show Business Nobody Knows* (New York: Bantam Books, 1973), 179; "Judge Rejects Bid to Avoid Second 'Confidential' Trial," *San Mateo (CA) Times*, October 23, 1957, 23; "Brown Now Officially Running for Governor," *Santa Rosa (CA) Press Democrat*, October 30, 1957, 1.

9. "Magazines Will Change Formats to Avoid Trial," *Corsicana (TX) Daily Sun*, November 12, 1957, 12; Maurice Zolotow, "Cleansing Agent: Cost of Law," *Variety*, January 8, 1958, 5.

10. "Confidential Announces New Magazine Format," *Kingsport (TN) Times*, November 12, 1957, 12; "Confidential Clean Up?," *Newsweek*, November 25, 1957, 81.

11. "Magazine Trials Cause Backfire," *L.A. Times*, November 23, 1957, 31.

12. "Brown Motives Backed in Dispute," *L.A. Times*, November 27, 1957, 20.

13. "Confidential, Whisper Convicted, Fined $5,000," *L.A. Times*, December 19, 1957, 5; "Confidential's Case Is Closed," *Reno (NV) Gazette-Journal*, January 16, 1958, 1; "Maureen O'Hara Drops $1,000,000 Libel Suit," *L.A. Times*, July 2, 1958, 2; "Errol Flynn Drops Magazine Suit," *Long Beach (CA) Independent*, July 9, 1958, 1; "Maureen Drops Confidential Suit," *Binghamton (NY) Press and Sun-Bulletin*, July 2, 1958, 4; "Liberace Accepts $40,000 in Libel," *Philadelphia Inquirer*, July 16, 1958, 28; "Liberace Paid by Confidential," *San Bernardino County (CA) Sun*, July 16, 1958, 4.

14. "Confidential's New Policy," *Confidential*, April 1958, 9.

15. "Worm Seeing How the Other Half Lives," *Janesville (WI) Daily Gazette*, February 8, 1958, 8; Art Ryon, "Ham on Ryon," *L.A. Times*, February 7, 1958, 41; Gabler, "*Confidential's* Reign of Terror," 190.

16. "High Price of Virtue," *Time*, May 26, 1958, 54; "Steirman to Publish Confidential Magazine," *Tuscon Arizona Daily Star*, May 22, 1958, 18; "Confidential, Whisper Sold Out by Harrison," *Tuscon Arizona Daily Star*, May 17, 1958, 7.

17. Hy Steirman, "Dear Reader," *Confidential*, October 1958, 6.

18. "Abby Says," *Gastonia (NC) Gazette,* December 5, 1959, 2; "The Press: Obscenity's Price," *Time,* December 27, 1963, 118.

19. Zolotow, "Cleansing Agent: Cost of Law," 5.

20. Jack D. Fox and William H. Rudy, "Rushmore, Ex-Editor of Confidential, Kills Wife and Himself in Taxi," *New York Post,* January 5, 1958, 3.

21. Ibid.

22. Ibid.

23. Wilson, "Failed in His Biggest Role," 16.

24. Ibid.

25. "Arrange Rites for Rushmore," *New York Mirror,* January 13, 1958, 13; Wolfe, "Public Lives," 87.

26. Rushmore, "I Worked for Confidential," 32.

27. Ibid.

Chapter 25: Conclusion

1. "The Public Is Much More Tolerant Nowadays," *Detroit Free Press,* October 6, 1957, 80; John Crosby, "Liz Taylor's Libel Suit," *Warren County (PA) Observer,* December 6, 1960, 4.

2. Goodman, *Fifty-Year Decline,* 78–79.

3. "Fan Magazines Copy Old 'Confidential,'" *Amarillo (TX) Globe-Times,* January 4, 1961, 20.

4. "Walter Winchell," *Cincinnati Enquirer,* December 17, 1957, 10; "Pardonable Confusion," *Camden (NJ) Courier-Post,* December 21, 1957, 8; Zolotow, "Cleansing Agent," 61.

5. "Tarnished Glitter," *Salem (MA) News,* January 16, 1958, 4; "Walter Winchell on Broadway: The Broadway Orbit," *Camden (NJ) Courier-Post,* December 17, 1957, 28.

6. "Tarnished Glitter," 4.

7. See generally D'Emilio and Freedman, *Intimate Matters*; David Allyn, *Make Love, Not War* (London: Little, Brown, 2001); Zolotow, "Cleansing Agent," 61.

8. "Hy Gardner Calling," *Ogden (UT) Standard-Examiner,* April 2, 1961, 6.

9. William B. Lockhart and Robert C. McClure, "Censorship of Obscenity: The Developing Constitutional Standards," *Minnesota Law Review* 45 (November 1960): 5–121; *Memoirs v. Massachusetts* 383 U.S. 413 (1966); Walker, *In Defense of American Liberties,* 235.

10. *New York Times Co. v. Sullivan,* 376 U.S. 254, 256–57 (1964); *Garrison v. Louisiana,* 379 U.S. 64, 69 (1964). The California criminal libel statute was held unconsti-

tutional in 1976 and repealed in 1986. See *Eberle v. Municipal Court*, 55 C.A.3d 423 (1976).

11. See Alan Betrock, *Sleazy Business: A Pictorial History of Exploitation Tabloids, 1959-1974* (Brooklyn: Shake Books, 1996), 4–5; Bernard Weinraub, "Decline and Fall of the Gossip Columnist," *New York Times*, May 14, 1967, 80.

12. "The Enquirer: Up From Smut," *Newsweek*, April 21, 1975; David E. Sumner, *The Magazine Century: American Magazines Since 1900* (New York: Peter Lang Publishing, Inc., 2010), 131.

13. Julie Creswell, "Richard J. Durrell, First Publisher of People Magazine, Dies at 82," *New York Times*, March 8, 2008, B16; People Magazine Advertisement, *New York Magazine*, November 14, 1977, 17.

14. "The People Perplex," *Newsweek*, June 6, 1977, 89; "Joining the People Parade," *Business Week*, May 16, 1977, 71; Barry Siegel, "People Prying into Private Lives," *L.A. Times*, May 6, 1976, E1; "Inside Look at People Magazine," *Time*, November 8, 1974, 58; Petersen, "Gossip Industry," 230; Linda Bird Franke, "Gossipmania," *Newsweek*, May 24, 1976, 56.

15. Jack Vitek, *The Godfather of Tabloid: Generoso Pope Jr. and the National Enquirer* (Lexington: University Press of Kentucky, 2010), 108, 182.

16. P. J. Corkery, "Exclusive! Inside the National Enquirer," *Rolling Stone*, June 11, 1981, 18ff; "Press: Hollywood Goes to War," *Time*, January 21, 1980, 70.

17. "Hollywood Goes to War," 70; Calder, *Untold Story*, 153.

18. "Hollywood Goes to War," 70; Franke, "Gossipmania," 63.

19. "Hollywood's Stars vs. the Enquirer," *Newsweek*, December 8, 1980, 86; Walls, *Dish*, 172.

20. "The Press: A Five Year Legal Toothache," *Time*, March 23, 1981, 90; "Enquirer Belted," *Time*, April 6, 1981, 77; "Carson Blasts 'Enquirer' on Tonight Show," *Rochester (NY) Democrat and Chronicle*, March 18, 1981, 1; Alex Beam, "Tabloid Law," *Atlantic*, August 1999, 55.

21. "Hollywood's Stars vs. the Enquirer," 86; Calder, *Untold Story*, 172–173; Beam, "Tabloid Law."

22. See David Kamp, "The Tabloid Decade," *Vanity Fair*, February 1999, 66; Jonathan Alter, "America Goes Tabloid," *Newsweek*, December 26, 1995, 34; Peter Carlson, "The Decade of Dishing Dirty Laundry," *Washington Post*, February 2, 1999, C2; Lawrie Mifflin, "Big Television Shocker: Tabloid Shows Go Soft," *New York Times*, January 18, 1999, C1.

23. Kamp, "Tabloid Decade," 66; Bill Carter, "Now It Can Be Told: Tabloid TV Is Booming," *New York Times*, December 23, 1991, D10; Mifflin, "Big Television Shocker."

24. See "The New Guy Makes the Tackle," *New York Times*, September 10, 2014, B9; "Daytime TV Impact Honorees," *Variety*, April 2, 2013; Allison Hope Weiner, "The Web Site Celebrities Fear," *New York Times*, June 25, 2007, C1; "A Star Watcher Has Star Power," *New York Times*, October 25, 2008, BU7.

25. Nicholas Schmidle, "The Digital Dirt," *New Yorker*, February 22, 2016.

26. Ibid.

27. See Michael Idov, "The Demon Blogger of Fleet Street," *New York Magazine*, September 26, 2010.

28. Julia Marsh, "Gawker's Internal Emails Show Callous Response to 'Rape' Victim," *New York Post*, March 11, 2016.

29. Andrew Ross Sorkin, "Peter Thiel, Tech Billionaire, Reveals Secret War With Gawker," *New York Times*, May 25, 2016, A1.

30. Goodman, *Fifty-Year Decline*, 53.

31. Burt Boyar, "Best of Broadway," *Philadelphia Inquirer*, July 21, 1958, 13; Wolfe, "Public Lives," 87.

32. Lee Mortimer, "Mortimer's New York Confidential," *Stroudsburg (PA) Pocono Record*, August 11, 1959, 14; "Dorothy Kilgallen," *Salt Lake Tribune*, January 21, 1962, 23.

33. Bob Harrison, *Naked New York* (New York: Paragon, 1961); "'Epic' Misses Real Low-Down on New York," *Indianapolis Star*, December 10, 1961, 135.

34. Wolfe, "Public Lives," 89.

35. Betrock, *Sleazy Business*, 6; "David Frost," *Salina (KS) Journal*, January 25, 1978, 22; Slide, *Inside the Hollywood Fan Magazine*, 180; "Robert Harrison, 73, Magazine Publisher," *New York Times*, February 20, 1978, 7.

36. Wolfe, "Public Lives," 157.

37. Ibid., 89.

SELECTED BIBLIOGRAPHY

Archives

ACLU Collection, Mudd Library, Princeton University.

Edmund G. Brown Collection, Bancroft Library, University of California, Berkeley.

FBI Investigation and Surveillance Records, Howard Rushmore, Marquette University Library.

National Archives and Records Administration, Kansas City.

Books and Articles

Aaker, Everett. *Encyclopedia of Early Television Crime Fighters: All Regular Cast Members in American Crime and Mystery Series, 1948–1959*. Jefferson, NC: McFarland, 2011.

Allyn, David. *Make Love, Not War*. London: Little, Brown, 2001.

Anderson, Christopher. *Hollywood TV: The Studio System in the Fifties*. Austin: University of Texas Press, 1994.

Arthur, William Reed, and Ralph L. Crosman. *The Law of Newspapers*. New York: McGraw-Hill, 1940.

Bacon, James. *Made in Hollywood*. New York: Warner Books, 1978.

Badman, Keith. *Marilyn Monroe: The Final Years*. New York: Thomas Dunne Books/ St. Martin's Griffin, 2013.

Baker, Jean H. *The Stevensons: A Biography of an American Family*. New York: W.W. Norton, 1997.

Balio, Tino. *Grand Design: Hollywood as a Modern Business Enterprise, 1930–1939*. Berkeley: University of California Press, 2007.

———. *Hollywood in the Age of Television*. New York: Routledge, 1990.

Barbas, Samantha. *The First Lady of Hollywood: A Biography of Louella Parsons*. Berkeley: University of California Press, 2006.

———. "How the Movies Became Speech." *Rutgers Law Review* 64 (2012): 665–745.

———. *Laws of Image: Privacy and Publicity in America.* Stanford, CA: Stanford Law Books, 2015.

———. *Movie Crazy: Fans, Stars and the Cult Of Celebrity.* New York: Palgrave, 2001.

Basinger, Jeanine. *The Star Machine.* New York: Vintage Books, 2009.

Bawden, James, and Ron Miller. *Conversations with Classic Film Stars: Interviews from Hollywood's Golden Era.* Lexington: University Press of Kentucky, 2016.

Bernstein, Lee. *The Greatest Menace: Organized Crime in Cold War America.* Amherst, MA: University of Massachusetts Press, 2009.

Bernstein, Samuel. *Mr. Confidential: The Man, His Magazine and the Movieland Massacre That Changed Hollywood Forever.* London: Walford, 2006.

Bessie, Simon Michael. *Jazz Journalism: The Story of the Tabloid Newspapers.* New York: Russell & Russell, 1969.

Betrock, Alan. *Sleazy Business: A Pictorial History of Exploitation Tabloids, 1959–1974.* Brooklyn, NY: Shake Books, 1996.

———. *Unseen America: The Greatest Cult Exploitation Magazines, 1950–1966.* Brooklyn, NY: Shake Books, 1990.

Black, Gregory D. *The Catholic Crusade Against the Movies, 1940–1975.* Cambridge, UK: Cambridge University Press, 2006.

Bogle, Donald. *Dorothy Dandridge: A Biography.* New York: Boulevard Books, 1998.

Brady, Kathleen. *Lucille: The Life of Lucille Ball.* New York: Hyperion, 1994.

Breines, Wini. *Young, White, and Miserable: Growing Up Female in the Fifties.* Chicago: University of Chicago Press, 2001.

Brown, Peter Harry, and Pat H. Broeske. *Howard Hughes: The Untold Story.* Cambridge, MA: Da Capo, 2005.

Buford, Kate. *Burt Lancaster: An American Life.* London: Aurum, 2008.

Buszek, Maria Elena. *Pin-Up Grrrls: Feminism, Sexuality, and the Pin-Up, 1860 to the Present.* Durham, NC: Duke University Press, 2003.

Calder, Iain. *The Untold Story: My 20 Years Running the National Enquirer.* New York: Miramax Books, 2004.

Casper, Drew. *Postwar Hollywood, 1946–1962.* Malden, MA: Blackwell, 2007.

"Censorship of Motion Pictures." *Yale Law Journal* 49 (1939): 87–113.

"Censorship of Obscene Literature by Informal Governmental Action." *University of Chicago Law Review* 22 (1954): 216–233.

Ciment, James. *Postwar America: An Encyclopedia of Social, Political, Cultural, and Economic History.* Armonk, NY: Sharpe Reference, 2007.

Clarke, Gerald. *Get Happy: The Life of Judy Garland.* New York: Delta, 2000.

Collins, Gail. *Scorpion Tongues: Gossip, Celebrity, and American Politics.* New York: Harper Perennial, 2007.

Conrad, Harold, and Budd Schulberg. *Dear Muffo: 35 Years In The Fast Lane.* New York: Stein and Day, 1982.

"Constitutionality of the Law of Criminal Libel." *Columbia Law Review* 52 (1952): 521–534.

Cramer, Richard Ben. *Joe DiMaggio; The Hero's Life.* New York: Simon & Schuster, 2005.

"Crime Comics and the Constitution." *Stanford Law Review* 7 (1955): 237–260.

Cuordileone, K.A. *Manhood and American Political Culture.* New York: Routledge, 2004.

Davis, Ronald L. *The Glamour Factory: Inside Hollywood's Big Studio System.* Dallas: Southern Methodist University Press, 1993.

———. *Van Johnson: MGM's Golden Boy.* Jackson: University Press of Mississippi, 2016.

Davis, Sammy, Jane Boyar, and Burt Boyar. *Sammy: An Autobiography: With Material Newly Revised from "Yes I Can" and "Why Me."* New York: Farrar, Straus and Giroux, 2000.

De Grazia, Edward. "Obscenity and the Mail: A Study of Administrative Restraint." *Law and Contemporary Problems* 20 (1955): 608–620.

DeCordova, Richard. *Picture Personalities: The Emergence of the Star System in America.* Urbana: University of Illinois Press, 2001.

D'Emilio John, and Estelle B. Freedman. *Intimate Matters: A History of Sexuality in America.* Chicago: University of Chicago Press, 2013.

Desjardins, Mary. "Fan Magazine Trouble: The AMPP, Studio Publicity Directors, and the Hollywood Press, 1945–1952." *Film History: An International Journal* 26 (2014): 29–56.

———. *Recycled Stars: Female Film Stardom in the Age of Television and Video.* Durham, NC: Duke University Press, 2015.

Dick, Bernard F. *Hollywood Madonna: Loretta Young.* Jackson: University Press of Mississippi, 2012.

Doherty, Thomas Patrick. *Hollywood's Censor: Joseph I. Breen and the Production Code Administration.* New York: Columbia University Press, 2009.

Douglas, George H. *The Golden Age of the Newspaper.* Westport, CT: Greenwood, 1999.

Earle, Peggy. *Legacy: Walter Chrysler Jr. and the Untold Story of Norfolk's Chrysler Museum of Art.* Charlottesville: University of Virginia Press, 2008.

Ehrenstein, David. *Open Secret: Gay Hollywood—1928–1998.* New York: Morrow, 1999.

Ellis, Douglas. *Uncovered: The Hidden Art of the Girlie Pulps.* Silver Spring, MD: Adventure House, 2003.

Ellroy, James. *L.A. Confidential.* New York: Grand Central, 2013.

Emerson, Thomas I. "The Doctrine of Prior Restraint." *Law and Contemporary Problems* 20 (1955): 648–671.

Evans, Peter, and Ava Gardner. *Ava Gardner: The Secret Conversations*. New York: Simon & Schuster, 2014.

Eyman, Scott. *Lion of Hollywood: The Life and Legend of Louis B. Mayer*. New York: Simon & Schuster, 2012.

Faderman, Lillian, and Stuart Timmons. *Gay L.A.: A History of Sexual Outlaws, Power Politics, and Lipstick Lesbians*. Berkeley: University of California Press, 2009.

Federal Writers' Project of the Works Progress Administration of Northern California. *California in the 1930s: The WPA Guide to the Golden State*. Berkeley: University of California Press, 2013.

Feeley, Kathleen A. "Gossip as News: On Modern U.S. Celebrity Culture and Journalism." *History Compass* 10 (2012): 467–482.

Finch, Christopher and Linda Rosenkrantz. *Gone Hollywood*. London: Weidenfeld and Nicolson, 1980.

Fishgall, Gary. *Gonna Do Great Things: The Life of Sammy Davis, Jr.* New York: Scribner, 2014.

Flynn, Errol. *My Wicked, Wicked Ways: The Autobiography of Errol Flynn*. New York: Cooper Square, 2002.

Foster, Richard. *The Real Bettie Page: The Truth about the Queen of the Pin-Ups*. New York: Citadel, 1999.

Freedland, Michael. *All The Way: A Biography of Frank Sinatra*. New York: St. Martin's, 2015.

Frost, Jennifer. *Hedda Hopper's Hollywood: Celebrity Gossip and American Conservatism*. New York: New York University Press, 2011.

Fuller, Samuel, Christa Fuller, and Jerome Rudes. *A Third Face: My Tale of Writing, Fighting, and Filmmaking*. New York: Alfred A. Knopf, 2002.

Gabler, Neal. *Winchell: Gossip, Power and the Culture of Celebrity*. New York: Knopf, 1994.

Giesler, Jerry, and Pete Martin. *Hollywood Lawyer: The Jerry Giesler Story*. New York: Pocket Books, 1962.

Gilbert, James Burkhart. *A Cycle of Outrage: America's Reaction to the Juvenile Delinquent in the 1950s*. New York: Oxford University Press, 1986.

Glick, Alvin. "Group Libel and Criminal Libel." *Buffalo Law Review* 1 (1951): 260–1.

Goodman, Ezra. *The Fifty-Year Decline and Fall of Hollywood*. New York: Macfadden Books, 1962.

Graham, Sheilah. *Hollywood Revisited: A Fiftieth Anniversary Celebration*. New York: St. Martin's, 1985.

Halberstam, David. *The Fifties*. New York: Random House, 1993.

Haney, Robert W. *Comstockery in America: Patterns of Censorship and Control*. New York: Da Capo, 1974.

Hempel, William J., and Patrick M. Wall. "Extralegal Censorship of Literature." *New York University Law Review* 33 (1958): 989–1026.

Hofler, Robert. *The Man Who Invented Rock Hudson: The Pretty Boys and Dirty Deals of Henry Willson*. New York: Carroll & Graf, 2005.

Holley, Val. *Mike Connolly and the Manly Art of Hollywood Gossip*. Jefferson, NC: McFarland, 2003.

Horowitz, Daniel. *Betty Friedan and the Making of the Feminine Mystique: The American Left, the Cold War, and Modern Feminism*. Amherst: University of Massachusetts Press, 2000.

Hudson, Rock, and Sara Davidson. *Rock Hudson: His Story*. New York: Carroll & Graf, 2007.

Hunt, William R. *Body Love: The Amazing Career of Bernarr Macfadden*. Bowling Green, OH: Bowling Green State University Popular Press, 1989.

Hunter, Tab, and Eddie Muller. *Tab Hunter Confidential: The Making of a Movie Star*. Chapel Hill, NC: Algonquin Books, 2006.

James, Brandon. *Jeanne Carmen: My Wild, Wild Life as a New York Pin Up Queen, Trick Shot Golfer and Hollywood Actress*. Bloomington, IN: IUniverse, 2008.

James, C. N. Paul, and Murray L. Schwartz. "Obscenity in the Mails: A Comment on Some Problems of Federal Censorship." *University of Pennsylvania Law Review* 106 (1957): 214–253.

Johnson, David K. *The Lavender Scare: The Cold War Persecution of Gays and Lesbians in the Federal Government*. Chicago: University of Chicago Press, 2010.

Kaplan, James. *Sinatra: The Chairman*. New York: Doubleday, 2016.

Kashner, Sam, and Jennifer MacNair. *The Bad and the Beautiful: Hollywood in the Fifties*. London: Time Warner Paperbacks, 2005.

Kelley, Kitty. *His Way: The Unauthorized Biography of Frank Sinatra*. New York: Bantam, 1986.

Kelley, N. Megan. *Projections of Passing: Postwar Anxieties and Hollywood Films, 1947–1960*. Jackson: University Press of Mississippi, 2016.

Kelly, Jerome Michael. *The Credibility of Confidential Magazine and the Newspaper Compared*. Master's thesis, Stanford University, 1957.

Kelly, John. "Criminal Libel and Free Speech." *University of Kansas Law Review* 6 (1958): 295–333.

Kinsey, Alfred C., Wardell Baxter Pomeroy, and Clyde E. Martin. *Sexual Behavior in the Human Male*. Bloomington: Indiana University Press, 1998.

Klurfeld, Herman. *Winchell, His Life and Times*. New York: Praeger, 1976.

Kuntz, Tom, and Phil Kuntz. *The Sinatra Files: The Secret FBI Dossier*. New York: Times Books, 2000.

Lait, Jack, and Lee Mortimer. *U.S.A. Confidential*. New York: Crown, 1952.

Leaming, Barbara. *If This Was Happiness: A Biography of Rita Hayworth*. London: Sphere, 1990.

———. *Marilyn Monroe*. New York: Three Rivers, 2000.

Leff, Leonard J., and Jerold L. Simmons. *The Dame in the Kimono: Hollywood, Censorship, and the Production Code*. Lexington: University Press of Kentucky, 2001.

Leflar, Robert. "Legal Remedies for Defamation." *Arkansas Law Review* 6 (1952): 423–454.

———. "Social Utility of the Criminal Law of Defamation." *Texas Law Review* 34 (1956): 984–1035.

Leider, Emily Wortis. *Becoming Mae West*. New York: Da Capo, 2001.

Lerner, Max. *The Unfinished Country: A Book of American Symbols*. New York: Simon & Schuster, 1959.

Lewis, Jon. *Hard Boiled Hollywood: Crime and Punishment in Postwar Los Angeles*. Berkeley: University of California Press, 2017.

Lewis, Judy. *Uncommon Knowledge*. New York: Pocket Books, 1995.

Lockhart, William B. "Literature, the Law of Obscenity, and the Constitution." *Minnesota Law Review* 38 (1954): 295–395.

———. "Censorship of Obscenity: The Developing Constitutional Standards." *Minnesota Law Review* 45 (1960): 5–121.

Lockhart, William B., and McClure, Robert C. "Obscenity in the Courts." *Law and Contemporary Problems* 20 (1955): 587–607.

Madsen, Axel. *Stanwyck: A Biography*. New York: Open Road Media, 2015.

———. *The Sewing Circle: Sappho's Leading Ladies*. New York: Kensington Books, 2002.

Malone, Aubrey. *Maureen O'Hara: The Biography*. Lexington: University Press of Kentucky, 2013.

Mann, William J. *How to Be a Movie Star: Elizabeth Taylor in Hollywood, 1941–1981*. London: Faber, 2011.

———. *Wisecracker: The Life and Times of William Haines, Hollywood's First Openly Gay Star*. New York: Penguin Books, 1999.

Mansfield, Stephanie. *The Richest Girl in the World: The Extravagant Life and Fast Times of Doris Duke*. New York: Kensington, 1994.

Mavity, Nancy Barr. *The Modern Newspaper*. New York: Holt, 1930.

May, Elaine Tyler. *Homeward Bound: American Families in the Cold War Era*. New York: Basic Books, 1988.

McDonald, Paul. *The Star System: Hollywood and the Production of Popular Identities*. London: Wallflower, 2000.

McNulty, Thomas. *Errol Flynn: The Life and Career.* Jefferson, NC: McFarland, 2012.

McLean, Adrienne L., and David A. Cook. *Headline Hollywood: A Century of Film Scandal.* New Brunswick, NJ: Rutgers University Press, 2001.

McLellan, Diana. *The Girls: Sappho Goes to Hollywood.* New York: St. Martin's Griffin, 2000.

Miller, Douglas T., and Marion Nowak. *The Fifties: The Way We Really Were.* Garden City, NY: Doubleday, 1977.

Moore, William Howard. *The Kefauver Committee and the Politics of Crime, 1950–1952.* Columbia: University of Missouri Press, 1974.

Mott, Frank Luther. *A History of American Magazines.* Cambridge, MA: Harvard University Press, 1970.

Murphy, Terrence J. *Censorship: Government and Obscenity.* Getzville, NY: William S. Hein, 2013.

Museum of Broadcasting. *Lucille Ball, First Lady of Comedy.* New York: Museum of Broadcasting, 1988.

Nasaw, David. *Children of the City: At Work And At Play.* Garden City, NY: Anchor/Doubleday, 1985.

Nord, David Paul, Joan Shelley Rubin, and Michael Schudson. *A History of the Book in America.* Vol. 5, *The Enduring Book: Print Culture In Postwar America.* Chapel Hill: University of North Carolina Press, 2015.

Odgers, William Blake, and Melville Madison Bigelow. *A Digest of the Law of Libel and Slander.* Boston: Little, Brown, 1881.

O'Hara, Maureen, and John Nicoletti. *'Tis Herself: An Autobiography.* New York: Simon & Schuster, 2005.

Oppenheim, Maurice. "Shall We Have Cameras In Our Courtrooms." *Student Lawyer Journal* 19 (1958): 75.

O'Steen, Sam, and Bobbie O'Steen. *Cut to the Chase: Forty-Five Years of Editing America's Favorite Movies.* Studio City, CA: Michael Wiese, 2002.

Otash, Fred. *Investigation Hollywood!* Chicago: H. Regnery, 1976.

Pack, Robert. *Edward Bennett Williams for the Defense.* Bethesda, MD: National Press Books, 1988.

Patterson, Karin. "Prince Modupe: An African in Early Hollywood." *Black Music Research Journal* 31 (2011): 29–44.

Paul, James C. N., and Murray L. Schwartz. *Federal Censorship: Obscenity in the Mail.* Westport, CT: Greenwood, 1977.

Petersen, Anne Helen. *The Gossip Industry: Producing and Distributing Star Images, Celebrity Gossip and Entertainment News 1910–2010.* PhD diss., University of Texas, 2011.

Peterson, Theodore. *Magazines in the Twentieth Century*. Urbana: University of Illinois Press, 1964.

Previn, André. *No Minor Chords: My Days in Hollywood*. Toronto: Bantam, 1993.

Pyron, Darden Asbury. *Liberace: An American Boy*. Chicago: University of Chicago Press, 2013.

Rarick, Ethan. *California Rising: The Life and Times of Pat Brown*. Berkeley: University of California Press, 2006.

Report of the Senate Interim Committee on Collection Agencies, Private Detectives and Debt Liquidators. Sacramento: Senate of the State of California, 1959.

Romano, Renee Christine. *Race Mixing: Black-White Marriage in Postwar America*. Cambridge, MA: Harvard University Press, 2009.

Rosten, Leo. *Hollywood: The Movie Colony, the Movie Makers*. New York: Harcourt, Brace, 1972.

Russo, Gus. *Supermob: How Sidney Korshak and His Criminal Associates Became America's Hidden Power Brokers*. New York: Bloomsbury, 2008.

Russo, Gus. *The Outfit*. New York: Bloomsbury, 2003.

Schatz, Thomas. *The Genius of the System: Hollywood Filmmaking in the Studio Era*. Minneapolis: University of Minnesota Press, 2010.

Schrenk, Susan D. *Confidential: The Demise of a 1950s Scandal Magazine*. Master's thesis, University of Washington, 2000.

Schultz, Henry E. "Censorship or Self Regulation?" *Journal of Educational Sociology* 215 (1949): 215–224.

Schwarz, Ted. *Marilyn Revealed: The Ambitious Life of an American Icon*. Lanham, MD: Taylor Trade, 2009.

Scott, Henry E. *Shocking True Story: The Rise and Fall of Confidential, "America's Most Scandalous Scandal Magazine."* New York: Pantheon Books, 2010.

Server, Lee. *Ava Gardner: Love Is Nothing*. London: Bloomsbury, 2010.

———. *Robert Mitchum: Baby I Don't Care*. New York: St. Martin's, 2013.

Sherry, Michael S. *Gay Artists in Modern American Culture: An Imagined Conspiracy*. Chapel Hill: University of North Carolina Press, 2007.

Shiel, Mark. *Hollywood Cinema and the Real Los Angeles*. London: Reaktion Books, 2012.

Shulman, Irving. *"Jackie"! The Exploitation of the First Lady*. New York: Trident, 1970.

Siebert, Fred S. *The Rights and Privileges of the Press*. Westport, CN: Greenwood, 1970.

Slide, Anthony. *Inside the Hollywood Fan Magazine: A History of Star Makers, Fabricators, and Gossip Mongers*. Jackson: University Press of Mississippi, 2010.

Smith, Lewis C. "The Truth Beaten Down." *College Composition and Communication* 4 (1953): 138–141.

Spiegel, Irwin O. "Defamation by Implication—In the Confidential Manner." *Southern California Law Review* 29 (1956): 306–321.

Spoto, Donald. *High Society: The Life of Grace Kelly*. New York: Harmony Books, 2009.

Stenn, David. *Clara Bow: Runnin' Wild*. New York: Cooper Square, 2000.

Stevens, John D. *Sensationalism and the New York Press*. New York: Columbia University Press, 1991.

Stewart, James B. "The Twelfth Annual Albert A. Destefano Lecture." *Fordham Journal of Corporate and Financial Law* 18 (2012).

Summers, Anthony. *Goddess: The Secret Lives of Marilyn Monroe*. London: Indigo, 2000.

Taraborrelli, J. Randy. *The Secret Life of Marilyn Monroe*. London: Pan, 2010.

Taschen Publishing. *1000 Pin-Up Girls*. Cologne: Taschen, 2008.

Tereba, Tere. *Mickey Cohen: The Life and Crimes of L.A.'s Notorious Mobster*. Toronto: ECW, 2013.

Terry, Jennifer. *An American Obsession: Science, Medicine, and Homosexuality in Modern Society*. Chicago: University of Chicago Press, 2010.

Thomas, Tony, Rudy Behlmer, and Clifford McCarty. *The Films of Errol Flynn*. Secaucus, NJ: Citadel Press, 1973.

Tuck, Jim. *McCarthyism and New York's Hearst Press: A Study of Roles in the Witch Hunt*. Lanham: University Press of America, 1995.

Van Doren, Mamie, and Art Aveilhe. *Playing the Field: My Story*. London: Headline, 1988.

Vitek, Jack. *The Godfather of Tabloid: Generoso Pope Jr. and the National Enquirer*. Lexington: The University Press of Kentucky, 2010.

Walker, Samuel. *In Defense of American Liberties: A History of The ACLU*. Carbondale: Southern Illinois University Press, 1999.

Walker, Stanley. *City Editor*. Baltimore: Johns Hopkins University Press, 1999.

———. *The Night Club Era*. Baltimore: Johns Hopkins University Press, 1999.

Waller, Theodore. "Paper-Bound Books and Censorship." *ALA Bulletin* 47 (1953): 474–476.

Walls, Jeannette. *Dish: How Gossip Became the News and the News Became Just Another Show*. New York: Perennial, 2001.

Williams, Edward Bennett. *One Man's Freedom*. New York: Atheneum, 1962.

Williams, John. *America's Mistress: The Life and Times of Miss Eartha Kitt*. New York: Quercus, 2014.

Wilson, Earl. *The Show Business Nobody Knows*. New York: Bantam Books, 1973.

Wilson, Hunter. "California's New Obscenity Statute: The Meaning of "Obscene" and the Problem of Scienter." *Southern California Law Review* 36 (1963): 513–545.

Wilson, Theo. *Headline Justice: Inside the Courtroom: The Country's Most Controversial Trials*. New York: Thunder's Mouth, 1996.

Wittern-Keller, Laura. *Freedom of The Screen: Legal Challenges to State Film Censorship, 1915–1981.* Lexington: University Press of Kentucky, 2008.

Zuckerman, Harvey Lyle. "Obscenity in the Mails." *Southern California Law Review* 33 (1960): 171–188.

INDEX

Page numbers in italics refer to captions and illustrations

ABC, 64, 259
Administrative Procedures Act (1946), 185
Alexander, Adolph, 238
Allen, Steve, 213
Allison, Dick, 287
Allyson, June, 109, 117–119
Amadril, Allen, 226
Amarillo Globe-Times, 220
America (magazine), 153
American Civil Liberties Union (ACLU), 179–182, 186, 189, 192, 243
Andreason, Mylee, 263
Annan, Ruth, 287
Archerd, Army, 63
Arnaz, Desi, vii, 105, 110–111, *112–113*, 114, 256
Association of Motion Picture Producers, 260
Astor, John Jacob, VI, 48, 156
Ausnit, Edgar, 131–132

Bacon, James, 130, 166, 201, 217
Baer, Buddy, 253
Bailey, Pearl, 47
Baker, Josephine, 38–39
Ball, Lucille, vii, 110–111, *112–113*, 114
Baltimore Afro-American, 268
Bankhead, Tallulah, 71
Barker, Lex, 72, 203
Barrymore, Diana, 283
Baule, Frederique "Frede," 120
Bautzer, Greg, 72, 127–128
Beatty, Warren, 287
Beauty Parade, 9–10, 11, 145

Becker, Ross & Stone, 101–102
Bee, The (Danville, Virginia), 230
Behind the Scene, 53
Bell, Rex, 98
Bellson, Louie, 47
Belser, Lee, 262
Bennett, Joan, 127
Benson, Lee, 205
Bergman, Ingrid, 65, 72–73
Berkeley, Busby, 167
Betts, Sandra Ann, 177
Bey, Turhan, 72
Billingsley, Sherman, 38, 39, 145
Birnbaum, H. L., 169
Blasgen, Virginia, 227
Bogart, Humphrey, viii, 127, 171–172
Bonwit, Paul, 97
Borchard, Albert, 240
Bow, Clara, 98
Brady, Kathleen, 114
Brady, Scott, 253
Brando, Marlon, 109, 163
Branton, Geri, 235
Branton, Leo, Jr., 234
Bravo, Jaime, 244
Breen, Jay, 32, 78, 79, 118, 168, 213–214
Brennan, William J., Jr., 263
Brevities: America's First National Tabloid Weekly, 98
Brinkman, Paul, 201–202, 206
Britton, Sherry, 14
Broadway Brevities and Society Gossip, 96–97
Brooklyn Daily Eagle, 53

Brown, Edmund G. "Pat," 215–216, 225, 231, 232, 235–236, 238, 243, 275–276
Bruce, Virginia, 63–64
Burke, Louis, 241, 244
Burnett, Carol, 288

Cabot, Bruce, 171
Calhoun, Rory, 133–135, 140, 253
Calvet, Corinne, 253, 260
Cannon, Jimmy, 82, 160
Carmen, Jeanne, 203
Carson, Johnny, 288
Carstairs, Jo, 120
CBS, 64, 216, 259
Celebrity, 286
Cercy, Ralph, 264
Chafee, Zechariah, 243
Chaney, William, 93
Chaplin, Charlie, 167
Chicago Confidential (Lait and Mortimer), 23
Chicago Defender, 47–48
Chicago Evening American, 259
Chicago Sun-Times, 145
Chicago Tribune, 159, 259
Chicago Worker, 259
Chotiner, Murray, 100
Christian Herald, 280
Chrysler, Walter, Jr., 156–157
Church of God Evangel (newsletter), 154
Churchill, Douglas, 64
City Detective and Guard Service, 122
Click, 29
Clow, Stephen G., 96–98
Coast Reporter, 98
Cockeyed: Confidential, Top Secret. Makes Up the Facts and Blames the Names, 147
Cohen, Mickey, 93, 99
Cohn, Harry, 89, 131, 265
Cohn, Roy, 43
Columbia Pictures, 131–132, 140, 217
Commonweal (magazine), 150
composographs, 7
Comstock Act (1873), 184, 185
Confidential, 23, 29–34, 46, 80, 89–90, 101–108, 121, 138–139, 196, 213–214, 281–285

appeal of, 150–152
banning of, 205–206
circulation and readership, 35, 40, 143–145, 148–149, 195, 204, 259
criticisms, 52–53, 145, 213–214
European bureau for, 204–205
under Hy Steirman, 277–278
imitators, knockoffs, and parodies, 53–54, 146–147
inspirations for, 21
mandated change of focus, 275, 277
production costs and profit, 144–145
regular topics in, 31, 47–51, 114, 155–156, 160
sources of information, 92–93, 197–198
staffing and contributors, 32, 45, 82, 84–87
use of photos, 105
See also Harrison, Robert
Confidential Inc., 231, 241–242
"Confidential" Story, The, 217
Connolly, Mike, 63, 82, 87, 89, 141, 175, 255
conspiracy charges, 242, 252
Cooper, Gary, 163, 195, 196, 197, 253
Cooper, Ted, 131
Coronet, 26, 110
Costello, Frank, 22, 188
Courtney, Geene, 211, 212
cover-ups, 24
Cox, Richard W., 241
Crain, Jeanne, 201–202, 206
Crane, Stephen, 72
Crawford, Joan, 71, 87
criminal libel, viii, 216, 235, 238, 241–243, 271
Crosby, John, 213
Crowley, Arthur, 95, 182–183, 227, 244, 247–248, 252–255, 257–258, 261, 263–268, 270–273
Crowther, Bosley, 66

Dailey, Dan, 74–76, 248
Daily Herald (Tyrone, PA), 153, 230
Daily Mirror (London), 237
Daily Variety, 275
Daily Worker, 41
Dale, Verena, 200–201
D'Amore, Patsy, 122
Dandolos, Nick (Nick the Greek), 206

Dandridge, Dorothy, 233–235, 241, 245, 268–269
Daniels, Billy, 47–48, 85
Daniels, Martha Braun, 47, 48
David, Leon, 183, 246
Davis, Sammy Jr., vii, 114–115, 164, 202
Dawson, Glory, 224
de Acosta, Mercedes, 120
De Scaffa, Francesca, 85–86, 90, 116–117, 240, 241, 244, 255
DeGeneres, Ellen, 291
Denton, Nick, 291
DeStefano, Al, 13, 102, 104, 106, 129–130, 202, 211, 233
Detroit Free Press, 220
Detroit Times, 259
Deutsch, Armand, 216–217
DeVoe, Daisy, 98
DeVorss, Billy, 9
Diamond, Jack, 133
Dietrich, Marlene, 71, 119–120, 125
Dillon, Josephine, 117, 141, 255, 260
DiMaggio, Joe, vii, 69–71, 120, 122–124, 224, 226
  See also Wrong Door Raid
Donahue, Jimmy, 48–49
Donahue, Troy, 133
Dors, Diana, 206
Dougherty, Father Denis, 259
Douglas, Melvyn, 86
Driben, Peter, 9
Drouet, LaGuerre, 266, 270, 273, 274
Duke, Doris, 172–175

Editor and Publisher, 7
Ekberg, Anita, 195, *196*, 197, 229
Ellroy, James, 93, 94, 95
Enquirer. See National Enquirer
Ernst, Morris, 15
Esquire, 7, 14, 86, 144, 203
Estherville Daily News (Iowa), 230
Expose, 38
exposé magazines. *See* scandal magazines
extortion, 25, 97–100, 130, 174, 258
Eyeful, 10

fan magazines, ix, 58–59, 61–62, 149, 282
Farrell, Edythe, 10–11, 54

Fellows, Robert, 217
Ferman, Irving, 182
Fidler, Jimmie, 63, 71
Fiore, Ray, 151
Fisher, Eddie, viii, 206, 282
Fishgall, Gary, 115
Flavettes, 49–50
Flirt, 10
Flynn, Errol, vii–viii, 167, 170–171, 260–261, 276, 283
Forrestal, James, 158
Fortune, 18
Francis, Vera, 93
Fred Otash Detective Bureau, 95
Freeman, Y. Frank, 129
Frew, June Shirley, 14, 86

Gable, Clark, 60, 61, 86, 109, 116–117, 141, 255
Gabler, Neal, 40
Gang, Martin, 224
Gardner, Ava, vii, viii, 68–69, 114–115, 126, 163
Gardner, Hy, 63, 211
Garland, Judy, 99
Garrison v. Louisiana (1964), 285
Gastonia Gazette, 154
Gates, Phyllis, 135
Gawker, 291
Gelien, Andrew Arthur. *See* Hunter, Tab
Giesler, Jerry, 95, 128, 160, 166–169, 172, 174, 178, 181–183, 215–216, 281
Gillespie, Dizzy, 115
girlie magazines, 9–10, 35
Girnau, Frederic, 98
Globe, 286
Goelet, Robert, 206
Goldberg, Frank, 93, 256
Goodman, Ezra, 82, 141, 282, 292
gossip columns, 35–36, 58, 62–63, 285, 289–291
Gould, Polly, 262–263
Govoni, Al, 29, 32, 105, 106, 107, 168, 200, 211–212, 235, 241, 276
Graham, Billy, 259–260
Graham, Sheilah, 63
Greenspan, Lou, 183, 275
Gregory, Paul, 164, 233, 257–258

Guild, Leo, 82, 89
Guinan, Texas, 97

Hagman, Larry, 287
Haines, William, 61
Hamilton, Dennis, 206
Harriman, W. Averell, 97
Harris, Lloyd, 224
Harris, Sydney, 150
Harrison, Robert, 3–4, 202–203, 213, 220,
    244–245, 261, 275–276
  death threats against, 211
  employment history, 4, 7–9
  fact-checking and, 90–91
  fear of libel, 101–104
  on female readership, 149
  girlie magazine publications, 9–12,
    14–16
  on imitators, 147–148
  lawsuits against, 235, 245
  on mistrial, 274
  personal traits, 13–14, 45
  physical characteristics, 14
  post-*Confidential* activities, 293–294
  retirement from publishing, 277–278
  signed editorial, 249
  work habits, 12–13
  See also Confidential
Harrison, Stephen, 159
Hartford Courant, 154, Hays, Will
Haymes, Dick, 78, 80
Hays, Will, 60, 98
Hays card, 63
Hayworth, Rita, 78–80
Heimer, Mel, 178
Hep, 234
Hicks, Joyce, 177
Hill, Percival, 97
Hill, Virginia, 22
Hogan, Frank, 130, 231
Hogan, Hulk, 291
Hollywood Detective Agency, 86
Hollywood Lowdown, 68, 98
Hollywood Nite Life, 99–100
Hollywood Ranch Market, 95
Hollywood Reporter, 82, 129

Hollywood Research Inc. (HRI), 81–95, 169,
    182–183, 209, 233–235, 241, 255,
    264–265
Hoover, J. Edgar, 37, 52, 159
Hope, Bob, 198, 202
Hopper, Hedda, 62, 69, 74, 140, 141–142,
    166, 178
House Un-American Activities Committee
    (HUAC), 17, 42, 125
Howland, Victor Huntington, 54
Hudson, Rock, 132–133, 135
Hughes, Howard, 67–68
Hull, Cordell, 207
Hunter, Tab, vii, 133, 135–137, *138*, 247, 253
Hush-Hush, 147

I Love Lucy, vii, 110
In the Know, 286
Independent Motion Picture Producers
    Association, 260
Inside News, 293
Inside Story, 146
interracial sex, 47, 114
Irwin, Phil, 122–124, 226
Israel, Sam, 128

Jaffe, Eddie, 9
Janis, Elsie, 97
Jeffries, Herb, 115
Jet, 47–48
Johnson, Erskine, 63, 76, 120, 197, 217, 282,
    283
Johnson, Evie Wynn, 77
Johnson, Van, vii, 76–78, 217
Johnston, Eric, 64–65, 184
Joyce, Peggy Hopkins, 97

Kable, Robert R., 241
Kable Printing Company, 107, 144, 186, 231,
    241, 246–247
Kanaly, Father Don, 134
Kansas City Star, 259
Karen, Billy, 122
Kaye, Danny, 111
Kefauver, Estes, 21
Kefauver committee hearings, 21–22
Kelly, Grace, 140, 172
Kelm, Arthur. *See* Hunter, Tab

Kempton, Murray, 82, 160
Khan, Prince Aly, 65, 78
Kilgallen, Dorothy, 63, 70, 74, 80
Kinsey, Alfred, 26, 151–152
Kitt, Eartha, 72, 283
Knight, Goodwin, 231
Korshak, Sidney, 128
Kostelanetz, Andre, 111
Kotz, Florence, 122
Kraft, Fred, 223, 224, 231
Kraft committee, 223–232

Ladd, Alan, 119, 134
Ladies' Home Journal, 144
LaGuardia, Fiorello, 9, 15
Lait, George, 131
Lait, Jack, 23–25, 27
Lamas, Fernando, 72
Lancaster, Burt, 115–116
Lanchester, Elsa, 258
Lanza, Mario, 73
Lasky, Jesse L., 97
Lasky, Victor, 182
Laughton, Charles, 164, 258
Laurents, Arthur, 76
Lawler, Anderson, 60
Lee, Gypsy Rose, 10
Lee, Jennie, 200
Lerner, Max, 213–214
LeRoy, Mervyn, 129, 229
Levin, Harvey, 290–291
libel. *See* criminal libel
Liberace, 236–238, *239*, 240, 246, 276
Life, 22, 69, 131, 132, 144, 187
Linn, Clarence, 232, 235, 236, 247–248, 253, 254, 257, 275, 280
Littell, Norman, 187
Look, 72, 131, 141, 201
Los Angeles Herald-Express, 168
Los Angeles Mirror-News, 141
Los Angeles Times, 68, 225, 244, 271
Lowdown, The, 147
Lyons, Leonard, 63, 160

Macfadden, Bernarr, 5, 6, 7
Madison, Guy, 133, 198
Madupe Mudge Paris, Prince David, 173–174

"Mae West's Open-Door Policy," 92, 241
Malin, Patrick Murphy, 182
Manheimer, Irving, 141–142
Mann, William, 75, 201
Mansfield, Stephanie, 174
Martin, Scott, 219
Mason, James, 172
Mature, Victor, viii, 201
Maxwell, Elsa, 206
Mayer, Louis B., 61, 76–77
McCarthy, Jerry, 87, 256
McCarthy, Joseph, 17, 42–43
McCoy, Marjorie Frances, 42
McDonald, Marie, 195, 208–209, 225
McGarraghy, Joseph C., 191, 192
McGrath, J. Howard, 18
McKesson, William, 225, 231–232, 257
Meade, Fred, 81, 88–92, 93, 182, 225, 233, 234, 241, 244, 255, 264–266
Meade, Marjorie, 81, 88–91, 92, 129, 182, 225, 233, 241, 244, *252*, 255
Metro-Goldwyn-Mayer (MGM), 58, 59, 60, 61, 63, 126, 141, 216–220
Mitchum, Robert, 164–170, 241, 258, 265–266
Modern Man, 15
Modern Screen, 62, 74, 135, 140, 178
Monroe, Marilyn, 69–71, 109, 120, *121*, 122–124, 209
Montalbán, Ricardo, 59
Montez, Maria, 147
Moore, Terry, 187
Moran, Earl, 9
Mordaunt-Smith, Michael, 204–205, 262
Morrison, Denis, 84
Mortimer, Lee, 23–25, 27, 46
Mosby, Aline, 82, 89, 99, 257
Motion Picture Industry Council (MPIC), 65, 260, 274
Motion Picture Producers and Distributors of America (MPPDA; MPAA), 60, 63, 129
Motion Picture Production Code, 8, 60
Muir, Florabel, 82, 84, 106, 255
Murphy, George, 223, 248, 260
Muscarella, Ray, 33
Myles, Meg, 202

Nader, George, 125
Naked New York (Harrison), 293
Nasaw, David, 4
National Enquirer, 285–288
National Examiner, 286
National Police Gazette, 5, 9, 10, 29, 35
Navaar, Jack, 133
NBC, 64
Neal, Bob, 198
Neal, Tom, 253
Near v. Minnesota (1931), 180, 191
New, Harry, 185
New Broadway Brevities, The, 98
New York Confidential (Lait and Mortimer), 23
New York Confidential (magazine), 293
New York Daily Mirror, 29, 212, 261
New York Daily News, 5, 29, 248, 286
New York Enquirer, 285
New York Evening Graphic, 4, 5
New York Post, 52, 261
New York Society for the Suppression of
    Vice, 15
New York Times, 64, 153, 169, 179, 215, 220,
    230, 259, 285, 286, 290
New York Times Co. v. Sullivan (1964), 285
New York World-Telegram and Sun, 175, 181
New Yorker, The, 135, 290
Newsweek, 82, 125, 127, 145, 146, 150, 151,
    215, 220, 276, 286
Nixon, Allan, 93, 253
Novak, Kim, viii, 131–132, 140, *196*
Novarro, Ramón, 61
"Nude Who Came to Dinner, The ,"
    164–165, 241

O'Brien, William C., 190
obscenity charges, viii, 15, 205, 231–232,
    235, 241, 242, 263–264, 284
O'Hara, Maureen, 209–211, 239, *239*, 241,
    245–246, 262, 267–268, 276
On the Q.T., 212
"Only the Birds and the Bees Saw What
    Dorothy Dandridge Did in the
    Woods," 233–235, 241
O'Reilly, Daniel, 235
Otash, Fred, 93–95, 105, 195, 227, *228*, 229,
    247–248
Outlook, 35

Padovani, Lea, 72
Page, Bettie, 10, 13
Pallette, Pilar, 212
Pantages, Alexander, 167
Paramount studios, 58, 65
Parker, William, 94, 95
Parra, Enrique, 211
Parsons, Louella, 62, 68, 69, 98–99, 140
Payton, Barbara, 197–198
Peale, Norman Vincent, 19
Pearson, Drew, 187, 236, 243
"Pega Palo—The Vine That Makes You
    Virile," 211, 241
People (magazine), 286
Perry, Joseph Sam, 247
Photoplay, 62, 76, 126, 140, 141–142, 170
Pidgeon, Walter, 253
"Pill That Ends Unwanted Pregnancy, The,"
    190, 231, 241
Police Gazette. See National Police Gazette
Pons, Lily, 111
Pope, Generoso Jr., 285, 287
Pottstown, Pennsylvania, 259
Power, Tyrone, 72
Preble, Bob, 133
Presley, Elvis, 287
Previn, André, 75
Price, Will, 211
prior restraints, 180, 191
private detectives, 93
Private Lives, 147
Publishers Distributing Corporation,
    107–108, 241, 247, 248
Putnam, George, 181, 237

Quigley, Martin Jr., 8
Quillan, Ronnie, 84–85, 110, 235, 240, 256

Rachevsky, Zina, 116
Radio Moscow, 259
Rand, Sally, 10
Rao (yogi), 173
Rave, 54, 127, 131, 171–172, 237
Ray, Johnnie, 31–32, 100, 147
Ray, Nicholas, 209
Reader's Digest, 144
Redbook, 134
Redke, Fred, 226

Redlands Daily Facts, 274
Reporter, The, 193
Rhinelander, Kip, 7
Rickard, Tex, 97
RKO studios, 58, 165, 166, 217
Robb, Inez, 174–175
Rochlen, Kendis, 82
Rockefeller, Bobo, 48
Rogers & Wells (law firm), 287
Roosevelt, Eleanor, 107
Ross, Barney, 99
Ross, Daniel G., 102, 104, 106, 160, 188, 190, 263–264
Rossellini, Roberto, 65, 72–73
Roth, Samuel, 263
Roth v. United States (1957), 263–264
Rubirosa, Porfirio, 86, 172
Ruditsky, Barney, 93, 122–124, 224, 226, 255
Rushmore, Howard, 40–45, 52, 76, 82, 87, 90, 103, 106–107, 142, 148, 160, 164, 225, 279–280
    anticommunist articles, 157–158
    Confidential blacklist and, 129–130
    disappearance, 158–159
    Harvard University and, 163
    lawsuits against, 168, 174
    pseudonymous articles, 51, 110, 136, 156, 176–177
    Rory Calhoun and, 133–135
    testimony, 240, 255
    trip to California, 83–84
Ruta, Reggie, 292

San Diego Union, 259
Sanders, Red, 226
Sanicola, Hank, 99, 122
Saturday Evening Post, 132, 282
Saturday Review of Literature, 103
scandal magazines, ix, 22–23, 127, 146–154, 171–172
    censorship of, 193
    industry pushback on, 216–217, 229
    legislation against, 181–182, 235–236
    resurgence of, 285–289
    sales of, 205–206
    See also tabloid newspapers
Schaefer, Hal, 120, 122–124
Schary, Dore, 65, 129–130, 166, 183

Scheff, Samuel, 142, 240
Schenck, Joe, 70–71
Scherer, Roy, Jr. *See* Hudson, Rock
Schulberg, Budd, 61
Scott, Lizabeth, 176–179, 183
Screen Actors Guild, 260
Screen Producers Guild, 260
Screenland, 73, 110, 132, 135–136
Senate Interim Committee on Collection Agencies. *See* Kraft committee
Sepia, 234
Server, Lee, 126
Shaw, Artie, 72
Sherman, Lowell, 97
Shreveport, Louisiana, 126
Shubert, Lee, 97
Shute, George, 147
Silva, Simone, 166
Simpson, O.J., 289
Sinatra, Frank, vii, viii, 23, 68–69, 99, 114, 120, 122–124, 198–200, 224, 226–227, 232
Skelton, Red, 73
Skolsky, Sidney, 177
Slander (1956), 217–219
Slatzer, Bob, 209
Smith, Liz, 293
Smithfield, North Carolina, 126
Sokolsky, George, 42
Spillane, Mickey, 93
St. Cyr, Lili, 103, 167
Star, 286
Starr, Eve, 168
Steirman, Hy, 277
Stern, Jack, 255
Stevenson, Adlai, 51–52
Stevenson, Ellen, 52
Stewart, Sheila, 122, 227
Storm, Tempest, 251
Strickling, Howard, 60–61, 141, 163–164
Stuart, Lyle, 38, 44, 103, 206
Studio One (tv series), 216–217
Summerfield, Arthur, 184, 185–186
Sun, 286
Suppressed, 54, 146
Supreme Court (US), 65, 180, 285
Swanson, Gloria, 71

tabloid newspapers, 4–5, 29, 38, 96–99, 285–289

See also scandal magazines

Tamm, Edward, 191

Taylor, Elizabeth, viii, 200–201, 282

Taylor, Robert, 61

Thiel, Peter, 291

Tilden, Big Bill, 51

Tillinger, Eugene, 54

Time, 26, 36, 45, 145, 157, 175, 278

tips and tipsters, 82, 87, 90, 92–95, 106, 129, 240, 290

Titter, 10, 11

TMZ.com, 289–291

Todd, Mike, viii, 265

Tolson, Clyde, 159

Tone, Franchot, 86

Top Secret, 54, 104, 146

Topping, Bob, 72

Tracy, Spencer, 60–61

True Story, 5

Tufts, Sonny, 253

Turner, Lana, viii, 68, 72, 253

Tuton, Robert, 92

TV Guide, 144

20th Century Fox, 58, 59, 69–70, 131

Uncensored, 146

Underwood, Agnes, 82, 89, 255

United Feature Syndicate, 175

United States v. Paramount Pictures, Inc. (1948), 65

Universal-International, 84

US Court of Appeals for the District of Columbia Circuit, 185

US District Court for the District of Columbia, 188

US Post Office Department, 101, 108, 184–194, 254

Us Weekly, 286

U.S.A. Confidential (Lait and Mortimer), 23, 25, 27

U.S.A. Inside Report, 293

Valentine, Paul, 103

Van Doren, Mamie, 128

Variety, 9, 39, 68, 220, 282, 283

von Wittenberg, H. L., 86, 89, 255, 256

Wadden, Tom, 188

Walker, Herbert V., 248–249, 251, 253, 256–257, 262, 263, 271–272, 273, 275

Wall Street Journal, 145

Wanger, Walter, 243

Warner Bros., 58, 66, 167

Washington Confidential (Lait and Mortimer), 23, 25

Washington Post, 212

Wayne, John, 109, 212

Wechsler, James, 38, 43, 52, 160

Weidman, Jerome, 217

Weldy, Dick, 211–212

Welles, Orson, 72, 86

Welles, Sumner, 207

Wellman, Gloria, 236

West, Mae, 91–92, 241, 260

Westover, Harry, 247

"When Maureen O'Hara Cuddled in Row 35," 209–211, 241

Wherry, Kenneth, 26

Whisper, 12, 15–16, 29, 102, 145, 146, 247

Whisper Inc., 241, 276

White, Walter, 38

Wilding, Mike, 200–201

Williams, Edward Bennett, 187–189, 191–193, 288

Willson, Henry, 133, 135, 136

Wilson, Earl, 14, 69, 205, 275

Winchell, Walter, 35–40, 43–44, 48, 49, 53, 54, 145, 157–158, 283

Wink, 10

Wolfe, Tom, x, 213, 293–294

Wright, Chalky, 91–92, 105, 263

Wrong Door Raid, vii, viii, 120, *121*, 122–124, 223, 224–226, 232, 240

Wynn, Evie. *See* Johnson, Evie Wynn

Young, Loretta, 60

Youngdahl, Luther, 190, 191, 192

Zanuck, Darryl, 60

Zilboorg, Gregory, 150

Zolotow, Maurice, 82–83, 278, 283–284